CLASSIC CASES IN NEUROPSYCHOLOGY,
VOLUME II

Brain Damage, Behaviour and Cognition:
Developments in Clinical Neuropsychology
Titles in Series

Classic Cases in Neuropsychology, Volume II

Edited by
Chris Code
Washington Singer Laboratories, University of Exeter, UK

Claus-W. Wallesch
Department of Neurology, Otto-von-Guericke University of Magdeburg, Germany

Yves Joanette
Faculty of Medicine, Université de Montréal, Canada

André Roch Lecours
Faculty of Medicine, Université de Montréal, Canada

Ψ Psychology Press
Taylor & Francis Group

HOVE AND NEW YORK

First published 2003 by Psychology Press
27 Church Road, Hove, East Sussex, BN3 2FA

Simultaneously published in the USA and Canada
by Psychology Press
29 West 35th Street, New York, NY 10001

Psychology Press is part of the Taylor & Francis Group

Typeset in Times by RefineCatch Limited, Bungay, Suffolk
Printed and bound in Great Britain by
Biddles Ltd, Guildford and King's Lynn
Cover design by Joyce Chester

British Library Cataloguing in Publication Data
A catalogue record for this book is available from the British Library

Library of Congress Cataloging-in-Publication Data
Classic cases in neuropsychology / Chris Code . . . [et al.].
    p. cm.
Includes bibliographical references and index.
ISBN 0-86377-891-7
    1. Clinical neuropsychology – Case studies.   I. Code, Christopher, 1942–   .

RC359.C537 2002
616.8—dc21   2002068118

ISBN 0-86377-891-7

This book is dedicated to Alan Parkin
Neuropsychologist
1950–1999

Contents

List of contributors

Claudius Bartels, Department of Neurology, Faculty of Medicine, Otto-von-Guericke University of Magdeburg, Leipziger Str. 44, D-39120 Magdeburg, Germany.

Patricia S. Bisiachi, Dipartimento di Psicologia, University of Trieste, Trieste, Italy.

John L. Bradshaw, Neuropsychology Research Unit, Department of Psychology, Monash University, Clayton, Victoria, 3168, Australia.

Brian Butterworth, Institute of Cognitive Neuroscience, University College London, Alexandra House, 17 Queen Square, London WC1N 3AR.

David Caplan, Neuropsychology, Massachusetts General Hospital, Fruit Street, Boston, MA 021141, USA.

Chris Code, School of Psychology, Washington Singer Laboratories, University of Exeter, Exeter EX4 4QG, UK
and
Brain Damage and Communication Research, School of Communication Sciences & Disorders, University of Sydney, Lidcombe, NSW 2141, Australia.

Margarete Delazer, University Klinik für Neurologie, Innsbruck, Austria.

Hadyn D. Ellis, School of Psychology, Cardiff University, PO Box 901, Cardiff CF10 3YG, UK.

Susanne Ferber, Department of Psychology, University of Western Ontario, London, Ontario N6A 5G2, Canada.

Emer M.E. Forde, Neuroscience(s) Research Institute (Psychology), Aston University, Aston Triangle, Birmingham B4 7ET, UK.

Luisa Girelli, Università degli Studi di Milano-Bicocca, Dipartimento di Psicologia, Edificio U6, Piazza dell'Ateneo Nuovo 1, 20126 Milano, Italy.

Nellie Georgiou-Karistianis, Experimental Neuropsychology Research Unit, School of Psychology, Psychiatry and Psychological Medicine, Monash University, P.O. Box 17, Clayton, Victoria 3800, Australia.

Georg Goldenberg, Department of Clinical Neuropsychology, Bogenhausen Hospital Engelschalkinger Str., 81925 Munich, Germany.

Peter W. Halligan, School of Psychology, Cardiff University, PO Box 901, Cardiff CF1 3YG, UK.

J. Richard Hanley, Department of Psychology, University of Essex, Wivenhoe Park, Colchester CO4 3SQ, Essex, UK.

Manfred Herrmann, Department of Neuropsychology/Behavioral Neurobiology, Center for Cognitive Sciences, University of Bremen, R 3350, Grazer Strasse 6, D-28359 Bremen, Germany.

Patricia Jelenic, Clinique Spécialisée de l'Autisme, Hôpital Rivière-des-Prairies, 7070 Bvd perras, Montréal, Québec H1E 1A4, Canada.

Yves Joanette, Centre de Recherche du Centre Hospitalier Côte-des-Neiges, 4565 Chemin de la Reine-Marie, Montréal, Quebec H3W 1W5, Canada.

B.L.J. Kaczmarek, Institute of Psychology, University of Maria Curie-Sklodowska, 20–080 Lublin, Plac Litewski 5, Poland.

Hans-Otto Karnath, Department of Cognitive Neurology, University of Tuebingen, Hoppe-Seyler-Strasse 3, D-72076 Tuebingen, Germany.

Janice Kay, School of Psychology, Washington Singer Laboratories, University of Exeter, Exeter EX4 4QG, UK.

A. Roch Lecours, Centre de Recherche, Centre Hospitalier Côtes-des-Neiges, 4565 Chemin-de-la-reine Marie, Montréal, Quebec H3W 1W5, Canada
and
Faculté de Médecine, Université de Montréal, C.P. 6128, Succ. A., Montréal, Quebec H3C 3J7, Canada.

Elyse Limoges, Clinique Spécialisée de l'Autisme, Hôpital Rivière-des-Prairies, 7070 Bvd perras, Montréal, Québec H1E 1A4, Canada.

Nadine Martin, Centre for Cognitive Neuroscience, Department of Communication Sciences, College of Allied Health Professions, Temple University, 1701 N. 13th Street, Philadelphia, Penn 19122, USA.

John C. Marshall, Neuropsychology Unit, Radcliffe Infirmary, University of Oxford, Woodstock Road, Oxford OX2 6HE, UK.

Laurent Mottron, Clinique Spécialisée de l'Autisme, Hôpital Rivière-des-Prairies, 7070 Bvd perras, Montréal, Québec H1E 1A4, Canada.

Constanza Papagno, Department of Psychology, University of Milano-Bicocca, Building U6, 20126 Milano, Italy.

Alan J. Parkin, Laboratory of Experimental Psychology, University of Sussex, Brighton BN1 9QG, UK.

Carlo Semenza, Dipartimento di Psicologia, Università degli Studi di Trieste, via S Anastasio 12, 34123 Trieste, Italy.

Giuseppe Vallar, Department of Psychology, University of Milano-Bicocca, Building U6, 20126 Milano, Italy.

Claus-W. Wallesch, Department of Neurology, Otto-von-Guericke University of Magdeburg, Leipziger Str. 44, D-39120 Magdeburg, Germany.

Series preface

From being an area primarily on the periphery of mainstream behavioural and cognitive science, neuropsychology has developed in recent years into an area of central concern for a range of disciplines. We are witnessing not only a revolution in the way in which brain–behaviour–cognition relationships are viewed, but a widening of interest concerning developments in neuropsychology on the part of a range of workers in a variety of fields. Major advances in brain-imaging techniques and the cognitive modelling of the impairments following brain damage promise a wider understanding of the nature of the representation of cognition and behaviour in the damaged and undamaged brain.

Neuropsychology is now centrally important for those working with brain-damaged people, but the very rate of expansion in the area makes it difficult to keep up with findings from the current research. The aim of the *Brain Damage, Behaviour and Cognition* series is to publish a wide range of books that present comprehensive and up-to-date overviews of current developments in specific areas of interest.

These books will be of particular interest to those working with the brain-damaged. It is the editors' intention that undergraduates, postgraduates, clinicians, and researchers in psychology, speech pathology and medicine will find this series a useful source of information on important current developments. The authors and editors of the books in this series are experts in their respective fields, working at the forefront of contemporary research. They have produced texts that are accessible and scholarly. We thank them for their contribution and their hard work in fulfilling the aims of the series.

CC and GH
Sydney, Australia and Birmingham, UK
Series Editors

Preface

Before the first volume of *Classic Cases in Neuropsychology* was published in 1996, we already knew that there were classic cases that we had not been able to include, for one reason or another. We were naturally pleased that the first volume was so well received by reviewers and readers, but it was soon made clear to us that not everyone's favourite case had been included. In Volume I we had been concerned to include those famous cases, like Broca's first cases Leborgne and Lelong, Phineas Gage and Marshall and Newcombe's first description of deep dyslexia, GR.

Volume II is the product of our attempts to put that right. Here we have asked some of the world's leading neuropsychologists to assess the place of a number of less famous, but particularly central, cases from the rich history of neuropsychology. As in Volume I, our main criterion for including a case was that it had a significant impact on neuropsychology and still has contemporary relevance, whether it is an old or a more modern case, whether it is well known, or less well known.

As in Volume I, we have asked each contributor to consider the place and influence of the cases they review in the history of neuropsychology. Some cases have had a positive impact and continue to have contemporary relevance, others undergo significant reassessment by contributors in the light of recent developments in theory and technology. The contents of this book should be of interest to students of neuropsychology at all levels. We would hope that researchers, teachers and practitioners in neurosciences, cognition, neurology, linguists and speech and language pathology would find some, if not all, chapters of relevance to their work.

Also as in Volume I, our attempts to group chapters into neat sections or parts has been difficult. We have chosen to group chapters into two main sections, Part One contains cases concerned mainly with language, calculation and memory and in Part Two we have grouped cases under perception, identification and consciousness.

At this happy stage, we forgive Caroline Osborne at Psychology Press for bullying us into Volume II and thank her, Rachel Brazil, and Kathryn Russel for their help, advice and continued patience. A special vote of thanks goes to Brian Butterworth for taking on the task of preparing our opening chapter. Mainly we thank our contributors for their work and their patience; some of whom may be forgiven for thinking that the book would never be finished. It is pleasing to us that many contributors from Volume I have contributed to Volume II. We are grateful for positive and constructive suggestions from Rita Sloan Berndt, Max Coltheart, and Neil Martin, who gave their time and energy to reading and reviewing the chapters. Finally, our appreciation goes to Dr Karen Eck for her major contribution to the Subject index, to Laura Monetta and Beatriz Mejia for their help with its preparation, and to Nathalie Walter for her assistance with the compilation of the Author index.

We have dedicated this volume to Professor Alan Parkin, who died suddenly during the early stages of preparation of the book. He was 49. Al's work, particularly on amnesia, has had a significant impact in neuropsychology. He contributed one of the best chapters to Volume I, on the famous amnesia case HM. He completed a first draft of his chapter on NA for Volume II shortly before he died. NA is the classic case of amnesia resulting from brain injury caused by a toy sword penetrating the brain through the nose. We are very grateful to Al's partner, Frances Aldrich, for her help in trying to track down a further draft of his chapter. The one we publish here is the earliest and the only one we have. Even so, it is an excellent first draft that received good reviews. We are pleased to be able to include it.

Chris Code is grateful to the Hanse Institute for Advanced Study, where he was a Fellow during the preparation of this book.

Chris Code
Claus-W. Wallesch
Yves Joanette
André Roch Lecours
9 October 2001

CHAPTER ONE

Windows on the mind

Brian Butterworth
Institute of Cognitive Neuroscience, University College London

Case studies of neurological patients have been of central importance to neuropsychology for the past 150 years. Indeed for most of that time they were the only way of studying the relationship between brain systems and those cortical functions that would not yield to animal models. However, one might ask why we need to look again at old neurological cases. In these old cases, the localisation of a lesion was often problematic because a long period might have elapsed between the behavioural tests and the examination of the patient's brain, while nowadays we can assess damage with some precision at the time the tests are made. What is more, in the old cases behavioural studies were rarely placed in the context of what we would now consider the necessary normal controls, or proper standardisation.

Perhaps the most striking difference between the scientific context of the studies reported in this volume and the situation today is that we have access to functional neuro-imaging that enables us to identify the brain systems active when carrying out the kinds of tasks the investigators found so instructive. Functional neuro-imaging appears to be a direct window on the mind. It seems as though we can actually see the processes of cerebration as they happen. We may therefore ask whether these classic cases can tell us anything about the brain and the organisation of cognition that we cannot find out better from a well-designed functional imaging study?

The situation seems to be analogous to Galileo's time, when astronomers began to use the telescope. This enabled them to see things previously invisible—like the moons of Jupiter—just as PET and fMRI enable us to see

1

human brain activity as it happens. Galileo did not have a proper theory of optics, and so he could only guess what it is was that projected on to the objective lens of his instrument. Similarly, we don't really have a good account of what we are observing in the fMRI camera: Is it neural spiking or is it local field potential? Recent evidence suggests the latter, but that still does not reveal how local field potentials and changes to them code mental representations and operations on them. What about the broad organisation of the mind? We know from brain imaging which brain areas are relatively active during a task, but can we tell which of these areas are necessary to carry out the task? Can we tell how these areas are functionally related? At the moment, the answer is no to both questions. For this, we still need the old 'window on the mind'; studies of individual people, each with their own particular mix of damaged and spared functions.

These case studies depend on 'experiments of nature' that are 'designed' to identify at least which are the necessary prerequisites for normal functioning, and which are not. For example, we may ask whether all the mechanisms for identifying letters are also necessary for identifying numbers. Monsieur C, Dejerine's alexic case (Chapter 5), shows that there is part of the mechanism that is specialised for letters and is not needed for numbers because this patient can identify numbers but not letters.

New technologies do not eliminate the need for careful and systematic observation of naturally occurring phenomena. Galileo's telescopic investigations did not make Tycho Brahe's observations of the positions of the stars and planets useless. Indeed, they told Galileo where he should be looking. In fact, descriptions of experiments of nature are vital to a whole range of sciences, from astronomy to zoology. What else are the stars and galaxies but experiments of nature? We certainly cannot recreate them in the lab (though we are getting closer to recreating some of the processes that drive the activities of stars). The theory of evolution of course depended on the careful annotation of, for example, species of finches in the Galápagos—another scientifically crucial experiment of nature.

Marshall and Halligan (Chapter 17) suggest that 'one definition of a classic paper is that the questions it raises continue to be of concern 20 (or more) years later'. This does not mean that the classic study was recognised as such when it was first published. For example, Freud's 1891 monograph on aphasia sold few copies and was rarely cited until Stengel's English translation, even though it contained original and important criticisms of the well-known Wernicke-Lichtheim model of disorders of language. It also contained Freud's first published discussion of slips of the tongue.

Some of the studies in this collection were recognised as of critical importance almost as soon as they were published, while the impact of others came much later, sometimes after the author was long gone. What is it that makes a paper have immediate impact, while others languish for decades before their importance is acknowledged? Two factors seem relevant. The first is what we would now call the 'impact factor' of the means of publication: major journal versus obscure journal; major scientific language versus a scientifically minor language; major publishing house with good distribution versus small publishing house, and so on. Secondly, was the world ready for the findings? That is, did the findings contribute to the development of any well-known theory, preferably with influential supporters?

Some papers had impact in a way that the author intended, while for others the case would be interpreted very differently today. Wernicke's cases presented by Wallesch, Herrmann, and Bartels (Chapter 2) are interesting precisely because a modern neuropsychologist is unlikely to class them as 'conduction' aphasic patients—a term invented by Wernicke himself. A cardinal symptom of conduction aphasia for us is poor repetition, but Wernicke's aphasia, at that time, seemed to be a failure to monitor and correct errors in one's own speech (a point, incidentally, that Freud drew attention to). Wernicke's PhD thesis, which described these patients, quickly became widely read.

Similarly, the implications of Warrington and Shallice's patient, JB, were quickly recognised, first and foremost because JB provided the double dissociation with amnesic patients whose short-term memory (STM) was spared. This should have driven a stake through the heart of single memory theories immediately, but many students of memory (especially in the United States) took no notice of neuropsychological findings in the 1970s. Martin's chapter (Chapter 3) draws attention to the fact that JB appeared to have intact speech, and thus could be distinguished from the conduction aphasic patients first clearly characterised by Lichtheim, a follower of Wernicke. However, debates still rage over the correct interpretation of cases like JB and PV. Is there a subtle language deficit that affects span tasks, as Alan Allport has claimed (Allport, 1984)? Does STM deficit affect language understanding, as Vallar, Baddeley, and many others have maintained (Vallar & Baddeley, 1984)? I confess an interest in this latter debate, having argued that it does not, on the basis of subjects with very poor performance on span tasks but intact comprehension (Butterworth, Campbell, & Howard, 1986).

Sometimes, indeed, a study can be highly influential in ways that would have appalled the authors, at least at the time of writing. This seems to have been the case with Caramazza and Zurif's study of aphasic comprehension. Caplan (Chapter 7) points out that the theory proposed turned out to be wrong, and the methodology flawed. In fact Caramazza himself would now disavow using groups of patients classified into syndromes to test cognitive hypotheses (Caramazza, 1986). Nevertheless, as Caplan notes: 'It is not unreasonable to argue that all the work that has gone on in the past 25 years on disorders of syntactic comprehension and the neural basis for this functional ability has its origin in this paper'. All of us make mistakes doing science, but it takes a special talent to make what the philosopher Austin called 'a ground-floor first-water mistake'.

Singer and Low's study of an acalculic patient (Chapter 4) described for the first time specific problems in transcoding from one form of numbers to another, a theme that was not taken up again for 50 years, but which is now seen to be separable from calculation. Even more dramatic is Wolff's description of what we now recognise as deep dyslexia (Chapter 6): some 70 years elapsed between the publication of this case and Marshall and Newcombe's (1973) classic paper outlining the theoretical basis of semantic errors in reading.

Ellis describes in detail (Chapter 16) three cases that for many years were thought to be within the remit of psychiatrists rather than neuropsychologists, but are now seen to reflect highly selective cognitive deficits with a potentially well-defined neuroanatomical basis.

Some papers are classics just because, as in other branches of science, the ingenuity of the experimenters throws new light on an old problem. One excellent example is Bisiach and Luzzatti's now famous 'Piazza del Duomo' experiment (Chapter 17). Their method of asking unilateral neglect patients to imagine a scene from different points of view enabled them to demonstrate convincingly that the phenomenon was not due to a sensory deficit. There is still a debate as to how best to explain it, more than 20 years on.

In their Preface to the first volume of *Classic Cases in Neuropsychology*, the editors wrote: 'Each chapter highlights the importance of the case for the development of neuropsychology . . . authors were asked to take particular care to put right any misunderstandings or misconceptions about an historical case that may have influenced neuropsychological development'. The authors in this volume have responded magnificently to the challenge of the previous volume. I am sure that all readers—neuropsychologists or not—will find their understanding both of the history of neuropsychology and the nature of the relationship between brain and cognitive functions greatly enriched by this splendid set of studies.

REFERENCES

Allport, A. (1984). Auditory-verbal short-term memory and conduction aphasia. In H. Bouma & D.G. Bouwhuis (Eds.), *Attention and performance X: Control of language processes*. Hillsdale, NJ: Lawrence Erlbaum Associates Inc.

Butterworth, B., Campbell, R., & Howard, D. (1986). The uses of short-term memory: A case study. *Quarterly Journal of Experimental Psychology, 38A*, 705–738.

Caramazza, A. (1986). On drawing inferences about the structure of normal cognitive systems from the analysis of impaired performance: The case for single-patient studies. *Brain & Cognition, 5*, 41–66.

Marshall, J., & Newcombe, F. (1973). Patterns of paralexia: A psycholinguistic approach. *Journal of Psycholinguistic Research, 2*, 175–199.

Vallar, G., & Baddeley, A.D. (1984). Phonological short-term store, phonological processing and sentence comprehension: A neuropsychological case study. *Cognitive Neuropsychology, 1,* 121–141.

PART ONE

Language, calculation, memory

CHAPTER TWO

Wernicke's cases of conduction aphasia

Claus-W. Wallesch and Claudius Bartels
Department of Neurology, Otto-von-Guericke University of Magdeburg, Germany

Manfred Herrmann
Department of Neuropsychology/Behavioral Neurobiology, University of Bremen, Germany

INTRODUCTION

In 1874, the 26-year-old psychiatrist-in-training, Carl Wernicke, published his MD thesis *Der aphasische Symptomencomplex*. This slim volume has probably become the most frequently quoted German medical thesis. Wernicke derived a model of language processing from the newly developed fibre anatomy of his time, which emphasised a role for the forebrain association fibres in the representation of cognitive processes, especially semantic representations. Wernicke attempted, as the subtitle of his thesis suggests, 'a psychological study with an anatomical foundation'. Based on the literature, Wernicke localises Broca's area in the foot of the third frontal convolution and hypothesises its function as a centre for speech movement concepts. From physiological data and conjecture, he assumes the presence of another language centre in the first temporal convolution, which he viewed as the cortical target of the acoustic nerve. Thus, Wernicke considered the temporal area to be a centre for auditory word images. It has to be noted that although Wernicke demonstrated the localisation and connections of these centres on a right hemisphere, he was aware of the left hemisphere dominance for language (p. 7). Even more curiously, Wernicke's diagram shows a monkey's brain.

In 1874, Wernicke explicitly did not localise more central language processes: 'The forebrain surface is a mosaic of such simple elements, which are characterised by their anatomical connections with the body's surface. All that exceeds these most simple functions, the integration of sensations to a concept, thinking, consciousness, is a function of the fibre masses, which connect areas on the forebrain surface with each other. These have been termed "association fibres" by Meynert.' (p. 4).

Using anatomical preparations, Wernicke (1874, pp. 17–19) described association fibres between the perisylvian structures that he assumed to provide connections between the sensory and the motor speech areas. He considered these especially important for language development by imitation (p. 13). In proficient speakers, lesion of these association fibres should result in the following (pp. 26–27; translation by Köhler et al., 1998):

> The patient comprehends all. . . . He can say everything, but the choice of correct words is impaired in a similar manner as just described [with aphasia resulting from lesion of the sensory language centre—the authors]. The auditory word image ('*Klangbild*') is preserved and can be accessed from those associations that form the word concept, but it cannot determine the correct choice of motor concepts (*Bewegungsvorstellungen*). . . . Therefore, words are confused. . . . However, here another form of correction is possible, which is little used in the normal speech process but which can completely exchange the unconscious by the conscious route. . . . Hearing is intact and the auditory perception is transmitted to the centre for auditory word images. The spoken word is perceived and found correct or wrong. If attentive, the patient knows that he spoke wrongly. . . . The patient will be able to practise what he wants to say by previous silent articulation; and if he is a strong-willed and attentive person, he will be able to compensate his deficit by conscious, laborious and time-consuming correction.

In the context of this passage, it has to be kept in mind that the concept of the phoneme was developed after the publication of Wernicke's thesis (Köhler, Bartels, Herrmann, Dittmann, & Wallesch, 1998). The linguistic unit Wernicke's production model was based upon was the syllable.

TWO CASES OF CONDUCTION APHASIA DESCRIBED BY WERNICKE

Altogether, Wernicke presents 10 cases in his thesis (see Table 2.1). Not surprisingly, attempts to classify the aphasia syndromes of Wernicke's patients according to modern criteria (e.g. Wallesch & Kertesz, 1993) give different results from Wernicke's interpretation. The case of Peter would probably not be considered as aphasia today, as all symptoms that are described can be accounted for by dysarthria and confusional state, and anarthria or mutism in the last days before death. Wernicke could not accept motor aphasia in the case of Itzigsohn, as the symptoms included agraphia and a comprehension deficit for prepositions. Seidel is analysed as a prototypical transcortical

TABLE 2.1
Case descriptions in Wernicke's *Der aphasische Symptomencomplex*

Name	*Aetiology*	*Wernicke's diagnosis*	*Probable modern classification*
Adam	Probable CVA	Sensory	Wernicke's
Rother	Infarct	Sensory	Wernicke's
Beckmann	Probable CVA	Conduction	Conduction
Kunschkel	Trauma	Conduction	Unclassifiable
Peter	Multiple infarcts	Motor	Dysarthria, then anarthria
Itzigsohn	Meningovascular syphilis	Unclassifiable	Probably Broca with some apraxia of speech
Seidel	Infarct	Insular aphasia	Transcortical motor
Funke	Probable CVA (haemorrhage?)	Not classified	Global
Zwettels	Probable CVA	Not classified	Insufficient data
Salmonsky	Abscess	Insular	Atypical Wernicke's

motor aphasia; Wernicke only uses a different name ('insular' aphasia). However, the same term is also used for Salmonsky's aphasia. Mainly because comprehension was largely spared, Wernicke draws a distinction from sensory aphasia in this case.

The two cases Wernicke diagnosed as conduction aphasia—Beckmann and Kunschkel—will be considered in more detail. In the description of his model, Wernicke does not predict repetition performance in conduction aphasia. Consequently, Wernicke focused in his case analyses not on a disorder of repetition but on the patients' attempts at self-correction resulting from lack of control of the motor centre.

The case of Beckmann

In the morning of 15 March 1874 this 64-year-old pharmacist noticed that he could not read properly and wrote even worse, although he could see perfectly well. On 18 March he went to Breslau to see an ophthalmologist. The same day the first language deficits emerged. Wernicke performed a clinical assessment on 20 March and found Beckmann physically fit but noticed some cardiac arrhythmia. His language behaviour is described (Wernicke, 1874, pp. 47–49) as follows:

> He comprehends all and answers questions correctly. He knows the use of objects. There is no hint of motor aphasia, as his knowledge of words is without limits. However, for many objects that he wants to name, the words are missing; he tries hard to find them, gets angry, and if the name is given to him, *he can repeat it faultlessly* [emphasis by present authors]. . . . Many productions

succeed, especially small talk; but then a critical word comes up and he gets
stuck; he struggles, gets angry, and almost every word that is now haltingly
produced is meaningless; he continues to correct himself, but the more he tries,
the worse it gets. . . . On the other hand, when in rage, it may happen that he
produces sentences that are grammatically correct but contain a totally different meaning from his intention. . . . Very frequently, he asks 'was that
correct?'.

On the street, he can read the signs in passing; however, when a specific word or
letter is indicated, he is unable to produce it. . . . There is agraphia, he can copy
everything, but cannot write on his own. . . He is more successful with digits,
but already two-digit numbers are a hard task for him.

Beckmann exhibited right homonymous hemianopia. In May, he was able to
read words, but not letters, and aphasia had much improved. When last seen
(no date given), agraphia had cleared, but alexia was still severe.

This patient, explicitly called a case of conduction aphasia by Wernicke,
was able to repeat with ease. Wernicke's description and theoretical account
focus upon Beckmann's futile attempts at production, the *'conduite
d'approche'*. The passage relating to this symptom has been quoted ('Many
productions succeed . . .', see above).

The case of Kunschkel

Kunschkel was a 50-year-old goldsmith who had suffered for 2 years from
bladder and stool incontinence. When admitted to hospital, he was aggressive
towards doctors and nurses and therefore was transferred to the psychiatric
ward. There he was uncooperative, irritable, and aggressive with temper
tantrums. Neurosyphilis seems to have been considered.

On 26 March 1874 there was a fight in the men's ward in which Kunschkel
received a blow to his right ear that rendered him right hemiparetic, right
hemianopic and aphasic. According at Wernicke (1874, p. 51, translation by
Köhler et al., 1998):

"He spoke adequately for quite a while, until finally at the end of a sentence,
there was an incorrect word. . . . When asked specifically about this word he had
just spoken, he attempts to correct, and produces a jumble of wrong words and
syllables . . ., a jargon that can hardly be recorded in writing. Occasionally, he
replies perfectly correct upon a question. As far as his command of language
reaches, his answers are correct and adequate. . . . He comprehends all and with
ease. There is alexia . . . and also agraphia.

Wernicke includes the following transcription of an interview with Kunschkel
(pp. 51–52):

W: Welche Jahreszahl haben wir? *(Which year is it?)*

K: 44

W: Lebt Ihr Vater noch? *(Is your father still alive?)*

K: Nein, der ist 46 gestorben. *(No, he died in 46.)*

W: Also wie lange her? *(So, how long is this past?)*

K: An die 29 Zaten Daten Diten. *(Some 29 /paraphasia/ data /paraphasia/).*

W: Haben Sie Geld? *(Do you have money?)*

K: Ja, ich habe den Luten eingelöst und meine Sachen. *(Yes, I have cashed the /paraphasia/ and my things.)*

W: Wie viel haben Sie dann? *(How much do you have then?)*

K: Nahe an 100 Thaler. Hätte ich 100 gehabt, dann hätte ich schon (stockt). *(Approximately 100 thalers. If I had had 100, then I had certainly [pause].)*

W: Was hätten Sie dann? *(What would you have done then?)*

K: Grätliche Hubel. *(/jargon/)*

W: Was ist das hier für ein Local? *(What type of building is this?)*

K: Das ist ein kaiserliches Kastel. *(This is an imperial castellion.)*

W: Was denn sonst? *(What else?)*

K: Nun es giebt kaisernes kis katen leben. Da haben Sie zum Beipiel ein königliches von der Elisabethkasetts, das heisst von allgemeiner Kasetts. *(Now, there are imperial (last syllable paraphasic) /paraphasia/ /paraphasia/ live. There, for example, you have a royal of the Elisabeth (rest paraphasic), this means of general /paraphasia/.)*

W: Möchten Sie gern nach Hause? *(Do you want to go home?)*

K: Ich bin jetzt schon 4 Wochen gar nicht von hier weggekommen. *(I have not been away from here for 4 weeks.)*

W: Was ist das? (Ein Taschentuch wird gezeigt). *(What is this? [A handkerchief is shown].)*

K: Das ist ein feines Filil. *(This is a fine /paraphasia/.)*

W: Filet? *(Fillet?)*

K: Nein Filet ist es nicht, das ist nicht so stark. *(No, it is not a fillet, this is not so strong.)*

W: Was ist es denn? *(What else is it then?)*

K: Taschentuch nennen wir's. *(We call it handkerchief.)*

W: Wie kann man es denn noch nennen? *(Is there another name for it?)*

K: Nun, wie man's in noblen Zweigen begreif ich in Adeln sich bewegt. *(Now, how one in noble branches it I do not understand in gentries moving (paragrammatic).)*

   [Ein Bleistift wird gezeigt.] *[A pencil is shown.]*

K: Ich dachte, es wäre ein kleiner Kolinomitz, aber es ist nicht. *(I thought it was a small /paraphasia/, but it is not.)*

W: Was ist es denn? *(What else is it, then?)*

K: Ich habe es immer unter dem Neumann Neu-Bleistift. *(I have it always under the name Newman (surname) New-pencil.)*

[Eine Brille wird gezeigt.] *[Spectacles are shown.]*

K: Das nennt man die Brücke, Brikke nennt man es. *(This is called bridge (malapropism), /paraphasia/ it is called.)*

W: Wozu brauch ich es denn, zum Spass? *(What do I need it for then, for fun?)*

K: Ach nein, um eben das meilige golden, um eben sein Ansehen zu ent-wickeln. *(Oh no, just for the /paraphasia/ golden, to advance one's reputation.)*

Wernicke notes rapid improvement of Kunschkel's aphasia. Paresis had completely resolved by 4 April. Aphasia could be detected only through a few imprecise or wrong speech sounds. Alexia had vanished, but agraphia was still present.

Wernicke's interpretation

Both latter cases obviously belong to each other. Both have full comprehension of what is said, both have retained their full lexicon, but access depends upon mood and situation in varying degree. One, Beckmann, is intellectually intact, the other, Kunschkel, is demented, talkative, without self-constraint and criticism. Consequently, Beckmann gets stuck in the middle of the sentence and wrestles for an expression, Kunschkel replaces what is missing by nonsense words or new combinations of syllables and is satisfied that he can close the sentence. He tries to correct himself, albeit weakly. Both exhibit the same type of alexia, and agraphia is more prominent than either aphasia or alexia.

(Wernicke, 1874, pp. 52–53)

The anatomical basis is both the foundation and the pinnacle of Wernicke's analysis. He continues (pp. 69–70):

The theory of aphasia that has been presented is able to integrate the various types of this disorder. This variety, which previously has amazed every observer, can now be calculated by use of the laws of combination. But all forms are characterized by an interruption of the psychic reflex ark that underlies normal language processing.

The interruption of conducting fibres that associate the psychic elements with each other by diseases of the forebrain white matter can cause psychic focal symptoms as was exemplified in aphasia. Diseases of the forebrain white matter often go unnoticed, and it is a great error to underestimate its function. All higher mental processes are probably conducted in the white matter of the forebrain.

In a later paper, Wernicke (1906) includes repetition performance in his description of conduction aphasia and states that automatic (echolalic) repetition and repetition of pseudo-words are rendered impossible by the lesion of the direct route between the sensory and motor speech centres. Meaningful words, however, were spared because of the intact indirect semantic route via the centre for concepts. This theory would predict meaning-related semantic paraphasias with repetition. A number of authors tested these predictions in their case analyses. Near semantic paraphasia with repetition was found by Heilbronner (1908) and Kleist (1916), but only occasionally.

THE NEUROANATOMICAL AND NEUROLINGUISTIC STATUS OF CONDUCTION APHASIA TODAY

In his seminal paper, 'Disconnexion syndromes in animals and man', Geschwind (1965) resuscitated the classical German (Lichtheim, 1885; Wernicke, 1874) theory of conduction aphasia resulting from a disconnection of the anterior from the posterior language area by lesion of the arcuate fasciculus. Damasio and Damasio (1980) added empirical support to this claim when analysing the lesions as shown by the CT of six patients with fluent speech with phonemic paraphasia and a repetition deficit that spared digits. On the other hand, the Damasios also pointed out that the lesion of quite a number of functional components of the language apparatus can account for deficits of repetition, so that the number of lesions possibly involved render it unlikely that all forms of conduction aphasia can be related to a single anatomical structure.

Caramazza, Basili, Koller, and Berndt (1981) suggested two types of conduction aphasia differing with respect to phonemic paraphasias in speech output and concluded that patients with repetition deficit but without output problems suffered from a pathological limitation of auditory-verbal short-term memory.

Like Wernicke, Kohn (1984) focused her interest in conduction aphasia upon phonemic paraphasia in non-repetition tasks. She proposed a disruption of a pre-articulatory programming stage so that the phonological representation of a word cannot immediately be transcribed into a phonemic string. Errors in these translations together with deficient output monitoring and error/or correction result in the characteristic, laborious sequences of self-corrections, the 'conduite d'approche'.

The modern literature is divided with respect to the critical or cardinal symptom(s) of conduction aphasia with neurologists mainly focusing on the repetition deficit (e.g. Benson et al., 1973; Geschwind, 1965; Kertesz, 1977) and neurolinguists on the phonemic disorder (e.g. Buckingham, 1992; Joanette, Keller, & Lecours, 1980; Kohn, 1984). Wernicke's (1906) prediction of the inability to repeat pseudo-words together with semantic paraphasia with repetition was confirmed repeatedly: the syndrome has been termed 'deep dysphasia' in analogy to deep dyslexia (Michel & Andreewsky, 1983).

The status of syndromes in aphasiology was critically reviewed in the 1980s (Caramazza, 1984; Poeck, 1983; Schwartz, 1984). Schwartz emphasised the polytypy of aphasic syndromes. She pointed out that it is not necessary that all members of a diagnostic category share any single attribute. Caramazza (1984) called this type of syndrome 'psychologically weak' and 'defined loosely as the co-occurrence of impairments to grossly defined functions'. In his view, groups of patients collected on the basis of such syndromatic categories are unsuitable for research into the mechanisms underlying pathological behaviour.

The existence of a syndrome of 'conduction aphasia', defined by repetition deficit, phonological disorder or polytypically cannot support either the psychological or the anatomical side of Wernicke's theory. With even greater certainty, it cannot support the close link Wernicke has formed between cognitive process and anatomical structure. Wernicke's theory as regards the anatomical basis of conduction aphasia seems to be neither provable nor disprovable, as Wernicke himself emphasises the plasticity of the association system represented in the fibre masses of the forebrain. Be that as it may, Wernicke (and other classic authors) provided us with insights, descriptions, and interpretations that are still valid today.

REFERENCES

Benson, D.F., Sherematta, W.A., Bouchard, A., Segarra, J.M., Prince, D., & Geschwind, M. (1973). Conduction aphasia: A clinicopathological study. *Archives of Neurology, 30*, 307–310.

Buckingham, H.W. (1992). The mechanisms of phonemic paraphasia. *Clinical Linguistics and Phonetics, 6*, 41–63.

Caramazza, A. (1984). The logic of neuropsychological research and the problem of patient classification. *Brain and Language, 21*, 9–20.

Caramazza, A., Basili, A.G., Koller, J.J., & Berndt, R.S. (1981). An investigation of repetition and language processing in a case of conduction aphasia. *Brain and Language, 14*, 235–271.

Damasio, H., & Damasio, A. (1980). The anatomical basis of conduction aphasia. *Brain, 103*, 337–350.

Geschwind, N. (1965). Disconnexion syndromes in animals and man. *Brain, 88*, 585–644.

Heilbronner, K. (1908). Zur Symptomatologie der Aphasie mit besonderer Berücksichtigung der Beziehungen zwischen Sprachverständnis, Nachsprechen und Wortfindung. *Archiv für Psychiatrie, 43*, 234–298.

Joanette, Y., Keller, E., & Lecours, A.R. (1980). Sequences of phonemic approximations in aphasia. *Brain and Language, 11*, 36–44.

Kertesz, A. (1977). *Aphasia and associated disorders*. Orlando, FL: Grune & Stratton.

Kleist, K. (1916). Über Leitungsaphasie und grammatische Störungen. *Monatsschrift Psychiatrie und Neurologie, 40*, 118–199.

Köhler, K., Bartels, C., Herrmann, M., Dittmann, J., & Wallesch, C.W. (1998). Conduction aphasia: 11 classic cases. *Aphasiology, 12*, 865–884.

Kohn, S. (1984). The nature of phonological disorder in conduction aphasia. *Brain and Language, 23*, 97–115.

Lichtheim, L. (1885). Über Aphasie. *Deutsches Archiv für Klinische Medizin, 36*, 204–294.

Michel, F., & Andreewsky, E. (1983). Deep dysphasia: An analogue of deep dyslexia in the auditory modality. *Brain and Language, 18*, 212–223.

Poeck, K. (1983). What do we mean by 'aphasic syndromes'? A neurologist's view. *Brain and Language, 20*, 79–89.

Schwartz, M. (1984). What the classical aphasia categories can't do for us, and why. *Brain and Language, 21*, 3–8.

Wallesch, C.W., & Kertesz, A. (1993). Clinical symptoms and syndromes of aphasia. In G. Blanken, J. Dittmann, A. Grimm, J.C. Marshall, & C.W. Wallesch (Eds.), *Linguistic disorders and pathologies*. Berlin: De Gruyter.

Wernicke, C. (1874). *Der aphasische Symptomencomplex*. Breslau: Cohn & Weigert.

Wernicke, C. (1906). Der aphasische Symptomencomplex. In E. von Leyden & F. Klemperer (Eds.), *Die Deutsche Klinik am Eingange des Zwanzigsten Jahrhunderts in akademischen Vorlesungen. Band VI: Nervenkrankheiten*. Berlin: Urban & Schwarzenberg.

CHAPTER THREE

PV and JB: Two cognitive neuropsychological studies of phonological STM impairment and their impact on theories of language and memory

Nadine Martin

Temple University, Philadelphia, USA and Moss Rehabilitation Research Institute

INTRODUCTION

In this chapter I will review two case studies of phonological short-term memory (STM) disturbance in the context of minimal language impairment; PV (Basso, Spinnler, Vallar, & Zanobio, 1982; Vallar & Baddeley, 1984a) and JB (Shallice & Butterworth, 1977; Warrington, Logue, & Pratt, 1971). These studies made substantial contributions to our understanding of relationships between language processing and verbal STM systems and more generally were an important influence in the field of cognitive neuropsychology. The evidence from these two cases provided support for the claim that phonological STM can be selectively impaired and that it is independent of the processes that generate language representations, an hypothesis first advanced by Warrington and Shallice (1969) in their seminal case report of KF. Warrington and Shallice's hypothesis motivated a series of cognitive neuropsychological investigations in the 1970s and 1980s of patients with presumably selective deficits of phonological STM. PV and JB are two of the more prominent of such case studies from that period. Each made important contributions to the development of cognitive neuropsychology as a science and helped to establish its role in mainstream cognitive psychology. Although their contributions are overlapping, they can each be credited with particular association to key developments in cognitive neuropsychology.

PV is a noteworthy case in part because of the sheer number of empirical investigations of her STM and language processing abilities. More important, these studies, in total, provide an outstanding example of the use of neuropsychological data to test assumptions of a cognitive model of working memory. Basso et al. (1982) first reported PV in 1982 and demonstrated that she exhibited a profound impairment of auditory short-term memory in the context of relatively preserved language and long-term learning abilities. Following that initial report, Vallar and colleagues (e.g. Vallar & Baddeley, 1984a, b; Vallar & Papagno, 1986) conducted a number of investigations of PV's short and long-term memory abilities within the framework of the working memory model of Baddeley (1986; Baddeley & Hitch, 1974). As a group, these studies represent an important example of the use of data from brain-damaged individuals to test a well-established model of verbal short and long-term memory. Investigations of JB were also impressive in this regard, but are important for another reason. Frequently, individuals with phonological STM disturbance also demonstrate mild to moderate language impairment, and thus, it is necessary to show that poor performance on span tasks is due to a deficit in verbal STM and not related to deficits (however mild) in language processing. Both PV and JB are relevant to this issue because, compared to many of the 'STM impaired' subjects studied during the 1970s and 1980s, they exhibited very little language impairment, and thus provided the strongest evidence of a 'selective' deficit of phonological STM. I will focus primarily on JB's case in regard to this issue, because he was the subject of studies that directly addressed the question of whether language and STM processes could be selectively impaired (Allport, 1984; Shallice & Butterworth, 1977). These studies were central to a debate in cognitive neuropsychology on the relationship between language processing and verbal STM that is still active today. In this chapter I will discuss these cases, their respective (and overlapping) contributions to the field of cognitive neuropsychology, and their relevance to current views of language and STM processes.

THE CASE OF PV

This case examines the use of cognitive neuropsychological data to test a model of short and long-term memory (Basso et al., 1982; Vallar & Baddeley, 1984a; Vallar & Papagno, 1986).

PV was 28 years old when she had a stroke that left her with a right hemiparesis and mild aphasic symptoms. A CT scan revealed a large hypodense area in the perisylvian region of the left hemisphere. Seven months post-onset, she was administered a language assessment that revealed mild difficulties in production (phonemic paraphasias and word finding difficulties in spontaneous speech). Also present were severe difficulties in sentence repetition and poor performance on a test examining the ability to follow directions of increasing complexity (the Token Test, DeRenzi & Vignolo, 1962). On subsequent administrations of this examination (at 14 and 23 months post-onset), the only language disorders remaining were a sentence repetition deficit and continued poor performance on the Token Test. Also remaining was a severe deficit in auditory-verbal span. Despite this remaining difficulty, PV has been able to manage a shop and care for her family in the years following her stroke.

PV's auditory-verbal span varied somewhat depending on the items to be recalled. Span for digits was 2 (at 90% correct) and for letters, only 1, while span for concrete, high frequency words was 3. Sentence repetition span was 6 words (8 syllables in total). Variance in span depending on the items to be recalled is not uncommon in individuals with span deficits (or indeed, normals, but with a different pattern of variance) and can be attributed to the influence of language processes on span performance. Auditory span for digits was also tested using a pointing response (written numbers 0–9) and found to be the same as with a verbal response. This argued against a deficit in covert speech production processes as a cause of the reduced span (Vallar & Baddeley, 1984a).

PV's span performance was affected by modality (another common feature of patients with auditory-verbal span impairment). Span improved considerably when stimuli were presented visually (digits = 4, letters = 4, words = 6). In contrast to the impaired span for auditorily presented materials, PV showed good performance on a task that measured memory for meaningful and non-meaningful visual sequences (a span of 8). Additionally, auditory-verbal span (but not visual span) was reduced when recall was postponed by a filled or unfilled delay (the Brown-Peterson paradigm). Basso et al. (1982) concluded that PV demonstrated an isolated disturbance of auditory-verbal STM. They ruled out language impairment as an instigator of the restricted auditory-verbal span because PV showed no disturbances in word comprehension or in spontaneous speech (at the time of testing). It has since been argued that the assessment of PV's language abilities may not have been stringent enough to reveal deficits that remained from her initial presentation of language impairment (Martin & Saffran, 1997). Nonetheless, it is clear that PV's primary deficit affected her ability to retain linguistic information in a short-term store, particularly phonological information. This deficit affected performance on verbal span tasks and language tasks that required retaining language information in a short-term store (e.g. Vallar & Baddeley, 1984b). It did not, however, affect performance on long-term learning tasks (paired associate learning, free recall of word lists, or prose recall) indicating a dissociation between phonological short-term memory and long-term memory (Basso et al., 1982).

Identifying the locus of impairment within a model of working memory

Vallar and Baddeley (1984a) conducted a number of experiments with PV to further pinpoint her STM deficit. As a framework, they used the revised version of Baddeley's (1966; Baddeley & Hitch, 1974) working memory model (Salame & Baddeley, 1982). This model is well known to cognitive psychologists and neuropsychologists who study STM. The model has two components that orchestrate the short-term retention of verbal input. The 'phonological short-term store holds auditory input in a non-articulatory phonological code and is subject to decay. This store is coupled with an 'articulatory' or 'phonological loop' that uses subvocal articulatory rehearsal to refresh the contents of the phonological store.[1] Non-verbal information is held in a comparable store and maintained in parallel fashion to the phonological loop by a mechanism termed the 'visuo-spatial scratch pad'. Finally, there is a third component of the model, the 'central executive', described by Baddeley (1996) as an attention controller. The full range of functions of the central executive have yet to be completely understood, but Gathercole and Baddeley (1993) note that it is responsible for regulation of the flow of information within working memory, retrieval of information from long-term memory and the processing and storage of information.

Baddeley's working memory model did not originally address the issue of the separation of language and memory systems, but does embody the basic assumption that verbal short-term memory and long-term memory of language are independent and dissociable. Thus, the model served quite naturally as a framework within which to interpret data from studies of verbal STM impairments. At the same time, the patient data afforded an as yet untapped opportunity to test the assumptions of the working memory model. The dissociation of short and long-term memory performance in STM-impaired patients had been explained as a deficit of the STM component of the working memory model (the phonological store and phonological or articulatory loop), leaving long-term learning and memory components intact (Baddeley, 1990). In two studies of PV, Vallar and Baddeley (1984a; Vallar & Papagno, 1986) tested assumptions of the working memory model by examining three phenomena associated with the operations of its STM components:

(1) *Phonological similarity effect.* Span for phonologically similar items is less than for phonologically dissimilar items (Baddeley, 1966; Conrad, 1964). Originally, this finding was attributed to confusions in articulatory codes for phonologically similar items, but in the revised version of the working memory model, it is attributed to coding of items in the input phonological store.

(2) *Word-length effect.* Span for longer words is reduced compared to span for shorter words (Baddeley, Thomson, & Buchanan, 1975). This phenomenon was attributed to the temporal limitations of the articulatory loop; fewer long words could be circulated by the loop than short words.

(3) *Articulatory suppression.* Repeated utterance of irrelevant speech during serial recall (auditory presentation) impairs performance in normals, diminishes the word length effect but does not affect the phonological similarity effect. The disappearance of the word length effect is attributed to its association with the operation of the articulatory loop. When the articulatory loop is engaged in articulating irrelevant speech, it is unavailable to circulate phonologically coded material through working memory. Phonological similarity effects remain, presumably because auditorily presented stimuli gain direct access to the phonological store, bypassing the articulatory loop. With visual presentation, effects of phonological similarity (Murray, 1968) and word length disappear (Baddeley, Lewis, & Vallar, 1984). The working memory model accounts for this by assuming that one function of the articulatory loop is to recode visual input into phonological codes that are then stored in the phonological store.

Vallar and Baddeley (1984a) explored these three phenomena in PV in order to pinpoint her deficit within the model. First, they predicted that if PV's phonological store was reduced in capacity, the effect of phonological similarity on span with auditory presentation would not be diminished. With respect to visual presentation, they also reasoned that if phonological similarity effects were not present, this would suggest that PV was not using subvocal rehearsal in span tasks. This pattern was predicted on the basis of evidence that phonological similarity effects are diminished in normals when subvocal rehearsal is prevented by concurrent articulation.

Vallar and Baddeley found that phonological similarity affected PV's span for letters with auditory presentation but not with visual presentation, suggesting that PV was not recoding visually presented material into phonological codes. PV's pattern of performance on the visually presented span measures was, in fact, better on phonologically similar lists (.60 sequences correct) than dissimilar lists (.10 sequences correct), a pattern opposite to that in normals. When concurrent articulation was applied to the visually presented span task, they found that PV did not show the normal effect of articulatory suppression; that is, it did not alter the effects of phonological similarity on her visual span performance. Vallar and Baddeley's (1984a) interpretation of PV's performance under conditions of articulatory suppression is somewhat incomplete. First, the standard effect of phonological similarity in visually presented verbal span tasks was not present in PV's performance, and so it is not quite clear what effects of concurrent articulation were expected. Secondly, there actually may have been an unexpected effect of articulatory suppression in the opposite direction to the normal effect. The trend for better performance on phonologically similar lists that was observed in the control condition became exaggerated in the concurrent articulation condition; more phonologically similar lists were recalled accurately for spans of 3, 4, and 5 items (30%, 40%, and 60% respectively). It is not clear why PV performed better on phonologically similar letter strings when they were presented visually, although one possibility is that the letters used in testing were easier to recall using a visually based strategy. For example, two of the stimulus items were P and V, the subject's initials, and also B, C, and D are in sequence within the alphabet. There is, of course, no way of knowing for certain that PV employed such strategies, but it would have been interesting to investigate further her better recall of visually presented phonologically similar letter strings.

Apart from PV's unexpected facility with phonologically similar visually presented letter lists, she showed the standard effect of phonological similarity when letter strings were presented auditorily, but not visually. This argues for the conclusion that PV did not use subvocal rehearsal but did use the input phonological store in auditory-verbal span tasks, although that store was reduced in capacity. PV's failure to use subvocal rehearsal was further substantiated in an experiment investigating the effects of word length on recall. Vallar and Baddeley reasoned that if PV was not using subvocal rehearsal, then the standard word length effect should not be present in her auditory-verbal STM performance. Word length had no effect on PV's performance and, in fact, she performed slightly better on strings of five-syllable words compared to two-syllable words. Also of interest is the observation that PV's span in this task was between 3 and 4 items compared to her span for digits (2) and letters (1). Vallar and Baddeley (1984a) note that this may be due to the fact that words may tap more semantic coding than numbers or letters. Although they did not expand on this point, it was an important observation that would influence subsequent studies of the links between language, STM, and learning. Specifically, it suggested that impairment in retaining phonological information did not preclude the influence of lexical and semantic processes on the capacity of the phonological STM store.

Finally, Vallar and Baddeley (1984a) showed that PV's articulation rate was normal and argued that this finding indicated that her articulation was normal. On this basis, they argued further that PV's failure to use subvocal rehearsal in span tasks could not be attributed to a deficit in articulation but rather was due to a strategy that compensated for the ineffectiveness of rehearsal given the impairment of the phonological store. This may be the case and it seems a reasonable conclusion, given the focus of the study. However, this interpretation begs another interesting question: in the absence of subvocal rehearsal, how are the influences of lexical and semantic processes on phonological STM (hinted at in the observation of PV's better span for words than letters or digits) mediated in the working memory model? The function of subvocal rehearsal is to refresh the contents of the phonological store. It is part of the phonological loop system that presumably connects with the central executive component of the working memory model and its links to long-term memory. Presumably, the benefit of richer coding of words compared to digits and letters is due to input from long-term lexical memory that is mediated by the phonological rehearsal loop's refreshment of representations in the phonological store. Alternatively (or additionally), the phonological store could have direct connections with long-term phonological, lexical, and semantic representations of words that are held in phonological code in the phonological short-term store (versions of this view have been proposed in several current models e.g., R. Martin & Lesch, 1996; N. Martin & Saffran, 1997). In such a case, if the phonological loop's operation was compromised, lexical and semantic influences on span would be mediated by these direct connections.

Vallar and Baddeley's (1984a) effort to pinpoint the locus of PV's deficit within a model of working memory is remarkable for two reasons. As mentioned earlier, it is an important example of the use of a cognitive model of memory to characterise neuropsychological data. The tasks chosen to test the model are logically and empirically linked to functions of various components of the model. Based on the working memory model's basic assumptions and the normal performance on the various span tasks, Vallar and Baddeley (1984a) systematically construct predictions about PV's performance and how it will locate the deficit within the model. This study is also noteworthy for features observed in PV's performance but not pursued in the present study. Given that the authors' intentions were quite specific (to pinpoint PV's deficit within a specified architecture of verbal memory), it would be imprudent for them to dwell on observations that are not immediately relevant to that purpose. Nevertheless, Vallar and Baddeley (1984a) make sufficient note of observations such as lexical influences on span or curious reversals of the normal effect of phonological similarity on span (visually mediated) to motivate future studies of these phenomena.

Using cognitive neuropsychological evidence to identify the source of recency effects in free recall

Whereas Vallar and Baddeley (1984a) used the working memory model to define PV's deficit, Vallar and Papagno (1986) demonstrated how data from PV could be used to test assumptions of the model. They attempted to discriminate between two accounts of a well-known characteristic of auditory-verbal STM—the recency effect (relatively good recall of the most recently presented items in a span). The recency effect in free recall of supraspan word lists has historically been attributed to an output of a short-term store with a limited capacity (Glanzer, 1972). An alternative hypothesis proposed by Tulving (1968) states that recency reflects the use of retrieval strategy that is sensitive to the temporal course of a sequence of items to be recalled (the 'temporal dating' hypothesis). This issue was addressed by Vallar and Papagno (1986) by examining effects of input modality (auditory versus visual) and recall order (free recall versus recall from the end) on PV's ability to freely recall lists of 10 unrelated words. Having identified the locus of PV's deficit in the phonological short-term store, they deduced that the short-term store account would predict a diminished recency effect in free recall with auditory, but not visual, presentation. In contrast, the temporal dating hypothesis would predict no difference between the two. With respect to effects of output order, they reasoned that a short-term store account would predict a reduced recency effect but a preserved ability to attempt recall from the end of the list. In contrast, the temporal dating hypothesis would predict impaired recall in both conditions.

PV showed reduced recency in free recall of word lists presented auditorily, but not visually. She also showed a reduction in recency with visual presentation, but was able to employ the required strategy of recalling last items first. The results of this experiment supported the short-term store account that recency effects in free recall of word lists presented auditorily reflect the output of a phonological short-term store. Ordinal retrieval strategies could be applied to this store, and in the case of PV, it was presumed that these strategies were unimpaired.

Use of cognitive neuropsychological data to define the role of short-term memory in comprehension and learning

PV was the subject of several additional studies that addressed questions concerning the role of phonological short-term memory in sentence comprehension (Vallar & Baddeley, 1984b) and in learning (Baddeley, Papagno, & Vallar, 1988). Their studies of PV's sentence comprehension concurred with other studies (e.g. Caramazza, Basili, Koller, & Berndt, 1981) indicating that the phonological short-term store plays a crucial role in sentence comprehension, particularly when the sentence structure requires holding on to information over intervening words in order to comprehend the sentence. Perhaps the most important of these later studies, however, addressed the role of STM in verbal learning. This topic is currently of considerable interest to investigators of memory and learning, and Baddeley et al.'s (1988) investigation of PV's learning ability can be credited with the application of innovative paradigms to investigate learning abilities in subjects with auditory-verbal STM impairments.

Basso et al. (1982) found that PV's ability to learn verbal material (e.g. supraspan word lists, paired associates) was comparable to that of normal controls. Baddeley et al. (1988) examined PV's learning abilities further and found a more complex relationship between her verbal STM and learning abilities. They examined PV's ability to learn a vocabulary in an unfamiliar language using a paired associates task. Although PV was able to learn meaningful paired associates in a familiar (native) language, she was unable to learn associations between unfamiliar words in an unfamiliar language and familiar words from her own language. Moreover, when the learning task was represented visually, her performance improved, but was still not within the range of the control subjects. They concluded that phonological STM provides critical support to the learning of *new* vocabulary and likely plays an important role in language learning.

Summary of studies of PV and their importance to cognitive neuropsychology

PV was the subject of many investigations and was studied over a fairly long period of time. This history is impressive in its own right. What makes the case studies of PV exceptional is that they systematically address assumptions and characteristics of an established and fairly well-articulated model of working memory. Working closely within such a model has both advantages and disadvantages. The phenomenon under study (impaired phonological STM) was only recently identified and not understood very well. The advantage of Vallar and Baddeley's approach was that the working memory model provided an empirically supported logical framework within which to make predictions about PV's performance on span tasks. This enabled a characterisation of PV's deficit within a model and subsequently led to the use of data from PV to test the assumptions of the working memory model (for example, the recency effect).

A potential disadvantage of this approach is that exploration of a poorly understood phenomenon may be restricted by the assumptions of a model. Many, if not all, cognitive models are initially underspecified with respect to the phenomena they attempt to explain, and the working memory model is no exception. This model is most explicit about the role of phonological components of language processing in STM and has considerably less to say about lexical, semantic, and syntactic coding or their influences on STM. The working memory model has evolved like most others, and some of the amendments to the model can be credited to cognitive neuropsychological data. Nonetheless, it remains disproportionately focused on the phonological components of STM despite early indications from patients like PV (and more recent demonstrations from many other patients (e.g. Martin, Shelton, & Yaffee, 1994) that lexical and semantic codes influence span performance.

Although I raise this concern, it is relatively minor and outweighed by the advantage of using a cognitive model to understand neuropsychological impairments and, in turn, using neuropsychological data to test and constrain our models of cognitive functions. This approach is now fairly standard practice in cognitive neuropsychological research, and although Vallar and colleagues were not the first or only researchers to develop these methods of model testing, their efforts are certainly among the most comprehensive. Moreover, Vallar and colleagues expanded their studies to aspects of PV's language and memory performance that were not addressed in the working memory model (e.g. sentence comprehension) and, as noted earlier, were careful to report observations not adequately accounted for in this model (e.g. lexical-semantic influences on span). In this respect, they made the best use of a well-established model of working memory.

THE CASE OF JB

This case examines the question of whether a phonological STM impairment is a storage problem, a phonological problem, or both, and the issue of relation of language and short-term memory (Allport, 1984; Shallice & Butterworth, 1977; Warrington, Logue, & Pratt, 1971).

In the discussion of PV's case, I briefly raised the issue of lexical and semantic influences on her verbal STM capacity. Early investigations of auditory-verbal STM focused primarily on the involvement of phonological representations in STM and claimed that information in short-term memory was phonologically coded. Although lexical and semantic influences were acknowledged, their influence was often attributed to input from long-term representations of language. In keeping with this perspective, it was important to demonstrate that the impairment of the phonological short-term store was independent of any language deficits (phonological, lexical, semantic, or syntactic) also present in the subject. This task was not simple because many of the subjects with STM impairment also had some language dysfunction. As would be expected, the view that a phonological STM store could be selectively impaired did not go unchallenged. In particular, proponents of the long-held view that repetition deficits in aphasia arose from a disconnection between input and output speech systems offered accounts of how a disconnection or phonological processing impairments could lead to reduced span performance (e.g. Kinsbourne, 1972; Strub & Gardner, 1974; Tzortzis & Albert, 1974). One of the more serious challenges to the selective STM deficits hypothesis emerged from a case study of JB (Allport, 1984, but first reported by Warrington et al., 1971). Allport (1984) proposed an alternative view that the STM deficit resulted from a more general disturbance affecting maintenance of phonological traces that support both the STM and language performance. This view was in turn challenged point by point in Shallice (1988).

The debate between Allport (1984) and Shallice (1988) concerning JB's phonological processing and storage abilities (to be elaborated below) highlights one of the more important questions in cognitive psychology: How are processes that generate language representations related to processes that store them? Although there are some exceptions—e.g. Craik and Lockhart's (1972) levels-of-processing theory—the language system and the STM system historically have been studied and modelled separately, a sensible practice when the goal is to define properties of each system. In the background of these efforts, however, there has always been the realisation that the interrelation of these two systems needs to be articulated. Language processing, even single-word processing, takes place over time, implying the need to integrate a means of temporarily maintaining linguistic representations over the course of generating these representations. Additionally, both language and verbal STM are fundamental capacities underlying one of the most important human cognitive capacities—verbal learning. It is essential that we learn how these processes work together. Moreover, our understanding of the links between verbal STM, language, and learning has a direct bearing on the treatment of word processing disorders in aphasia (including repetition and word span abilities).

Cognitive neuropsychological investigations are particularly suited to questions concerning the relation of two cognitive capacities. Identification of associations and dissociations of impairments can provide insight into the interrelationship of two seemingly separate systems such as language and STM. Moreover, this relationship can be investigated by close examination of patients with impaired language and/or STM as they perform tasks that invoke both capacities. JB's case offers an excellent example of this approach.

Case report

JB, a right-handed female, incurred language and STM deficits at the age of 23 following surgical removal of a meningioma in the area of the left angular gyrus. Prior to that surgery and from the age of 12, JB had experienced periodic episodes of alterations of consciousness accompanied by some expressive dysphasia. These attacks lasted about 3 minutes and occurred every 3 or 4 weeks. The dysphasic component of the attacks became more prominent by the age of 18. A language assessment 3 weeks following the operation revealed fluent, but paraphasic speech production, difficulties in comprehension and in writing. Most of these impairments cleared within a short period following this assessment.[2] Remaining deficits were in repetition and, to a lesser extent, comprehension (from Warrington, Logue, & Pratt,

1971). Warrington et al. (1971) reported a detailed study of JB's language and short-term memory abilities some years after her operation (at the age of 35). Their evaluation of JB indicated that the primary deficit remaining was one of a restricted auditory-verbal STM. Auditory span for digits was 3 to 4, for letters, 2 to 3, and for words, 2 to 3. Performance on the Token Test (De Renzi & Vignolo, 1962) indicated some language comprehension deficits when sentences entailed recalling three or four disconnected items. In spite of this mild difficulty in comprehending complex sentences, JB demonstrated good performance on tasks of long-term learning. Naming abilities also were found to be within the normal range, and speech production was fluent and accurate. On the basis of several factors, Warrington et al. (1971) attributed JB's repetition difficulties to a selective deficit of auditory-verbal STM. First and foremost was the presence of a severe deficit of auditory-verbal span in the context of relatively spared language ability. JB's performance on span tasks was also affected by modality of presentation (improved span with visual presentation). Secondly, JB showed rapid forgetting of auditorily presented letter sequences when recall was delayed by as little as 5 seconds (the Brown-Peterson task) but not when the letter sequences were presented visually. Perceptual factors were ruled out as a factor in JB's span impairment, because she performed well on auditory word categorisation tasks. Also, production processes were ruled out because JB's span was impaired when tested on a probe memory task that involved recognition memory rather than recall.

Shallice and Butterworth (1977) carried out a study of JB's spontaneous speech to rule out any involvement of the speech production system in her span impairment. In a straightforward examination of the fluency of JB's spontaneous speech, Shallice and Butterworth showed that her speech production was comparable to normals with respect to number of pauses, the overall rate, and the number of errors. They concluded that the auditory-verbal short-term store was not used by the speech production system and suggested that JB's reduced repetition span was due to impairment of input auditory store. An alternative possibility is that the auditory-verbal short-term store could be used in spontaneous speech, but that the requirements for speech transmission are small and not taxed by JB's span. Shallice and Butterworth dismissed this possibility because such an argument implies that the auditory store exists primarily to subserve some other function besides storage. It is unclear why this possibility is objectionable. That fact that storage of linguistic representations in the short-term store is 'temporary' implies a subservient or facilitative role in the execution of any task involving language processing (e.g. word retrieval, sentence processing, span performance, and learning). Nevertheless, the fact remains that JB's spontaneous production was unaffected by her restricted span and, also, that her language comprehension was not compromised until the stimuli to be processed exceeded JB's span. Thus, JB represents one of the clearest cases of what appears to be a selective deficit in auditory-verbal STM.

In 1984, Allport challenged Shallice and Butterworth's conclusion about JB's STM deficit. Allport agreed that it was likely that auditory STM was an input store, but he suggested that processes responsible for temporary main-tenance of transitory phonological representations were also responsible for processing speech input—a notion related to Craik and Lockhart's (1972) levels-of-processing theory. Allport tested JB on a phonological discrimin-ation task (same–different judgements of nonsense syllable pairs) and found impaired performance on this task. He proposed that JB's span deficit was related to a more general phonological processing impairment. Allport's argument was not that the processing deficit caused the span deficit, but rather that both were the result of an impairment affecting the temporary maintenance of phonological traces. Shallice (1988) argued that these data do not confirm a common deficit affecting JB's span and phonological dis-crimination. The phonological discrimination task that Allport used con-sisted of same–different judgements of nonsense syllable pairs. Shallice cites Saffran and Marin's (1975) argument that difficulty in retaining nonsense syllables would be expected when auditory-verbal STM is severely impaired.

A second test of JB's input processing is more difficult to refute as evi-dence of a phonological processing impairment (and so acknowledged by Shallice, 1988). Allport (1984) administered an auditory lexical decision test using names of familiar, picturable objects. Non-word foils were derived from the words by altering one consonant. JB's performance on this task was impaired (20% of the non-word foils and 7% of the words) indicating a mild phonological processing deficit. Although the identification of co-occurring phonological and STM deficits does not prove absolutely that the two deficits arise from the same deficit, it does indicate that the two functions (proces-sing and storage of phonological traces) are intimately linked. Moreover, Allport's investigation reminds us that in order to rule out involvement of language processes in STM, language and span tasks must be carefully matched so that they exploit the same level of linguistic representation. JB's good performance on auditory word categorisation tasks, comprehension tasks, and learning (Warrington et al., 1971) does not indicate an absence of a perceptual deficit. Rather, PV's impaired performance on the phonological judgement and lexical decision tasks indicates that the comprehension can proceed in spite of difficulties with auditory perception, probably with the aid of top-down lexical-semantic processes.

Allport examined JB's performance on yet another task that is relevant to the issue of language and STM relations: repetition of single and multiple word sequences using words of both high and low frequency and image-ability. A striking feature of JB's performance on this task was the proportion of phonemic paraphasias produced in repetition of three-word sequences, particularly when words were low in frequency and imageability. This finding, like the one mentioned earlier in relation to PV's repetition span, suggests that lexical and semantic processes influence the capacity of the short-term store. Moreover, this study highlights the importance of examining language and span abilities under a number of conditions in order to understand the involvement of one with the other.

Allport's investigations of JB's phonological and lexical abilities represent a reasonable challenge to the view that phonological STM can be selectively impaired, and yet, this issue may be one that remains unresolved. Because linguistic and memorial processes are invoked in all language tasks, it is likely that disruption of both language and auditory-verbal span performance would result from an impairment to one of two independent systems, *or* from an impairment to a common process supporting both functions. Distinguishing between the two accounts empirically is difficult, at best. Moreover, it is somewhat counterproductive, at this stage, to focus on the potential isolability of the phonological store. For example, evidence can be amassed to demonstrate that word processing impairments characteristic of aphasia are on a severity continuum with what appear to be selective disturbances of auditory-verbal STM (e.g. Martin, Saffran, & Dell, 1996; Martin & Saffran, 1997). This information is valuable in its potential to reveal important intricacies of language processing and storage relations, but it can never prove that the two systems share common processes. There is, perhaps, one avenue of inquiry that might succeed in teasing the two accounts apart. That is, to distinguish between error patterns on span and language tasks that arise from a selective STM impairment that compromises language processing and those that arise from an impairment to a common maintenance process that disrupts both language and STM performance. Although the prospect of making such a fine distinction may seem remote, the effort potentially will be facilitated by the use of computationally instantiated models to make predictions about error patterns associated with cognitive lesions.

It might appear that Allport (1984) and Shallice's (1988) debate on the organisation of language and STM ended in a stalemate. Nevertheless, this does not diminish the importance of their studies and discussions of JB, and the impact these have had on subsequent investigations of language and STM impairments in aphasia. In fact, JB's case represents a juncture at which attention began to shift from the quest to isolate short-term memory processes to a focus more on the links between STM and language processes. Consider, for example, papers in Vallar and Shallice (1990) that focus on lexical and semantic components of STM—e.g. Berndt and Mitchum (1990); Saffran and Martin (1990). In the 1990s there was a virtual explosion of interest in this issue and the decade witnessed some remarkable advances in empirical investigations of language involvement in STM impairments. R. Martin and colleagues (e.g. Martin et al., 1994; Martin & Lesch, 1996) distinguished between semantically based and phonologically based STM impairments and Martin (N.) and Saffran (1997) demonstrated that semantic and phonological impairments have different consequences for what has been held to be a characteristic specific to STM (serial position effects). Interest in the relations between STM and language processing shows no signs of fading and is not limited to the study of individuals with acquired brain damage. Investigators of developmental learning disorders also are actively engaged in the study of connections between STM impairments, language, and learning disorders (e.g. Gathercole & Baddeley, 1989; Service, 1992). Evidence from developmental and brain-damaged populations complements early studies of normal subjects that indicate linguistic influences on STM (e.g. Shulman, 1971; Baddeley, Thomson, & Buchanan, 1975; Watkins & Watkins, 1977).

An important outcome of this recent surge of interest in the relations between STM and language systems is the resultant evolution of Baddeley's working memory model. For much of the model's history, the phonological loop and rehearsal components were its most often investigated and most thoroughly articulated aspects. More recent investigations and theoretical discussions of this model focus on the role of the central executive and attentional processes in linking working memory with comprehension and production of language (e.g. Gathercole & Baddeley, 1993). As Baddeley and his colleagues continue development of the working memory model, other researchers offer new models that attempt to account for STM–language relations. Armed with empirical data to support such a relationship and computational modelling as a theoretical testing tool, a number of investigators have proposed new models to account for links between language processes and auditory-verbal STM (e.g. Gupta & MacWhinney, 1997; Hartley & Houghton, 1996; Houghton, 1990; Page & Norris, 1998; Vousden, Brown, & Harley, 2000). These developments in cognitive neuropsychology have their roots in single case studies of individuals with auditory STM impairments such as PV and JB. The investigators of these case studies began the discussion and defined the issues that are still of interest to cognitive psychologists and important to our understanding of cognition.

CONCLUSION

I have chosen two cases, the impact of which on the field of cognitive neuropsychology is as relevant today as it was when they were first studied. PV and JB were similar cases in that both subjects evolved from a profile of mild language impairment accompanied by auditory STM deficits to one of primarily an auditory STM deficit. Both were subjects of thorough investigations to pinpoint their deficits within a model of verbal STM (although PV's investigation is more explicitly directed towards this end). In this respect, both PV and JB are prominent examples of the cognitive case study approach that uses a cognitive model to guide the investigation of a neuropsychological impairment. Moreover, these cases were relevant, indeed central, to a debate in cognitive neuropsychology that has paved the way for what is currently an active and productive line of research, discerning the mechanisms linking language, STM and learning. In these two respects, PV and JB can be considered classic cases who have contributed to both the empirical and theoretical development of cognitive neuropsychology.

ACKNOWLEDGEMENTS

Preparation of this chapter was supported by grants from the National Institutes on Deafness and Other Communication Disorders to Temple University School of Medicine: R01 DC01924–07 (N. Martin) and R01 DC01910–17 (E.M. Saffran).

REFERENCES

Allport, A. (1984). Auditory-verbal short-term memory and conduction aphasia. In H. Bouma & D.G. Bouwhuis (Eds.), *Attention and performance X: Control of language processes.* Hillsdale NJ: Lawrence Erlbaum Associates Inc.

Baddeley, A.D. (1966). Short-term memory for word sequences as a function of acoustic, semantic and formal similarity. *Quarterly Journal of Experimental Psychology, 18*, 362–365.

Baddeley, A.D. (1986). *Working memory.* Oxford: Clarendon Press.

Baddeley, A.D. (1990). The development of the concept of working memory: Implications and contributions of neuropsychology. In G. Vallar & T. Shallice (Eds.), *Neuropsychological impairments of short-term memory.* Cambridge: Cambridge University Press.

Baddeley, A.D. (1996). The concept of working memory. In S.E. Gathercole (Ed.), *Models of short-term memory* (pp. 1–27). Hove, UK: Psychology Press.

Baddeley, A.D., & Hitch, G.J. (1974). Working memory. In G.H. Bower (Ed.), *The psychology of learning and motivation* (Vol. 8). New York: Academic Press.

Baddeley, A.D., Lewis, V., & Vallar, G. (1984). Exploring the articulatory loop. Quarterly *Journal of Experimental Psychology, 36A*, 233–252.

Baddeley, A.D., Papagno, C., & Vallar, G. (1988). When long-term learning depends on short-term storage. *Journal of Memory and Language, 27*, 586–595.

Baddeley, A.D., Thomson, N., & Buchanan, M. (1975). Word length and the structure of short-term memory. *Journal of Verbal Learning and Verbal Behavior, 14*, 575–589.

Basso, A., Spinnler, H., Vallar, G., & Zanobio (1982). Left hemisphere damage and selective impairment of auditory-verbal short-term memory: A case study. *Neuropsychologia, 20*, 263–274.

Berndt, R.S., & Mitchum, C. (1990). Auditory and lexical information sources in immediate recall: Evidence from a patient with deficit to the phonological short-term store. In G. Vallar & T. Shallice (Eds.), *Neuropsychological impairments of short-term memory* (pp. 115–144). Cambridge: Cambridge University Press.

Caramazza, A., Basili, A.G., Koller, J.J., & Berndt, R.S. (1981). An investigation of repetition and language processing in a case of conduction aphasia. *Brain and Language, 21*, 9–20.

Conrad, R. (1964). Acoustic confusion in immediate memory. *British Journal of Psychology, 55*, 75–84.

Craik, F.I.M., & Lockhart, R.S. (1972). Levels of processing: A framework for memory research. *Journal of Verbal Learning and Verbal Behavior, 11*, 671–684.

DeRenzi, E., & Vignolo, L.A. (1962). The Token Test: A sensitive test to detect receptive disturbances in aphasics. *Brain*, *85*, 665–678

Gathercole, S., & Baddeley, A.D. (1989). Evaluation of the role of phonological STM in the development of vocabulary in children: A longitudinal study. *Journal of Memory and Language*, *28*, 200–213.

Gathercole, S., & Baddeley, A.D. (1993). *Working memory and language*. Hove, UK: Lawrence Erlbaum Associates Ltd.

Glanzer, M. (1972). Storage mechanisms in recall. In G.H. Bower (Ed.), *The psychology of learning and motivation (Vol. 5)*. New York: Academic Press.

Gupta, P., & MacWhinney, B. (1997). Vocabulary acquisition and verbal short-term memory: Computational and neural bases. *Brain and Language*, *59, 267–333*.

Hartley, T., & Houghton, G. (1996). A linguistically constrained model of short-term memory for non-words. *Journal of Memory and Language*, *35*, 1–31.

Houghton, G. (1990). The problem of serial order: A neural network model of sequence learning and recall. In R. Dale, C. Mellish, & M. Zock (Eds.), *Current research in natural language generation*. New York: Academic Press.

Kinsbourne, M. (1972). Behavioral analysis of the repetition deficit in conduction aphasia. *Neurology*, *22*, 1126–1132.

Martin, N., & Saffran, E.M. (1997). Language and auditory-verbal short-term memory impairments: Evidence for common underlying processes. *Cognitive Neuropsychology*, *14*, 641–682.

Martin, N., Saffran, E.M., & Dell, G.S. (1996). Recovery in deep dysphasia: Evidence for a relation between auditory-verbal STM capacity and lexical errors in repetition. *Brain and Language*, *52*, 83–113.

Martin, R.C., & Lesch, M.F. (1996). Associations and dissociations between language impairment and list recall: Implications for models of STM. In S.E. Gathercole (Ed.), *Models of working memory* (pp. 149–178). Hove, UK: Psychology Press.

Martin, R.C., Shelton, J., & Yaffee, L. (1994). Language processing and working memory: Neuropsychological evidence for separate phonological and semantic capacities. *Journal of Memory and Language*, *33*, 83–111.

Murray, D.J. (1968). Articulation and acoustic confusability in short-term memory. *Journal of Experimental Psychology*, *78*, 679–684.

Page, M., & Norris, D. (1998). Modeling immediate serial recall with a localist implementation of the primacy model. In J. Grainger & A. M. Jacobs (Eds.), *Localist connectionist approaches to human cognition* (pp. 227–256). Mahwah, NJ: Lawrence Erlbaum Associates Inc.

Salame, P., & Baddeley, A.D. (1982). Disruption of short-term memory by unattended speech: Implications for the structure of working memory. *Journal of Verbal Learning and Verbal Behavior*, *21*, 150–164.

Saffran E., & Marin, O.S.M. (1975). Immediate memory for word lists and sentences in a patient with deficient auditory short-term memory. *Brain and Language*, *2*, 420–433.

Saffran, E.M., & Martin, N. (1990). Neuropsychological evidence for lexical involvement in short-term memory. In G. Vallar & T. Shallice (Eds.), *Neuropsychological impairments of short-term memory* (pp. 145–166). Cambridge: Cambridge University Press.

Service, L. (1992). Phonology, working memory, and foreign-language learning. *Quarterly Journal of Experimental Psychology*, *45A*, 21–50.

Shallice, T. (1988). *From neuropsychology to mental structure*. Cambridge: Cambridge University Press.

Shallice, T., & Butterworth, B. (1977). Short-term memory impairment and spontaneous speech. *Neuropsychologia*, 15, 729–735.

Shulman, H.G. (1971). Similarity effects in short-term memory. *Psychological Bulletin*, *75*, 399–415.

Strub, R.L., & Gardner, H. (1974). The repetition deficit in conduction aphasia: Mnestic or linguistic? *Brain and Language*, *1*, 241–255.

Tulving, E. (1968). Theoretical issues in free recall. In T.R. Dixon & D.L. Horton (Eds.), *Verbal behavior and general behavior theory* (pp. 2–36). Englewood Cliffs, NJ: Prentice-Hall.

Tzortzis, D., & Albert, M.L. (1974). Impairment of memory for sequences in conduction aphasia. *Neuropsychologia, 12*, 355–366.

Vallar, G., & Baddeley, A.D. (1984a). Fractionation of working memory: Neuropsychological evidence for a phonological short-term store. *Journal of Verbal Learning and Verbal Behavior, 23*, 151–161.

Vallar, G., & Baddeley, A.D. (1984b). Phonological short-term store: Phonological processing and sentence comprehension. *Cognitive Neuropsychology, 4*, 55–78.

Vallar, G., & Papagno, C. (1986). Phonological short-term store and the nature of the recency effect. *Brain and Cognition, 5*, 428–442.

Vallar, G., & Shallice, T. (Eds.) (1990). *Neuropsychological impairments of short-term memory*. Cambridge: Cambridge University Press.

Vousden, J.I., Brown, G.D.A., & Harley, T.A. (2000). Serial control of phonology in speech production: A hierarchical model. *Cognitive Psychology, 41*, 101–175.

Warrington, E.K., Logue, V., & Pratt, R.T.C. (1971). The anatomical localisation of selective impairment of short-term memory. *Neuropsychologia, 9*, 377–387.

Warrington, E.K., & Shallice, T. (1969). The selective impairment of auditory verbal short-term memory. *Brain, 92*, 885–896.

Watkins, O.C., & Watkins, M.J. (1977). Serial recall and the modality effect. *Journal of Experimental Psychology: Human Learning and Memory, 3*, 712–718.

NOTES

1. The original STM model focused primarily on an articulatory loop mechanism that refreshed contents of an output buffer. This was modified to include an input phonological store, in part, on the basis of evidence from patient JB, whose fluency of spontaneous speech was normal (Shallice & Butterworth, 1977).

2. It has been rightly pointed out by an anonymous reviewer that the mildness and transience of JB's language impairment is a bit surprising given the size and locus of her lesion (left retrorolandic areas). In right-handed individuals, the left hemisphere and this particular area is usually specialised for some language function. The fact that JB's transient dysphasia episodes began (or, at least were first observed) at age 12 suggests the possibility that JB's neural organisation favoured lateralisation of language in the right hemisphere (an unusual combination with right-handedness). Alternatively, it is conceivable, given the early onset of language difficulty, that neural reorganisation of language functions occurred, shifting much of the responsibility for language to the right hemisphere. Although this account is speculative, JB's case should be noted by those interested in factors contributing to reorganisation of functions in the brain.

CHAPTER FOUR

Singer and Low's case of acalculia: Foresight of modern theories on number processing

Luisa Girelli
Department of Psychology, University of Milano-Bicocca, Milan, Italy

INTRODUCTION

In 1933 Singer and Low, two neurologists working in London and Chicago respectively, reported a detailed investigation of the residual abilities of a patient with multiple difficulties in the numerical domain. This study was not the first describing an acquired numerical disorder, neither was the proposed interpretation of the patient's deficit a breakthrough in the development of theoretical accounts of acalculia. However, unlike in the majority of early reports, the assessment of the patient's numerical difficulties covered a wide range of competencies; the evaluation of these, together with some poignant observations of the patient's performance, foresaw some of the key issues in current theories of number processing and calculation. Singer and Low's study has indeed been recognised as one of the first and more remarkable attempts to systematically investigate acquired numerical disorders (e.g. McCloskey, Caramazza, & Basili, 1985; Seron & Noel, 1992). Its merits, however, have been largely overlooked and the priority on one single observation only among the many Singer and Low introduced—i.e. the specific breakdown of transcoding rules in the writing of Arabic numerals—is now attributed to them. Given the great attention that has been recently paid to numerical cognition, a closer examination and acknowledgement of their contribution is of particular interest.

Before describing in detail the case study and discussing its implications for current theories of numerical processing and calculation, the contributions that preceded and influenced Singer and Low's investigation will be briefly presented.

Anecdotic descriptions of disorders in numbers skills were first reported in research on aphasia in the last decades of the 19th century (e.g. Bastian, 1898). The researchers noticed that aphasic patients occasionally presented an inability to read and write numbers and to calculate, but these difficulties were always considered part of the aphasic syndrome. The first case of selective calculation deficit was reported by Lewandowsky and Stadelmann in 1908. Their patient, following the removal of an haematoma from the left occipital lobe, showed a severe inability to perform simple calculation despite good reading and writing of numbers as well as mostly preserved language and more general intellectual efficiency. The authors attributed the deficit to a disorder of the 'optic representation of number' and concluded that an impairment in calculation may occur as an isolated cognitive deficit following specific cerebral lesions. Thereafter, other cases of calculation disorders were reported (Peritz, 1918; Poppelreuter, 1917; Sittig, 1917), most of which confirmed the involvement of the left retrorolandic areas in numerical skills and indicated that these deficits may be associated not only with language problems but also with visuo-spatial difficulties.

It was only in 1919 that calculation disorders were systematically investigated and the term acalculia was introduced by Henschen. His arguments were grounded on a detailed examination of a vast number of published case reports and of his own clinical experience. He postulated the existence of specific cortical centres dedicated to different aspects of calculation: the third frontal convolution involved in the pronunciation of numbers; the angular gyrus and fissura intraparietalis involved in number reading; and the angular gyrus involved in number writing. Besides these anatomical speculations, Henschen advanced more important and general considerations. He suggested that acalculia was not a unitary syndrome and that it could be differentiated from language disorders as well as from general intelligence. Moreover, he promoted the idea, subsequently confirmed by Gerstmann (1927), that acalculia and number agraphia were correlated and associated with lesions to the left angular gyrus.

The concept of acalculia was then refined by Hans Berger (1926) who introduced the critical distinction between primary and secondary acalculia. The latter would frequently occur in patients with language, attentional, or memory deficits; primary or 'pure' acalculia, on the other hand, does not relate to any other cognitive deficit. Berger also noted that the dissociation between calculation ability and general intelligence, observed in some idiot savants as well as in cerebral-lesioned patients, indicated their functional autonomy. In a further attempt to identify the factors determining acalculia, Goldstein (1919) proposed a distinction between (1) an abstraction deficit, responsible for the loss of number meaning and of the understanding of the arithmetical operation and (2) a mechanical disturbance of unspecified type—e.g. visual, linguistic, or motor, the consequences of which on numerical skills may vary.

Shortly before Singer and Low's contribution, the role of spatial and constructional difficulties in acalculic disorders was emphasised by Lange (1930, 1933). He reported that written calculation was more frequently compromised than oral calculation and he identified a major source of calculation difficulties in the spatial organisation of numbers and in the manipulation of their relative position. This account had a great impact on later studies as indicated by the work of Kleist (1934) and Krapf (1937) who proposed the existence of a 'constructive acalculia' where the primary deficit would involve the spatial manipulation of numbers.

Thus, by the time Singer and Low carried out their investigation, acalculia was already recognised as a selective cognitive deficit (e.g. Henschen, 1919, 1920) but the theoretical accounts proposed were still controversial and underspecified.

CASE DESCRIPTION

Singer and Low's patient was a well-educated 44-year-old man with no significant clinical history, who worked as an assistant superintendent in a firm. He could reliably accomplish his work, which required him to keep track of time and the wages of the employees and to estimate the cost of jobs. Following accidental carbon monoxide poisoning, he disclosed multiple neuropsychological difficulties of which dyscalculia, agraphia, and apraxia were the most severe. The language evaluation indicated only mild anomic difficulties with preserved repetition and reading abilities. His writing was almost illegible at the beginning of the testing but improved after daily training. An accurate analysis of the errors he produced (e.g. anticipations, juxtapositions), whether in spontaneous, copied, or dictated writing, indicated that the major source of his difficulties was an inability to handle spatial elements. The patient himself complained that 'everything seemed left-sided'; moreover, in the absence of any hemianopia or scotoma, the difficulties he disclosed in several everyday situations (e.g. dressing himself) clearly indicated some form of right hemineglect. The observation that he was unable to handle tools he could recognise suggested the occurrence of constructional apraxia, further evaluated with several tasks. The patient's drawing from copy and from memory did not differ: in both cases he was markedly more impaired with asymmetric figures (e.g. shoe, church) than with symmetrical arrangements (e.g. apple, table) except when the latter were of higher complexity (e.g. hexagon), in which case his attempts were a total failure. As in writing, a constant displacement on the right of the vertical line and above or below the horizontal line was observed. His apraxia was further documented by a failure to reproduce visually presented arrangements with small sticks, a task originally developed by Strauss (1924).

In addition to the above, the patient was severely impaired in answering even very simple arithmetical operations, such as adding five and six. Therefore, his numerical skills were carefully evaluated with several tasks that tackle distinct aspects of numerical knowledge. Like the majority of early neuropsychological studies, quantitative data about the number of stimuli presented and the errors observed were not systematically reported; however, the variety of tasks adopted and the meticulous qualitative observations of the patient's performance disclosed Singer and Low's intuition into the complex and multi-componential nature of numerical abilities. As indicated by the brief review of the contemporary contributions, in the 1930s theories on numerical disorders were neither exhaustive nor explicitly formulated. Though the important distinctions between number processing and calculation abilities and, within this latter, between memory retrieval and computational strategies, were put forward early on (Lewandowsky & Stadelmann, 1908), no attempts to further refine the functional structure of numerical abilities were yet accomplished. In this respect, Singer and Low's investigation offers an original and invaluable contribution: the inventive methodology they adopted in evaluating the patient's difficulties clearly reflects their own theoretical insight on number processing and calculation skills.

From the authors' comments, we may infer that the evaluation of the patient's acalculia was undertaken several months after the onset of his illness, during which he underwent daily training for his calculation difficulties. No information on the type of instructions he received was given, but the effect of training on the single tasks was often reported.

CALCULATION SKILLS

The assessment of calculation abilities included multiple tasks, the comparison of which allowed the investigators to disentangle the effect of several critical factors, such as type of operation, problem difficulty, presentation modality, and context effect in the application of arithmetical knowledge. The importance of these factors is nowadays well established but it is worth noting that they have been overlooked not only in previous reports but also long after this study.

The patient's ability to answer simple subtractions and divisions was totally lost and did not improve over the training. On the other hand, he could answer correctly addition problems the sum of which was less than 10, as well as larger problems when an addend was 10 or 20 (e.g. 10 + 8). Any other sum as well as three single-digit addend problems (e.g. 1 + 3 + 4 = 6) were incorrectly answered. Interestingly, multiplication tables were the only operation to benefit from the training and, even if the performance was not error-free, the known problems were answered promptly. Written calculation (all operations but division) did improve over the training, though from the few given examples we may not infer to what extent this improvement concerned the execution of arithmetical procedures (e.g. use of carry) or the retrieval of simple calculations.

The authors attempted a reaction time analysis, the most intriguing observation of which was the differential speed improvement for simple addition and multiplication problems. Addition problems, even when consistently correct since the outset (e.g. $3 + 4 = 7$), required an average of 4 seconds, possibly suggesting that some form of inner counting strategies were applied to reach the solution. Multiplications, on the other hand, '. . .were regularly solved instantaneously, with hardly a measurable time interval. . .' and '[multiplication] had become a mechanically mastered process . . . The patient had no longer to calculate and deliberate, but could reproduce the learned result from memory . . . That this result was achieved in multiplication only is apt to throw light on a basic difference between this operation and the others' (p. 472).

Indeed, the distinction between different types of operations in terms of level of automaticity and preferred solution strategies is nowadays a matter of debate. All current cognitive models postulate two distinct components devoted to calculation; namely, the arithmetical facts system, that includes operations the solution of which may be directly retrieved from memory, and the functionally independent mastery of arithmetical procedures required in complex written calculation (e.g. Dehaene, 1992; Dehaene & Cohen, 1995; McCloskey et al., 1985). The internal organisation of the arithmetical facts system has been clarified recently by several case studies. Patients who showed selective deficit in one operation (e.g. multiplication) and preserved knowledge of others (e.g. addition and subtraction) have been repeatedly reported and it has been shown that the pattern of spared and impaired operations may vary considerably (e.g. Dagenbach & McCloskey, 1992; Delazer & Benke, 1997; Hittmair-Delazer, Semenza, & Denes, 1994; McNeil & Warrington, 1994; Pesenti, Seron, & van der Linden, 1994). Dissociations between different operations have been interpreted both in terms of segregated memory representation (Dagenbach & McCloskey, 1992) and in terms of different representation format (Dehaene & Cohen, 1995). According to this latter approach, which simply reformulated what psychologists and educators had for long postulated (Clapp, 1924; Thorndike, 1922), because overlearned multiplications and additions are systematically taught, they might be considered rote verbal memories; on the other hand, other operations like subtraction are more likely to rely on the execution of back-up strategies (e.g. counting) or on the internal manipulation of quantities (Dehaene & Cohen, 1997).

Singer and Low's observations of the patient's mastery of simple arithmetic fits nicely in this debate, indicating a clear-cut dissociation between impaired subtraction and division problems, procedure-based mastery of simple addition, and automatised multiplication tables. The authors also attributed the 'greater tendency [of multiplication tables] to become automatised' (p. 494) to the more extensive school training on these compared to other operations. The authors did not directly address the issue of the format representation. They noted that the patient's overall accuracy and type of errors did not vary according to the problems being presented in verbal or written modality. However, the observation that errors in multiplication often included the repetition of the second operand (e.g. $5 \times 4 = 24$, $6 \times 7 = 47$), seems to suggest that problems were indeed verbally recoded and that the naming of the factors intruded in the answer (cf. Campbell, 1994; Campbell & Clark, 1992).

Further systematic errors emerged from the authors' attempt to analyse the patient's qualitative performance. In addition problems the answer sometimes corresponded to the number following the larger addend (e.g. $16 + 6 = 17$ or $5 + 7 = 8$). The patient was thus counting from the larger addend but did not successfully complete the procedure. Of a less clear origin were the errors that corresponded to the reversal of one of the factors, as in $23 + 6 = 32$ or $13 + 6 = 31$. Finally, in both addition and multiplication problems, substitutions of operation errors were observed. In these cases, the patient produced an error that corresponded to the correct answer to a different operation between the same factors—e.g., $2 + 4 = 8$, $2 \times 5 = 7$. The misrecognition of arithmetical signs has been more recently described as an isolated source of calculation difficulties (Ferro & Silveira Botelho, 1980). Interestingly, the patient was able to write the signs to dictation but, despite being specifically instructed about the meaning of the arithmetical signs, still confused them in the context of calculation. Moreover, unexpected substitution occurred when the patient answered addition problems as subtractions—e.g. $8 + 5 = 3$ or $9 + 3 = 6$. In fact, when explicitly requested, the patient was unable to answer any subtraction problems. Similarly, he spontaneously added three digits when he had simply to read them aloud, while he never performed a similar sum if specifically asked to do so. These observations led Singer and Low to draw a distinction between spontaneous and task-elicited performance. In the former, the patient was 'exercising a function being unaware of it' (p. 493), while in the latter the very same function had to be activated as a requirement of the task. This fine differentiation is in line with current explanations of selective preservation and loss of knowledge in terms of 'incidental' and 'intentional' retrieval of information (Jacoby, 1984) as well as in terms of 'explicit' or conscious and 'implicit' recollection (Schacter, 1985, 1987).

Besides various structural factors, such as type of operation and size of the problem, Singer and Low also evaluated the impact of contextual effects on calculation proficiency. Retention of numbers and arithmetical signs within or out of mathematical context was evaluated by asking the patient to repeat the problem he had to answer previously as well as to simply retain equally long numerical stimuli with no specific instructions. Unfortunately, the potentially interesting disadvantage of the former task, that was interpreted as an index of context-specific difficulty in the manipulation of numbers (for a discussion of task effects in number processing see Cohen & Dehaene, 1995), may not be considered conclusive given that the answer modality was not matched across the tasks—i.e. the patient answered verbally to the former and in written form to the latter. It was also observed that when addition problems were dictated to the patient, he constantly wrote down the larger addend first (e.g. $6 + 3$), regardless of the relative order of the addends in the given problem (e.g. $3 + 6$). The spontaneous inversion of the addends was interpreted as a strategy to facilitate the task, in line with the observation that he used to count on from the larger addend in order to solve a sum. Indeed, the effect of the relative order of the addends in addition problems was reported since the very early studies on arithmetic skills (Browne, 1906) and confirmed in developmental (e.g., Siegler, 1987) as well as in neuropsychological investigation (Warrington, 1982).

Finally, the patient was presented with arithmetical text problems where numbers were no longer abstract entities but had concrete referents. The problems had very simple schemata and required computations matched for difficulty with the ones presented in pure calculation tasks. The performance in verbal text problems (e.g. 'A man has 5 automobiles and 3 trucks. How many vehicles?') was compared to the manipulation of real objects (e.g. 'Here are 6 beans and 5 beans. How many beans all together?'). It was observed that concrete problems were better mastered than verbal ones and that these latter yielded even more errors than abstract calculation. Within the concrete category, problems requiring the manipulation of money were easier than others. Singer and Low attributed these differences to the facilitation effect that a familiar situation (e.g. manipulation of money) may have on the execution of the computation itself, a suggestion that has now received further support from both developmental (e.g. Fuson, 1992; Resnick, 1992) and neuropsychological studies (Dehaene & Cohen, 1997). In fact, developmental studies have shown that the ability to reason about numbers at a formal level is acquired later on than the ability to manipulate quantities of objects or physical material (Resnick, 1992). A similar dissociation between the manipulation of formal numbers and of numbers with concrete referents has been observed recently in a case of acquired dyscalculia. Dehaene and Cohen (1997) described a patient who could compute calculation with hours that he was no longer able to compute in the abstract. For example, he could work out how much time elapsed between two hours but he could not answer any similar subtraction.

COUNTING

Once the extent of the patient's calculation difficulties was established, the authors attempted to identify the factors responsible for them by evaluating distinct competencies considered prerequisite for the mastery of calculation.

Following the assumption, shared by current psychologists (e.g. Fuson, 1992; Geary, Brown, & Samaranayake, 1991), that counting abilities have a great impact on the mastery of computational skills, the former were carefully evaluated. The knowledge of the counting sequence was assessed by asking the patient to count forward and backward, starting from 1 but also from any other number (e.g. 990), counting by 2 or by 3, and finally by identifying errors in orally presented sequences. Other automatic ordered sequences (e.g. days of the week, months of the year) were also tested (cf. Deloche & Seron, 1984). The patient was also required, given a number, to produce the one that comes before (e.g. '19' answer 18). Mental counting was then compared to counting of continuous series of objects or acts, which was evaluated in a series of extremely original tasks such as counting flashlight bursts in quick succession, finger tapping, and even blindfold counting of pills ('tactile counting'). Finally, counting of grouped pills, varying in pattern or shape, was also tested. In this case, the presentation of groups of equal numerosity (e.g. 4 groups of 5 pills) would have been expected to induce the application of strategies, such as counting the first group and multiplying; not surprisingly, this strategy was not adopted because it implies good arithmetical knowledge.

Overall, the patient showed selective difficulties in counting discontinuous series of large numerosities (over 10) possibly due to the greater spatial and attentional requirements of the task. Unfortunately, the authors did not report any observation of the patient's counting behaviour (e.g. pointing, oral counting) which would facilitate a more accurate interpretation of his deficit. Nevertheless, the implied distinction between mental counting and object counting has now been acknowledged to be of critical importance (e.g. Fuson, 1988). The former may be accomplished by simply reciting an automatic verbal sequence, while the latter requires the matching of the verbal sequence to distinct counting entities, a task that implies several constitutive principles (e.g. Gelman & Gallistel, 1978). Cerebral-lesioned patients may fail in object counting for different reasons related to the multiple aspects of the task (e.g. verbal production, spatial analysis, conceptual counting principles; Seron et al., 1991); in this respect, the performance of acalculic patients may be particularly revealing (e.g. Delazer & Butterworth, 1997). Nevertheless, this fundamental skill is still not routinely evaluated in patients with numerical disorders.

NUMBER PROCESSING

Number processing skills were evaluated in reading, writing, and recognition tasks. The patient was able to read up to 3-digit Arabic numerals as well as longer stimuli when constituted by 2 digits and multiplier (e.g. 25.000). He could easily read ordinals (e.g. 1st, 4th) and non-numerical signs (e.g. %, $). Number recognition difficulties were excluded on the basis of his correct performance in tasks where he was asked to identify a target stimulus between several visually similar alternatives (e.g. 257, 275, 725). Similarly, he was able to identify a specific numeral in a sequence of random spoken verbal numbers.

In writing Arabic numerals to dictation, however, his performance was disturbed for any number above 100. His errors consisted in the literal transcoding of each individual word of the verbal numerals—e.g., 'two hundred forty-two' was written as 20042. Interestingly, when dictated with 'two thousand five hundred' he wrote 2000500, but 'twenty-five hundred' was correctly transcoded as 2500 suggesting a clear effect of the verbal structure of the stimuli on the production of Arabic numerals (Noel & Seron, 1995). When the patient had to compose a given spoken numeral with cards representing single digits, he similarly failed in the writing task—i.e. producing lexicalisation errors. His performance was characterised by a further factor: digits were frequently arranged from right to left as in 050020001 as 'one thousand two hundred and fifty'. This result was attributed to an inability to manipulate spatial arrangement that led to a disturbed knowledge of 'place value'. The corresponding task in verbal modality was performed flawlessly—e.g. given 'one, eight, three' he said 'one hundred eighty-three'.

Analogue difficulties have been systematically reported in three modern single-case studies that elucidated the mechanisms underlying this phenomenon (e.g. Cipolotti, Butterworth, & Warrington, 1994; Delazer & Denes, 1998; Noel & Seron, 1995). In all these cases, lexicalisation errors of the type observed by Singer and Low were attributed to disturbed syntactic mechanisms—i.e. mechanisms devoted to the processing of the relative position of the digits within a numeral (e.g. Deloche & Seron, 1982; McCloskey et al., 1985) in the production of Arabic numerals. In particular, this error pattern has been interpreted as a misapplication of specific transcoding rules that operate in the production system (Power & Longuet-Higgins, 1978). The 'concatenation rule' is applied in transcoding verbal numerals in product relationship (e.g. two hundred, that means '2 times 100' → 200) while the 'overwriting rule' is applied in transcoding verbal numerals in sum relationship (e.g. two hundred and twenty, that means '200 plus 20' → 220). In all reported cases, the insertion of zeros (e.g. 20042) was interpreted as determined by an inability to master the overwriting operation. Analogue difficulties are indeed frequently observed in the production of Arabic numerals by young children (e.g. Power & Dal Martello, 1990; Seron, Deloche, & Noel, 1992; Seron & Fayol, 1994).

NUMBER KNOWLEDGE AND ESTIMATION

The standard task for evaluating number comprehension consists in the comparison of numerical values. Singer and Low were among the first to thoroughly present the patient with a series of tasks where pairs of Arabic numerals, but also fractions, times, and monetary values, had to be compared. The patient was always correct in pointing to the larger item and he also satisfactorily defined odd and even numbers, showing overall a well-preserved knowledge of 'number concept'.

To rule out the possibility of a gross inability to estimate quantities being responsible for poor arithmetic, the patient was requested to estimate visually presented quantities in an original series of tasks. He correctly ordered three piles of sticks as well as glasses containing different amounts of water. Then, presented with 200 pills, he had to sort heaps of different value (e.g. 60) without counting and to divide them in two equal parts. His performance was good, except when large amounts were involved (e.g. 235 pills to be divided in two). He was equally skilled in mental estimates, such as estimating the length of his middle finger, the time needed to go from Chicago to New York, or the average speed of an automobile. It is worth noticing that analogue questions are included in a 'cognitive estimates' test devised by Shallice and Evans in 1978. This task, originally developed as an executive functions test, is now routinely adopted to tap residual numerical estimation abilities in acalculic patients (Cipolotti, Butterworth, & Denes, 1991; Dehaene & Cohen, 1997; Warrington, 1982).

Following the assumption that memory is a critical component in the execution of any computation (but see Butterworth, Cipolotti, & Warrington, 1996), the authors attempted an evaluation of the patient's memory capacity. The patient was able to repeat three numbers immediately but failed after a short delay (3 minutes). He could keep in mind two 2-digit numbers to be underscored on a sheet of paper where 42 numbers were written down. However, when asked to repeat sentences that contained numbered objects, he retained the objects but not the numbers (e.g. 'A man has 250 horses and 30 cows', he repeated as 'A man has 50 horses and 25 cows'). The authors concluded that the patient could repeat and retain isolated numbers but not numbers in their mathematical context (e.g. text problems) and this difficulty might have played a role in his poor calculation. However, the few given examples indicate that the length of the stimuli was not balanced across the tasks, thus undermining the validity of their conclusion.

FURTHER TESTS

Among the various non-numerical abilities that were specifically investigated for their possible role in the patient's acalculia, the following are of particular interest.

Simultaneous perception

Tachistoscopic presentation of Arabic numerals, patterns of points, and words indicated great difficulty in simultaneous perception. The patient could read single-digit numbers but longer stimuli were only partially correct (e.g. 472 was read 1–47). He failed to recognise any pattern of points, even though with unlimited presentation he could always enumerate them. Monosyllabic words also required repeated exposures before being correctly read. Interestingly, highly familiar words (e.g. the patient's name) were recognised with no hesitation.

Chronognosis

The patient was well oriented in time and his time estimations were always adequate; also, he could answer general questions about specific dates. However, when asked to read the time from a watch, he correctly answered half hours only (e.g. 11.30). His errors mainly consisted of reading the symmetrically opposed time (e.g. 12.15 instead of 11.45) and similar mistakes occurred when he had to indicate the time on a dummy watch. His preserved understanding of time concept and the specific nature of the errors suggested that his difficulties were determined by the spatial requirement of the task.

Apperception

In a series of various tasks that included solution of logical inferences, verbal fluency, production of synonyms, opposites, and semantic similarities, the patient's performance was adequate. A further task modified from Buehler (1913) required the patient to identify letters or numbers within integrated figures. He did the task with ease and the authors concluded that his apperceptive processes were clearly efficient and not responsible for his calculation deficiency.

SINGER AND LOW'S DISCUSSION OF THE CASE

In discussing their findings, Singer and Low were very cautious in drawing definitive conclusions. They believed that further systematic studies as well as a refinement of the testing methods would both contribute to understanding the primary causes of acalculia more than a premature formulation of a theory.

In an attempt to interpret the results, the authors tried to connect the multiple deficits showed by the patient by identifying a common underlying cause. They rejected the possibility that a single factor was responsible for the observed profile, but at the same time they discussed all the patient's difficulties, among which poor calculation, defective numbers writing, poor tachistoscopic reading, and poor drawing, with an emphasis on the apparent link between them. Above all, Singer and Low were influenced by Lange's suggestion that an inability to 'manipulate the category of direction of space' was the core deficit in numerical disorders (Lange, 1933). Likewise, they recognised the 'inability to construct a continuous total out of discontinuous parts', otherwise defined as a 'difficulty to synthesise' (e.g. grasping of part of the stimuli in tachistoscopic presentation) and the 'inability to maintain spatial direction' (e.g. in writing and drawing) as main factors underlying the patient's disorders. The authors found an ideal framework to connect the patient's acalculia with what they defined as his 'general spatial agnosia' in Natorp's theory of calculation (1910). According to Natorp, all numerical operations have as a starting referent point the 'zero', from which one has to count in a forward direction to set the value of any given factor. Thus, for example, in order to add 3 plus 2, one will proceed from zero counting to 2 and keeping in mind this value one will go back to zero and count to 3.[1] While the counting procedure would contain the element of 'direction', the combination of these separate counts contains the element of 'construction'. According to Singer and Low, this original model of calculation would thus account for most but not all of the patient's difficulties.

SUMMARY AND CONCLUSIONS

In the past decades, the study of numerical disorders has begun to attract the attention of cognitive neuropsychologists and a substantial number of systematic single-case studies has appeared in the literature. This cumulative evidence has provided the basis for inferences about the structure and functioning of normal number processing and calculation (Cipolotti & Butterworth, 1995; Dehaene & Cohen, 1995; McCloskey et al., 1985). Current models of numerical cognition may well provide new insight into the early studies of acalculia, among which Singer and Low's is certainly of extreme significance.

Singer and Low's patient was clearly not a pure case and his constellation of symptoms was likely to be determined by multiple deficits. Though in some of the numerical tasks his poor performance could have been partially attributed to his apraxia as well as visuo-spatial difficulties, he showed deficits specific to the numerical domain.

Within number processing, the patient's ability to compare the magnitude of Arabic numerals contrasted with his selective difficulties in writing Arabic numerals to dictation. The latter was not secondary to deficit in the comprehension of spoken verbal stimuli given that he was able to match verbal to Arabic numerals. Thus, the patient showed a clear dissociation between intact number comprehension and impaired number production, a pattern that since then has been repeatedly reported (e.g. Benson & Denckla, 1969; McCloskey et al., 1985) and embodied in all current models where cognitive mechanisms for number comprehension and number production are unquestionably distinct (Figure 4.1). More specifically, the patient's difficulty was limited to the production of Arabic numerals, whether in writing numbers to dictation or in composing them by cards representing single digits. Furthermore, Singer and Low's observations of the patient's errors in the production of Arabic numerals adequately support a further dissociation between lexical and syntactic mechanisms within the number production system (e.g. Deloche & Seron, 1982; McCloskey et al., 1985). In fact, the patient never failed to select the individual digits—i.e. the lexical elements of the number (e.g. 2, 4, 2 in 242)—but he consistently produced a number of a wrong magnitude (e.g. 20042 instead of 242). As previously discussed, specific syntactic difficulties in the production of Arabic numerals have recently been investigated in three single-case studies (Cipolotti, Butterworth, & Warrington, 1994; Delazer & Denes, 1998; Noel & Seron, 1995). In all these cases, the errors observed were analogous to the ones reported by Singer and Low, consisting in a word-by-word transcoding of the verbal numeral in the corresponding Arabic form (e.g. two thousand and five hundred → 2000500). Indeed, the specific effect of the verbal structure of the numbers (e.g. 'two thousand and five hundred' versus 'twenty-five hundred') in the production of Arabic numerals reported by Singer and Low has been replicated and systematically investigated only, in recent times, by Noel and Seron (1995). The analysis of a larger corpus of these errors has now provided insight into the interpretation of this phenomenon. In particular, within the framework of Power et al.'s number production model (Power & Dal Martello, 1990; Power & Longuet-Higgins, 1978), lexicalisation errors are assumed to derive from the misapplication of specific rules supporting the transcoding of verbal numerals into Arabic numerals, namely the concatenation rule operating on verbal numerals in product relationship (e.g., three hundred = $3 \times 100 = 3\&00$) and the overwriting rule, operating on verbal numerals in sum relationship (e.g. one thousand and two = $1000 + 2 = 100\&2$). In summary, though Singer and Low's observations remained only descriptive and no explanation of their patient's number writing difficulties was attempted, their detailed evaluation of his number transcoding abilities allowed them to identify an extremely specific deficit that has been systematically reported and interpreted only 60 years later.

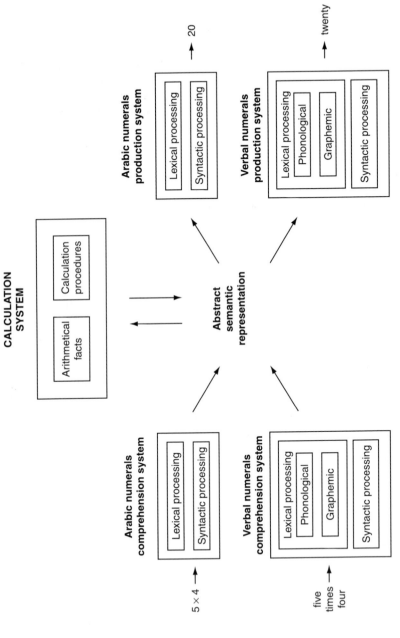

Figure 4.1 Schematic depiction of the main processing components in number processing and calculation posited by McCloskey, Caramazza, and Basili (1985).

Singer and Low's case study provides original observations also with regard to various aspects of calculation abilities. The patient's difficulties mainly concerned subtraction and division problems, while simple addition and multiplication were better preserved. The relevance of this dissociation within arithmetical operations and its impact on subsequent research has been previously discussed. In the last few years, several case studies have been reported indicating various patterns of impaired and spared operations (e.g. Dagenbach & McCloskey, 1992; Hittmair-Delazer et al., 1994; McCloskey, Harley, & Sokol, 1991; McNeil & Warrington, 1994; Pesenti, Seron, & van der Linden, 1994). Though these operation-specific deficits were first interpreted in terms of the relative difficulty or strength of the representations of the different operations (McCloskey, Harley et al., 1991), selective preservations of subtraction (e.g. Lamply, Eshel, Gilad, & Sarova-Pinhas, 1994) or multiplication (e.g. Delazer & Benke, 1997), generally considered difficult operations, have undermined this interpretation. At present, two alternative accounts for operation-specific deficits have been put forward. Some authors have postulated separate memory representation for different operations that can be selectively damaged (Dagenbach & McCloskey, 1992; Pesenti, Seron, & van der Linden, 1994). On the other hand, it has been proposed that dissociations within the four operations simply reflect a different level of processing: multiplication and addition, being systematically taught at school, would depend on rote verbal memory, while subtraction and division would rely on the use of back-up strategies or manipulation of quantities (Dehaene & Cohen, 1995, 1997). In line with this approach, Dehaene and Cohen (1997) described two patients, BOO and MAR, who presented opposite patterns of performance: BOO was more accurate in addition and subtraction than in multiplication; MAR was significantly better in multiplication and addition than in division and subtraction. The hypothesis of deficits at a different level of processing was further supported by BOO's general deficit in reciting stored verbal knowledge (e.g. rhymes or poems) and MAR's difficulties in all tasks based on quantitative numerical knowledge. Interestingly, Singer and Low's patient partially mimics MAR's performance, though his pattern of deficit within simple calculation was not associated with difficulties in the manipulation of quantities (e.g. number comparison).

Besides the dissociation within arithmetic operations, Singer and Low's qualitative analysis of the patient's performance disclosed several mechanisms and strategies subserving calculation, the role of which has been only recently recognised (e.g. McCloskey, 1992). They discussed the patient's performance in simple calculation, distinguishing automatic memory retrieval—effortless, accurate, and fast processing—from the use of back-up strategies and calculation procedures. The importance of this distinction is nowadays acknowledged and implemented in all current models of calculation (e.g. Dehaene & Cohen, 1997; McCloskey, 1992). Moreover, Singer and

Low drew their inferences from the accurate qualitative analysis of the errors in a similar way to what is now routinely done to interpret patients' performance in numerical tasks (e.g. Hittmair-Delazer et al., 1994; Sokol, McCloskey, Cohen, & Aliminosa, 1991).

Finally, the pattern of impaired exact calculation and preserved estimation abilities observed in Singer and Low's patient has also been replicated and more carefully investigated in recent studies (e.g. Dehaene & Cohen, 1991; Warrington, 1982). In a seminal paper, Warrington (1982) described the case of DRC, a patient with a severe deficit in basic arithmetic but otherwise preserved calculation skills. Though he was no longer able to answer promptly a simple sum, he could provide an estimate of the results—e.g. presented with $5 + 7$ he answered '13 roughly'. DRC could also adequately estimate large quantities of dots arranged on a card, showing preserved approximation abilities. The dissociation between exact calculation and estimation abilities was further documented in a case study by Dehaene and Cohen (1991). Their patient, NAU, had marked difficulties in all tasks requiring symbolic number processing (e.g. reading, calculation) but showed preserved approximate calculation abilities. The latter was documented, among other ways, by his ability to reject grossly false calculations (e.g. $2 + 2 = 9$) and by his normal performance in a task requiring him to locate a given numeral (e.g. 64) on a 1 to 100 number scale. On the basis of this evidence, the authors proposed the hypothesis, further developed in subsequent works (Dehaene, 1992; Dehaene & Cohen, 1997), of the existence of two routes mediating number processing: the first, operating on number symbols, that subserves exact calculation; the second, manipulating approximate magnitudes in analogic form, that is used in all tasks requiring estimation of quantities.

In conclusion, the significance of Singer and Low's case is well reflected in the fact that many of their observations have been replicated in successive case studies. The contribution of their study to the neuropsychology of numbers is not so much related to the authors' interpretation of the case as to the methodological procedures they adopted. The analytic approach they followed in the examination of the patient's difficulties allowed them to detect several phenomena, the importance of which has been confirmed by current theory of numerical cognition. Moreover, their underestimated merit was to introduce a number of paradigms that are now systematically used in the clinical assessment of numerical disorders and that entail a refined and articulated conception of the mechanisms underlying numerical abilities.

ACKNOWLEDGEMENTS

Preparation of this chapter was partially carried out while Luisa Girelli was at the Department of Psychology at the University of Trieste. The support of that institution, and particularly of Carlo Semenza, is gratefully acknowledged.

REFERENCES

Bastian, H.C. (1898). *A treatise on aphasia and other speech defects*. London: Lewis.

Benson, D.F., & Denckla, M.B. (1969). Verbal paraphasia as a source of calculation disturbance. *Archives of Neurology, 21*, 96–102.

Berger, H. (1926). Uber Rechenstorungen bei Herderkrankungen des Grosshirns. *Archive für Psychiatrie und Nervenkrankheiten, 78*, 238–263.

Browne, C.E. (1906). The psychology of simple arithmetic processes. *American Journal of Psychology, 17*, 1–12.

Buehler, K. (1913). *Die gestaltwarhrnehmung*. Stuttgart: W. Spernann.

Butterworth, B., Cipolotti, L., & Warrington, E.K. (1996). Short-term memory impairment and arithmetical ability. *Quarterly Journal of Experimental Psychology, 49A*, 251–262.

Campbell, J.I.D. (1994). Architecture for numerical cognition. *Cognition, 53*, 1–44.

Campbell, J.I.D., & Clark, J.M. (1992). Cognitive number processing: An encoding-complex perspective. In J.I.D. Campbell (Ed.), *The nature and origins of mathematical thinking* (pp. 457–491). Amsterdam: Elsevier Science.

Cipolotti, L., & Butterworth, B. (1995). Toward a multiroute model of number processing: Impaired transcoding with preserved calculation skills. *Journal of Experimental Psychology: General, 124 (4)*, 375–390.

Cipolotti, L., Butterworth, B., & Denes, G. (1991). A specific deficit for numbers in a case of dense acalculia. *Brain, 114*, 2619–2637.

Cipolotti, L., Butterworth, B., & Warrington, E.K. (1994). From 'one thousand nine hundred and forty-five' to 1000945. *Neuropsychologia, 32(4)*, 503–509.

Clapp, F.L. (1924). *The number combinations: Their relative difficulty and frequency of their appearance in textbooks. Research Bulletin, N.1*. Madison, W1: Bureau of Educational Research.

Cohen, L., & Dehaene, S. (1995). Number processing in pure alexia: The effect of hemispheric asymmetries and task demands. *Neurocase, 1*, 121–137.

Dagenbach, D., & McCloskey, M. (1992). The organisation of arithmetical facts in memory: Evidence from a brain-damaged patient. *Brain and Cognition, 20*, 345–366.

Dehaene, S. (1992). Varieties of numerical abilities. *Cognition, 44*, 1–42.

Dehaene, S., & Cohen, L. (1991). Two mental calculation systems: A case study of severe dyscalculia with preserved approximation. *Neuropsychologia, 29*, 1045–1074.

Dehaene, S., & Cohen, L. (1995). Towards an anatomical and functional model of number processing. *Mathematical Cognition, 1*, 83–120.

Dehaene, S., & Cohen, L. (1997). Cerebral pathways for calculation: Double dissociation between rote verbal and quantitative knowledge of arithmetic. *Cortex, 33*, 219–250.

Delazer, M., & Benke, T. (1997). Arithmetical facts without meaning. *Cortex, 33*, 697–710.

Delazer, M., & Butterworth, B. (1997). A dissociation of number meanings. *Cognitive Neuropsychology, 14(a)*, 613–636.

Delazer, M., & Denes, G. (1998). Writing Arabic numerals in an agraphic patient. *Brain and Language, 64(2)*, 257–266.

Deloche, G., & Seron, X. (1982). From one to 1: An analysis of a transcoding process by means of neuropsychological data. *Cognition, 12*, 119–149.

Deloche, G., & Seron, X. (1984). Semantic errors reconsidered in the procedural light of stack concepts. *Brain and Language, 21*, 59–71.

Ferro, J.M., & Silveira Botelho, M.A. (1980). Alexia for arithmetical signs. A cause of disturbed calculation. *Cortex, 16*, 175–180.

Fuson, K. (1988). *Children's counting and concepts of number*. New York: Springer.

Fuson, K. (1992). Relationship between counting and cardinality from age 2 to age 8. In

J. Bideau, C. Meljac, & J.P. Fisher (Eds.), *Pathways to number* (pp. 127–149). Hillsdale, NJ: Lawrence Erlbaum Associates Inc.

Gallistel, C.R., & Gelman, R. (1992). Preverbal and verbal counting and computation. *Cognition, 44*, 43–74.

Geary, D.C., Brown, S.C., & Samaranayake, V.A. (1991). Cognitive addition: A short longitudinal study of strategy choice and speed-of-processing differences in normal and mathematically disabled children. *Developmental Psychology, 27*, 787–797.

Gelman R., & Gallistel, C.R. (1978). *The child's understanding of number*. Cambridge, MA: Harvard University Press.

Gerstmann, J. (1927). Fingeragnosie und isolierte Agraphie, ein neues Syndrom. *Zeitschrift für die Gesamte Neurologie un Psychiatrie, 108*, 152–177.

Goldstein, K. (1919). *Die Behanlung, Fusorg und Bequtachtung der Hirnverletzten*. Leipzig: Vogel.

Henschen, S.E. (1919). Uber Sprach, Musik, und Rechenmechanismen und ihre Lokalisationen in Grosshirn. *Zeitschrift für die Gesamte Neurologie und Psychiatrie, 52*, 273–298.

Henschen, S.E. (1920). *Klinische und anatomische Beitrage zu Pathologie des Gehirns* (Vol. 5). Stockholm: Nordiska Bokhandeln.

Hittmair-Delazer, M., Semenza, C., & Denes, G. (1994). Concepts and facts in calculation. *Brain, 117*, 715–728.

Jacoby, L.L. (1984). Incidental versus intentional retrieval: Remembering and awareness as separate issues. In L.R. Squire & N. Butters (Eds.), *Neuropsychology of memory* (pp. 145–156). New York: Guilford Press.

Kleist, K. (1934). *Gehirnpathologie*. Leipzig: Barth.

Krapf, E. (1937). Uber Akalkulie. *Sweizerische Archives für Neurologie und Psychiatrie, 39*, 330–334.

Lamply, Y., Eshel, Y., Gilad, R., & Sarova-Pinhas, I. (1994). Select alcalculia with sparing of the subtraction process in a patient with left parietotemporal hemorrhage. *Neurology, 44*, 1759–1761.

Lange, J. (1930). Fingeragnosie und Agraphie. *Monatsschrift für Psychiatrie und Neurologie, 76*: 129–188.

Lange, J. (1933). Probleme der Fingeragnosie. *Zeitschrift für die Gesamte Neurologie und Psychiatrie, 147*, 594–610.

Lewandosky, M., & Stadelmann, E. (1908). Uber einen bemerkenswerten Fall von Hirnbluntung und uber Rechenstorungen bei Herderkrankung des Gehirns. *Journal für Psychologie und Neurologie, 11*, 249–265.

McCloskey, M. (1992). Cognitive mechanisms in numerical processing: Evidence from acquired dyscalculia. *Cognition, 44*, 107–157.

McCloskey, M., Aliminosa, D., & Sokol, S.M. (1991). Facts, rules and procedures in normal calculation: Evidence from multiple single-patient studies of impaired arithmetic fact retrieval. *Brain and Cognition, 17*, 154–203.

McCloskey, M., Caramazza, A., & Basili, A. (1985). Cognitive mechanisms in number processing and calculation: Evidence from dyscalculia. *Brain and Cognition, 4*, 171–196.

McCloskey, M., Harley, W., & Sokol, S.M. (1991). Models of arithmetical fact retrieval: An evaluation in light of findings from normal and brain-damaged subjects. *Journal of Experimental Psychology: Learning, Memory and Cognition, 7*, 377–397.

McNeil, J., & Warrington, E.K. (1994). A dissociation between addition and subtraction within written calculation. *Neuropsychologia, 32*, 717–728.

Natorp, P. (1910). *Die logischen Grundlagen der exakten Wissenschaften*. Leipzig: B.G. Teubner.

Noel, M.P., & Seron, X. (1995). Lexicalisation errors in writing Arabic numerals: A single-case. *Brain and Cognition, 29*, 151–179.

Peritz, G. (1918). Zur Pathopsychologie des Rechnens. *Deutsche Zeitschrift für Nervenheilkunde, 61*, 234–340.

Pesenti, M., Seron, X., & van der Linden, M. (1994). Selective impairment as evidence for mental organisation of arithmetical facts: BB, a case of preserved subtraction. *Cortex, 30(4)*, 661–671.

Poppelreuter, W. (1917). *Die Psychischen Schaedigungen durch Kopfschuss im Kriege 1914–1916*. Leipzig: Voss.

Power, R.J.D., & Dal Martello, M.F. (1990). The dictation of Italian numerals. *Language and Cognitive Processes, 5*, 237–254.

Power, R.J.D., & Longuet-Higgins, H.C. (1978). Learning to count: A computational model of language acquisition. *Proceedings of the Royal Society of London, B.200*, 391–417.

Resnick, R. (1992). From protoquantities to operators: Building mathematical competence on a foundation of everyday knowledge. In G. Leinhardt, R. Putman, & R.A. Haltrup (Eds.), *Analysis of arithmetic for mathematical teaching* (pp. 373–425). Hillsdale, NJ: Lawrence Erlbaum Associates Inc.

Restle, F. (1970). Speed of adding and comparing numbers. *Journal of Experimental Psychology, 83*, 274–278.

Schacter, D.L. (1985). Multiple forms of memory in humans and animals. In N.M. Weinberger, J.L. McCaugh, & G. Lynch (Eds), *Memory systems of the brain* (pp. 351–358). New York: The Guilford Press.

Schacter, D.L. (1987). Implicit memory: History and current status. *Journal of Experimental Pschology: Learning, Memory and Cognition, 13*, 501–507.

Seron, X., Deloche, G., Ferrand, I., Cornet, J.A., Frederix, M., & Hirsbrunner, T. (1991). Dot counting by brain-damaged subjects. *Brian and Cognition, 17*, 116–137.

Seron, X., Deloche, G., & Noel, M.P. (1992). Number transcribing by children: Writing Arabic numbers under dictation. In J. Bideau, C. Meljac, & J.P. Fisher (Eds.), *Pathways to number*. Hillsdale, NJ: Lawrence Erlbaum Associates Inc.

Seron, X., & Fayol, M. (1994). Number transcoding in children. A functional analysis. *British Journal of Child Development, 12*, 281–300.

Seron, X., & Noel, M.P. (1992). Language and numerical disorders: A neuropsychological approach. In J. Alegria, D. Holender, J. Junca de Morais, & M. Radeau (Eds.), *Analytic approaches to human cognition*. Amsterdam: Elsevier.

Shallice, T., & Evans, M. (1978). The involvement of the frontal lobes in cognitive estimation. *Cortex, 14*, 294–303.

Siegler, R. (1987). The perils of averaging data over strategies: An example from children's addition. *Journal of Experimental Psychology: General, 116*, 250–264.

Singer, H.D., & Low, A.A. (1933). Acalculia (Henschen): A clinical study. *Archives of Neurology and Psychiatry, 29*, 477–498.

Sittig, O. (1917). Uber Storungen des Ziffernschreibens bei Aphasishen. *Zeitschrift für Pathopsychologie, 3*, 298–306.

Sokol, S.M., McCloskey, M., Cohen, N.J., & Aliminosa, D. (1991). Cognitive representations and processes in arithmetic: Inferences from the performance of brain-damaged subjects. *Journal of Experimental Psychology: Learning, Memory, and Cognition, 17(3)*, 355–376.

Strauss, H. (1924). Konstruktive Apraxia. *Monatsschrift für Psychiatrie und Neurologie, 56*, 65.

Thorndike, E.L. (1922). *The psychology of arithmetic*. New York: Macmillan.

Warrington, E.K. (1982). The fractionation of arithmetical skills: A single case study. *Quarterly Journal of Experimental Psychology, 34A*, 31–51.

NOTE

1. A model of simple calculation that invokes the mapping of numbers on an oriented number line has been proposed by Restle (1970). and more recently by Gallistel and Gelman (1992).

CHAPTER FIVE

Monsieur C: Dejerine's case of alexia without agraphia

J. Richard Hanley and Janice Kay
Department of Psychology, University of Exeter, Exeter, UK

MONSIEUR C: CASE DETAILS

In 1887, Monsieur C was a wealthy, intelligent and well-educated former textile merchant who was living with his wife in retirement in Paris. He had enjoyed excellent health throughout the 68 years of his life. On 19 October, however, he started to experience mild speech problems and short bouts of numbness and weakness in his right arm and leg. This did not prevent him from continuing to take his customary long walks through the city, and on 23 October he distinctly remembered reading signs and posters in shop windows. Over the next couple of days, the weakness in his arm and leg increased. At some point he noticed that 'he was no longer able to read a single word, all the while writing and speaking very well and distinguishing the objects and people that surrounded him as well as before'.

Two weeks later, in the belief that his reading problem might be the consequence of a peripheral visual problem that could be resolved by wearing appropriate spectacles, Monsieur C consulted an ophthalmologist, Dr. E. Landolt. Landolt carried out a detailed investigation of his visual skills, and of his ability to process letters, numbers, and words. Landolt reported that Monsieur C 'speaks fluently without fault, listens and easily understands everything one says to him'. However, he found Monsieur C unable to read letters or words, and capable of reading three-digit numbers only slowly one digit at a time. He could write 'whatever he wishes from memory' but 'he can never read through what he has written himself, even individual letters are lifeless for him'. Landolt discovered that Monsieur C had a partial right-sided homonymous hemianopia (loss of vision in the right visual field) with total hemiachromatopsia (colour blindness) in the right visual field. However, the problems in processing written symbols could not possibly have been the consequence of a basic visual problem because Monsieur C's visual acuity, colour vision, and object recognition were good when objects were presented in his preserved left visual field. Moreover, he could clearly see and copy letters even though he did not appear to recognise them as familiar written symbols.

Landolt therefore referred Monsieur C to the great neurologist Jules Dejerine. When he first saw Monsieur C, Dejerine was 38 years old and had recently been promoted to the rank of professor despite the initial opposition of Charcot, perhaps the most distinguished French neurologist of his generation. Charcot was head physician at the Salpetriere Hospital, and in 1882 had been appointed to a specially created chair in neurology in the Faculty of Medicine in Paris. In 1887, Dejerine was in the first year of a ground-breaking eight-year stay as the head of a clinical neurology ward at Bicetre Hospital (Bub, Arguin, & Lecours, 1993). At the time, Bicetre was 'the proving ground of the Salpetriere, and more precisely of those who aspired to Charcot's chair' (Bub et al., 1993, p. 534), the position to which Dejerine was finally elected some 20 years later.

Dejerine saw Monsieur C for the first time on 15 November 1887. For the next two-and-a-half months, they met twice a week. They then continued to meet once every four to six weeks until 1891, either at Bicetre or in Dejerine's home. Over that period, Monsieur C spent his days walking in Paris with his wife. Later in the day, they would play music together, she would read to him, and they would play a game of cards. They would also engage in conversation with friends in which Monsieur C would always take an active role. However, his reading ability never returned, and the impairment apparently left him bewildered and at times close to suicide.

On 5 January 1892 Monsieur C complained once again of numbness in his right arm and leg, of dizziness, and of difficulty in articulating words. The next day he could walk around his apartment without apparent difficulty. However, he started to make paraphasic speech errors and was alarmed to find himself no longer able to write letters or words accurately. Intellect and spoken comprehension appeared to be preserved, but for the next 10 days he was unable to speak. On 16 of January he fell into a coma and died soon after. The following day, Dejerine carried out an autopsy in the patient's home.

DEJERINE'S PRESENTATION OF MONSIEUR C

Dejerine presented the case of Monsieur C to the Biological Society in Paris on 20 February 1892. A written account of this presentation (Dejerine, 1892), from which the case details described earlier are taken, was published later in the same year in the *Mémoires de la Société de Biologique*. A translation in English of several important extracts from Dejerine's original article has been published by Eling (1994).[1] Monsieur C was presented by Dejerine as a case of '*cécité verbale pure*' (*cécité* means 'blindness', *verbale* has been generally been translated as 'word', and *pure* has the same meaning in English and French) '*avec intégrité de l'écriture*' (with preserved writing). We shall refer to it henceforth as either *pure alexia* or as *alexia without agraphia*.

Although Dejerine's (1892) paper provided by far the most detailed documented account of the functional impairments observed in a case of pure alexia that had ever been published, this was not its chief purpose.[2] Dejerine's main goal was to distinguish both functionally and anatomically between alexia *without* agraphia as observed in the case of Monsieur C, and a case of alexia *with* agraphia that Dejerine had reported to the Society the previous year (Dejerine, 1891). Dejerine wrote that Henschen (1890) had reported a case of alexia with agraphia 'in which the autopsy showed two restricted lesions, one sited on the angular gyrus, the other at the bottom of the second frontal convolution'. Henschen had speculated that the lesion in the angular gyrus might be the cause of the reading problem while the lesion in the frontal convolution might be the cause of the writing problem. In opposition to this suggestion, Dejerine pointed out that the absence of any frontal lesion in both his own case and in two subsequent reports of alexia with agraphia (Berkhan, 1891; Serieux, 1892) ruled out such an interpretation.

Dejerine's view was that both the alexia and the agraphia seen in cases such as these are the consequence of a single lesion to the left angular gyrus, which he believed to be 'the centre for the optical images for letters'.[3] In alexia *without* agraphia, however, Dejerine argued that the angular gyrus was preserved but 'could no longer be brought into play by a visual stimulus'. Hence the patient was unable to read. The fact that such a patient remained able to write and to produce and understand speech indicated that these visual representations of written letters and words in the angular gyrus could still be accessed from intact stored representations of *spoken* words. As Dejerine acknowledged, this account of pure alexia and alexia with agraphia was functionally similar to views that had been expressed previously by Wernicke (see Wernicke, 1886/1989). What the case of Monsieur C offered was anatomical evidence that could be used to substantiate it.

Critically, Dejerine's autopsy of Monsieur C revealed evidence of two quite distinct sets of lesions both confined to the left hemisphere. Dejerine reported that the more recent lesions 'occupied the angular gyrus and the inferior parietal lobe. That is the area in which we are accustomed to seeing lesions in alexia with agraphia. It explains perfectly the symptoms observed during the last days of this patient's life' when Monsieur C was unable to read or write. The earlier lesions were 'sited on the lingual lobe, the fusiform lobe, the cuneus, the tip of the occipital lobe, and the fold of the corpus callosum.' The right hemianopia was caused, according to Dejerine, by the lesion to the cuneus and by degeneration of the optic radiations. It meant that all visual information from the right visual field, including letters, was disconnected from the left angular gyrus. Dejerine believed that the alexia occurred because visual information entering the right hemisphere from the left visual field was also disconnected from the left angular gyrus. Although Dejerine's account was endorsed by Hinshelwood (1895) in his contemporary discussion of the anatomical correlates of acquired dyslexia, more recent accounts from Geschwind (1965) to Saffran and Coslett (1998) argue that this disconnection occurs as a direct consequence of a lesion to the callosal pathways. Although he believed that the left and right cunei must be directly linked by callosal fibres in order that visual information from the two visual fields could be integrated, Dejerine did not believe the callosal lesion to be of any importance in explaining Monsieur C's alexia. Instead, he argued that the lesion to the left cuneus that disconnected the angular gyrus from the visual centres in the left occipital lobe also made it impossible for visual information from the occipital lobe in the right hemisphere to access the angular gyrus.

Untouched by the original lesions were the pathways between Broca's convolution ('articulatory memory centre for words') and the first temporal convolution ('auditory memory centre for words'), as was the connection between the first temporal convolution and the angular gyrus. In addition to storing visual representations of letters, Dejerine (1892) argued that the angular gyrus also contained representations of familiar visual word forms. Preserved connections from the first temporal convolution to the angular gyrus therefore explained Monsieur C's preserved ability to access the spellings of words during writing even though he could not read them. In addition, the connections between the left angular gyrus and the motor areas in both the left hemisphere and the right hemisphere (via the corpus callosum) were intact. This, in Dejerine's view, allowed Monsieur C to continue to write letters and words following his first illness.

In discussing this issue soon afterwards, Hinshelwood (1895) commented that there was a widely held belief at the time that 'by constant and prolonged practice the motor images of writing had become so deeply imprinted upon the graphic motor centre that without any aid from the visual centre the revival of these motor images was quite sufficient to guide the hand to form these letters correctly' (p. 1569). As Hinshelwood pointed out, Dejerine's investigation of Monsieur C contradicted this view by demonstrating that preservation of the graphic motor centre would not in itself permit normal writing in pure alexia. The case of Monsieur C made it clear that preservation of the *visual* representations of words and letters was also necessary for writing, because it was when they were damaged as a result of his final illness that Monsieur C lost the ability to write.

In conclusion, therefore, Dejerine had made a convincing case that alexia without agraphia as observed in the case of Monsieur C could be parsimoniously explained in terms of the angular gyrus becoming disconnected from visual information entering both the left and right hemispheres. The consequence of this was that stored knowledge about letters and words was preserved in the left angular gyrus but could no longer be accessed during reading. At the same time, the connections between the angular gyrus and areas responsible for production and perception of spoken language in the left frontal and temporal regions remained intact, explaining his preserved ability to write and spell words he could not read. When the angular gyrus itself suffered damage shortly before his death, Monsieur C showed both alexia and agraphia.

THE FUNCTIONAL ARCHITECTURE OF DEJERINE'S THEORY OF READING

Dejerine's (1892) belief that the brain stores representations of familiar visual word forms was an extension of Wernicke's model of language processing that the great German neurologist did not himself originally accept (Bub et al., 1993). Wernicke's (1886/1989) position at that time was that written words were recognised by sounding out their individual letters.[4] Today, however, it is almost universally acknowledged that a reading route based on rules of letter–sound association is unworkable for deep alphabetic orthographies such as English or French. This is because it would be unable to provide the correct pronunciation of the relatively large number of exception words that these writing systems contain (e.g. *have* in English, *monsieur* in French). As Bub et al. (1993) mention, however, this point might have been more salient to Dejerine than to Wernicke because German, unlike French, has a relatively shallow orthography in which grapheme–phoneme relationships are much more straightforward.

Dejerine's view is, however, a precursor to the belief, now widely held among cognitive neuropsychologists (e.g. Coltheart, 1978; Morton, 1979), that reading a familiar word involves activating its representation in an orthographic lexicon. Dejerine did not go as far as to claim that visual word forms could directly access word meanings stored in the 'ideational centre' (the semantic system in contemporary terminology). Unlike most modern cognitive neuropsychologists (see Caramazza, 1997; Shelton & Caramazza, 1999), Dejerine argued that the visual word form first had to activate its phonological representation in the auditory and articulatory memory centres for words before the meaning of the word could be retrieved. In today's terms, borrowing the terminology of Patterson (1982), this means that Wernicke believed in obligatory phonological mediation on the basis of *assembled* phonology, while Dejerine believed in obligatory phonological mediation on the basis of *addressed* phonology. Although Dejerine's position represented an important advance over Wernicke's, the recent literature suggests that neither account can adequately explain the ability of certain patients with severe phonological processing impairments to access the meaning of written words (e.g. Hanley & McDonnell, 1997). The presence of a reading route that directly links print and meaning is now a feature of virtually all models that make a serious attempt to explain the neuropsychology of reading (e.g. Coltheart, Curtis, Atkins, & Haller, 1993; Plaut, McClelland, Seidenberg, & Patterson, 1996).

It is obvious from his account of pure alexia that Dejerine considered the visual representations of letters and words that are used in reading to be the same representations that are accessed during writing ('there is no need to hypothesise for writing the existence of a so-called special graphic centre'). In this respect at least, Dejerine's views are much closer to those contemporary theorists who argue that the same orthographic units are used for reading and spelling (e.g. Allport & Funnell, 1981; Plaut et al., 1996), than those who postulate the existence of separate systems for input (reading) and output (spelling) (e.g. Ellis & Young, 1996). It is interesting to note that even though the case of Monsieur C represents a quite startling dissociation between preserved writing and impaired reading, there is nothing about Monsieur C's reading and spelling performance that would call into question the single lexicon account.

Although the precise role of the left angular gyrus in reading and writing has not yet been established, Dejerine's interpretation of alexia without agraphia has proved enormously influential. As Bub et al. (1993) make clear, the only major change that Geschwind (1965) made to Dejerine's account was that Geschwind considered that it was the callosal lesion that was primarily responsible for disconnecting reading areas in the left hemisphere from visual information being processed in the right.[5] For the rest of this chapter, however, we wish to shift the focus away from anatomical issues, and concentrate instead on the precise nature of the striking reading impairment experienced by Monsieur C.[6]

Over the past 20 years, letter-by-letter reading and pure alexia have attracted an immense amount of attention from many of the world's leading cognitive neuropsychologists. How closely does the pattern of performance observed in Monsieur C resemble recent accounts of pure alexia? How readily can it be explained by contemporary theoretical accounts? Bub et al. published an extremely interesting discussion of this issue in 1993. Their conclusion was rather downbeat: 'Would the current degree of understanding have greatly impressed him (Dejerine) or left him somewhat disappointed? We cannot speak for Dejerine, of course, but we do know our present grasp of pure alexia is sufficiently imperfect that we would probably do best to wait a few more years before we speculate on the answer.' Almost a decade later, has our understanding of the causes of pure alexia advanced, and does it permit a more clear-cut cognitive interpretation of Monsieur C's impaired reading ability?

MONSIEUR C'S READING DEFICIT

Dejerine did not report the results of any formal tests of Monsieur C's spelling performance. Nevertheless, it would appear from Dejerine's description of his writing to dictation and spontaneous writing as being 'perfect' that Monsieur C's spelling was entirely preserved. Despite his preserved ability to write, Dejerine reported that Monsieur C's ability to read was *entirely* abolished: 'Verbal blindness is just as marked for printed letters as for handwritten letters. He is unable to recognise a single printed letter or word'. At most, all that appeared left to Monsieur C is what is today referred to as logographic reading by developmental psychologists such as Frith (1985) and Ehri (1992). In the earliest stages of reading acquisition, very young children appear to be able to recognise environmental print such as brand-name logos by processing them as pictures rather than written words. For example, the colour of a logo is often more important for a child reading logographically than is the identity of any of the individual letters that the logo contains. In such a way, Monsieur C may have been able to identify his daily newspaper: 'On showing him the newspaper which he used to read the patient says: "Its *Le Matin*, I recognise it by its form", but he was not able to read any of the letters in the title'. Alternatively, he may have recognised *Le Matin* from its font or from its layout.

In fact what is most striking about Monsieur C's reading deficit, as Landolt's investigation showed, was his *total* inability to name visually presented letters. Performance was equally poor regardless of whether letters were printed or handwritten. 'Placed facing the Snellen chart he is not able to name any of the letters; however he maintains that he can see them perfectly'. He said that Z looked like a 'serpent', P looked like a 'buckle', and A resembled an 'easel'. Extremely limited ability to name visually presented letters has consistently been observed in subsequent reports of patients with pure alexia. Caplan and Hedley-White (1974) and Coslett and Saffran (1989, 1992), for example, have described patients who were totally unable to produce the name of visually presented letters or words.

Monsieur C's letter-processing deficit appeared to be confined to visual recognition, however, because he could slowly identify and name individual letters if he was allowed to trace over their visual form with his finger. The speed at which he could achieve letter recognition by tracing was unfortunately insufficient to allow words to be recognised during reading. This strategy has occasionally been observed in more recent accounts of pure alexia. For example, Case 3 (Benson, Brown, & Tomlinson, 1971) sometimes identified a misnamed letter by tracing it with his finger. Maher, Blayton, Barrett, Schober-Peterson, and Rothi (1998) reported that a treatment for alexia based on finger spelling led to a 50% increase in reading speed with 100% accuracy.

As Coltheart (1998) points out, however, finger spelling is not the compensatory strategy that has been most commonly reported in recent accounts of patients with alexia. Instead, many of them adopt what is known as letter-by-letter (LBL) reading, by which words are often read aloud correctly but extremely slowly, with some patients taking over 16 seconds to read three- and four-letter words (Patterson & Kay, 1982; Warrington & Shallice, 1980). Reading times increase linearly with the number of letters in a word, and patients will sometimes overtly name each letter individually before they read a word aloud. Was Monsieur C suffering from a condition that is analogous to that observed in letter-by-letter reading?

There is now overwhelming evidence that, like Monsieur C, patients who read letter-by-letter also experience problems in processing letters. In a major review of LBL reading, Behrmann, Plaut, and Nelson (1998) pointed out that 50/57 of cases they surveyed showed clear evidence of slow and error prone letter processing when single letters were presented in isolation to them. The other seven were not tested on speeded tasks. As Behrmann et al. (p. 23) put it, 'there is no single subject in whom letter recognition is definitively normal'. The critical issue is whether the letter-processing deficit found in letter-by-letter readers is qualitatively similar to that experienced by patients such as Monsieur C.

We believe that a careful examination of the literature suggests that there may be some important differences. First of all, the severity of the letter-naming deficit is nothing like as extreme in letter-by-letter reading as was observed with Monsieur C. For example, Binder and Mohr (1992) reported that the naming rates of letters presented as single capitals by five LBL readers were 96%, 96%, 100%, 100%, and 100%. This raises the possibility that letter-by-letter reading is actually contingent on reasonably accurate letter naming and that it is their extremely limited ability to *name* visually presented letters that prevents patients such as Monsieur C from reading words letter-by-letter. A paper by Hinshelwood (1895), that appeared only three years after the publication of Dejerine's account of Monsieur C, provides evidence that is consistent with this suggestion. Hinshelwood's (1895, 1900) case bore striking similarities to Monsieur C (sudden and complete loss of the ability to read any words or letters; preserved speech production and comprehension; preserved writing; right homonymous hemianopia; unimpaired intellect). After approximately six months, however, the patient started to attempt to relearn the alphabet. He practised daily, and gradually came to read words 'only slowly and laboriously, spelling out the words letter by letter' (Hinshelwood, 1900, p. 13). Subsequently Hinshelwood (1917, p. 5) reported that this man did not persevere with reading in this way because it 'required such intense mental effort'. When re-tested seven years later, he could still write, but had lost all ability to read letters and words. It appears, therefore, that alexic patients who are unable to read words aloud are more severely impaired at letter naming than letter-by-letter readers, and this may be the reason why they are unable to employ letter-by-letter reading as a compensatory strategy.

A second potential difference is that the letter recognition impairment in letter-by-letter reading almost certainly occurs at an earlier stage of processing than letter naming. The results of recent experimental work strongly suggests that letter-by-letter readers have difficulty in recognising the *abstract identity* of visually presented letters (e.g. Arguin & Bub, 1994; Reuter-Lorenz & Brunn, 1990). Although some have argued (Hanley & Kay, 1992; Kay & Hanley, 1991) that this deficit is more evident when letters are processed simultaneously than when they are processed sequentially, the idea of an impairment in accessing abstract identities of letters is consistent with virtually all recent attempts to explain letter-by-letter reading (e.g. Behrmann et al., 1998; Saffran & Coslett, 1998). Key evidence for this claim is the observation that letter-by-letter readers tend to be extremely slow (Behrmann & Shallice, 1995; Hanley & Kay, 1996; Reuter-Lorenz & Brunn, 1990) or extremely inaccurate (Perri, Bartolomeo, & Silveri, 1996) at cross-case matching of visually presented letters (e.g. does 'D' = 'b' or 'd'?). It is important to point out that this task does not require that the letters are named; a patient with preserved ability to recognise the abstract identity of letters should be able to perform cross-case matching accurately even if they were totally unable to recall the name of visually presented letters.

Did Dejerine provide any evidence as to whether or not Monsieur C's problems in letter naming were the consequence of an impairment in accessing the abstract identities of visually presented letters? Although Monsieur C was never given a test of cross-case matching, Dejerine was clearly of the opinion that he could *not* recognise letters as familiar visual forms. Dejerine's conclusion rested on two separate lines of evidence. Unfortunately neither line of evidence is particularly convincing. One of these was the fact that Monsieur C could write the code that his textile firm employed to disguise the price of clothing from potential customers. In this code, the numbers 1, 2, 3, 4, 5, 6, 7, 8, 9, 0 were represented by the letters c, t, o, i, f, a, m, e, u, x, respectively. This enabled the price of a garment to be revealed surreptitiously by a string of letters. When asked by Dejerine, Monsieur C could apparently 'place under each letter the corresponding number but he is unable to read the individual letters that make it up'. Unfortunately, this pattern of performance does not necessarily indicate an ability to recognise letters even as surrogates for numbers, however. As Bub et al. (1993) point out, it is not clear exactly how this task was administered. Dejerine believed that Monsieur C was capable of processing letters quite normally, so long as this did not involve treating them as linguistic units. If Monsieur C had been able to put numbers next to a randomly ordered sequence of these 10 letters, then Dejerine's view would have been confirmed. The evidence that Dejerine provided merely showed that Monsieur C could write from memory both the letters and the numbers in their correct order. It did not show that production of the correct number was in any sense contingent on recognising the written letters.

The second piece of evidence emerged from a detailed examination of the written forms that Monsieur C produced when he was asked to copy written words. Dejerine concluded that the copies that Monsieur C made resembled pictures rather than the letters that he would produce in spontaneous writing: 'In effect he copies mechanically and in the same way that he would copy any drawing'. Monsieur C would make an exact copy of the shape of the letters as they were formed in the words that he was looking at rather than the letter shape that he would produce when writing spontaneously. Moreover, the shapes that he produced differed when he was copying cursive writing from when he was copying print. If his impairment was simply an inability to access the name of a letter from its visual form, Dejerine reasoned, then Monsieur C should nevertheless have been able to recognise the letter as he was copying, and produce the same form that he would produce when he was writing spontaneously. Unfortunately, though, these data are somewhat equivocal. Bub et al. (1993) point out quite correctly that in some of the examples that Dejerine provided of Monsieur C's copies, Monsieur C did undoubtedly produce a visual form that matched more closely his own cursive form than the shape of the letter he had been asked to copy. We must therefore reluctantly conclude that there is no evidence that demonstrates unequivocally whether or not Monsieur C was capable of recognising the abstract identity of visually presented letters.

Do more recent investigations of alexic patients who are unable to read words letter-by-letter shed any further light on this issue? The pure alexic patients described by Sevush and Heilman (1984) and Miozzo and Caramazza (1998) were impaired at cross-case matching. Caplan and Hedley-White's (1974) pure alexic could correctly realign letter tiles that had been rotated away from their normal orientation. Unfortunately, this patient was not administered any cross-case matching tasks, so it is not possible to determine whether or not he could access abstract letter identities. However, Coslett and Saffran (1992) reported a patient who scored 10/10 at cross-case letter matching despite being unable to name any letters aloud. We ourselves have recently seen a patient (Mycroft, Hanley, & Kay, 2002) who could distinguish correctly aligned letters from mirror reversals and could also perform cross-case matching of visually presented letters despite a complete inability to name them.[7] Performance by these two patients on letter-processing tasks of this kind appears to be much better than that which is sometimes observed in letter-by-letter readers (e.g. Perri et al., 1996).

The evidence is therefore preliminary, but it does appear possible for at least some pure alexics of this kind to recognise the abstract identity of letters more accurately than some letter-by-letter readers. We would therefore tentatively claim that although the locus of the deficit in letter-by-letter readers appears to be at the level of recognising the abstract identity of visually presented letters, the key impairment in pure alexic patients such as Monsieur C may be somewhat different. In our view, by far the best contemporary explanation of this impairment is provided by Saffran and Coslett's (1998) right hemisphere account of pure alexia.

Saffran and Coslett (1998) have argued that at least some alexic patients are able to make use of a right hemisphere reading system. They believe that this is the reason why a number of studies have observed alexic patients who can comprehend words presented at rates so fast that they could not be recognised overtly or read aloud. Their suggestion is that under appropriate circumstances the right hemisphere can perform lexical decisions and can make decisions about the semantic properties of visually presented words at above chance levels even when words are presented for short durations. However, they claim that the right hemisphere is unable to provide the names of any words or letters. If words or letters are to be named by pure alexic patients, information about letter identity must be transferred across the corpus callosum to the left hemisphere.

Our conclusion, therefore, is that there may be two distinct sub-types of 'pure' alexia. Pure alexia of the kind described by Dejerine (1892) may arise because left hemisphere reading mechanisms are disconnected from visual input in the right visual field by a right homonymous hemianopia, and from reading mechanisms in the right hemisphere by impaired inter-hemispheric transfer. These patients are unable to read words and letters aloud because even when the right hemisphere can establish the identities of words and letters, it is unable to name them (Saffran & Coslett, 1998). The ability of letter-by-letter readers to name words and letters suggests that they, on the other hand, *can* access left hemisphere reading mechanisms. Their problem is that the left hemisphere cannot generate the abstract identity of simultaneously presented letters either accurately enough or fast enough to permit normal reading aloud of words.

It is interesting to note that a theoretical framework of this kind would have been quite alien to Dejerine who believed the right hemisphere to be totally incapable of linguistic processing of any kind. In some ways it is closer to Wernicke's rival view of pure alexia according to which the right hemisphere was able to recognise letters but was prevented by the callosal lesion from transmitting this knowledge to the speech system. It is therefore ironic that Monsieur C's callosal lesion, undamaged right hemisphere, and total inability to read words overtly would have made him an ideal case in whom the right hemisphere view of pure alexia could be evaluated. According to the right hemisphere hypothesis, one would predict that Monsieur C should have been able to distinguish written words from written nonwords and perform cross-case matching of visually presented letters under forced choice testing conditions.

MONSIEUR C'S VISUAL PROCESSING DEFICIT

The only additional impairment that Monsieur C (a skilled musician both before and after his illness) experienced in addition to reading words, copying words, and reading numbers containing more than one digit was a difficulty in reading musical scores. He remained able to sing and play well-learned pieces on the piano as efficiently as before, and he could even write musical notation. He was also able to learn to sing new pieces with which he had been unfamiliar prior to his illness. There were therefore close parallels between his alexia without agraphia and the impairment to his musical skills. This impairment has subsequently been observed in some patients with alexia (e.g. Assal, 1983; Horikoshi et al., 1997), and is often referred to as music alexia. It is now clear, however, that music alexia can be observed without alexic reading, and that alexic reading can be observed without music alexia (Basso & Capitani, 1985; Gates & Bradshaw, 1977). It therefore seems that Dejerine was incorrect when he suggested that the musical and reading problems that Monsieur C experienced might both be the consequence of the same visual processing deficit.

As we have seen, Monsieur C showed no evidence of problems in comprehending or producing spoken language: 'never did this man show the slightest sign of word deafness, never did he show the slightest difficulty in speech'.[8] Equally remarkably, he had no signs of agnosia 'if one shows him some objects, he names them without difficulty' or face-processing impairment. Dejerine also reported that 'his sense of direction is perfectly preserved' for places he knew both before and after his illness. Most striking of all, Landolt reported that Monsieur C was able to read aloud single Arabic numerals satisfactorily despite his problems with naming letters. This dissociation provides evidence that written numbers and letters may be processed by mechanisms that at some level are functionally distinct. However, Monsieur C was only able to read aloud three-digit numbers by reading the individual numerals one number at a time: 'He cannot recognise the value of several numbers at the same time; on seeing the number 112 he declares "it's a 1, 1 and 2", but it is only by writing that he manages to say one hundred and twelve.' The key point here is that Monsieur C appeared to have problems in processing numbers only when they had to be recognised in parallel. A similar pattern of performance was reported in two LBL readers by Cohen and

Dehaene (1995). Such cases suggest that the speed with which alexics can identify numbers, both singly and when they contain more than one digit, is worth detailed investigation.

The highly selective nature of his impairment led Dejerine to conclude that Monsieur C suffered from a visual impairment that was purely ortho-graphic in nature. He certainly would not have accepted the view that pure alexia is the consequence of a subtle low level visual processing problem (Behrmann et al., 1998; Chialant & Caramazza, 1998; Farah & Wallace, 1991; Patterson & Lambon Ralph, 1999; Rapp & Caramazza, 1991) that is not confined to the processing of letters. It is impossible to rule out unequivo-cally a visual processing disorder in the absence of any tests of Monsieur C's ability to process tachistoscopically presented non-linguistic material under speeded conditions. However, some pure alexics, at least, appear to perform normally in such circumstances (Arguin & Bub, 1993), so the evidence to date is certainly not inconsistent with Dejerine's view that the deficit in pure alexia is orthographic in nature (see Farah, 2000, for an interesting and balanced recent discussion of this issue).

WORD BLINDNESS OR *LETTER* BLINDNESS?

In conclusion, therefore, we know of no evidence that would contradict Dejerine's view that Monsieur C's pure alexia was the consequence of a lesion or lesions that prevented visual analyses of written material from mak-ing contact with representations of letters and visual word forms stored in the left hemisphere. However, we interpret Monsieur C's complete inability to read words or letters as occurring because information about the abstract identity of visually presented letters could not be transferred from the right to the left hemisphere. We would suggest that this is a different form of pure alexia from that which is observed in patients who read words letter-by-letter. The reasonably well-preserved ability of letter-by-letter readers to name words and letters suggests that they *can* access left hemisphere reading mech-anisms but cannot generate the abstract identity of simultaneously presented letters either accurately enough or fast enough to permit normal reading aloud of words.

Although debate may continue over the precise nature of the letter-processing deficit that Monsieur C experienced, it is important to conclude by pointing out that his primary impairment is clearly at the letter level rather than at the word level. It is certainly the case that his first illness prevented Monsieur C from recognising words as familiar visual units, and meant that written words could not access their pronunciations within the speech system. Nevertheless, the breakdown clearly occurred well before the point at which visual *word* level representations are accessed in the left hemisphere. Dejerine (1892) did not postulate the existence of an impairment to word level representations themselves in the case of Monsieur C. Indeed, as we have seen, his account of Monsieur C's preserved *writing* was critically dependent on the absence of any word level impairment. Why then did Dejerine use the term *word* blindness ('*cécité verbale*') when he referred to Monsieur C?

'Word blindness' was a term in common use in Europe around the turn of the 20th century (e.g. Hinshelwood, 1895, 1900, 1917; Kussmaul, 1877). Hinshelwood (1917) applied it to both acquired dyslexia and developmental dyslexia ('congenital word blindness') to refer simply to people who were not blind but could not read. He offered the following definition: 'By the term word blindness is meant a condition in which with normal vision and therefore seeing the letters and words distinctly, an individual is no longer able to interpret written or printed language. With a clear understanding of this definition there is nothing misleading about the term which I think has now become permanently fixed in our medical vocabulary'. (Hinshelwood, 1917, p. 2.)

However, it is interesting to note that Hinshelwood (1895) experienced some misgivings about whether or not word blindness was a 'sufficiently precise' term for pure alexia. When discussing his own alexic patient, he commented that: 'There are different forms of word blindness which must be carefully distinguished from one another. The case just reported is really one of letter blindness—i.e. the inability to recognise individual letters' (p. 1565). This is a critically important point. '*Letter*' blindness would have been a much more appropriate term than 'word' blindness to apply in the case of Monsieur C because word blindness deflects attention away from the fact that Monsieur C's primary impairment is clearly at the written *letter* level not the word level. *Verbal* blindness, as '*cécité verbale*' was translated by Binder and Mohr (1992), would also have been preferable to word-blindness, as it is at least neutral with regard to the locus of the functional impairment. If a term other than word blindness had been used to describe the 19th-century cases of pure alexia, then the more recent, and, in our opinion, mistaken view that pure alexia is caused by damage to the word form system (e.g. Warrington & Shallice, 1980) might never have become influential.

REFERENCES

Allport, D.A., & Funnell, E. (1981). Components of the mental lexicon. *Philosophical Transactions of the Royal Society (London)*, *B295*, 397–410.

Arguin, M., & Bub, D.N. (1993). Single character processing in a case of pure alexia. *Neuropsychologia*, *31*, 435–458.

Assal, G. (1983). Aphasie de Wernicke sans amusie chez un pianiste. *Revue Neurologique*, *129*, 251–255.

Basso, A., & Capitani, E. (1985). Spared musical abilities in a conductor with global aphasia and ideomotor apraxia. *Journal of Neurology, Neurosurgery and Psychiatry*, *48*, 407–412.

Behrmann, M., Plaut, D.C., & Nelson, J. (1998). A literature review and new data supporting an interactive view of letter by letter reading. *Cognitive Neuropsychology*, *15*, 7–51.

Behrmann, M., & Shallice, T. (1995). Pure alexia. An orthographic not spatial disorder. *Cognitive Neuropsychology*, *12*, 409–454.

Benson, D.F., Brown, J., & Tomlinson, E.B. (1971). Varieties of alexia: Word and letter blindness. *Neurology*, *21*, 951–957.

Berkhan, O. (1891). Ein fall von subcorticale "Alexie (Wernicke)". *Archives für Psychiatrie und Nervenkrausen*, *23*, 558–564.

Binder, J.R., & Mohr, J.P. (1992). The topography of callosal reading pathways. *Brain*, *97*, 1807–1826.

Broadbent, W.H. (1896). Note on Dr Hinshelwood's communication on word-blindness and visual memory. *The Lancet*, *3*, 18.

Bub, D.N., Arguin, M., & Lecours, A.R. (1993). Jules Dejerine and his interpretation of pure alexia. *Brain and Language*, *45*, 531–559.

Caplan, L.R., & Hedley-White, T. (1974). Cueing and memory function in alexia without agraphia: A case report. *Brain*, *115*, 251–262.

Caramazza, A. (1997). *Access of phonological and orthographic forms: Evidence from dissociations in reading and spelling.* Hove, UK: Psychology Press.

Chialant, D., & Caramazza, A. (1998). Perceptual and lexical factors in a case of letter-by-letter reading. *Cognitive Neuropsychology*, *15*, 167–201.

Cohen, L., & Dehaene, S. (1995). Number processing in pure alexia: The effect of hemispheric asymmetries and task demands. *Neurocase*, *1*, 121–137.

Cohen, L., & Dehaene, S. (2000). Calculating without reading: Unsuspected residual abilities in pure alexia. *Cognitive Neuropsychology*, *17*, 563–583.

Coltheart, M. (1978). Lexical access in simple reading tasks. In G. Underwood (Ed.), *Strategies of information processing* (pp. 151–216). London: Academic Press.

Coltheart, M. (1998). Seven questions about letter-by-letter reading. *Cognitive Neuropsychology*, *15*, 1–6.

Coltheart, M., Curtis, B., Atkins, P., & Haller, M. (1993). Models of reading aloud: Dual-route and parallel-distributed processing approach. *Psychological Review*, *100*, 589–608.

Coslett, H.B., & Saffran, E.M. (1989). Preserved object recognition and reading comprehension in optic aphasia. *Brain*, *112*, 1091–1110.

Coslett, H.B., & Saffran, E.M. (1992). Optic aphasia and the right hemisphere: A replication and extension. *Brain and Language*, *43*, 148–161.

De Bleser, R., & Luzzatti, C. (1989). Models of reading and writing and their disorders in classical German aphasiology. *Cognitive Neuropsychology*, *6*, 501–513.

Dejerine, J. (1891). Sur un cas de cécité verbale avec agraphie suivi d'un autopsie. *Memoires de la Societe Biologique*, *3*, 197–201.

Dejerine, J. (1892). Contribution a l'étude anatomo-pathologique et clinique des différentes variétés de cécité verbale. *Mémoires de la Société Biologique*, *4*, 61–90.

Dingwall, W.O. (1993). The biological bases of human communicative behavior. In J.B. Gleason & N.B. Ratner (Eds.), *Psycholinguistics* (pp. 42–88). Orlando FL: Harcourt Brace.

Ehri, L.C. (1992). Reconceptualizing the development of sight word reading and its relationship to recoding. In P.B. Gough, L.C. Ehri, & R. Treiman (Eds.), *Reading acquisition* (pp. 107–143). Hillsdale, NJ: Lawrence Erlbaum Associates Inc.

Eling, P. (1994). *Reader in the history of aphasia: From Gall to Geschwind.* Amsterdam: John Benjamin's Publishing Company.

Ellis, A.W., & Young, A.W. (1996). *Human cognitive neuropsychology: A textbook with readings.* London: Taylor & Francis.

Farah, M. (2000). *The cognitive neuroscience of vision.* Malden, MA: Blackwell.

Farah, M., & Wallace, M. (1991). Pure alexia as a visual impairment: A reconsideration. *Cognitive Neuropsychology*, *8*, 313–334.

Fisher, J.H. (1905). Case of congenital word-blindness. (Inability to learn to read). *Opthalmic Review*, *24*, 315–318.

Frith, U. (1985). Beneath the surface of developmental dyslexia. In K.E.Patterson, M.Coltheart, & J.C.Marshall (Eds.), *Surface dyslexia: Neuropsychological and cognitive studies of phonological reading* (pp. 301–330). Hove, UK: Lawrence Erlbaum Associates Ltd.

Gates, A., & Bradshaw, L. (1977). The role of the hemispheres in reading. *Brain and Language*, *4*, 403–431.

Geschwind, N. (1965). Disconnexion syndromes in animals and man. *Brain*, *88*, 237–294, 585–644.

Hanley, J. R., & Kay, J. (1992). Does letter-by-letter reading involve the spelling system? *Neuropsychologia*, *30*, 237–256.

Hanley, J.R., & Kay, J. (1996). Reading speed in pure alexia. *Neuropsychologia*, *34*, 1165–1174.

Hanley, J.R., & McDonnell, V. (1997). Are reading and spelling phonologically mediated? Evidence from a patient with a speech production impairment. *Cognitive Neuropsychology*, *14*, 3–33.

Henschen, S.E. (1890). Observation, avec autopsie, de Margaretha Anderson. *Klinisch und anatomische beitrage zur pathologie des Gehirns. Ersther Theil.* Stockholm: Nordiska Bokhandel.

Hinshelwood, J. (1895). Word blindness and visual memory. *The Lancet*, *2*, 1564–1570.

Hinshelwood, J. (1900). *Letter, word, and mind-blindness.* London: Lewis & Co. Ltd.

Hinshelwood, J. (1917). *Congenital word-blindness.* London: Lewis & Co. Ltd.

Horikoshi, T., Asari, Y., Watanabe, A., Nagaseki, Y., Nukui, H., Sasaki, H., & Komiya, K. (1997). Music alexia in a patient with mild pure alexia: Disturbed visual perception of nonverbal meaningful figures. *Cortex*, *33*, 187–194.

Howard, D. (1997). Language in the human brain. In M.D. Rugg (Ed.), *Cognitive neuroscience.* Hove, UK: Psychology Press.

Kay, J., & Hanley, J.R. (1991). Simultaneous form perception and serial letter recognition in a case of letter-by-letter reading. *Cognitive Neuropsychology*, *8*, 249–273.

Kean, M-L. (1994). Norman Geschwind. In P. Eling (Ed.), *Reader in the history of aphasia: From Gall to Geschwind* (pp. 349–387). Amsterdam: John Benjamin's Publishing Company.

Kussmaul, A. (1877). *Die storungen der sprache.* Leipzig: F.C.W.

Maher, L.M., Clayton, M.C., Barrett, A.M., Schober-Peterson, D., & Rothi, L.J.G. (1998). Rehabilitation of a case of pure alexia: Exploiting residual abilities. *Journal of the International Neuropsychological Society*, *4*, 636–647.

Miozzo, M. & Caramazza, A. (1998). Varieties of pure alexia: The case of failure to access graphemic representations. *Cognitive Neuropsychology*, *15*, 203–238.

Morgan, W.P. (1896). A case of congenital word blindness. *British Medical Journal*, *2*, 1378.

Morton, J. (1979). Facilitation in word recognition: Experiments causing change in the logogen model. In P.A. Kolers, M. Wrolstad, & H. Bouma (Eds.), *Processing of visible language* (pp. 259–268). New York: Plenum.

Mycroft, R., Hanley, J.R., & Kay, J. (2002). Preserved access to abstract letter identities despite abolished letter naming in a case of pure alexia. *Journal of Neurolinguistics*, *15*, 99–108.

Patterson, K. (1982). The relation between reading and phonological coding: Further neuropsychological observations. In A.W. Ellis (Ed.), *Normality and pathology in cognitive function* (pp. 77–112). London: Academic Press.

Patterson, K., & Kay, J. (1982). Letter-by-letter reading: Psychological descriptions of a neurological syndrome. *Quarterly Journal of Experimental Psychology*, *34A*, 411–441.

Patterson, K., & Lambon Ralph, M. (1999). Selective disorders of reading?. *Current Opinion in Neurobiology*, *9*, 235–239.

Perri, R., Bartolomeo, P., & Silveri, M.C. (1996). Letter dyslexia in a letter-by-letter reader. *Brain and Language, 53*, 390–407.

Plaut, D, McClelland, J., Seidenberg, M., & Patterson, K. (1996). Understanding normal and impaired word reading. *Psychological Review, 103*, 56–115.

Rapp, B.C., & Caramazza, A. (1991). Spatially determined deficits in letter and word processing. *Cognitive Neuropsychology, 8*, 275–311.

Reuter-Lorenz, P.A., & Brunn, J.L. (1990). A prelexical basis for letter-by-letter reading. *Cognitive Neuropsychology, 7*, 1–20.

Saffran, E.M., & Coslett, H.B. (1998). Implicit vs. letter-by-letter reading in pure alexia: A tale of two systems. *Cognitive Neuropsychology, 15*, 141–165.

Serieux, P. (1892). Sur un cas de surdité verbale pure. *Revue de Medicine, 13*, 733–750.

Sevush, S.P. & Heilman, K.M. (1984). A case of literal alexia. *Brain and Language, 22*, 92–108.

Shelton, J.R., & Caramazza, A. (1999). Deficits in lexical and semantic processing: Implications for models of normal language. *Psychonomic Bulletin and Review, 6*, 5–27.

Warrington, E.K., & Shallice, T. (1980). Word-form dyslexia. *Brain, 103*, 99–112.

Wernicke, C. (1886/1989). Neurology: Recent contributions on aphasia. *Cognitive Neuropsychology, 6*, 547–569.

NOTES

1. The quotations in English come from our own unpublished translation of Dejerine's original article.
2. According to Dingwall (1993), the first documented account of alexia without agraphia was as long ago as 1588.
3. The earliest published case reports of acquired and developmental dyslexia in Britain (Fisher, 1905; Hinshelwood, 1900; Morgan, 1896) also expressed the view that the angular gyrus plays a major role in reading by storing visual representations of words and letters.
4. See De Bleser and Luzzatti (1989) for further discussion of Wernicke's views on reading.
5. According to Kean (1994), Geschwind regarded Dejerine's (1892) paper as a masterpiece, and it had a profound influence on his thinking in the period that led up to the publication of his 1965 article on disconnection syndromes.
6. See Binder and Mohr (1992) for evidence concerning the anatomical location of the lesions observed in patients with pure alexia. See Howard (1997) for discussion of the results of cerebral blood flow studies in normal readers that have attempted to uncover brain areas involved in reading.
7. Cohen and Dehaene (2000) have recently described a pure alexic who performed analogously with numbers. For example, their patient could decide accurately which of two Arabic numerals was larger despite being unable to name either of them.
8. This was an important observation because there were those at this time (e.g. Broadbent, 1896) who argued that an inability to name words always co-occurred with an inability to name visually presented objects.

CHAPTER SIX

Deep dyslexia: The case of Frau Fretz (Wolff, 1903)

Claudius Bartels and Claus-W. Wallesch
Department of Neurology, Otto-von-Guericke University of Magdeburg, Germany

INTRODUCTION

To our knowledge, the first case of deep dyslexia—a reading disorder of aphasic patients with the key features of semantic errors when attempting to read, derivational and visually (word-form) related errors, and pronounced deficits in reading function words and pseudo-/nonwords—was described in 1903 by the Swiss physician, later ophthalmologist, Gustav Wolff, in his patient Frau Fretz. In 1903, when Wolff published his study 'Zur Pathologie des Lesens und Schreibens', Wolff was '*Privatdozent*' (a senior lecturer who fulfilled the academic qualifications for a professorship) at Basle University and assistant physician (registrar) at the Basle Hospital for the Insane.

FRAU FRETZ

Frau Fretz, born in 1870, was admitted to the Basle Hospital for the Insane on 2 June 1902. Previously, she had repeatedly suffered from rheumatism of the joints which resulted in cardiac (probably mitral) valve disease. On 20 June 1900 she had suffered a first stroke with aphasia and right hemiparesis, from which she partially recovered. The next 'fit' ('*Anfall*') occurred on 14 March 1902, with right-sided paresis, aphasia, and confusion. She was admitted to the Bürgerspital (citizens' hospital). Over the next weeks, hemiparesis improved, confusion fluctuated, and aphasia remained.

At admission to the psychiatric hospital, clinical investigations revealed a strong systolic murmur over the cardiac apex, right hemiparesis, normal visual fields, and proteinuria. Frau Fretz was fully oriented. Her mood was described as depressed.

Wolff (1903, pp. 524–529) describes his patient's aphasia as follows:

Perception and apperception are intact. She has full language comprehension and follows commands. She can give the name for all sensorily perceived objects. Therefore, there is no motor language disorder. On the other hand, she has greatest difficulties in finding nouns without sensory perception. With exceptions, she cannot answer questions such as: What (which instrument) cuts meat?, What (which animal) draws a cart? What is used for writing? With much more ease, she can tell properties. When asked 'what is the oven for?', she replies 'warm', when asked 'what is the taste of sugar', she says 'sweet' and so on. Forced to rely on the association of her memory images, she is often unable to find the word. A necessary consequence of this defect is that her ability to speak spontaneously is almost abolished. The store of words that she can use spontaneously is greatly limited. I collected them carefully, but have listed so far only the following: *yes*, *no*, *Leim*, *St. Jakob* (boroughs in Basle), *Wolf*, *railway* (her husband works at the 'Wolf freight train station' in Basle), *away*.

Especially intriguing are her deficits of reading and writing. Most words cannot be read, regardless of whether presented in German or Latin print or script. However, as she can read a number of words, we will compare a list of words that she can read in German script or print to those that she cannot. [See Table 6.1.]

It has to be noted that . . . of the list [in column two of Table 6.1] can be increased ad infinitum, which cannot be said for [the list in column one]. It is much more difficult to find a word that she can read than one that she cannot. The next question must be, whether there is a characteristic feature in these two categories of words by which words that can be read differ from those that cannot.

It is obvious that the first column includes only nouns, adjectives and few verbs, but lacks the other word classes. Articles, pronouns, prepositions, conjuctions etc. cannot be read. This fact exemplifies that not the form but the meaning of a word is crucial for legibility. As the patient cannot read words that consist of only two letters such as 'in' and 'so', but can read words with a much greater number of letters such as 'Eierkuchen' or 'Löffelstiel', it is clear that not the processing demands of the written form but something relating to the meaning of the word causes the difficulties she has in reading. In order to define this something, we ask, whether there is a general difference among words of the same class that belong to one or the other of the lists. With respect to the nouns, it cannot be ignored that those of column [one] correspond to objects that are familiar to a common class woman. 'Spoon, bible, eye, garden, heaven, hell, wood, table' are more familiar to her than 'delivery, isle, Babylon, commisery, history'. This difference is not as clear with all words. The words 'blood' or 'nettle' denote things, of which one should assume that their mental image is as much embedded in a simple mind as are the words 'island, century, point'. But generally, the characteristic difference can hardly be overlooked.

TABLE 6.1
Words that Frau Fretz could and could not read in German script or print:
From Wolff (1903)

Words the patient reads correctly	Words the patient cannot read
Löffel (spoon)	*Gewehr* (gun)
Löffelstiel (spoon-handle)	*Babel* (Babylon)
Bibel (bible)	*Lieferung* (delivery)
Garten (garden)	*vollauf* (completely)
Eierkuchen (egg cake)	*Katechismus* (catechism)
schreiben (to write)	*Blut* (blood)
lesen (to read)	*Geschichte* (story/history)
hören (to hear)	*Brennessel* (nettle)
sehen (to see)	*der* (the)
Welt (world)	*Beileid* (commisery [sympathy])
Himmel (heaven)	*Eiland* (isle/islet)
Hölle (hell)	*evangelisch* (protestant)
Auge (eye)	*katholisch* (catholic)
heiss (hot)	*israelitisch* (israelitic/jewish)
Holz (wood)	*oder* (or)
Pult (writing table)	*viel* (much)
Spitze (point)	*mehr* (more)
gut (good)	*wenig* (little; adverb)
fest (hard)	*welcher* (which)
freuen (to enjoy)	*andere* (others)
schon (already)	*sie* (she)
lustig (funny)	*steht* (stands, third person singular)
froh (happy)	*gelang* (succeded)
Herr (master/mister)	*selten* (rare)
treu (true)	*Theil* (part)
lästig (bothersome)	*eidgenössisch* (Swiss)
Eier (eggs)	*zu* (to/too)
Tisch (table)	*verstehen* (to understand)
Jahrhundert (century)	*auf* (on)
Insel (island)	*in* (in)
	oben (on top)
	über (above)
	wenn (when/if)
	kein (no/none)
	so (so)
	ich (I)
	eben (flat/of course)
	hat (has)
	vor (before)
	bei (at, close to)
	mein (my)
	sein (his)
	ihr (her, also second person plural)
	sauber (clean)
	erworben (acquired)
	plötzlich (suddenly)
	wertvoll (valuable)
	friedlich (peaceful)
	zweiter (second).

Here, Wolff describes two characteristic symptoms of the syndrome of deep dyslexia, namely that his patient is least impaired when reading familiar nouns and is unable to read function words. Next, Wolff analyses the patient's paralexias:

> Another observation seems to give special insight into the patient's reading ability. Besides words that she can and cannot read, there are a number of others which she reads differently to their written presentation. We have to add to [Table 6.1] above [Table 6.2] that contains on the left side the word as presented to the patient and on the right the word as it was read.
>
> The table demonstrates that, with many words, the patient reads something entirely different to what was presented. Frequently, what was read was more or less similar to the presentation, e.g. with the words *rein—reinig, glatt—glätten*. With these examples, there is similarity with respect to form as well as meaning. In other instances, there is similarity only for form (*schüchtern—düster, mässig—mühselig, Altar—Alter*). However, what is the connection between

TABLE 6.2
Words as presented to Frau Fretz and the words as read: From Wolff (1903)

Presented was:	Read was:
wieder (again)	*Wiederhall* (echo)
Gebetbuch (prayer book)	*Betbuch* (prayer book)
Waschfrau (laundress)	*waschen* (to wash)
Freund (friend)	*Traute* (courage)
Feuer (fire)	*Feueranzünder* (lighter)
Werk (factory)	*Maschine* (machine) (on a later day, she read: *Werkzeug* (tool))
Vorbilder (role models)	*Bilderbuch* (picture book) (on a later day: *Fortbildungsschule* (adult college))
Hacke (hoe)	*Morgenrock* (dressing gown)
Altar (altar)	*Alter* (age)
Geschwür (ulcer)	*Schwür* (oath, with paraphasia u: ü)
glatt (smooth)	*glätten* (to smoothen)
schüchtern (timid)	*düster* (dark)
rein (clean)	*reinig* (non-existent; derivation, *reinigen*: to clean)
entstanden (derived)	*auferstanden* (resurrected)
Christus (Christ)	*Lehre* (teaching) (on another day: *christlich* (christian))
grossmüthig (generous) (literally: great-minded)	*Kleinod* (gem), on another *day: kleinnöthig* (paraphasia containing '*klein*': small)
niederländisch (netherlandic)	*vaterländisch* (patriotic)
begabt (gifted)	*Schulgabe* (school gift)
mässig (limited)	*mühselig* (effortful)
Allgemeine Zeitung (General Newspaper)	*Konsum* (consum) [see later]
Rothwand (Red wall: local mountain)	*Rother Turm* (red tower)

Hacke and *Morgenrock*, between *grossmüthig* and *Kleinod*, between *Allgemeine Zeitung* and *Konsum*?

Wolff thus identifies both derivational (correct stem morpheme transposed into another word class) and visually (word-form) related paralexias. Both features are characteristic for the syndrome of deep dyslexia.

> The latter example seems to be the key for these characteristic alterations that happen to the words during reading. *Konsum* is the colloquial name in Basle for the shops of the *Allgemeine Konsumverein* (General Consum Society), which is printed above many shops and which denotes something for which the patient knows only the name *Konsum*. With other examples, the link between presentation and reading is not as easily perceived. There is an analogy for *Rothwand* and *Rother Turm*; *Rother Turm* is the name of a well-known building in Basle. Without certainty, a similar connection can be assumed between *Christus* and *Lehre* (*Christenlehre?*—Sunday school) or *Werk* and *Maschine* (*Maschinenwerke?*—machine works). I cannot understand, however, the link between *grossmüthig* and *Kleinod*, but one can assume a similar connection based on the visual experiences of the patient.

On the basis of these observations, Wolff formulates a theory of his patient's reading strategy, namely that Frau Fretz relies on word-form reading:

> We conclude that the patient does not really read even those words, where her spoken reaction hits the target, but that a general effect of the form of the written word activates similar engrams of written words in her consciousness together with the corresponding object images. . . . With our patient, letter-by-letter reading is of no importance at all, word-form reading is the only available strategy. . . . This is supported by the fact that the patient can read only a minority of letters. Only a, b, d, f, l are correctly indentified . . ., although not consistently.
>
> There is a marked difference between letters and numbers. She can read all digits and numbers between 10 and 20.

Wolff reports further that Frau Fretz could copy and transpose script and print but could neither write to dictation nor write down names of objects including those she could name orally.

Interestingly, Wolff compared Frau Fretz's post-stroke written language deficits with the developmental disabilities of three other patients who could read but (almost) not write (except for copying) and who exhibited some degree of a whole-word reading strategy. According to Wolff, these patients suffered from intellectual impairment since early childhood, and Wolff explains their written language performance quite convincingly as an adaptation to enforced school requirements.

Frau Fretz's cognitive status remained constant until she suffered a second stroke on 4 December 1902. Autopsy revealed an old infarct of about 4 cm diameter in the region of the third left frontal convolution that extended to the ventricle, and a fresh ventricular haemorrhage. The right hemisphere appeared normal.

DEEP DYSLEXIA

The book *Deep Dyslexia*, edited by Coltheart, Patterson, and Marshall (1980), has been one of the most influential for cognitive neuropsychology and neurolinguistics. In their introductory chapter, Marshall and Newcombe (1980) describe the symptoms of deep dyslexia that they found in their patient GR as follows:

> The most striking aspect of the behaviour of the patient that we studied (Marshall & Newcombe, 1966) was that he would produce surprising numbers of frank semantic errors when attempting to read aloud individual words. [p. 1; e.g. uncle—cousin.]

> In addition, GR would sometimes make derivational errors, misreading, for example, an adjective or verb as its related nominal (or vice versa). [p. 1; e.g. strange—stranger.]

> Errors in which there was a clear visual (shape) similarity between stimulus and (the written form of) his (oral) response were also common. [p. 2; e.g. stock—shock.]

> A syntactic hierarchy could also be observed such that concrete nouns stood the best chance of being read correctly. Adjectives, verbs and abstract nouns were of intermediate difficulty, and function words were rarely read correctly. [p. 2.]

> Finally, we note that GR can never read aloud a nonword—an orthographically legal character string which happens not to have found a semantic niche in the English language. [p. 2–3.]

Wolff did not confront Frau Fretz with nonwords. All the other characteristics of deep dyslexia are addressed in his paper and were found to be present with Frau Fretz. Concreteness, which surprisingly was not considered in Marshall and Newcombe's (1966) first paper on the subject, somehow corresponds to Wolff's concept of 'object familiarity'.

We will not discuss the impact the concept of deep dyslexia had for cognitive neuropsychology as this has been analysed by others (e.g. Barry, 1996).

It is interesting, however, to compare Frau Fretz with other deep dyslexic cases from the classic literature. Marshall and Newcombe (1980) cite cases of Franz (1930), Beringer and Stein (1930), Low (1931), Goldstein (1948), Simmel and Goldschmidt (1953), and Faust (1955), and compare their performance with respect to the presence of semantic, derivational, and visual errors and impaired reading of function and nonwords. Only the cases of Low and of Goldstein have been described in similar detail as Frau Fretz. They seem to fulfil the criteria for the diagnosis of deep dyslexia. It must be questioned whether the cases of Franz, Beringer and Stein, and Faust correspond to our notion of deep dyslexia at all. Low's and Goldstein's explanations of their patient's deficit relate to Gestalt theory, to the part–whole relation (Low) and the holistic–sequential dichotomy (Goldstein). Wolff, as we have seen, proposes that Frau Fretz's deficits are related to preserved and prominent visual experiences of word forms that are part of the semantic representation. His theoretical account bears some relationship to Patterson's (1978, 1979) theory of the mechanisms behind semantic and visual paralexia.

Although overlooked by the modern literature, probably because of its publication in a journal that is difficult to access today, the case of Frau Fretz and Wolff's interpretation of her deficits hallmark the beginning of the history of the concept of 'deep dyslexia'.

REFERENCES

Barry, C. (1996). G.R., the prime 'deep dyslexic': A commentary on Marshall and Newcombe (1966). In C. Code, C.-W. Wallesch, Y. Joanette, & A.E. Lecours, (Eds.), *Classic cases in neuropsychology* (pp. 189–202). Hove, UK: Psychology Press.

Beringer, K., & Stein, J. (1930). Analyse eines Falles von 'reiner' Alexie. *Zeitschrift für Gesamte Neurologie und Psychiatrie, 123,* 472–478.

Coltheart, M., Patterson, K., & Marshall, J.C. (Eds.). (1980). *Deep dyslexia.* London: Routledge & Kegan Paul.

Faust, C. (1955). *Die zerebralen Herdstörungen bei Hinterhauptsverletzungen und ihre Beurteilung.* Stuttgart: Thieme.

Franz, S.I. (1930). The relations of aphasia. *Journal of General Psychology, 3,* 401–411.

Goldstein, K. (1948). *Language and language disturbances.* New York: Grune & Stratton.

Low, A.A. (1931). A case of agrammatism in the English language. *Archiv für Neurologie und Psychiatrie, 25,* 556–597.

Marshall, J.C., & Newcombe, F. (1966). Syntactic and semantic errors in paralexia. *Neuropsychologia, 4,* 169–176.

Marshall, J.C., & Newcombe, F. (1980). The conceptual status of deep dyslexia: An historical perspective. In M. Coltheart, K. Patterson, & J.C. Marshall (Eds.), *Deep dyslexia* (pp. 1–21). London: Routledge & Kegan Paul.

Patterson, K.E. (1978). Phonemic dyslexia: Errors of meaning and the meaning of errors. *Quarterly Journal of Experimental Psychology, 30,* 587–601.

Patterson, K.E. (1979). What is right with 'deep' dyslexic patients. *Brain and Language, 8,* 111–129.

Simmel, M.L., & Goldschmidt, K.H. (1953). Prolonged post-eclamptic aphasia: Report of a case. *Archiv für Neurologie und Psychiatrie, 69,* 80–83.

Wolff, G. (1903). Zur Pathologie des Lesens und Schreibens. *Zeitschrift für Psychiatrie, 60,* 509–533.

CHAPTER SEVEN

Caramazza and Zurif's (1976) studies of aphasic patients with syntactic comprehension deficits

David Caplan
Neuropsychology Laboratory, Department of Neurology, Massachusetts General Hospital, Boston, USA

THE CONTEXT

In 1976, when Caramazza and Zurif published the paper to be discussed here, most aphasiologists in North America were heavily influenced by the work of what may be called the 'Boston School' of aphasiology. This approach to understanding aphasia had its roots in the German 'Connectionist' models of the late 19th century (Lichtheim, 1885; Wernicke, 1874). These models postulated the existence of a relatively small number of aphasic syndromes, each linked to lesions in particular brain locations. This class of models held, among other things, that disorders of language comprehension resulted from lesions in the cortex surrounding the primary receptive cortical areas and disorders of language production from lesions in cortex surrounding the primary motor areas of the cortex. This theory applied to single words; other levels of the language code, such as words with internal structure, sentences, and discourse, were not much discussed in this literature.

This approach was widely criticised and lost followers in the second quarter of the 20th century. By the 1960s, there were many strains of thought in the United States that followed other paths, especially Goldstein (1948). However, following an influential paper by Geschwind (1965), neo-Connectionist aphasiology rapidly became established in the United States (less so elsewhere). While neo-Connectionist aphasiology departed from its 19th century predecessors in certain ways, it retained the vital features of focusing on single, simple words in its theoretical claims about language and the brain, and in maintaining the links between sensory and motor association cortex and language perception/comprehension and production, respectively.

At the same time as neo-Connectionist aphasiology was being developed, theoretical linguistics was consolidating a far more radical change. Noam Chomsky and his colleagues had laid the foundations for a formal model of language structure, at the centre of which lay a generative syntactic component. Chomskian linguistics emphasised the sentence as a basic linguistic unit, and syntactic structure as the determinant of sentential ('propositional') meaning.

Caramazza and Zurif's (1976) paper in *Brain and Language* in a sense brought these two lines of research together. Caramazza and Zurif studied the ability to use syntactic structures to determine aspects of sentence meaning in aphasic patients. Other authors had previously studied syntactic features of language—subject–verb agreement, the presence of errors affecting function words and morphological endings in agrammatism and paragrammatism—but Caramazza and Zurif were the first to emphasise the role of syntactic structure in determining basic aspects of sentence meaning, such as thematic roles, and in this they situated themselves very much within the Chomskian model. Caramazza and Zurif found that Broca's aphasics had disturbances of this functional ability. This indicated that the relationship between brain regions and language comprehension and production was more complex than the Connectionists had claimed. At the sentence level, lesions in motor association cortex could produce impairments of syntactically based sentence comprehension. New models of language–brain relationships would be needed to accommodate this finding.

THE PAPER

Caramazza and Zurif (1976) described not a single case, but rather a series of aphasic patients. They studied the sentence–picture matching abilities of these patients. They found that these patients could match sentences to pictures under some conditions but not others. The conditions under which the patients could match sentences to pictures were when (a) the thematic roles in the sentence (who is the agent or actor; who is the theme or recipient of the action; etc.) could be inferred from lexical meaning and real world knowledge, and (b) the sentences were syntactically simple. The patients could not match sentences to pictures when the sentences were syntactically complex and the thematic roles in the sentences could not be inferred from lexical meaning and real world knowledge.

Specifically, these patients could match sentences such as 1 and 2 to pictures, but not sentences such as 3:

1. The boy is eating a red apple.
2. The apple the boy is eating is red.
3. The girl the boy is chasing is tall.

These patients also systematically misunderstood nonsensical sentences, assigning thematic roles according to real world likelihood rather than syntactically dictated meaning in sentences such as 4:

4. The boy the apple is eating is tall.

The authors concluded that these patients had lost an 'algorithmic' method of interpreting sentences. By the term 'algorithmic,' they had in mind a mechanism that assigned the syntactic structure of a sentence and determined thematic roles by integrating lexical meanings into that structure. They claimed that the patients retained 'heuristic' methods of interpreting sentences, assigning thematic roles according to the likely interactions of the items referred to by lexical items in the real world.

These interpretations of these data have stood essentially intact for over 20 years. It is now commonplace to use the combination of a deficit in understanding semantically reversible syntactically complex sentences and the retained ability to understand semantically irreversible sentences with the same syntactic structures as the criterial attribute of a disorder of syntactic comprehension.

Problems with the paper

In retrospect, Caramazza and Zurif's logic was flawed. Caramazza and Zurif used both lexical foils (pictures with an incorrect lexical item) and syntactic foils (pictures depicting the reversed, syntactically unlicensed, interpretation of a sentence). For semantically irreversible sentences (sentences 1 and 2) and implausible sentences (sentence 4), when syntactic foils were used, one picture depicted an implausible or impossible event; for semantically reversible sentences (sentence 3), both pictures depicted plausible events. Caramazza and Zurif reported that subjects rarely chose lexical foils, but this does not establish that the patients could assign *thematic roles* heuristically, only that they retained the lexical knowledge needed to identify the items referred to by the words in the sentences. Conversely, the patients' pattern of choice of syntactically correct pictures and syntactic foils does not prove that they could not assign syntactic structure. This pattern could simply reflect a bias towards choosing semantically plausible pictures. This would lead to systematic correct responses to sentences 1 and 2, systematic errors to sentence 4, and chance performance on sentence 3—exactly the pattern of responses found. Therefore, Caramazza and Zurif's results did not demonstrate that their

patients had a disorder affecting syntactic processing. The way to demonstrate a disorder of syntactic comprehension is to show that subjects can
understand some syntactic structures and not others.

It is frequently claimed that Caramazza and Zurif did this: that they
showed that there are aphasic patients who could understand simple syntactic
structures but not more complex ones. It is also frequently claimed that
Caramazza and Zurif claimed that these patients use simple syntactically
based heuristics, such as assigning agency to an immediately preverbal noun,
to determine thematic roles. Neither of these beliefs about this paper is correct. No syntactically simple semantically reversible sentences were presented
in the study.

The aftermath of the paper

It is fortunate that the problems with the Caramazza and Zurif paper escaped
the reviewers' notice, because this paper inaugurated all the ensuing work on
syntactic comprehension disorders. This work has pursued both the characterisation of disorders of syntactic comprehension and the neural basis of
syntactic processing in sentence comprehension. The characterisation of disorders of syntactic comprehension began with quite general models, and then
focused more and more on the evidence for deficits restricted to specific syntactic operations in particular patients and groups of patients. The search for
the neural basis for syntactic processing began with a focus on Broca's area,
and still remains very focused on this region. I shall review some major trends
in this research, commenting on data and theory as I go. I have not attempted
to cover the entirety of the field. Rather, my focus is on work done by
researchers whose ties have been to Caramazza and Zurif. It transpires that
this encompasses most major issues in this field.

THE OVERARCHING DEFICIT HYPOTHESIS

The first issue was raised by Caramazza and Zurif themselves. This pertains
to the relationship between the (putative) disorder affecting syntactic processing seen in their cases and the patients' speech output disorder. Four of
Caramazza and Zurif's cases had Broca's aphasia. Caramazza and Zurif
argued that these patients had what Zurif later frequently referred to as an
'overarching' deficit affecting the construction of syntactic form (see, e.g.,
Zurif, 1982), in which syntactic algorithms could not be applied in either
sentence production or sentence comprehension.

Caramazza and Zurif attributed both the syntactic disorder in production
and that in comprehension in their Broca's aphasics to disorders affecting the
use of function words. Their paper was published at a time when there
seemed to be a good rationale for claiming that a disorder affecting accessing

function words would affect syntactic processing in both the input and the output modalities. Garrett's (1976) work on sentence production identified different patterns of speech errors affecting function words and content words and had related accessing function words to accessing syntactic structures. Early work on parsing (e.g. Wanner & Maratsos, 1978) drove the creation of phrase structure off information in the function word and morphological vocabularies. Apparently confirmatory evidence for Caramazza and Zurif's position came from Bradley et al.'s (1980) finding of abnormalities in lexical decision tasks for function words and morphological forms in Broca's aphasics but not fluent aphasics.

Nonetheless, the overarching hypothesis has not been sustainable. One problem is that there has never been a characterisation of the overarching deficit. Other than implicating function words in building syntactic structures, Caramazza and Zurif did not put forward a model of the overlap between the algorithms responsible for the production of syntactic form in sentence production and the construction of syntactic forms in sentence comprehension, and it is not clear that any model with significant overlap is defensible.

The function word/bound morpheme access version of the overarching deficit analysis has also not been accepted. At the level of theories of syntactic processing, contemporary models of both sentence production and sentence comprehension relate the construction of syntactic structure to information contained in critical open-class items, not solely to algorithms triggered by the closed-class vocabulary (see Levelt, 1989, in the area of production, and MacDonald, Pearlmutter, & Seidenberg, 1994, in the area of comprehension). Empirically, Bradley's data were not replicated (Gordon & Caramazza, 1983) and, upon reanalysis, did not show what they had been thought to show (Gordon & Caramazza, 1982, 1983). What Bradley et al. (1980) took to be sparing of function words is more likely to be sparing of high-frequency words, whether function or content in type.

Despite the absence of clear models of how accessing the function word/ bound morpheme vocabulary is similar in production and comprehension and how its access affects syntactic processing, one could approach Caramazza and Zurif's hypothesis empirically. Agrammatic patients vary with respect to the morphological and syntactic forms they can produce (Menn & Obler, 1990), and one could capitalise on this fact to see if there is some relationship between the constructions that a patient can produce and those he or she can understand, and if deficits in these two domains can be plausibly related to the patient's disturbance of function words and bound morphemes. To my knowledge, this approach has not been pursued. It is therefore possible that Caramazza and Zurif's overarching hypothesis is correct for some patients, who have a disorder of syntactic processing that affects both production and comprehension of sentences because of an impairment of lexical access for function words and bound morphemes. However, this is an area that has not been pursued vigorously empirically.

This emphasis on an overarching deficit had important effects. It focused attention on Broca's aphasics as the set of aphasics who had disturbances in syntactic comprehension and on Broca's area as the site of syntactic processing in sentence comprehension. The 'mixed anterior aphasics' in Caramazza and Zurif's study, whose performances were identical to those of the Broca's aphasics, were ignored. This focus on Broca's aphasics and Broca's area is part of the legacy of this paper.

THE COMPLETE PARSING FAILURE HYPOTHESIS

Zurif and Caramazza spoke of a deficit in algorithmic processes underlying computation of syntactic form and associated propositional meaning. In the immediate aftermath of their paper, several authors argued that this deficit was complete: that it affected the ability to construct all syntactic structures. Typical of this point of view was the 1980 paper by Berndt and Caramazza that postulated a total disruption of the parser in agrammatic patients. Subsequent work indicated that this was too broad a characterisation of the deficit in many patients, though, again, it may be a correct description of some patients' impairments (Caplan, Baker, & Dehaut, 1985).

THE MAPPING DEFICIT HYPOTHESIS

The polar opposite to the view that agrammatic patients had complete failures of the parser was put forward by Linebarger and her colleagues (Linebarger, 1995; Linebarger, Schwartz, & Saffran, 1983a, b). These researchers (Linebarger et al., 1983a, b) demonstrated that four agrammatic patients could make grammaticality judgements about many sentence types, and concluded that their parsing abilities must be intact. The deficit in these patients, these authors suggested, lay not in constructing syntactic structures but in using them to determine aspects of meaning—a 'mapping' deficit.

The claim that agrammatic patients retain the ability to parse sentences and lose the ability to map syntactic structures on to meaning is too sweeping. In their original work, Linebarger and colleagues themselves noticed that their patients performed less well on some grammatical structures than others, notably ones in which wellformedness depended upon morphophonological agreement of items when the second item occurred at a distance from the first and was unheralded by previous material, such as agreement of pronouns in tag questions. It is not clear that the patients constructed these latter structures. Other researchers (Caplan, 1995; Grodzinsky, 2000) have argued that, in some instances, Linebarger's patients' good grammaticality judgement abilities could have resulted from their sensitivity to some very basic aspects of syntactic/semantic form, such as the fact that a verb can only assign a specific thematic role to one noun phrase. The application of this principle would allow subjects to accept sentences such as *The boy that the girl chased hugged the baby* and reject sentences such as *The boy that the girl chased the woman hugged the baby*—a pattern of performance that Linebarger and her colleagues attributed to integrity of structuring syntactic form and a failure of mapping. Mapping failures likely do account for some part of the abnormal performances of some patients, but the extent to which they do so remains unknown.

THE SHORT-TERM MEMORY HYPOTHESIS

The possibility that limitations in short-term memory abilities might underlie some disorders of syntactic comprehension surfaced earlier, in the observation that separation of items that bore morphophonological agreement resulted in poor grammaticality judgement performances in Linebarger's patients. However, the issue is more general: parsing frequently requires relating items at a distance and psychologists interested in short-term memory argued that parsing deficits reflected disturbances of this memory system. This viewpoint was given additional life by the replacement of models of short-term memory by models of working memory, which was conceived of as a short-duration, limited-capacity verbal memory system, the function of which was to retain representations in an active state while computations were performed on them. Baddeley (1976, 1986) gave the working memory model a form: verbal working memory consisted of a 'central executive' that carried out computations and retained some representations in an abstract form, and a 'slave system', the 'articulatory loop', which kept representations active in a phonological form by a combination of decay-subject storage (the 'phonological store') and rehearsal. Parsing deficits were argued to result from impairments of this system, either its phonologically based slave system (Vallar & Baddeley, 1984) or its central executive component (Miyake, Carpenter, & Just, 1994).

There is, however, considerable evidence that this is not the case. Patients with impaired rehearsal and phonological storage have been described with excellent syntactic comprehension (Martin, 1987; Waters, Caplan, & Hildebrandt, 1991). Alzheimer's and Parkinson's patients with extremely limited central executive capacities also have excellent syntactic comprehension (Caplan & Waters, 1997a; Rochon, Waters, & Caplan, 1994; Waters, Caplan, & Rochon, 1995). Though memory factors into parsing deficits, it appears that the memory system involved is *sui generis*—specialised for parsing and possibly related aspects of on-line language comprehension (see Caplan & Waters, 1999, for a discussion).

APHASIC SYNDROMES AND SPECIFIC DEFICITS

A theme that runs through the above discussion is that the initial character-isations of the syntactic deficits in patients as overarching, complete parsing, mapping and/or STM/WM deficits were too broad. When it comes to theor-etical formulations regarding the nature of syntactic comprehension deficits, bigger (i.e. more general) is not better. Many patients have selective disorders. Work stemming from the 1976 paper has developed this line of research.

Grodzinsky (1990, 1995, 2000) has argued for the view that agrammatic aphasics have a selective deficit in co-indexing traces. Traces are elements postulated in Chomsky's syntactic theory (Chomsky, 1986, 1995). In this theory, traces are noun phrases that are not pronounced. They are found in sentences in which a noun phrase has to be related to a distant syntactic position to receive a thematic role. This occurs, in Chomsky's model, because a noun phrase has moved from an original position. There are two types of traces in Chomsky's theory: Wh-traces and NP-traces. Wh-traces are found in sentences with 'wh-words'—interrogatives and relative clauses. For instance, in the sentence *John saw the man who the police wanted [t]*, accord-ing to Chomsky's theory, *the man* originally was located in the syntactic position of object of the verb *wanted*. As part of the formation of the relative clause, *the man* moved from its original position as theme of *wanted* leaving a trace, noted as [t]. *The man* must be related to its trace to receive its thematic role as theme of *wanted*, according to this theory. NP-traces are similar. According to Chomsky, they are found in sentences such as passives (*The man was found [t]*) and 'Raising' sentences (*The man seemed[t] to run quickly.*) In Chomsky's model, *the man* originated in the positions marked by [t] in these sentences, moved to its final syntactic position, left a trace, and receives its thematic role around these verbs by virtue of being co-indexed with that trace.

Grodzinsky and his colleagues have argued that only Broca's aphasics, and not other aphasics, do not co-index traces normally in comprehension tasks, leading to systematic misinterpretations of object-relativised clauses and pas-sive sentences, and that this problem in co-indexing traces is the only syn-tactic processing problem that Broca's aphasics have. This is known as the 'trace deletion hypothesis'. The trace deletion hypothesis has been extensively debated. In my view, there is no support for it, but Grodzinsky and his colleagues feel otherwise. I shall briefly review the evidence, as I see it.

It is true that many Broca's aphasics have shown a pattern of comprehen-sion that is partially consistent with the trace deletion hypothesis. This pat-tern consists of good performance on semantically reversible syntactically simple sentences that do not contain traces that have undergone long-distance movement, and poor performance on semantically reversible syn-tactically more complex sentences that do contain traces that *have* undergone such long-distance movement. Sentences such as actives are in the first group, and passives and object-relativised sentences in the second. Note that this is the pattern of performance often said to have been documented by Caramazza and Zurif (1976) but not actually tested for in their paper.

However, this is only partial evidence for the trace deletion hypothesis. In addition to showing that Broca's aphasics can understand sentences without traces that have undergone long-distance movement, advocates of the hypothesis have to show that these patients can understand sentences containing other elements that need to be related to noun phrases at a distance, such as reflexives and possibly pronouns. A few Broca's aphasic patients have been studied on these structures and been shown to have this ability, but only very few. At this stage of research, detailed case studies are needed to demonstrate that Broca's patients always retain these abilities.

A second prediction of the trace deletion hypothesis is that all Broca's aphasics will show this pattern. But this, too, is not the case. Many Broca's aphasics perform above chance on passive sentences (Berndt, Mitchum, & Haendiges, 1996).

Thirdly, the trace deletion hypothesis predicts that other aphasic patients will not show this pattern. Again, this is not what has been found. Both case studies (Caplan & Hildebrandt, 1988a, b; Caplan, Hildebrandt, & Makris, 1996; Hildebrandt, Caplan, & Evans, 1987) and group studies (even those from Grodzinsky's lab—e.g. Balogh & Grodzinsky, 2000) show that both loss and sparing of the ability to co-index traces follow all types of aphasia.

Grodzinsky (2000) has replied to these arguments. To the argument that Broca's aphasics may not perform well on other structures, he replies that, because a small number of Broca's aphasics have been shown to be able to understand these baseline structures, all Broca's aphasics can be assumed to understand them. In my view, this assumption is unwarranted at this stage of our understanding of patients' performances. All groups of patients show great within-group individual differences in what they can understand (Caplan et al., 1985, 1996, 1997). As stated above, detailed case studies are necessary to show this.

To the argument that some Broca's aphasics show poor (chance) performance on some structures, such as passive, he argues that performances of patients with Broca's aphasia are normally distributed around chance, implying that good performance in individual cases is a random occurrence. This is an interesting type of argument. It maintains that, even though a single patient's performance *seems* to be above chance when only that patient is considered, it may not be if one looks at that patient as part of a larger group of patients. To illustrate this, Grodzinsky, Pinango et al. (1999) compared the distribution of responses in a series of Broca's aphasics to that produced by tossing an unbiased coin, with the number of tosses being equal to the number of trials each patient was tested on. They claimed that the similarity between the simulation and the patients' performances was 'striking'. However, it turns out that the two patterns are not the same. Caramazza, Capitani, Rey, and Berndt (2001) carried out five statistical analyses that showed that the patients' performances were not, in fact, statistically random; there really are Broca's aphasics whose performance on reversible sentences is at above chance levels, and this contradicts the trace deletion hypothesis (for additional discussion see Berndt & Caramazza, 1999; Caplan, 2001a; Drai, Grodzinsky, & Zurif, 2001; Zurif & Pinango, 1999).

An additional problem that Grodzinsky's reply raises is that it requires that a patient's performance be set in the context of performances by other patients of the same type. But what defines the 'type' of patient whose performances are relevant is unclear. Grodzinsky and his colleagues are ambiguous about whose performances can be generalised over. At times they say the relevant group are agrammatic aphasics, but at other times they say it consists of Broca's aphasics, non-fluent aphasics, or 'anterior' aphasics. Unless we know what group is referred to, this approach to analysing individual subjects' performances cannot be applied (see Caplan, 2001a, for a discussion)

To the final claim that other aphasic patients have disorders that also affect sentences requiring the co-indexation of traces, Grodzinsky (2000) replies that similar off-line performances of fluent and Broca's aphasics are due to different 'on-line' processing mechanisms. This claim leads to the next topic.

ON-LINE DEFICITS IN SYNTACTIC PROCESSING IN APHASIA

On-line processing refers to what happens in real time as language users listen to a sentence: they find certain parts of a sentence hard to structure, they refer back to earlier portions, etc. There are numerous ways to study on-line processing. One task that has been used for this purpose in aphasia is cross-modal lexical priming.

In the cross-modal lexical priming task, subjects listen to a sentence and make a lexical decision about a word presented visually at a point in the ongoing sentence. Cross-modal lexical priming consists of faster reaction times to a visually presented word that is related to a word in the sentence. In the critical experiments cited by Grodzinsky, the visually presented words occurred at the point of a trace in the sentence and either were or were not semantically related to the noun phrase that the trace referred to. Normal subjects show priming for related words at this point (and not just before this point); i.e. they show priming for a word such as *doctor* at point 2 (but not at the control point 1) in sentences such as 5 and 6.

5. The nurse serving on the renal transplant unit [1] who [2] administered the injection replaced the vial.

6. The nurse serving on the renal transplant unit [1] who the injection dismayed [2] replaced the vial.

Grodzinsky and others (e.g. Zurif et al., 1993) claim that Broca's aphasics do not show cross-modal lexical priming for these related words at this point, whereas Wernicke's aphasics do. This forms the basis of claims that, whatever the similarities in off-line performances of Broca's and other aphasic patients, their underlying deficits differ. The studies that support this claim warrant close attention.

In the first study (Zurif et al., 1993), four Wernicke's patients who showed cross-modal lexical priming effects for traces also performed better on off-line tests of the ability to co-index traces than the four Broca's aphasics who did not show the cross-modal lexical priming effect. The differences in on-line performance might have been due to the relative impairment of the patients rather than their lesion site or aphasia type (Caplan, 1995). This leaves only one cross-modal lexical priming study (Swinney, Zurig, Prather, & Love, 1996), of only four Wernicke's and four Broca's aphasics, that serves as the basis for arguing that similar off-line performances in these patient groups is due to disturbances of different on-line operations. In addition, a study by Blumstein et al. (1998) contradicts the Swinney/Zurif results. Blumstein and her colleagues repeated the Swinney study using purely auditory materials (the target word was presented in the voice of a speaker of the opposite sex from the speaker of the sentence). They found priming for words semantically related to the antecedent of a trace in eight Broca's aphasics, but no priming for words separated from a prime by an equal number of syllables in control sentences without traces. Balogh et al. (1998) argued that the Blumstein et al. results reflect end-of-sentence 'wrap up' re-activation of previously presented lexical items, not syntactically based co-indexation of traces. However, this cannot be true of two sentence types in Blumstein et al.'s experiment 1. Five fluent (Wernicke's) aphasics did *not* show priming in the Blumstein study; also the opposite result from that reported by Swinney and his colleagues. Overall, the data do not support the claim that Broca's and Wernicke's aphasics differ with respect to their performance on cross-model lexical priming tasks, or in on-line processing of syntactic structures more generally.

NEUROLINGUISTIC ISSUES

Caramazza and Zurif's patients fell into two groups: as noted, four had Broca's aphasia, and four had 'mixed anterior' aphasia. Caramazza and Zurif emphasised the disorder in the Broca's aphasics, as noted above, on theoretical psycholinguistic lines. This emphasis quickly translated itself into the claim that Broca's area was involved in syntactic parsing. This claim was widely adopted in the neurological literature, sometimes with the modification that Broca's area is the most important part of a widespread neural net responsible for this functional ability (see Damasio, 1992; Mesulam, 1990, for examples of these claims). It was modified by Grodzinsky to claim that Broca's area is responsible for the co-indexation of traces.

From the point of view of deficit–lesion correlational analyses, this claim falters because of the lack of specificity in the relationship between syntactic comprehension disorders and aphasic syndromes, discussed above. It is also exposed on the neurological side. Many authors at first assumed patients with Broca's aphasia had lesions in Broca's area (Caramazza & Zurif, 1976; Grodzinsky, 1990), but lesions in these patients were later found to usually extend well beyond Broca's area (Mohr et al., 1978) and at times not to affect this area at all (Vanier & Caplan, 1990). Lesion location is inaccurate in many of the studies. For instance, in some studies, CT and MR images have been analysed by purely subjective techniques that yield poor inter-observer reliability (Hayward, Naeser, & Zatz, 1977; Naeser & Hayward, 1978). Other studies use more accurate techniques to analyse CT or MR scans, but study relatively small numbers of cases (Dronkers et al., 1994; Tramo, Baynes, & Volpe, 1988). Metabolic effects of lesions invariably affect tissue not seen to be damaged on CT and standard MR scans, which may contribute to deficits, but few studies have measured cerebral metabolism in patients with syntactic comprehension deficits, and those that have done so suffer from a choice of inappropriate tests of syntactic processing (Karbe et al., 1989; Kempler et al., 1991; Metter et al., 1990).

New imaging approaches provide a different way to investigate the functional neuroanatomy of language. One approach is to use ERPs. I will omit discussion of the P600 or 'syntactic positive shift (SPS)' because it arises posteriorly and I wish to focus on Broca's area, which is most clearly related to the Caramazza and Zurif (1976) paper (for discussion of the P600/SPS, see Osterhout & Hagoort, 1999). A second wave—the 'left anterior negativity (LAN)' or 'early left anterior negativity (ELAN)'— arises in relation to a wide variety of syntactic anomalies roughly over Broca's area (Coulson, King, & Kutas, 1998a, b; Friederici, Pfeifer, & Hahne, 1993; Gunter, Stowe, & Mulder, 1997; Munte & Heinze, 1994; Munte, Heinze, & Mangun, 1993; Munte, Matzke, & Johannes, 1997; Neville et al., 1991; Osterhout & Mobley, 1995). Friederici (1995, 1999) has suggested that the LAN and the ELAN reflect early, automatic, 'first-pass' building of syntactic structure. Kluender and Kutas (1993a, b) described a LAN when subjects processed object-relativised clauses, which they ascribed to the working memory load in these sentences. Assuming that the LAN and ELAN originate in or close to Broca's area, Friederici's structure-building hypothesis about this wave contradicts Grodzinsky's trace-localisation hypothesis, while Kluender and Kutas' results are at least broadly consistent with his hypothesis, though, as noted, they interpret them in a very different framework.

In the past 12 years, studies of regional cerebral blood flow (rCBF), initially using positron emission tomography (PET) and now also based on functional magnetic resonance imaging (fMRI), have become a major source of data regarding the location of the neural tissue involved in language processing. A minority of these studies focus on sentence level comprehension. Several studies compare sentence processing against a range of baseline tasks (Bavelier et al., 1997; Bookheimer et al., 1993; Chee et al., 1999; Mazoyer et al., 1993; Stowe & Wijers, 1994) or have varied task demands while keeping sentence structure constant (Dapretto, Bookheimer, Strojwas, & Cohen, 1998; Nichelli & Grafman, 1995). The implications of these studies for the functional neuroanatomy of syntactic processing are limited because the rCBF effects are likely to reflect differences in task demands. More focused studies have compared different syntactic structures in the same tasks. Several of the studies have focused on relative clauses, which are relevant to the 'Broca's area does traces' hypothesis. Studies using plausibility judgement tasks in PET have shown consistent activation of Broca's area in high performing young subjects, precuneal activation in young subjects who perform less well, left inferior parietal activation in elderly subjects, and variable activation of midline frontal structures (Stromswold et al., 1996; Caplan, Alpert, & Waters, 1998, 1999; Caplan, Alpert, Waters, & Olivieri, 2001; Caplan, 2001b). A study using a statement verification task with fMRI reported an increase in rCBF in both Broca's area and in Wernicke's area of the left hemisphere, as well as smaller but reliable increases in rCBF in the homologous regions of the right hemisphere (Just et al., 1996). Despite the fact that passive sentences are affected in Broca's aphasics according to Grodzinsky's hypothesis, we have not found activation for passive compared to active sentences (Caplan, 2001b).

Overall, the ERP and functional neuro-imaging literatures are consistent with the view that there is a preferred site for some aspects of syntactic processing, which may differ in different groups. Broca's area—the focus of attention—may be such a site for processing relative clauses in young proficient language users. However, there are many loose ends to tie up here.

A REASSESSMENT OF A SEMINAL PAPER

This brief review of studies since the Caramazza and Zurif (1976) paper illustrates the range of work that has been spawned by that paper. The paper is truly seminal; as I said earlier, it is not unreasonable to argue that all the work that has gone on in the past 25 years on disorders of syntactic comprehension and the neural basis for this functional ability has its origin in that paper.

In this chapter, I have focused on hypotheses that have followed that paper in the writings of researchers closely affiliated with that original work. In my view, these researchers have articulated very strong hypotheses that have not received empirical support. But, even if the hypotheses are wrong, enunciating and defending them has been valuable. It has incorporated concepts from theoretical linguistics and sophisticated methods from psychology into studies of aphasia. It has highlighted methodological and interpretative considerations in aphasiology itself. And, though it does not look promising to me, some of these hypotheses may, of course, turn out to be right.

Seminal papers do not resolve issues; they open up areas for study. Virtually none of the issues raised in the Caramazza and Zurif (1976) paper regarding the nature of syntactic deficits in sentence comprehension, their neural basis, and the neural basis of syntactic processing in normal subjects have been resolved. The legacy of Caramazza and Zurif's work is that they are being studied.

ACKNOWLEDGEMENTS

The research reported here was supported by a grant from NIDCD (DC00942).

REFERENCES

Baddeley, A.D. (1976). *The psychology of memory*. New York: Basic Books.

Baddeley, A.D. (1986). *Working memory*. New York: Oxford University Press.

Balogh J.E. & Grodzinsky, Y. (2000). Levels of linguistic representation in Broca's aphasia: Implicitness and referentiality of arguments. In R. Bastiaanse & Y. Grodzinsky (Eds.), *Grammatical disorders in aphasia: A neurolinguistic perspective*. London: Whurr Publications.

Balogh, J., Zurif, E.B., Prather, P., Swinney, D., & Finkel, L. (1998). Gap filling and end of sentence effects in real-time language processing: Implications for modeling sentence comprehension in aphasia. *Brain and Language, 61*, 169–182.

Bavelier, D., Corina, D., Jezzard, P., Padmanabhan, S., Clark, V.P., Karni, A., Prinster, A., Braun, A., Lalwani, A., Rauschecker, J.P., Turner, R., & Neville, H. (1997). Sentence reading: A functional MRI study at 4 Tesla. *Journal of Cognitivie Neuroscience, 9*, 664–686.

Berndt, R., & Caramazza, A. (1980). A redefinition of the syndrome of Broca's aphasia. *Applied. Psycholinguisties, 1*, 225–278.

Berndt, R.S., & Caramazza, A. (1999). How 'regular' is sentence comprehension in Broca's aphasia? It depends on how you select the patients. *Brain and Language, 67*, 242–247.

Berndt, R., Mitchum, C.C., & Haendiges, A.N. (1996). Comprehension of reversible sentences in 'agrammatism': A meta-analysis. *Cognition, 58*, 289–308.

Blumstein, S., Byma, G., Kurowski, K., Hourihan, J., Brown, T., & Hutchison, A. (1998). On-line processing of filler-gap constructions in aphasia. *Brain and Language, 61(2)*, 149–169.

Bookheimer, S.Y., Zeffiro, T.A., Gallard, W., & Theodore, W. (1993). Regional cerebral blood flow changes during the comprehension of syntactically varying sentences. *Neuroscience Society Abstracts, 347.5*, 843.

Bradley, D.C., Garrett, M.F., & Zurif, E.B. (1980). Syntactic deficits in Broca's aphasia. In D. Caplan (Ed.), *Biological studies of mental processes* (pp. 269–286). Cambridge, MA: MIT Press.

Caplan, D. (1995). Issues arising in contemporary studies of disorders of syntactic processing in sentence comprehension in agrammatic patients. *Brain and Language, 50*, 325–338.

Caplan, D. (2001a). The measurement of chance performance in aphasia, with specific reference to the comprehension of semantically reversible passive sentences: A note on issues raised by Caramazza, Capitani, Rey, and Berndt (2001) and Drai, Grodzinsky, and Zurif (2001). *Brain and Language, 76*, 193–201.

Caplan, D. (2001b). Functional neuroimaging studies of syntactic processing. *Journal of Psycholinguistic Research, 30*, 297–320.

Caplan, D., Alpert, N., & Waters, G. (1998). Effects of syntactic structure and propositional number on patterns of regional cerebral blood flow. *Journal of Cognitive Neuroscience, 10*, 541–552.

Caplan, D., Alpert, N., Waters, G., & Olivieri, A. (2001). Activation of Broca's area by syntactic processing under conditions of concurrent articulation. *Human Brain Mapping.*

Caplan, D., Alpert, N., Waters, G., & Olivieri, A. (in press b). Brain organization for syntactic processing studied with positron emission tomography. In A. Galaburda & S. Kosslyn (Eds.), *The languages of the brain.* Paris: Springer-Verlag.

Caplan, D., Baker, C., & Dehaut, F. (1985). Syntactic determinants of sentence comprehension in aphasia. *Cognition, 21*, 117–175.

Caplan D., & Hildebrandt, N. (1988a). *Disorders of syntactic comprehension.* Cambridge, MA: MIT Press.

Caplan D., & Hildebrandt, N. (1988b). Disorders affecting comprehension of syntactic form. Preliminary results and their implications for theories of syntax and parsing. *Canadian Journal of Linguistics, 33*, 477–505.

Caplan, D., Hildebrandt, N., & Makris, N. (1996). Location of lesions in stroke patients with deficits in syntactic processing in sentence comprehension. *Brain, 119*, 933–949.

Caplan, D., & Waters, G. (1997a). Working memory and on-line sentence comprehension in patients with Alzheimer's disease. *Journal of Psycholinguistic Research, 26(4)*, 377–400.

Caplan, D., & Waters, G.S. (1999). Verbal working memory and sentence comprehension. *Behavioral and Brain Sciences, 22*, 77–94.

Caplan, D., Waters, G., & Hildebrandt, N. (1997). Determinants of sentence comprehension in aphasic patients in sentence-picture matching tasks. *Journal of Speech and Hearing Research, 40*, 542–555.

Caramazza, A., Capitani, E., Rey, A., & Berndt, R.S. (2001). Agrammatic Broca's aphasia is not associated with a single pattern of comprehension performance. *Brain and Language, 76*, 158–184.

Caramazza, A., & Zurif, E.B. (1976). Dissociation of algorithmic and heuristic processes in language comprehension: Evidence from aphasia. *Brain and Language, 3*, 572–582.

Chee, M., Caplan, D., Soon, C.S., Sriram, N., Tan, E., & Thiel, T. (1999). Processing of visually presented sentences in Mandarin and English studied with fMRI, *Neuron, 23*, 127–137.

Chomsky, N. (1986). *Knowledge of language.* New York: Praeger.

Chomsky, N. (1995). *The minimalist program.* Cambridge, MA: MIT Press.

Coulson, S., King, J.W., & Kutas, M. (1998a). ERPs and domain specificity: Beating a straw horse. (Part A). *Language and Cognitive Processes, 13*, 653–672.

Coulson, S., King, J.W., & Kutas, M. (1998b). Expect the unexpected. Event-related brain potentials to morphosyntactic violations. (Part B). *Language and Cognitive Processes, 13*, 21–58.

Damasio, A.R. (1992). Aphasia. *The New England Journal of Medicine, 326*, 531–539.

Dapretto, M., Bookheimer, S., Strojwas, M., & Cohen, M. (1998). An fMRI study of syntactic processing using a selective attention paradigm. *Neuroimage, 7*, S1.

Drai, D., Grodzinsky, Y., & Zurif, E. (2001). Broca's aphasia is associated with a single pattern of comprehension performance: A reply. *Brain and Language, 76*, 185–192.

Dronkers, N.F., Wilkins, D.P., van Valin, R.D., Redfern, B.B., & Jaeger, J.J. (1994). A reconsideration of the brain areas involved in the disruption of morphosyntactic comprehension. *Brain and Language, 47*, 461–463.

Friederici, A. (1995). The time course of syntactic activation during language processing: A model based on neuropsychological and neurophysiological data. *Brain and Language, 50*, 259–281.

Friederici, A.D. (1999). Diagnosis and reanalysis: Two processing aspects the brain may differentiate. In J.D. Fodor & F. Ferreira (Eds.), *Reanalysis in sentence processing* (pp. 177–200). New York: Kluver.

Friederici, A.D., Pfeifer, E., & Hahne, A. (1993). Even-related brain potentials during natural speech processing: Effects of semantic, morphological and syntactic violations. *Cognitive Brain Research, 1*, 183–192.

Garrett, M.F. (1976). Syntactic processes in sentence production. In R. Wales & E. Walker (Eds.), *New approaches to language mechanisms* (pp. 231–256). Amsterdam: North-Holland.

Geschwind, N. (1965). Disconnection syndromes in animals and man. *Brain, 88*, 237–294, 585–644.

Goldstein, K. (1948). *Language and language disturbances*. New York: Grune and Stratton.

Gordon, B., & Caramazza, A. (1982). Lexical decision for open- and closed-class words: Failure to replicate differential frequency sensitivity. *Brain and Language, 15*, 143–160.

Gordon, B., & Caramazza, A. (1983). Closed- and open-class lexical access in agrammatic and fluent aphasics. *Brain and Language, 19*, 335–345.

Grodzinsky, Y. (1990). *Theoretical perspectives on language deficits*. Cambridge, MA: MIT Press.

Grodzinsky, Y. (1995). A restrictive theory of agrammatic comprehension. *Brain and Language, 50*, 27–51.

Grodzinsky, Y. (2000). The neurology of syntax: Language use without Broca's area. *Behavioral and Brain Sciences, 23*, 47–117.

Grodzinsky, Y., Piñango, M.M., Zurif, E., & Drai, D. (1999). The critical role of group studies in neuropsychology: Comprehension regularities in Broca's aphasia: *Brain and Language, 67*, 134–147.

Gunter, T.C., Stowe, L.A., & Mulder, G. (1997). When syntax meets semantics. *Psychophysiology, 34*, 660–676.

Hayward, R., Naeser, M.A., & Zatz, L.M. (1977). Cranial computer tomography in aphasia. *Radiology, 123*, 653–660.

Hildebrandt, N., Caplan, D., & Evans, K. (1987). The man left without a trace: A case study of aphasic processing of empty categories. *Cognitive Neuropsychology, 4(3)*, 257–302.

Just, M.A., Carpenter, P.A., Keller, T.A., Eddy, W.F., & Thulborn, K.R. (1996). Brain activation modulated by sentence comprehension. *Science, 274*, 114–116.

Karbe, H., Herholz, K., Szelies, B., Pawlik, G., Wienhard, K., & Heiss, W. (1989). Regional metabolic correlates of Token Test results in cortical and subcortical left hemispheric infarction. *Neurology, 39*, 1083–1088.

Kempler, D., Curtis, S., Metter, E.J., Jackson, C.A., & Hanson, W. (1991). Grammatical comprehension, aphasic syndromes and neuroimaging. *Journal of Neurolinguistics, 6*, 301–318.

Kluender, R., & Kutas, M. (1993a). Bridging the gap: Evidence from ERPs on the processing of unbounded dependencies. *Journal of Cognitive Neuroscience, 5*, 196–214.

Kluender, R., & Kutas, M. (1993b). Subjacency as a processing phenomenon. *Language and Cognitive Processes, 8*, 573–633.

Levelt, W.J.M. (1989). *Speaking: From intention to articulation*. Cambridge, MA: MIT Press.

Lichtheim, L. (1885). On aphasia. *Brain, 7*, 433–484.

Linebarger, M.C. (1995). Agrammatism as evidence about grammar. *Brain and Language, 50*, 52–91.

Linebarger, M.C., Schwartz, M.F., & Saffran, E.M. (1983a). Sensitivity to grammatical structure in so-called agrammatic aphasics. *Cognition, 13*, 361–392.

Linebarger, M.C., Schwartz, M.F., & Saffran, E.M. (1983b). Syntactic processing in agrammatism: A reply to Zurif and Grodzinsky. *Cognition, 15*, 207–214.

MacDonald, M.C., Pearlmutter, N.J., & Seidenberg, M.S. (1994). Lexical nature of syntactic ambiguity resolution. *Psychological Review, 101*, 676–703.

Martin, R.C. (1987). Articulatory and phonological deficits in short-term memory and their relation to syntactic processing. *Brain and Language, 32*, 159–192.

Mazoyer, B.M., Tzourio, N., Frak, V., Syrota, A., Murayama, N., Levrier, O., Salamon, G., Dehaene, S., Cohen, L., & Mehler, J., (1993). The cortical representation of speech. *Journal of Cognitive Neuroscience, 5(4)*, 467–479.

Menn, L., & Obler, L. (Eds.) (1990). *Agrammatic aphasia: A cross-language narrative sourcebook.* Philadelphia, PA: John Benjamins.

Mesulam, M.-M. (1990). Large-scale neurocognitive networks and distributed processing for attention, language, and memory. *Annals of Neurology 28(5)*, 597–613.

Metter, E.J., Hanson, W.R., Jackson, C.A., Kempler, D., van Lancker, D., Mazziotta, J.C., & Phelps, M.E. (1990). Temporoparietal cortex in aphasia: Evidence from positron emission tomography. *Archives of Neurology, 47*, 1235–1238.

Miyake, A., Carpenter, P., & Just, M. (1994). A capacity approach to syntactic comprehension disorders: Making normal adults perform like aphasic patients. *Cognitive Neuropsychology, 11*, 671–717.

Mohr, J.P., Pessin, M.S., Finkelstein, S., Funkenstein, H., Duncan, G.W., & Davis, K.R. (1978). Broca aphasia: Pathologic and clinical. *Neurology, 28*, 311–324.

Munte, T.F., & Heinze, H. (1994). ERP negativities during syntactic processing of written words. In H.J. Heinze & G.R. Mangun (Eds.), *Cognitive electrophysiology* (pp. 211–238). La Jolla, CA: Birkhauser Boston, Inc.

Munte, T.F., Heinze, H., & Mangun, G.R. (1993). Dissociation of brain activity related to syntactic and semantic aspects of language. *Journal of Cognitive Neuroscience, 5*, 335–344.

Munte, T.F., Matzke, M., & Johannes, S. (1997). Brain activity associated with syntactic incongruities in words and pseudo-words. *Journal of Cognitive Neuroscience, 9*, 318–329.

Naeser, M.A., & Hayward, R.W. (1978). Lesion localization in aphasia with cranial computed tomography and the Boston Diagnostic Aphasia Exam. *Neurology, 28*, 545–551.

Neville, H., Nicol, J.L., Barss, A., Forster, K.I., & Garret, M.F. (1991). Syntactically based sentence processing classes: Evidence from event-related brain potentials. *Journal of Cognitive Neuroscience, 2*, 151–165.

Nichelli, P., & Grafman, J. (1995). Where the brain appreciates the moral of a story. *NeuroReport, 6*, 2309–2313.

Osterhout, L., & Hagoort, P. (1999). A superficial resemblance doesn't necessarily mean that you're part of a family: Counter arguments to Coulson, King, and Kutas (1998) in the P600/SPS-P300 debate. *Language and Cognitive Processes, 14(1)*, 1–14.

Osterhout, L., & Mobley, L.A. (1995). Event-related brain potentials elicited by failure to agree. *Journal of Memory and Language, 34*, 739–773.

Rochon, E., Waters, G.S., & Caplan, D. (1994). Sentence comprehension in patients with Alzheimer's disease. *Brain and Language, 46*, 329–349.

Stowe, L.A., & Wijers, A.A., (1994). PET-studies of language: An assessment of the reliability of the technique. *Journal of Psycholinguistic Research, 23*, 499–527.

Stromswold, K., Caplan, D., Alpert, N., & Rauch, S. (1996). Localization of syntactic comprehension by positron emission tomography. *Brain and Language, 52*, 452–473.

Swinney, D., Zurif, E., Prather, P., & Love, T. (1996). Neurological distribution of processing resources underlying language comprehension. *Journal of Cognitive Neuroscience, 8,* 174–184.

Tramo, M.J., Baynes, K., & Volpe, B.T. (1988). Impaired syntactic comprehension and production in Broca's aphasia: CT lesion localisation and recovery patterns. *Neurology, 38,* 95–98.

Vallar, G., & Baddeley, A.D. (1984). Phonological short-term store, phonological processing, and sentence comprehension: A neuropsychological case study. *Cognitive Neuropsychology, 1,* 121–142.

Vanier, M., & Caplan, D. (1990). CT-scan correlates of agrammatism. In L. Menn & L.K. Obler (Eds.), *Agrammatic aphasia* (pp. 97–114). Amsterdam: Benjamins.

Wanner, E., & Maratsos, M. (1978). An ATN approach to comprehension. In M.M. Halle, G. Miller, & J. Bresnan (Eds.), *Linguistic theory and psychological reality.* Cambridge, MA: MIT Press.

Waters, G.S., Caplan, D., & Hildebrandt, N. (1991). On the structure of verbal short-term memory and its functional role in sentence comprehension: Evidence from neuropsychology. *Cognitive Neuropsychology, 8(2),* 81–125.

Waters, G. S., Caplan, D., & Rochon, E. (1995). Processing capacity and sentence comprehension in patients with Alzheimer's disease. *Cognitive Neuropsychology, 12,* 1–30.

Wernicke, C. (1874). *Der Aphasische Symptomenkomplex.* Breslau: Cohn & Weigart. [Reprinted in translation in *Boston Studies in Philosophy of Science, 4,* 34–97.]

Zurif, E.B. (1982). The use of data from aphasia in constructing a performance model of language. In M.A. Arbib, D. Caplan, & J.C. Marshall (Eds.), *Neural models of language processes* (pp. 203–207). New York: Academic Press.

Zurif, E.B., & Pinango, M.M. (1999). The existence of comprehension patterns in Broca's aphasia. *Brain and Language, 70,* 133–138.

Zurif, E., Swinney, D., Prather, P., Solomon, J., & Bushell, C. (1993). An on-line analysis of syntactic processing in Broca's and Wernicke's aphasia. *Brain and Language, 45,* 448–464.

CHAPTER EIGHT

Low-velocity intra-nasal penetrating head injury: Case NA

Alan J. Parkin
Laboratory of Experimental Psychology, University of Sussex, Brighton, UK

INTRODUCTION

Instances of penetrating head injury are much rarer than their counterpart, closed-head injury. Within the penetrating variety lies an even rarer subset—'low-velocity intra-nasal penetrating injuries', i.e. penetration of the skull and brain by means of a slow-moving object passing up the nostril. Although very uncommon, the literature contains several instances of this kind of injury. One source comes from cases of ritual suicide that involve ramming a chopstick up the nose (Yamamoto, Yamada, & Sato, 1985). In addition, de Tribolet, Guignard, and Zander (1979) reported a young boy who suffered a transcranial injury when a paint brush went up his nose. Rawlinson, Russell, Coakham, and Byrnes (1988) described a man who, following a dispute about a snooker match, was held to the floor by his opponent and a snooker cue was pushed up his left nostril. This injury resulted in damage to the mammillary bodies and hypothalamus (Dusoir, Kapur, Byrnes, McKinstry, & Hoare, 1990).

Penetrating head injuries have a certain 'appeal' to neuropsychologists because they produce relatively circumscribed neuropathology rather than the diffuse and extremely variable character of closed-head injury. This point was made forcibly by Teuber, Milner, and Vaughan (1968) in their study of the most famous case of a slow nasally mediated head injury. The patient, NA, suffered a bizarre accident involving a miniature fencing foil. Many years later NA recounted the episode in his own words:

I was working at my desk. . . . My room-mate had come in [and] he had taken one of my small fencing foils off the wall and I guess he was making like Cerano de Bergerac behind me. . . . I just felt a tap on the back. . . . I swung around . . . at the same time he was making the lunge. I took it right in the left nostril, it went up and punctured the cribiform area of my brain. (Parkin, 1997; transcript of TV interview.)

This account, despite its clarity, is only partly correct because the foil entered the right nostril, but it did take a path slightly to the left of the midline.

The incident occurred in 1960 but the first report on the case did not appear until eight years later (Teuber et al., 1968): interestingly Teuber et al. refer to NA as having been involved in a 'duel', another deviation from NA's own account. The clinical characteristics are of particular interest because of their relevance to subsequent debate about NA, and in particular, the site of his lesion. On neuropsychological examination NA was found to have two persisting deficits, a profound anterograde amnesia and Parinaud's Syndrome. The latter is an occulo-motor disorder in which the patient is incapable of upward gaze. Finally, NA also exhibited autoscopy—an out-of-body experience. In one instance his mother was sitting by him in bed when he remarked 'why are you paying so much attention to the fellow on the bed instead of paying attention to me?'. In addition, his pupils remained unresponsive to light and accommodation.

Teuber et al.'s study compared NA with a group of controls, the famous bilateral temporal lobectomy amnesic HM (for a recent overview of this case see Parkin, 1996), and patient groups with penetrating head injuries in either the frontal, parietal, temporal, or occipital cortical areas. NA exhibited no deficits on perceptual tests or the Wisconsin Card Sorting Test and his post-morbid intelligence was considered to be comparable to his post-morbid ability. However, NA was impaired on maze learning although, notably, he did learn, albeit slowly, whereas HM failed completely. Copying of the Rey Figure was normal but with substantial forgetting after 40 minutes. On Kimura's recurring nonsense figures, NA showed a degree of impairment but his deficit was far more marked with verbal and numeric materials. This contrast was very marked in comparison with HM: on verbal materials HM and NA performed similarly but NA far exceeded HM on nonsense figures.

THE IMPORTANCE OF CASE NA

The case of NA was initially considered important on both a psychological and a neuroanatomical level. At the psychological level NA's deficit was markedly material-specific due to the left-sided nature of his lesion. Material-specific deficits were, of course, well known from cases of unilateral temporal lobectomy. NA's case was unusual in that no involvement of the temporal lobes was suspected in NA's neuropathological profile. The initial study of Teuber et al. did not have the benefit of neuroradiologic findings. However, the entry point of the wound, and trajectory of the foil, suggested that damage to the midline structures had most likely occurred—a fact supported by known links between autoscopic experience and damage in the region of the third ventricle including the peduncle. Furthermore, the presence of Parinaud's Syndrome inferred, on the basis of animal lesion studies, that the superior quadrigeminal region was affected. Finally, disturbance of pupillary reflex was taken to indicate some involvement of the pretectal region. Teuber et al. thus concluded that the lesion 'may thus have been quite circumscribed' (p. 279) but allowed for the fact that vascular disruption and infection due to rhinorrhea could have resulted in more widespread damage.

Despite these reservations, Teuber et al. nonetheless acknowledged that the concentration of apparent midline damage in case NA was qualitatively different to case HM's bilateral temporal damage and, as a consequence, supported 'the belief that amnestic syndromes can be produced by interfering with diverse parts of a complex anatomical system' (p. 279).

THE SQUIRE INVESTIGATIONS

Investigation of NA was continued in the work of Squire and his colleagues. Squire and Slater (1978) used a short-term memory distractor task and confirmed previous findings that NA was much more impaired for verbal than visual information (in this case spatial location). The first investigation of NA had indicated an initial retrograde amnesia for about two years, which, with recovery, shrank to around two weeks after two-and-a-half years. Using a variety of tests for public events, Squire and Slater confirmed that NA's premorbid event memory (i.e. pre-1960) was intact (except for performance on one test) whereas his post-morbid memory was extremely impaired. However, a subsequent report did indicate a much more substantial retrograde amnesia showing that NA's recall of events was restricted to the period of his life between age 10 and 20 but that recall was poor in the 2 years previous to the injury (Zola-Morgan, Cohen, & Squire, 1983). This, in combination with NA's acknowledged failure on another test of remote memory, undermined the previous view that NA's deficit was purely one of encoding new information. However, ad hoc arguments were produced that these relatively mild deficits could stem from the mediating effects of ongoing anterograde impairment that prevented NA from reflecting on, and hence reinforcing, his recent pre-morbid memory.

It was not until 1979 that the first neuroradiological evidence appeared about NA's lesion. Squire and Moore (1979) reported the outcome of three CT scans. Their conclusion, which subsequently proved controversial, was as follows (p. 504):

The available history of the injury and the findings on the CT scan suggest that the fencing foil penetrated the right nostril and entered the cranial cavity through the ethmoid bone. The probable course of the foil was to cross the midline and pass through the orbito-frontal cortex, the rostrum of the corpus callosum, the anterior horn of the left ventricle, and through the neostriatum into the thalamus. . . . The discrete nature of the lesion provides support for attributing this patient's memory deficit to damage of the left thalamus and suggests that the damage is largely localised to the dorso-medial nucleus. A precise definition of the lesion cannot be determined without pathological confirmation. Nevertheless, the findings on CT scan provide a reasonable basis for the conclusions presented here.

Despite the cautionary note implied in the above conclusion, subsequent studies wrote up NA as a patient with a specific pathology in the left dorso-medial nucleus of the thalamus and no other apparent damage (e.g. Kaushall, Zetin, & Squire, 1981). Assumption of this discrete lesion was particularly important in a study reported by Squire (1982) in which NA was compared with Korsakoff patients on a variety of tests. Squire had laid considerable emphasis on the critical role of dorso-medial thalamic lesions in the generation of Korsakoff Syndrome, so comparison with NA might enable differentiation of Korsakoff deficits mediated by thalamic involvement from other influences of Korsakoff deficits—notably frontal involvement. Result showed that Korsakoffs were different to NA, being impaired on release from proactive interference, and judgements of temporal order.

DOUBTS ABOUT NA'S LESION

In an article published in 1985 Weiskrantz cast severe doubts on the lesion interpretation of NA put forward by Squire and Moore and subsequently assumed in later articles (Weiskrantz, 1985). Weiskrantz's point was a simple one and one that was extremely difficult to refute—how could the tip of the fencing foil end up in the dorso-medial nucleus without damaging tissue on the way? Moreover the route of the foil assumed by Squire and Moore would have to have been 'parabolic' rising upwards through the orbito-frontal cortex into the corpus callosum and then down through the internal capsule and into the thalamic region. Weiskrantz argued that this route was highly unlikely and, even if correct, why was there no evidence of damage other than that to the dorso-medial nucleus?

Figure 8.1 shows Weiskrantz's 1985 diagram of his estimation of the fencing foil's path through the brain. Of interest is the fact that the straight path is extremely ventral taking in the lowest part of the orbito-frontal cortex but passing through the cerebral peduncle and terminating in the corpora quadrigemina. A trajectory of this kind would almost certainly affect the mammillary bodies as well. These assumed neuroanatomical findings were

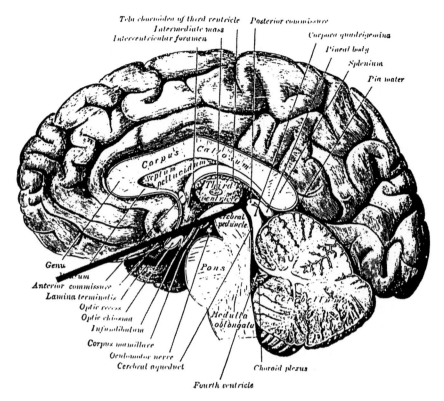

Tela choroidea of third ventricle   Posterior commissure
Intermediate mass
Intercentricular foramen   Corpora quadrigemina
Pineal body
Splenium
Pia mater

Corpus Callosum
septum pellucidum
Third ventricle
cerebral peduncle
Genu
um
Anterior commissure
Lamina terminalis
Optic recess
Optic chiasma
Infundibulum
Corpus mamillare
Oculomotor nerve
Cerebral aqueduct
Pons
Medulla oblongata
Cerebellum
Choroid plexus
Fourth ventricle

Figure 8.1 Estimated path of a fencing foil approximately 2.25 mm diameter, entering nostril and reaching posterior commissure on a direct path avoiding optic chiasm and with minimal damage to frontal lobes. (Drawing of brain from H. Gray, *Anatomy of the Human Body*, 30th edition, C.D. Clemente, Ed. Philadelphia: Lea & Febiger, 1985, p. 989. Reprinted by permission.)

more consistent with NA's overall pathology—i.e. the presence of both Parinaud's Syndrome, autoscopy, and anterograde amnesia. However, Weiskrantz took his argument further by arguing that the assumption of a difference between HM and NA was invalid because HM would 'almost certainly have thalamic degeneration' due to damage of the hippocampal formation affecting the substantial afferent supply to the mammillary bodies and subsequent thalamic structures via the fimbria-fornix. Weiskrantz rejected the CT scan evidence from Squire and Moore as lacking adequate detail and adopted a strong position that all amnesic patients shared a common lesion site.

In a somewhat macabre sequel to this dispute, Zola-Morgan and Squire (1985) attempted to replicate the fencing foil incident on an adult male cadaver. They made three attempts; two passed through the frontal cortex and ended in the corpus callosum and a third ended in the anterior thalamus. In no instance, contrary to Weiskrantz's predictions, did any of the trajectories affect the mammillary bodies and, moreover, the cadaver experiment could not replicate the ventral trajectory suggested by Weiskrantz although they acknowledged that a more ventral route had been achieved in a 'failed suicide by intra-nasal chopstick' reported by Yamamoto et al. (1985).

STRUCTURAL MRI IN CASE NA

Although heroic in some sense, the cadaver experiment was of little value because of the enormous variation across individuals in nasal structure. The real answer to determining NA's lesion required structural neuro-imaging and to this end an MRI study was published in 1989 (Squire, Amaral, Zola-Morgan, Kritchevsky, & Press, 1989). The key findings were as follows:

- In the left thalamus there is damage to a substantial number of nuclei including the ventral aspect of the dorso-medial nucleus. It is also likely that the mammillo-thalamic tract is damaged.
- The posterior hypothalamus is damaged and the mammillary bodies are completely missing.
- The right anterior temporal lobe is damaged subcortically running from the pole into the amygdala.
- The hippocampal formation appears intact bilaterally.

The results of the MRI seem to vindicate Weiskrantz's concerns about NA's lesion. First the loss of the mammillary bodies and the absence of cortical damage is consistent with the ventral pathway of the foil proposed by Weiskrantz. In addition, there was no evidence for the parabolic pathway implied in the account of Squire and Moore (1979).

It may be recalled that Weiskrantz also suggested that deafferentiation of the mammillary bodies might lead to their degeneration in case HM thus minimising important differences between the pathologies of HM and NA. This also seems confirmed in that a recent MRI study of HM has shown that, along with damage to polar cortex of the temporal lobe, amygdaloid complex, entorhinal cortex, and hippocampal formation, HM also has shrunken mammillary bodies (Corkin, Amaral, Gonzalez, Johnson, & Hyman, 1997).

CONCLUSION

What are we to make of this episode in the history of neuropsychology? The basic lesson appears to be that neuropsychologists interested in the relationship between brain structure and function are at the mercy of the neuroradiological methods they use. This is as true now as it was when Squire and Moore were using CT scans with NA. Thus the new technology of functional neuroimaging seems to be fraught with difficulty. There is, for example, controversy about the relation between anterior and posterior hippocampal regions and encoding versus retrieval (Schacter & Wagner, 1999). In addition, the previously accepted 'hemispheric encoding retrieval asymmetry' hypothesis (HERA: Tulving, Kapur, Craik, Markowitsch, & Houle, 1994) now seems in need of serious revision (Nolde, Johnson, & D'Esposito, 1998; Wagner et al., 1998).

Returning to NA, it is clear that this patient's neuropathology extends beyond the dorso-medial nucleus of the thalamus and that the prescient comments of Weiskrantz were wholly justified. It is also true that Squire and Moore placed all their faith in the evidence produced by the then new and exciting CT image and that other behavioural indicators of NA's likely lesion site(s) were set to one side—e.g. the presence of Parinaud's Syndrome and autoscopic hallucination, plus, it has to be said, the unlikely trajectory of the fencing foil that was proposed.

The moral, then, is that the primacy given to neuroradiological evidence in so much recent neuropsychology might be misguided. A potential example of this is recent work concerning language impairments in HM which have been evident from data collected as early as the 1970s (MacKay, Burke, & Stewart, 1998). The authors of this study attribute HM's language problems to various linguistic deficits such as sentence planning and lexical access and that these deficits stem from hippocampal pathology. It is said that whenever two neuropsychologists discuss the hippocampus at least three new theories about its function emerge. Nonetheless, the idea that the hippocampus has direct involvement in sentence planning etc. is, to say the least, novel. The motivation, of course, is that the recent MRI study of HM is taken as sacrosanct—it must be correct so, *ipso facto*, the hippocampus must have the proposed linguistic functions. Perhaps this is wrong. Perhaps a PET or fMRI study of HM might show hypometabolism in other regions deemed unaffected on the basis of MRI—it is very often the case that structural MRI fails to show up lesions underlying serious cognitive deficiency (e.g. Parkin, 1988). At the end of the day it is perhaps wiser to place neuroradiological evidence on an equal footing with other sources of evidence such as the patterns of behaviour observed in experiments derived from theoretical 'dry' models of cognitive function. In the case of NA this might have led to more investigation of his proposed encoding deficit and how this might have explained his modest retrograde amnesia.

REFERENCES

Corkin, S., Amaral, D.G., Gonzalez, R.G., Johnson, K.A., & Hyman, B.T. (1997). H.M.'s medial temporal lobe lesion: Findings from MRI. *Journal of Neuroscience, 17*, 3964–3979.

De Tribolet, N., Guignard, M.D., & Zander, E. (1979). Brain abscess after trans-nasal intra-cranial penetration of a paint-brush. *Surgical Neurology, 11*, 187–189.

Dusoir, H., Kapur, N., Byrnes, D.P., McKinstry, S., & Hoare, R.D. (1990). The role of dien-cephalic pathology in human memory disorder. *Brain*, *113*, 1695–1706.

Gray, H. (1985). Anatomy of the Human Body.

Kaushall, P.I., Zetin, M., & Squire, L.R. (1981). A psychosocial study of chronic, circumscribed amnesia. *The Journal of Nervous and Mental Disease*, *169*, 383–389.

MacKay, D.G., Burke, D.M., & Stewart, R. (1998). H.M.'s language production deficits: Impli-cations for relations between memory, semantic binding, and the hippocampal system: Erratum. *Journal of Memory and Language*, *38*, 28–69.

Nolde, S.F., Johnson, M.K., & D'Esposito, M.D. (1998). Left prefrontal activation during episodic remembering: An event-related fMRI study. *NeuroReport*, *9*, 3509–3514.

Parkin, A.J. (1996). H.M.: The medial temporal lobes and memory. In C. Code, C-W Wallesch, Y. Joanette, & A. Roch Lecours (Eds.), *Classic cases in neuropsychology* (pp. 337–347). Hove, UK: Psychology Press.

Parkin, A.J. (1997). *Memory and amnesia*. Hove, UK: Psychology Press.

Rawlinson, J.N., Russell, T., Coakham, H.B., & Byrnes, D.P. (1988). Trans-nasal hypophysec-tomy: An unusual sporting injury. *Surgical Neurology*, *30*, 311–315.

Schacter, D.L., & Wagner, A.D. (1999). Medial temporal lobe activations in fMRI and PET studies of episodic encoding and retrieval. *Hippocampus*, *9*, 7–24.

Squire, L.R. (1982). Comparisons between forms of amnesia: Some deficits are unique to Korsa-koff's syndrome. *Journal of Experimental Psychology: Learning, Memory, and Cognition*, *8*, 560–571.

Squire, L.R., Amaral, D.G., Zola-Morgan, S., Kritchevsky, M., & Press, G. (1989). Description of brain injury in the amnesic patient N.A.: Based on magnetic resonance imaging. *Experi-mental Neurology*, *105*, 23–35.

Squire, L.R., & Moore, R.Y. (1979). Dorsal thalamic lesion in a noted case of human memory dysfunction. *Annals of Neurology*, *6*, 503–506.

Squire, L.R., & Slater, P.C. (1978). Anterograde and retrograde memory impairment in chronic amnesia. *Neuropsychologia*, *1*, 313–321.

Teuber, H.L., Milner, B., & Vaughan, H.G., Jr. (1968). Persistent anterograde amnesia after stab wound of the basal brain. *Neuropsychologia*, *1*, 267–282.

Tulving, E., Kapur, S., Craik, F.I.M., Markowitsch, H.J., & Houle, S. (1994). Hemispheric encoding/retrieval asymmetry in episodic memory: Positron emission tomography findings. *Proceedings of the National Academy of Sciences*, *91*, 2016–2020.

Wagner, A.D., Poldrack, R.A., Eldridge, L.L., Desmond, J.E., Glover, G.H., & Gabrieli, J.D.E. (1998). Material-specific lateralisation of prefrontal activation during episodic encoding and retrieval. *NeuroReport*, *9*, 3711–3717.

Weiskrantz, L. (1985). On issues and theories of the human amnesic syndrome. In N.M. Wein-berger, J.L. McGaugh, & G. Lynch (Eds.), *Memory systems of the brain* (pp. 380–415). New York: Guilford Press.

Yamamoto, I., Yamada, S., & Sato, O. (1985). Unusual craniocerebral penetrating injury by a chopstick. *Surgical Neurology*, *23*, 396–398.

Zola-Morgan, S., Cohen, N.J., & Squire, L.R. (1983). Recall of remote episodic memory in amnesia. *Neuropsychologia*, *21(5)*, 487–500.

Zola-Morgan, S., & Squire, L.R. (1985). Complementary approaches to the study of memory: Human amnesia and animal models. In N.M. Weinberger, J.L. McGaugh, & G. Lynch (Eds.), *Memory systems of the brain: Animal and human cognitive processes* (pp. 463–477). New York: Guilford Press.

CHAPTER NINE

The control of speech in the adult brain: The disconnected right hemispheres of PS, VP, and JW

Chris Code
School of Psychology, University of Exeter, UK and School of Communication Sciences and Disorders, University of Sydney, Australia

Yves Joanette
Centre de Recherche du Centre Hospitalier Cote-des-Neiges, Montreal, Canada

INTRODUCTION

One of the most central and intriguing questions throughout the history of neuropsychology has concerned the nature of the relationship between the cerebral hemispheres. This question has at the same time concerned itself with the contribution of a hemisphere to a mental activity, the putative superordinate *roles* of the hemispheres, the ontogenic development of hemispheric specialisation, and the potential for a hemisphere to take on responsibility for functions previously controlled by the other damaged hemisphere.

Indeed, the question of inter-hemispheric relationships found early voice in Broca's 1865 description of his patient 'Tan', the case study we generally consider to mark the very beginnings of neuropsychology and dominance theory. For Tan, Broca considered the role of his right hemisphere significant in producing his speech automatism (i.e. 'tan, tan' repeated). Despite this early interest in the possibility of right hemisphere involvement in language and recovery from aphasia, language processing was essentially associated with the left hemisphere. For nearly 100 years (from the 1860s to the 1960s), the right hemisphere of right handers was denied any contribution to language. This was mainly because the effects of a right hemisphere lesion on language processing was seen to be much less dramatic. Until the pioneering work of Eisenson (1962), impairments in communication following right hemisphere damage were undetected. The dominance model has taken a beating in recent years and we acknowledge a significant role for the right hemisphere in behaviour. This is not in question. We are familiar too with the idea that both hemispheres have a role in language, even if we are a long way from complete theoretical accounts of the nature and extent of that involvement. There is a strong meaning of *dominance* where the left hemisphere is seen as a controller for both hemispheres, and part of this role involves inhibition or suppression of the right hemisphere, but it is the control of speech production that has been the hallmark of dominance theory and the canonical left hemisphere function.

Despite a clear superiority in left hemisphere speech production and encoding, there is converging evidence for the involvement of the right hemisphere in aspects of nonpropositional speech production from aphasic subjects, from adults who have undergone left hemispherectomy (surgical removal of the left hemisphere), and from neuro-imaging studies with neurologically normal subjects (Code, 1996, 1997).

While the study of aphasia following left hemisphere damage has amassed a battalion of classic cases, some of the most interesting and significant being featured in this volume and the first volume of *Classic Cases in Neuropsychology*, the question of the contribution of the right hemisphere to language too has its classic cases, albeit fewer. The cases discussed in this chapter are special. Unlike the majority of the classic cases, who have lesions from stroke or injury, these individuals have undergone special forms of brain surgery. We examine the role of the right hemisphere in speech production from the perspective of three important cases whose hemispheres have been disconnected by surgery. This operation is carried out to prevent the interhemispheric spread of seizures in people with severe epilepsy who do not respond to pharmaceutical intervention and would not benefit from focal surgery. What is particularly remarkable about these three people, and sets them aside from the other split-brain cases investigated intensively over the years, is that their right hemispheres have an apparent ability to develop speech encoding over time, and it is for this reason that we claim they are classic.

Early psychological investigations of split-brain patients were disappointing (see Sauerwein & Lassonde, 1996, in the first volume of *Classic Cases*) in the quality and amount of their contribution of the hemispheres to language processing, but Roger Sperry (who received the Nobel Prize for his work in 1982), Joseph Bogen, Michael Gazzaniga, and others developed unique methods and procedures to examine the separate contributions of the hemispheres to cognition and behaviour. These methods entailed the controlled presentation of stimuli to the separate hemispheres through lateralised visual-field presentation, as well as auditory dichotic presentation and tactile presentation.

The split-brain studies had a massive impact on both scientific and popular understanding of the contribution of the right hemisphere to mental life, particularly to language and speech (see Code, 1987, and Joanette, Goulet, & Hannequin, 1990, for a review). However, it became clear that there were major questions concerning the reliability and validity of the findings of split-brain research. These concern the nature of the neurological history of the subjects, the extent of the surgery, and the reliability of the lateralisation methods used. People who undergo split-brain surgery have a history of epilepsy that often goes back many years into early infancy, and brain organisation is generally accepted to develop differently in the brain that is unaffected by epilepsy. Epilepsy can cause major lateral shifts in hemispheric processing, such that the right hemisphere can become a great deal more involved in language and speech than in the brain unaffected by epilepsy. Consequently, we cannot base our understanding of right hemisphere language solely on the results of investigations of split-brain patients. What we need to observe is a convergence of evidence from several different sources. In other words, we would want to observe agreement or support between studies producing evidence from different populations.

A further significant variable we discuss in this chapter is *time*. Hundreds of studies have been completed on a very small number of split-brain patients and over a very long time period. Some subjects have been tested intensively over as much as 20 years. Time is an important factor in neuropsychology—time post-onset of neurological impairment, time since surgery, recovery of function over time, and development of neural and cognitive compensation mechanisms over time.

Our major assumption is that the right hemisphere disconnected by split-brain surgery or isolated by left hemispherectomy does not operate in the same way as the normally functioning right hemisphere working in typical collaboration with the left hemisphere. While generating useful insights and posing interesting questions concerning the lateralisation of language and the plasticity of the brain, the right hemisphere language abilities observed following split-brain surgery in epileptic patients do not represent the language abilities of the normally functioning right hemisphere, interacting naturally with the left hemisphere. Evidence for right hemisphere language skills resulting from the split-brain research, therefore, can be considered as revealing the linguistic *potential* of the right hemisphere, rather than reliable evidence for a normal right hemisphere language capacity (Joanette & Goulet, 1998). Despite these provisos, damage to the right hemisphere (as following a stroke) on linguistic abilities should show some sort of convergence with the potential of the right hemisphere for language, as observed in split-brain research.

PS, VP, and JW have experienced not only epilepsy and split-brain surgery, but also intense examination and experimentation by Michael Gazzaniga and his co-workers, much of which has concentrated on investigation of the emergence with time post-surgery of a right hemisphere speech production capability. Each underwent a two-stage callosotomy (sectioning of the corpus callosum only) and not a full commisurotomy (sectioning of the corpus callosum and the anterior commissure, the massa intermedia and the right fornix), and this fact impacts on our interpretation of the results of the research. It is the primary aim of this chapter to examine the impact of this putative right hemisphere speech capability for neuropsychology, especially for our ideas of recovery and treatment following brain damage. We start with a sketch of right hemisphere language and then examine the general language capabilities of these three people. We then examine the speech production capabilities of their right hemispheres and finally discuss the implications of the studies.

THE NATURE OF RIGHT HEMISPHERE LANGUAGE

Research has examined the question of right hemisphere language in a large range of populations using a range of methodologies. The data from these studies often do not converge well, and are often inconclusive with a lack of agreement between studies and a poor replication record. There appear also to be significant individual differences in brain organisation and representation of language (Ojemann, 1979), in cerebral circulation (Hart, Lesser, Fisher, Schwerdt, Bryan, & Gordon, 1991) and in cognitive style and response to experimental tasks (Segalowitz & Bryden, 1983).

The complex question of right hemisphere language can be approached with reference to more than one standard linguistic framework. The study of aphasic symptomatology over the last 100 years or so confirms that the left hemisphere's role in language has been characterised through traditional formal unit-and-rule, structuralist linguistic descriptions. Left hemisphere damaged aphasic individuals can have problems at phonological, morphological, syntactic, lexical, and semantic levels. In contrast, the essential characteristics of the right hemisphere's involvement in language processing are not covered by these 'straight' linguistic processes. Serial, analytical, segmental processing has been said to underlie the syntactic, morphological, and phonological processing associated with the left hemisphere (Bradshaw & Nettleton, 1981; Wapner, Hamby, & Gardner, 1981), whereas right hemisphere processing is holistic, parallel, contextual. So, left hemisphere damage produces problems in context-free linguistic processes (e.g. syntax, phonology) whereas right hemisphere damage effects context-dependent complex linguistic entities like verbal jokes, metaphors, narratives, indirect speech acts, as well as semantic discrimination and intonation (for reviews see Beeman & Chiarrello, 1998; Code, 1987; Joanette et al., 1990).

However, dichotomising mental activity into processing 'modes' for the right and left hemispheres does not satisfy everyone (see Bradshaw &

Nettleton, 1981, and accompanying commentaries). While elementary, the right hemisphere appears to have some straight linguistic competence. It cannot process active versus passive, future tenses, or distinguish singular from plural. However, it appears to be able to differentiate affirmatives and negatives and to comprehend concrete nouns, adjectival phrases, and object definitional phrases. Assessment of the right hemispheres of split-brain and hemispherectomy subjects using standardised norm-referenced tests, appears to show a vocabulary roughly equivalent to a 13-year-old child (Zaidel, 1978), but syntactic competence is around the 5-year-old level. While the right hemisphere appears to have some auditory verbal comprehension ability, it appears to have little facility for processing segmental phonological and phonetic information (Ivry & Lebby, 1998).

The right hemisphere seems to have particular skills in processing semantic information. Right hemisphere damage can cause impairments in comprehending the meaning of individual words (Eisenson, 1962; Gainotti, Caltagirone, & Miceli, 1983), and in the understanding of connotative but not denotative meaning (Gardner & Denes, 1973; Brownell, Potter, Michelow, & Gardner, 1984). Sidtis (1985) too demonstrated semantic priming across the hemispheres. However, it does not appear to have the skills to make judgements of semantic relatedness involving picture–word matching (Hart et al., 1991). A significant role for the right hemisphere in discourse processing is established (Brownell & Martino, 1998; Stemmer & Joanette, 1998) and a striking feature of right hemisphere damage can be a pragmatic impairment—a breakdown in the context-dependent processing of communication intent by the individual or his or her interlocutor(s).

A recurrent view is that while the right hemisphere has abilities to comprehend incoming linguistic material, it has little or no ability to encode or produce language. However, right hemisphere lesioned patients can present with production impairments at the word (Joanette & Goulet, 1998) and discourse levels (e.g. Joanette et al., 1990). Hughlings Jackson's (1874) observations of brain-damaged patients convinced him that speech production could be characterised in terms of its propositionality and automaticity. He introduced the idea that the left hemisphere was responsible for processing propositional speech whereas both right hemisphere and left hemisphere were involved in processing nonpropositional speech. The idea that speech can be distinguished in terms of its automaticity and propositionality has been utilised by a number of workers since Jackson (Code, 1987, 1996; Goldman-Eisler, 1968; Goldstein, 1948; Van Lancker, 1987, 1993; Wray, 1992). It is argued (Van Lancker, 1987, 1993; Wray, 1992) that nonpropositional, holistically processed, formulaic kinds of speech do not entail straight linguistic, unit-and-rule analysis and synthesis and do not engage components of a generative linguistic system. They are produced in pre-programmed holistic chunks.

The main features of more nonpropositional and automatic language are invariance of production and a non-segmental and holistic construction. Recitation, counting, listing the days of the week and the months of the year, and rote repetition of arithmetic tables are low in propositionality and more automatically produced; they do not involve the generation and processing of new ideas and their conversion into original utterances, and they are highly familiar. Clearly, in normal behaviour the hemispheres normally cooperate to process a dynamic stream of propositional and nonpropositional language. However, following brain damage language can be fractionated in various ways and we can observe dissociations between propositional and nonpropositional language. The nonpropositional speech production capabilities of the few adults who have had their left hemisphere surgically removed—left hemispherectomy—are discussed in Volume One (Code, 1996).

To conclude this brief review, there is now a large body of research showing that the right hemisphere is engaged in the processing of various supra-segmental features of prosody (Ross, 1981) as well as emotional prosody and emotional language (Borod, Bloom, & Santschi-Haywood, 1998; Ley & Bryden, 1981), although the weight of evidence strongly indicates that prosody is a complicated behaviour involving both hemispheres (see, for instance, Pell, 1998; Van Lancker & Breitenstein, 1999, Van Lancker & Sidtis, 1992).

We next turn our attention to three very special human beings, and focus our discussion on their emerging speech production capabilities. Of the 40 or so people reported in the literature who have had split-brain surgery, only three right handers, so far, have shown a consistent right hemisphere speech capability. We will consider explanations for this phenomenal development and consider the limitations of the findings for models of neural representation of language and speech. We will be concerned particularly to examine the factor of time—time since onset of the epilepsy which precipitated the callosotomy, time between the onset of the epilepsy and the surgery, and time between surgery and speech 'emerging' from the right hemisphere. We will consider also the degree to which very intensive experimentation over many years can be seen as stimulation and possessing some of the essential features of successful 'treatment'.

EMERGING SPEECH AND LANGUAGE FROM THE DISCONNECTED RIGHT HEMISPHERE: SPLIT-BRAIN CASES PS, VP, AND JW

Before we focus on speech production, we summarise first the general linguistic capabilities of the right hemispheres of these individuals. These abilities appear to be superior to those of the neurologically normal right hemisphere.

An interesting finding to emerge from some of the early studies on the linguistic capabilities of the disconnected right hemisphere of split-brain patients was that verbs were not processed by this hemisphere (Gazzaniga, 1970). This finding has been disputed, where it has been shown that when word frequency and age of acquisition are taken into account, the right hemisphere can understand verbs just as well as nouns (Zaidel, 1978). The right hemisphere of these subjects is capable of understanding visually presented verbs (Sidtis et al., 1981b; Zaidel, 1982), and just like the left hemisphere, the right hemisphere can also understand visually presented nouns, choosing the appropriate picture depicting a written action name, and executing complex verbal commands such as 'Stand like a boxer!' (Gazzaniga, LeDoux, & Wilson, 1977). When action verbs were presented to the right hemisphere, only patients PS and VP were able to understand and carry out simple verbal commands (Gazzaniga, 1983). Because of this difficulty in carrying out verbal commands (Gazzaniga & Hillyard, 1971; Sidtis et al., 1981b), it has been concluded that it is more difficult for the right hemisphere to understand verbs than to understand nouns.

The semantic abilities of the right hemisphere have also been demonstrated in these cases. When a word that was semantically related to a target word had to be identified from a set of three words, the right hemisphere of PS was able to match frequently associated words (e.g. clock–time, porch–house, devil–hell), as well as words with opposite meanings (e.g. boy–girl, angel–devil) (Gazzaniga et al., 1977). VP and JW were administered a task in which a target word was presented in the left visual half-field, followed by a series of four words in free-field presentation. They were instructed to point with the left hand to the word that illustrated either one of the following semantic relations with the initial word: (1) synonymy (e.g. boat–ship), (2) antonymy (e.g. day–night), (3) hyponymy (e.g. lake–water), (4) hyperonymy (e.g. tree–oak), and (5) function (e.g. clock–time) (Sidtis & Gazzaniga, 1983). Performance on this task showed that the semantic capacities of the right hemisphere were usually inferior to those of the left hemisphere. JW's right hemisphere was always inferior to that of VP, whereas the performance of the two left hemispheres was almost identical. The performance of both JW and VP varied very little from one semantic relation to another. For four of the five relation types, the inter-type variation was 4% for VP and 10% for JW (Sidtis & Gazzaniga, 1983). Antonymy was the most difficult relation for VP, whereas synonymy was the most difficult one for JW. Not only were these semantic relations associated with the poorest right hemisphere performance, but they were also the ones for which the left hemisphere was the least competent. Thus, this difference between the right hemisphere and the left hemisphere appeared to be more quantitative than qualitative.

In a further study of the semantic processing of the disconnected right hemisphere, Gazzaniga et al. (1984) administered three language tasks to VP and JW to examine the semantic fields of four target words: 'ant', 'eye', 'bed', and 'bunny'. In the first task, the target word was presented in either the left or right visual field. VP and JW were asked to choose which of two test words, presented in either the same visual field or the contralateral field, was more closely associated with the previously presented target word. In the second task, the subjects had to indicate if there was an association between the target word, presented in either the right or left visual field, and a test word that was subsequently presented in either the same or the opposite visual half-field. The third task was somewhat similar to the second, except that the two words were presented simultaneously: the target word appeared at the point of fixation, while the test word appeared in either the right or the left visual half-field. Once again, the subjects had to indicate if the test word was associated with the target word. Results revealed that the subjects were performing at chance level in the contralateral conditions of the first two tasks—i.e. when the target word and the test word were presented in opposite visual half-fields (Gazzaniga et al., 1984). We might therefore conclude that there was no efficient inter-hemispheric transfer in these two conditions. In contrast, when both the target and the test words were presented in the same visual half-field, the right hemisphere seemed to be sensitive to various semantic relations: (a) hyponymy (e.g. ant–insect), (b) co-hyponymy (e.g. ant–bee), (c) attribute (e.g. ant–small), and (d) function (e.g., ant–crawl).

In fact, VP's right hemisphere performed almost as well as her left hemisphere in the first task. The performance of JW's right hemisphere was inferior to the performance of his left hemisphere for the first two tasks only. Performance of the right hemisphere was better for the third task than for the second task, and better for the second and third tasks than for the first task, where performance was at chance level. On the basis of these results, it can be said that the degree of the right hemisphere's semantic competence varies between VP and JW. In this case, VP's right hemisphere lexicon appears to be more efficient and/or complete than JW's. However, in both subjects, the right hemisphere lexicon appears to be smaller and not as rich as the left hemisphere lexicon (Gazzaniga et al., 1984). It might be that the lexicons of the two hemispheres are similar, but that access to the right hemisphere lexicon is more difficult. It could also be that this apparent asymmetry is in fact a reflection of the particular nature of the semantic judgements required in these tasks (Gazzaniga et al., 1984). The results for task three clearly indicate that the nature of the task had an effect on the semantic judgements of JW's right hemisphere (Gazzaniga et al., 1984).

Gazzaniga et al. (1984) assessed VP's and JW's knowledge of current events in order to examine each hemisphere's ability to acquire new information since disconnection of the hemispheres. A word was presented to either the left or the right visual half-field and the subjects had to select an associated word from a set of six written choices. For example, following the presentation of the word 'hostage', the subjects had to decide which one of the following words was associated with the target word: Iran, Russia, England, Australia, and Cuba. The association to be made here concerned the taking of American hostages in Iran. It is interesting to note the connotative nature of the meaning given to the target word—in other words, the word 'hostage' is not associated with Iran *a priori*. Both VP's and JW's right hemisphere and left hemisphere performed equally well on this task. Moreover, the two hemispheres tended to miss the same trials. This similarity in the performance of the two hemispheres is quite remarkable.

SPEECH PRODUCTION FROM THE DISCONNECTED RIGHT HEMISPHERE

PS

PS was the subject of several years of examination with a large range of published papers. PS is male, right-handed, with onset of severe convulsions at 2 years, focused in the left temporal region. At 15 years he underwent complete sectioning of the corpus callosum. A complete medical history is available in Wilson, Reeves, Gazzaniga, and Culver (1977).

An apparent right hemisphere speech capability began to emerge at approximately 2 years post-surgery. Over a period from 18 months to 36 months his object-naming abilities on presentation of stimuli to his left visual field (right hemisphere) improved from 0 to 100% correct. Over this same period the single-word reading aloud capabilities of his right hemisphere improved from 0 to nearly 90% correct.

Complex visual scenes were also presented to PS's left or right visual field. The responses following exposure of these scenes to PS's right hemisphere show an interesting pattern of response, as can be seen in Table 9.1. His left hemisphere responds in the expected way (e.g. the picture of a man with a handgun correctly produces *Guy with a gun* from PS's left hemisphere). In almost all cases in Table 9.1 PS's right hemisphere identifies and names a central part of the picture correctly with one word. However, the subsequent production, while logically related to the correctly produced word, is unrelated in fact to the picture. We examine this phenomenon further below.

VP

VP (Gazzaniga et al., 1984; Sidtis et al., 1981b) was the next split-brain subject whose right hemisphere began to develop the power to produce propositional speech some time following surgery. VP is a right-handed female who experienced her first epileptic attack at 6 years. (Baynes & Eliassen, 1998; Sidtis et al., 1981b) or 9 years (Gazzaniga, 1983; Gazzaniga et al., 1984) with surgery at 27 years of age. At 27 years she underwent a two-stage

TABLE 9.1
PS's verbal responses to complex pictures shown only to his right hemisphere
(adapted from Gazzaniga et al., 1979)

Right hemisphere stimuli	Verbal response
A piece of layer cake	Cake . . . it was a whole vanilla cake with chocolate icing, silverware is there too.
Exploding firework	Smoke . . . coming out of a chimney, it's a small house.
Man, shearing sheep	Man . . . he is walking through the woods.
Couple dancing	Some . . . guys working on building together.
Man with handgun	Gun . . . hold up . . . he has a gun and is holding up a bank teller, a counter separates them.

callosotomy. In a footnote on the last page of their paper concerned with the language abilities of VP and JW, Sidtis et al. (1981b) state: 'At our first evaluation (4 months post-operative) she could not name any stimuli presented to her left sensory field. By the 12th post-operative month, however, she named 32% of the left visual field words presented in one test' (p. 330). 'Naming words' here presumably means 'reading words aloud'.

More detailed examination of VP's speech at 12 months post-surgery was reported by Gazzaniga et al. (1984) who showed she could read aloud 38/40 simple nouns or verbs. As with PS, the right hemisphere and left hemisphere of VP were presented with 13 complex pictorial scenes for description. Her responses are particularly illuminating. When a scene of an athlete jumping a hurdle was exposed to her left hemisphere, she correctly and fairly completely responded with: *I don't know if he's an athlete or not, but he is a man running over hurdles. He's got gym shorts on, and I don't know for sure if he had a shirt on. Think he did . . . and tennis shoes, jogger's shoes.* However, her right hemisphere responds with: *An athlete . . . a basketball guy? . . . had a uniform. His back was facing me, and he was on an angle. He looked like he had been walking, and he was gonna take another step because one foot was like more out.*

Like for PS, both hemispheres can describe the basic features of the picture, but the pictures shown to the right hemisphere are then embellished upon. What appears to be happening with exposure of the scene to her right hemisphere is an embellishment by the left hemisphere of initially correct right hemisphere naming. The left hemisphere 'hears' the initial right hemisphere response and then guesses, infers, confabulates. This strategy is an example of 'cross-cuing' where, following the correct right hemisphere identification of *an athlete*, the left hemisphere, which has heard this response, cannot resist guessing *a basketball guy?*. The right hemisphere apparently sees the sporting kit the athlete is wearing. While it is hard to see where *his back was facing me* comes from, the *angle* of the picture is unusual and the right hemisphere has seen that. The right hemisphere has also seen the outstretched leg of the athlete – *one foot was like more out.* But the left hemisphere was unable to infer a hurdler from this. It seems like the left hemisphere's interjection may have put the right hemisphere off course.

JW

The third split-brain case with emerging right hemisphere speech, JW, described only within the last seven years (Baynes, Wessinger, Fendrich, & Gazzaniga, 1995; Gazzaniga, Eliassen, Nisenson, Wessinger, Fendrich, & Baynes, 1996), while perhaps stretching the notion of 'classic' case in temporal terms, certainly qualifies as a classic in terms of his apparent significance. In 1984 in a paper describing some of the results from testing VP and JW, Gazzaniga, Smylie, Baynes, Hirst and McCleary state: 'Case JW possessed no ability to generate speech from the right hemisphere' (p. 215). JW contrasts interestingly with PS and VP in that his apparent right hemisphere speech did not emerge until 11 years post-surgery. Additionally, JW was an adult when he experienced his first epileptic seizures. He is a right-handed male whose epileptic problems did not start until he was 19 years of age with surgery (two-stage callosotomy) 7 years later when he was 26 years of age. JW has been seen regularly since 1979, and weekly since 1988.

JW then has a very different history to the two earlier cases, PS and VP, who were much younger than JW and pre-pubescent when their epilepsy began. PS was just 20 months old and VP was 6 years of age. The potential for the right hemisphere taking on the major role in language following an epileptically disturbed left hemisphere for PS and VP was therefore much increased. What is particularly interesting about JW was that despite his age (37 years) and the lateness of his surgery, his right hemisphere has still been able, apparently, to make a contribution to language and, particularly, speech production.

JW's naming of pictures presented to his left visual field improved from 21% correct for colour and 26% for standardised line drawings (Snodgrass & Vanderwart, 1980). His right hemisphere was able to read aloud 20% of short nouns increasing to 48% correct with a larger font (Baynes et al., 1995).

Baynes et al. (1995) report on the naming and reading aloud error types of JW's right and left hemispheres. The majority of naming and reading errors for JW's right hemisphere were random with no apparent relationship to the stimuli. In naming 44% had either a superordinate or associate relationship to the stimuli and there were no visual errors. For reading, 79% of right hemisphere errors were random, with 5 superordinate and associated errors and 3 visual. The left hemisphere made too few errors to show any pattern but there appears to be the same general spread of error types. Worth mention is that of the 9 errors made by the left hemisphere on reading aloud, 5 were visual. The high number of random errors may result from a high degree of left hemisphere guessing. JW is always encouraged to guess rather than not respond. He often says he sees nothing but a flash during the hemi-field presentation, despite correct identification. JW's guesses are often correct.

JW's right hemisphere was shown the complex scene of a woman standing by an old-fashioned wash tub and the interaction between JW and the experimenter follows; we have indicated which hemisphere appears to be responsible for the utterance:

JW: It was a person *(right hemisphere)* . . .
       Would it be someone hanging out their laundry *(left hemisphere)*?
       One person *(left hemisphere)*.
       Must have been a woman *(left hemisphere)*.
Exp: Did you see any laundry?
JW: I think so. I think she was reaching up and that's what she was doing . . . *(left hemisphere)*.

There appears to be a correct right hemisphere identification of the person in the scene followed by a left hemisphere confabulation (*someone hanging out their laundry*). This cannot come from the left hemisphere via cross-cuing because there is no connection between the first statement and this one. The right hemisphere must perceive the scene and its contents, it has problems making a connection between the separate objects. The right hemisphere is inferring *laundry* from the *washing machine*, which the right must have seen, although JW does not apparently name the *washing machine*. But the left hemisphere could have made the connection between a *person/someone hanging out laundry* to state *one person* and to infer that it *must have been a woman*. This liberated left hemisphere knows that men don't do the washing. The final response to the experimenter's question would appear to be a confirmation of confabulation. The woman was not reaching up.

Another scene shown to JW's right hemisphere was of one woman standing behind another who was sitting at a table crying. There was a stove and a sink in the background.

JW: The first thing I thought of was a woman baking. I don't know why . . .
Exp: Was she sitting or standing?
JW: Standing up by a table or something.

We know why JW's right hemisphere *thought of a woman baking* when shown the scene, or we think we know. It was presumably because the right hemisphere saw the stove and maybe at least one woman and again makes the reasonable, if sexist, inference that a stove (not explicitly named) and *a woman* can mean *baking*. The *woman* may have also been inferred from the stove. It cannot have been the left hemisphere responding because it is JW's first statement. The right hemisphere may also know that *the woman* was standing, although the two-item forced-choice means he may also have responded with 'sitting' *at a table or something*. Either right or left hemispheres could have seen the *table or something*, but it could also have been inferred from *baking*. The right hemisphere also missed the second crying woman and therefore did not access the emotional tone of the scene. The left hemisphere inferred 'baking' from these clues.

While PS, VP, and JW share the experience of epilepsy and split-brain surgery, they are different in many respects, although speech emerged from the right hemispheres of both PS and VP at about the same time after their surgery—18 and 12 months respectively. Even more interesting is the more recently described JW, whose right hemisphere has taken 11 years after separation of the hemispheres to seemingly develop speech (see Table 9.2).

TABLE 9.2
Summary of onset of epilepsy, age of surgery, and emergence of right hemisphere speech in the three cases

	PS (Male)	*VP (Female)*	*JW (Male)*
Onset of problems	2 years	6 or 9 years	19 years
Age of surgery	15 years	22 or 27 years	25/26 years
RH speech emerged post-operatively	18 months	12 months	11 years

DISCUSSION

Gazzaniga (1983) suggested that of the approximately 40 individuals who have undergone split-brain surgery, at that time, only a few have been shown to possess right hemisphere language. Those that do possess it, he suggests, show widely different language organisation, reflecting the extent of left hemisphere damage caused by pre-operative epilepsy and, presumably, the extent of the surgery separating the hemispheres. Only these three right-handers, so far, have developed right hemisphere speech. Given the suspected ability of the hemispheres to exchange information despite separation of the corpus callosum, can these three cases tell us anything useful, particularly about the involvement of the right hemisphere in speech production? We address this question by examining three or four possible explanations for the observed right hemisphere speech in these cases: the neural transfer of information via intact putative routes, the use of 'cross-cuing' strategies during experiments, and the possible effects of time on the development of a right hemisphere speech production capability.

First, the number of people who have undergone the split-brain operation with significant right hemisphere speech (3/40 or so) is similar to the percentage of right-handers having a right hemisphere that apparently contributes more than usual to language (around 5%), as suggested by the occurrence of so-called crossed aphasia[1] in right-handers (Joanette, 1989). This may indirectly support the view that the right hemispheres of these three individuals enjoyed a speech production capacity prior to their surgery. However, the fact that this right hemisphere language capacity took many months to emerge would not support such an interpretation.

How does the speech of the separated right hemisphere contrast with that of the completely isolated right hemisphere, as in left hemispherectomy? Is there any basis for supposing the existence of two, dissociable, speech production systems? A very few right-handed people have had a complete left hemispherectomy in adulthood. The completely isolated right hemispheres of left hemispherectomy cases EC and NF are, without doubt, able to speak (Code, 1996). These men had staged surgery in their 40s (EC was 49 and NF was 41). In contrast to the three cases discussed here, their reported speech was predominantly nonpropositional and nonreferential. EC apparently had some referential naming ability and could produce modal phrases and expletives consisting of several words (e.g. *Yes, but I cannot . . .*) and had some ability to repeat words said to him, although with laboured articulation. NF too was able to produce longer utterances such as *You got a match?* and *Yes, it was okay*, when asked if he enjoyed his lunch. So the left hemispherectomy patient may be telling us that there is a (surgically separable) right hemisphere speech production system, predominantly nonpropositional, which is at least partially represented in the right hemisphere.

The apparent single-word production of the split-brain right hemisphere suggests a reluctance by the left to relinquish control to the right. The left appears to take all and every opportunity to interject. It appears to have no choice. All its actions appear to be at an unconscious level.

A right hemisphere single-word capacity?

According to Gazzaniga et al. (1996, p. 1260), 'A possible explanation for JW's difficulty in producing complex scene descriptions is that those stimuli could not be characterised properly by a single-word response.' The right hemisphere in these cases simply produces a string of single words—a list (as often observed in non-fluent aphasia following left hemisphere damage)—and this may be due to left hemisphere control enabled through cross-cuing, which we discuss further below. (The 'listing' ensues for many people with aphasia, apparently, because left hemisphere capability is severely compromised by the left hemisphere damage.)

If Gazzaniga's explanation is correct, does it mean that the right hemisphere of this split-brain subject has no capacity to produce more than a single word or that this single-word response represents all that any separated right hemisphere is capable of? The left hemispherectomy evidence appears to contradict the latter interpretation; the isolated right hemisphere is liberated from the dominance of its neighbour. Paradoxically, the conscious and unconscious strategies adopted by the split-brain individual and their left hemisphere following callosotomy may actively inhibit a clearer view of right hemisphere language.

But how might a single-word right hemisphere capacity in split-brain speakers be accommodated? The right hemisphere can hold and access the complex scene, but it has little or no access to the left hemisphere's auditory verbal working memory storage capacity, so it is unable to generate a phonological response longer than one word. The complex scene responses suggest several attempts by the right hemisphere to generate single words. Both hemispheres are required for language, as seems to be the case for other aspects of cognition. The organisation of language in the brain is not the mere addition of the respective and isolated contributions of the left hemisphere and the right hemisphere. If that were the case, it follows that it is probably impossible to expect one isolated hemisphere to behave as it would normally in the intact brain. So, it might be the case that the separated right hemisphere is only capable of isolated words just because the processes necessary to link and combine words (e.g. morphology, syntax, auditory-verbal working memory) are not available to it. However, this does not preclude the possibility that the right hemisphere has some direct input to the organisation of word meaning in a coherent discourse, despite its inability to cope with word linking. If this were the case, then the right hemisphere's limited ability to produce only single words does not mean that it has nothing to contribute to the more general semantic-based organisation of single words.

Problems of interpretation and reliability in split-brain research

The neurological history of the split-brain cases is of particular importance because, in most cases, the neurological problem has its roots in pre-pubescent infancy and it is highly unlikely that the right hemisphere of the split-brain case has not been significantly affected by the neurological condition. Consequently, the relationship between the hemispheres is not the same as it is in a neurologically intact brain. The isolated right hemisphere is not therefore representative of the normal right hemisphere and is not directly comparable to the right hemisphere of the left hemispherectomy case or the unilaterally left hemisphere damaged aphasic person.

It is important to stress that inter-hemispheric transfer of information is known to take place during split-brain experiments. All three cases discussed here have undergone sectioning of the corpus callosum only and there may be other possible routes between the hemispheres for exchange of information. Gazzaniga, Sidtis, Volpe, Smylie, Holtzman, and Wilson (1982) suggest that the anterior commissure (intact in all three cases) may allow the right hemisphere access to the left hemisphere's speech production system. Whether this possible access occurs earlier or later in the speech production process is not clear. In addition, cross-cuing between hemispheres in split-brain subjects is well known, as described above. Cases who have undergone complete commisurotomy and have developed right hemisphere speech have not been described.

Baynes et al. (1995) examined cross-cuing in JW. They presented a series of restricted predictable sets of digits for naming to separate visual fields and JW's right hemisphere performed at 95% accuracy. However, a second series of digits with the digit 9 substituted for other expected digits was prepared. JW's performance was unchanged and 9s were never correctly named. It was apparent that the hemisphere that was actually initiating the speech was not aware of the digit displayed. In this experiment at least, cross-cuing of some kind was taking place. In this experiment the right hemisphere was identifying the digit and providing some kind of information to the left, which was producing the spoken response. Analysis of error types on this task suggested that information might have been transferred visually or using some kind of manual signalling to inform the left hemisphere of the correct digit. There was evidence that visual confusions might have accounted for some of the errors in the LVF and JW made more errors on the higher digits 6,7,8 in the LVF, suggesting a possible manual counting strategy.

Baynes et al. (1995) also conducted a series of experiments to determine whether responses to left visual field presentation were generated by the right hemisphere or whether orthographic and phonemic information was being transferred over to the left via subcortical structures or the intact anterior commissure. Matching (GOAT–GOAT) and non-matching (GOAT–GOTE) visual pairs and matching (GOAT–GOAT) and non-matching phonemic pairs (GOAT–CAKE) were presented within visual fields (i.e. both members of the pair to one field) and between visual fields (one member of the pair to the LVF and one to the RVF). JW was required to press a key to indicate if the words looked alike or sounded alike. The within-fields task assesses each hemisphere's ability with orthographic or phonemic matching and the between-fields task assesses the transfer of orthographic or phonemic information between the hemispheres. On both of the between-fields tasks JW only performed at chance, indicating that it was unlikely that his ability to name stimuli presented to his LVF—his right hemisphere—was due to transfer of orthographic, phonemic, or visual information.

Of course, because JW and other split-brain subjects do utilise cross-cuing to complete experimental tasks, does not mean that they always do, as Baynes et al.'s results suggest. Nonetheless, cross-cuing suggests that callosotomy does not prevent collaboration between the hemispheres, as in the normally functioning brain.

Has the separated right hemisphere been trained?

Is the apparent increasing capacity for speech in the right hemisphere of these patients the result of intensive stimulation of the right hemisphere brought about through intensive long-term experimentation? JW has been seen regularly since 1979 and weekly since 1988. This adds up to a great deal of intensive stimulation over many years. Animal work has shown clearly that stimulation results in learning and new neural growth (e.g. Kolb, 1996). To what extent can we view this as intensive long-term 'training' or even of so-called 'spontaneous' recovery over time? Certainly, the intensive stimulation that aphasic people receive through aphasia therapy (Katz et al., 2000) is a tiny fraction of the stimulation that JW, in particular, has received. Has the right hemisphere of JW and the other split-brain subjects been stimulated and 'trained' to such a degree that it has developed a speech production capacity? The inter-hemispheric availability of at least subtle semantic information (priming data) may allow the development of more useful inter-hemispheric interactions over time, as documented during the period of partial disconnection in JW by Sidtis et al. (1981a). One could conceive of this as a hybrid between cross-cuing and training (Sidtis, personal communication).

There have been a variety of approaches to enrolling the right hemisphere in aphasia therapy (and attempts have been made to directly cause learning in the right hemisphere of aphasic people, Code, 1994). While it has not been established that the right hemisphere can be involved directly in aphasia therapy, there is a range of evidence that the right hemisphere does take on a larger role in language following left hemisphere damage in some patients (Calvert et al., 2000; Code, 1987; Gainotti, 1993; Weiler et al., 1995).

What seems clear from the extensive split-brain literature is that there are numerous forms of cognitive and spatial interactions even after complete section of the corpus callosum. In a sense, these interactions might be the best model for 'unconscious processing' because they are generally not available for oral report under standard conditions (Sidtis, personal communication). The studies with PS, VP, and JW are important because they force us to question our notions about the relationship between language, and in particular speech production, and the cerebral hemispheres. There may be significant implications from the work, with JW in particular, for the treatment of aphasia following left hemisphere damage. It is an established axiom of neuropsychology that 'recovery' can take place for people with younger, more plastic, nervous systems but that it is less likely, even impossible, for older nervous systems (the Kennard principle). JW demonstrates that we need to reassess this position. The adult brain is more plastic than previously thought. The adult brain is capable of learning and the adult right hemisphere may even be capable, with sufficient training, of developing significant language, and even some speech production.

ACKNOWLEDGEMENT

We are grateful to John Sidtis for particularly useful comments on an earlier draft of this chapter.

REFERENCES

Baynes, K., & Eliassen, J.C. (1998). The visual lexicon: Its access and organisation in commissurotomy patients. In M. Beeman & C. Chiarello (Eds.), *Right hemisphere language comprehension: Perspectives from cognitive neuroscience* (pp. 79–104). Mahwah NJ: Lawrence Erlbaum Associates Inc.

Baynes, K., Wessinger, M., Fendrich, R., & Gazzaniga, M.S. (1995). The emergence of the capacity to name left visual field stimuli in a callosotomy patient: Implications for functional plasticity. *Neuropsychologia, 33*, 1225–1242.

Beeman, M., & Chiarello, C. (Eds.) (1998). *Right hemisphere language comprehension: Perspectives from cognitive neuroscience.* Mahwah NJ: Lawrence Erlbaum Associates Inc.

Borod, J.C., Bloom, R.L., & Santschi-Haywood, C. (1998). Verbal aspects of emotional communication. In M. Beeman & C. Chiarello (Eds.), *Right hemisphere language comprehension: Perspectives from cognitive neuroscience* (pp. 285–307). Mahwah NJ: Lawrence Erlbaum Associates Inc.

Bradshaw, J.L., & Nettleton, N.C. (1981). The nature of hemispheric specialisation in man. *The Behavioural and Brain Sciences, 4*, 51–91.

Brownell, H., & Martino, G. (1998). Deficits in inference and social cognition: The effects of right hemisphere brain damage on discourse. In M. Beeman & C. Chiarello (Eds.), *Right hemisphere language comprehension: Perspectives from cognitive neuroscience* (pp. 309–328). Mahwah, NJ: Lawrence Erlbaum Associates Inc.

Brownell, H., Potter, H.H., Michelow, D., & Gardner, H. (1984). Sensitivity to lexical denotation and connotation in brain-damaged patients: A double dissociation? *Brain and Language, 22*, 253–265.

Calvert, G.A., Brammer, M.J., Morris, R.G., Williams, S.C.R., King, N., & Matthews, P.M. (2000). Using fMRI to study recovery from acquired dysphasia. *Brain and Language, 71*, 391–399.

Code, C. (1987). *Language, aphasia, and the right hemisphere.* Chichester, UK: Wiley.

Code, C. (1994). Role of the right hemisphere in the treatment of aphasia. In R. Chapey (Ed.), *Language intervention strategies in adult aphasia* (*3rd Edition*). Baltimore: Williams & Wilkins.

Code, C. (1996). Speech from the isolated right hemisphere? Left hemispherectomy cases EC and NF. In C. Code, C-W. Wallesch, Y. Joanette, & A. Roch Lecours (Eds.), *Classic cases in neuropsychology* (pp. 319–336). Hove, UK: Psychology Press.

Code, C. (1997). Can the right hemisphere speak? *Brain and Language, 57*, 38–59.

Eisenson, J. (1962). Language and intellectual modification associated with right cerebral damage. *Language and Speech, 5*, 49–53.

Gainotti, G. (1993). The riddle of the right hemisphere's contribution to the recovery of language. *European Journal of Communication Disorders, 28*, 227–246

Gainotti, G., Caltagirone, C., & Miceli, G. (1983). Selective impairment of semantic-lexical discrimination in right-brain-damaged patients. In E. Perecman (Ed.), *Cognitive processing in the right hemisphere* (pp. 149–167). London: Academic Press.

Gardner, H., & Denes, G. (1973). Connotative judgements by aphasic patients on a pictorial adaptation of the semantic differential. *Cortex, 9*, 183–196.

Gazzaniga, M., LeDoux., J.E., & Wilson, D.H. (1977). Language, praxis, and the right hemisphere: Clues to some mechanisms of consciousness. *Neurology, 27*, 1144–1147.

Gazzaniga, M.S. (1970). *The bisected brain*. New York: Appleton-Century Crofts.

Gazzaniga, M.S. (1983). Right hemisphere language following brain bisection: A 20-year perspective. *American Psychologist, May*, 525–537.

Gazzaniga, M.S., Eliassen, J.C., Nisenson, L., Wessinger, M., Fendrich, R., & Baynes, K. (1996). Collaboration between the hemispheres of a callosotomy patient: Emerging right hemisphere speech and left hemisphere interpreter. *Brain, 119*, 1255–1262.

Gazzaniga, M.S., & Hillyard, S.A. (1971). Language and speech capacity of the right hemisphere. *Neuropsychologia, 9*, 273–280.

Gazzaniga, M.S., Sidtis, J.J., Volpe, B.T., Smylie, C., Holtzman, J., & Wilson, D. (1982). Evidence for paracallosal verbal transfer after callosal section: A possible consequence of bilateral language organisation. *Brain, 105*, 53–63.

Gazzaniga, M.S., Smylie, C.S., Baynes, K., Hirst., W. & McCleary., C., (*trans.*) (1984). Profiles of right hemisphere speech following brain bisection. *Brain and Language, 22*, 206–220.

Gazzaniga, M.S., Volpe, B.T., Smylie, C.S., Wilson, D.H., & LeDoux. (1979). Plasticity in speech organization following commissurotomy. *Brain, 102*, 805–815.

Goldman-Eisler, F. (1968). *Psycholinguistics: Experiments in spontaneous speech*. London: Academic Press.

Goldstein, K. (1948). *Language and language disturbances*. New York: Grune and Stratton.

Hart, J., Lesser, R.P., Fisher, R.S., Schwerdt, P., Bryan, R.N., & Gordon, B. (1991). Dominant-side intracarotid amobarbital spares comprehension of word meaning. *Archives of Neurology*, 48, 55–58.

Ivry, R., & Lebby, P.C. (1998). The neurology of consonant perception: Specialised module or distributed processors? In M. Beeman & C. Chiarello (Eds.), *Right hemisphere language comprehension: Perspectives from cognitive neuroscience*. Mahwah NJ: Lawrence Erlbaum Associates Inc.

Jackson, J.H. (1874). On the nature of the duality of the brain. In J. Taylor (Ed.) (1958), *Selected writings of John Hughlings Jackson: Volume II*. London: Staples Press.

Joanette, Y. (1989). Aphasia in left-handers and crossed aphasia. In F. Boller & J. Grafman (Eds.), *Handbook of neuropsychology, Vol. 2*, (pp. 173–183). Amsterdam: Elsevier Science.

Joanette, Y., & Goulet, P. (1998). Right hemisphere and the semantic processing of words: Is the contribution specific or not? In E.G. Visch-Brink & R. Bastiaanse (Eds.), *Linguistic levels in aphasiology* (pp. 19–34). San Diego, CA: Singular Publishing Group, Inc.

Joanette, Y., Goulet, P., & Hannequin, D. (1990). *Right hemisphere and verbal communication*. New York: Springer-Verlag.

Katz, R.C., Hallowell, B., Code, C., Armstrong, E., Roberts, P., Pound, C., & Katz, L. (2000). Comparison of aphasia management practices in five healthcare systems. *International Journal of Language and Communication Disorders, 35*, 303–314.

Kolb, B. (1996). *Brain plasticity and behavior*. Hillsdale, NJ: Lawrence Erlbaum Associates Inc.

Ley, R.G., & Bryden, M.P. (1981). Consciousness, emotion and the right hemisphere. In G. Underwood & R. Stevens (Eds.), *Aspects of consciousness, Volume II: Structural issues*. London: Academic Press.

Ojemann, G.A. (1979). Individual variability in cortical localisation of language. *Journal of Neurosurgery, 50*, 164–169.

Pell, M.D. (1998). Recognition of prosody following unilateral brain lesion: Influence of functional and structural attributes of prosodic contours. *Neuropsychologia, 36*, 8701–8715.

Ross, E. (1981). The aprosodias: Functional-anatomic organisation of the affective components of language in the right hemisphere. *Archives of Neurology (Chicago)*, *38*, 561–567.

Sauerwein, H.C., & Lassonde, M. (1996). Akelaitis investigations of the first split-brain patients. In C. Code, C-W. Wallesch, Y. Joanette, & A. Roch Lecours (Eds.), *Classic cases in neuropsychology* (pp. 305–318). Hove, UK: Psychology Press.

Segalowitz, S.J., & Bryden, M.P. (1983). Individual differences in hemispheric representation of language. In S.J. Segalowitz (Ed.), *Language functions and brain organisation* (pp. 341–372). London: Academic Press.

Sidtis, J.J. (1985). Bilateral language and commissurotomy: Interactions between the hemispheres with and without the corpus callosum. In A. Reeves (Ed.), *Epilepsy and the corpus callosum* (pp. 369–380). New York: Plenum Press.

Sidtis, J.J., & Gazzaniga, M.S. (1983). Competence versus performance after callosal section: Looks can be deceiving. In B. Hellige (Ed.), *Cerebral hemisphere asymmetry: Method, theory, and application*. New York: Praeger.

Sidtis J.J., Volpe B.T., Holtzman J.D., Wilson D.H., & Gazzaniga, M.S. (1981a). Cognitive interaction after staged callosal section: Evidence for transfer of semantic activation. *Science*, *212*, 344–346.

Sidtis, J.J., Volpe, B.T., Wilson, D.H., Rayport, M., & Gazzaniga, M.S. (1981b). Variability in right hemisphere language function after callosal section: Evidence for a continuum of generative capacity. *The Journal of Neuroscience*, *1*, 323–331.

Snodgrass, J.G., & Vanderwart, M. (1980). A standardised set of 200 pictures: Norms for name agreement, imagery agreement and familiarity and visual complexity. *Journal of Experimental Psychology: Human Learning and Memory*, *6*, 174–215.

Stemmer, B., & Joanette, Y. (1998). The interpretation of narrative discourse of brain-damaged individuals within the framework of a multilevel discourse model. In M. Beeman & C. Chiarello (Eds.), *Right hemisphere language comprehension: Perspectives from cognitive neuroscience* (pp. 329–348). Mahwah, NJ: Lawrence Erlbaum Associates Inc.

Van Lancker, D. (1987). Nonpropositional speech: Neurolinguistic studies. In A.W. Ellis (Ed.), *Progress in the psychology of language, Vol. III* (pp. 49–118). London: Lawrence Erlbaum Associates Inc.

Van Lancker, D. (1993). Nonpropositional speech in aphasia. In G. Blanken, J. Dittmann, H. Grimm, J.C. Marshall, & C-W. Wallesch (Eds.), *Linguistic disorders and pathologies* (pp. 215–225). Berlin: Walter de Gruyter.

Van Lancker, D., & Breitenstein, C. (1999). Emotional dysprosody and similar dysfunctions. In J. Bougousslavsky & J. L. Cummings (Eds.), *Disorders of behavior and mood in focal brain lesions*. Cambridge: Cambridge University Press.

Van Lancker D., & Sidtis J.J. (1992). The identification of affective-prosodic stimuli by left and right hemisphere damaged subjects: All errors are not created equal. *Journal of Speech and Hearing Research*, *35*, 963–970.

Wapner, W., Hamby, S., & Gardner, H. (1981). The role of the right hemisphere in the apprehension of complex linguistic materials. *Brain and Language*, *14*, 15–33.

Weiler, C., Isensee, C., Rijntjes, M., Huber, W., Muller, S., Bier, D., Dutschka, K., Woods, R.P., North, J., & Diener, H.C. (1995). Recovery from Wernicke's aphasia: A positron emission tomography study. *Annals of Neurology*, *37*, 723–732.

Wilson, D.H., Reeves, A., Gazzaniga, M.S., & Culver, C. (1977). Cerebral commissurotomy for the control of intractable seizures. *Neurology (NY)*, *27*, 708–715.

Wray, A. (1992). *The focusing hypothesis*. Amsterdam: John Benjamins Publishing Company.

Zaidel, E. (1978). Auditory language comprehension in the right hemisphere following cerebral commissurotomy and hemispherectomy: A comparison with child language and aphasia. In A. Caramazza & E.B. Zurif (Eds.), *Language acquisition and language breakdown*. Baltimore: Johns Hopkins University Press.

Zaidel, E. (1982). Reading by the right hemisphere: An aphasiological perspective. In Y. Zotterman (Ed.), *Dyslexia: Neuronal, cognitive and linguistic aspects.* Oxford: Pergamon Press.

NOTE

1. 'Crossed' aphasia can occur, rarely, following a right hemisphere lesion in a right-handed person (Joanette, 1989).

CHAPTER TEN

The fractionation of mental life: Luria's study of Lieutenant Zasetsky

B.L.J. Kaczmarek
Institute of Psychology, University of Maria Curie-Sklodowska, Lublin, Poland

Chris Code
School of Psychology, University of Exeter, UK and School of Communication Sciences and Disorders, University of Sydney, Australia

Claus-W. Wallesch
Department of Neurology, Otto-von-Guericke University of Magdeburg, Germany

> Perhaps someone with expert knowledge of the human brain will understand my illness, discover what a brain injury does to a man's mind, memory and body, appreciate my effort, and help me avoid some of the problems I have in life.
>
> —Lieutenant Zasetsky (Luria, 1975, p. 18)

INTRODUCTION

The Russian psychologist Aleksander Romanovich Luria (1902–1977) contributed a number of most influential books to neuropsychology. His *Traumatic Aphasia* (1970), *Higher Cortical Functions in Man* (1980), and *The Working Brain* (1973a) include classic descriptions of his clinically based and influential theory on higher brain functions. However, his most popular works are two little books about two unique individuals. *The Mind of a Mnemonist* (1968) describes the neuropsychological function in a man with a very powerful memory and an unhappy life, who had not suffered from brain damage. The subject of this chapter, however, is the story of Lieutenant Zasetsky, a brain-damaged survivor of the World War II. His profound story is told in *The Man With a Shattered World* (1972/1975), largely by himself, but with interpretations by Luria.

There have been many books before and since this one about the impact of brain damage on the mental, emotional, and social life of individuals who have survived brain damage. But *The Man With a Shattered World* is one of the best because it brings together the real difficulties of a life shattered by brain damage as reported by Zasetsky and a powerful theoretical framework that allows the reader some understanding and insight into the nature of the bewildering range of functional losses. Zasetsky (Z) is important for a number of reasons: we get a unique insight into the personal experience of brain damage from the journal that Z kept over many years and one of the most powerful descriptions of the fractionation of cognition leading to the disabilities and handicaps that can accompany cerebral lesions. Further, Z describes the effects of his rehabilitation from his own experience, and finally, Luria's analysis of Z's problems provides a unique and powerful demonstration of his clinical approach and his theory of the cerebral basis of higher mental functions.

A.R. Luria's historical position in neuropsychology and rehabilitation is both unique and difficult to assess. Although many of his theoretical positions are related to Kurt Goldstein's (1948, 1995; see Noppeney & Wallesch, 2000), his background is quite different from this great neurologist's and includes both psychoanalysis and Marxism.

Luria graduated in 1921 with a degree in biological and social sciences and founded the Kazan Psychoanalytic Society in 1922 (Sigmund Freud sent a letter of congratulation). When moving to Moscow in 1923, Luria became a member of the Russian Psychoanalytic Society. In Moscow, he joined Kornilov's Institute of Experimental Psychology (Van de Veer & Valsiner, 1991). Subsequently, after an attempt to reconcile Freudian theory and Marxism, he became critical of psychoanalysis, both for scientific and ideological reasons. Both in the Russian Psychoanalytic Society and at the Kornilov Institute, Luria started a fruitful collaboration with a unique thinker, Lev Vygotsky (1896–1934), who from pedagogy, experimental psychology, and many other influences (neurophysiology, gestalt psychology, linguistics, comparative psychology, ethology) derived a highly original theory of cognition, semantics, and emotions (see Van de Veer & Valsiner, 1991). The Kornilov Institute's aim was to replace the old 'idealistic' psychology with a truly Marxist psychology founded on empirical evidence. The Institute fell into disgrace during the reign of Stalin.

Luria died in 1977. His peculiar historical position was noted in Karl Pribram's (1978, p. 137) obituary:

Luria first came to the attention of the scientific community through his book on conflict. Already he had established the first psychoanalytic institute in Russia, and had initiated a magnificent collaboration with Vygotsky and Leontiev. Vygotsky's early death was to be balanced by the lifelong friendship which

Leontiev provided. The Luria, Leontiev, Vygotsky triumvirate successfully bridged the gap between 19th century and current Soviet psychology. During the interim, a reductive physiology reigned. It is another of those contradictions that characterises Luria therefore that as a psychologist proclaiming the importance of social factors he should become one of the world's foremost neuropsychologists. However, he related physiology and psychology in a truly dialectic fashion, to transcend the duality of mind and brain in a sophisticated single discipline.

Luria's entry into neuropsychology was probably his collaboration with Vygotsky on developmental psychology. They also did some studies of aphasic patients to gain better insight into the relationship between thought and language. Furthermore, the idea of complex psychological systems can be found already in Vygotsky's writing:

> In the process of the psychic development of a child ... not only internal reorganisation and improvement of separate functions takes place, but also inter-functional links and relations are qualitatively changed. As a result, new psychological systems emerge that unite in complex coordination a number of elementary functions. These unities of a higher kind, that come to replace homogeneous, elementary functions we tentatively name higher psychic functions. (Vygotsky (1930/1984); quoted in Van de Veer & Valsiner, p. 175).

It is also worth pointing out that Luria frequently stressed his intellectual debt to Vygotsky.

Luria's methods were more qualitative than quantitative. He developed a neuropsychological process model based on syndrome analysis that 'seeks out the most important traits or primary basic factors that have immediate consequences of these basic underlying factors. Only after these basic factors and their consequences have been identified can the entire picture become clear. The object of observation is thus to ascertain a network of important relations. When done properly, observation accomplishes the classical aim of explaining facts, while not losing sight of the romantic aim of preserving the manifold richness of the subject' (Luria, 1979, p. 178). Through observation and testing, syndrome analysis aims to identify a pattern of disturbances or symptoms indicating an underlying impairment (Luria, 1973b).

The complexity of neuropsychological investigation is probably best exemplified in Luria's book *Higher Cortical Functions in Man* (1980). For circumscribed lesions, it stresses the need to reveal a clinical picture of inter-relating symptoms that constitute a syndrome typical of a dysfunction of specific brain areas. This approach requires a theory of brain functions and their cerebral representation in order to relate symptoms and findings to structure and function.

Luria introduced the concept of functional brain systems to replace narrow localisation of function. For Luria, a lesion does not destroy a function but disrupts a functional system. Three basic systems are related to (1) energetic, (2) informative, and (3) regulative/control functions.

(1) The energetic system involves the activity of the brainstem and other subcortical structures, the 'old brain' which arose during the phylogenic development of mammals. These structures not only regulate physiological functions but are also important in emotional processes. A structure of central importance is the reticular formation of the brainstem, which plays the role of a biological clock responsible for the states of sleep and wakefulness. Most significant, however, is that these structures maintain the tonus of the cerebral cortex, thus serving the proper functioning of the cortex.

(2) The informative system provides for the input, transformation, and storage of information. It is concerned with the information that comes to the brain from both outside and inside the body. The system comprises the posterior region of the brain including the temporal, parietal, and occipital lobes. These lobes constitute central parts of individual analysers, which are connected with corresponding receptors (ears, eyes, skin). Thus, the temporal lobe processes auditory sensations through its primary, secondary (association), and finally its tertiary cortices or zones; the parietal lobe elaborates impulses coming from our skin, viscera and tendons through primary, secondary, and tertiary cortices/zones, while the occipital lobe is concerned with visual analysis. Interaction is possible between these systems through their shared tertiary zones, where the three lobes meet in the area of the occipitoparietotemporal junction.

(3) The regulatory system involves the frontal lobes. This system is concerned with programming and regulating the course of complex actions. In other words it plays an executive role that is secured by its multiple reciprocal connections with other cerebral structures. Language plays a particular role in the controlling activity of the frontal lobes.

Luria's theory of the organisation of the functional systems underlying higher cognitive functions provided the framework for interpreting and understanding Z's complex range of difficulties. These days academic neuropsychology focuses on the 'fractionation' of cognitive functions following brain damage. The apparent independence of functions, as illustrated by the relative loss or survival of functions following different kinds of brain damage, permits the building of neuro-cognitive models. Examination of the performance of people with brain damage has provided us with unique insights into the organisation of cognition. Z's cognition was so fractionated that

Luria used the term 'shattered' to describe it. Of course, *shattered* has a more romantic ring to it than the colder term *fractionated*, and, with his book on Z, Luria wanted to revive a more romantic approach to science (Sacks, 1990).

LIEUTENANT ZASETSKY

Z was a young man with a promising future. He was a third-year student at an Institute of Mechanics when he joined the army at the outbreak of the Soviet–German war. During a battle near Smolensk he was wounded by a bombshell, which destroyed the parietal lobe of his left hemisphere. Here is an extract from his case history (Luria, 1972/1975, p. 31):

> Sub-lieutenant Zasetsky, aged 23, suffered a head injury on 2 March 1943 that penetrated the left parieto-occipital area of the cranium. The injury was followed by a prolonged coma and, despite prompt treatment in a field hospital, was further complicated by inflammation that resulted in adhesions of the brain to the meninges and marked changes in the adjacent tissues. The formation of scar tissue altered the configurations of the lateral ventricles by pulling the left lateral ventricle upwards and producing an incipient atrophy of the medulla[1] of this area.

This passage indicates that pneumencephalography, the only method of (indirect) brain imaging available at the time, had been performed on Z. From both Z's and Luria's statements, it seems that Z suffered right homonymous hemianopia, a right hemisensory deficit, and probably focal seizures in addition to his neuropsychological deficits. Hemiparesis is not mentioned and probably was not prominent.

Despite his language disability, Z decided to keep a journal describing what had happened to him and his struggles to overcome the damage to his brain. He worked on this journal day after day. Sometimes it took him an entire day to write half a page as he had to search hard for every word and to read each sentence several times to become certain that it was correct. He first called his journal *The Story of a Terrible Brain Injury*, but later changed it to *I'll Fight On*. He started the journal before the end of the war and continued for over 25 years. After years of everyday struggle with his language and memory it had come to little more than 3000 pages. Luria edited the text and added comments of his own to produce *The Man With a Shattered World*.

Z'S COGNITIVE SYMPTOMS

In the book, Z and Luria describe symptoms from both the acute and chronic stages after Z's brain injury and also some experiences from Z's rehabilitation. We shall try to organise their reports according to neuropsychological functions. (We quote from the Jonathan Cape edition, 1973, and the British Penguin edition, 1975.) Used with permission.

Language

(1) 'The first time he entered my office in the rehabilitation hospital, I was struck by how young he looked. He seemed scarcely more than a boy, who looked at me with a puzzled smile and tilted his head awkwardly to one side. (Later I learned that the vision on his right side was gone and, in order to see, he had to shift sideways.) I asked how he was getting on, and after some hesitation he replied shyly, "Okay". The question of when he had been wounded, however, left him at a loss.
"Well, you see . . . it's, it's . . . a long time already . . . must be two, three . . . what's the word? . . ."
What town was he from?
"At home . . . there's . . . I want to write . . . but just can't."
Did he have any relatives?
"There's . . . my mother . . . and also—what do you call them?"'
(p. 29).

(2) 'I tried to think of the word before the need for it came. I had run through words that came to mind—doctor? . . . no, I knew that wasn't right . . . sister? (I couldn't think of the word nurse either and used sister instead) . . . bird . . . no, it's bedpan! Suddenly I remembered about that bird or duck, the word we used for bedpan.' (p. 80)

(3) 'But I always forget where my forearm is located: Is it near my neck or my hands? The same thing happens with the word buttocks. I forget where this is, too, and get confused. Is it in my leg muscles above my knees? My pelvic muscles? The same sort of thing happens with many other parts of my body. What's more, I still can't remember the words for them. . . . It takes me a long time to remember what the word eye means. Finally I do, but then I have the same problem with the word nose.' (p. 48)

(4) 'I also had troubles with expressions like: "Is an elephant bigger than a fly?" . . . Naturally I know what an elephant and a fly are, which is large and which is small. But I just didn't understand the words smaller and bigger in those expressions.' (pp. 110–111)

Semantic knowledge of the world

(5) 'I can't understand how wood is manufactured, what it is made of.' (p. 87)

(6) 'I don't understand how plants grow, what nourishes them, or how

you grow a new plant by cutting off a leaf and putting it in water.' (p. 93)

(7) 'He referred to his major disability as a loss of "speech-memory". And he had good reasons to do so. Before he was wounded, words had distinct meanings which readily occurred to him. Each word was part of a vital world to which it was linked by thousands of associations, each aroused a flood of vivid and graphic recollections.' (p. 89)

Reading

(8) 'I went into the hall to look for a bathroom I'd been told was next door. I went up to the room and looked at the sign on the door. But no matter how long I stared at it and examined the letters, I couldn't read a thing. Some peculiar, foreign letters were printed there—what bothered me most was that they weren't Russian.' (p. 61)

(9) 'When I just look at a letter, it seems unfamiliar and foreign to me. But if I strain my memory and recite the alphabet loud, I definitely can remember what the letter is.' (p. 62)

(10) 'Suddenly I got up, looked at the newspaper, and immediately saw a photograph of Lenin and was overjoyed to recognise that familiar face. Still, I couldn't read any of the print, not even the largest type in the word Pravda.' (p. 63)

(11) 'After a few months I could remember the whole alphabet. However, I still couldn't identify any of the letters immediately. When the teacher asked me to point to the letter k, I'd have to think for a while and recite the alphabet until I got to k! For some reason, I still knew how to recite the alphabet and could run through it without a hitch.' (p. 66)

(12) 'I read printed material letter by letter. When I first started to read again, I often couldn't recognise a letter at first and had to run through the alphabet until I found it. . . . Often after I've worked out the letters in a word, I forget the word itself and have to read every letter over again in order to understand it.' (p. 66)

Writing

(13) 'I'd forgotten how to use a pencil. I'd twist it back and forth but I just couldn't begin to write. I was shown how to hold it and asked to write something. But when I picked up the pencil all I could do was draw some crooked lines across the paper.' (p. 68)

(14) 'At first I had just as much trouble with writing—that is, even after I thought I knew the letters, I couldn't remember how they were formed. Each time I wanted to think of a particular letter I'd have to run through the alphabet until I found it. But one day a doctor . . .

asked me to write automatically – without lifting my hand from the paper. . . . It turned out I could write only short words automatically—short ones. . . . But still, after the doctor showed me how to write quickly, automatically, and not letter by letter, I was able to get one word down after the other without having to think about it.' (p. 69)

Arithmetic

(15) 'He had difficulty not only with complex systems of ideas like geometry, physics and grammar, but with the simple arithmetical processes taught in the first years of elementary school.' (p. 120)

(16) 'I was always confusing numbers and couldn't get the answers when I tried to add or subtract in my head.' (p. 122)

(17) 'So I don't try to work out money myself when I buy food at the store.' (p. 123)

Visuo-spatial functions

(18) 'Once when I left my room and was walking in the corridor, I'd no sooner taken a few steps than I suddenly banged my right shoulder and the right side of my forehead against the wall and got a huge bump on my forehead.' (p. 44)

(19) 'Ever since I was wounded I've had trouble sometimes sitting down in a chair or on a couch. I first look to see where the chair is, but when I try to sit down I suddenly make a grab for the chair since I'm afraid I'll land on the floor. Sometimes that happens because the chair turns out to be further to one side than I thought.' (p. 50)

(20) (During an ophthalmological examination, Z was required to indicate on which side a semi-circle was open): 'When I finally understood what she was asking, I looked at the semi-circle but couldn't judge since I didn't know what "left" or "right" meant. It seems that ever since I was wounded I can't understand such expressions.' (p. 56)

(21) 'These problems also occurred in his reactions to sounds. When someone called him in the hospital corridor he was unable to tell which direction the sound was coming from.' (p. 56)

(22) 'I've been living at home now for almost two years, but when I go for a walk I still can't seem to remember the streets, even the nearest ones. Although the town is so small . . ., the architectural layout doesn't make sense to me.' (p. 59)

Praxis and gnosis

(23) (In occupational therapy): 'I took the thread in one hand, the needle in the other, but couldn't understand what to do with them. How was I to thread a needle? I twisted it back and forth but hadn't the slightest idea what to do with any of these things. When I first looked at those objects, but hadn't yet picked them up, they seemed perfectly familiar—there was no reason to think about them. But as soon as I had them in my hands, I was at a loss as to how to work out what they were for. I'd lapse into a kind of stupor and wouldn't be able to associate these two objects in my mind.' (p. 51)

(24) 'I'd set a stump of wood in a place, pick up an axe, swing, and miss, so that the axe hit the floor. . . . I seldom manage to hit the centre of the block but usually land somewhere to the right or left of it, as though some mysterious power were twisting my swing to one side.' (p. 52)

(25) 'When I went any distance from my house, I couldn't recognise my own house. All the houses looked alike to me and I was afraid I'd get lost.' (p. 59)

(26) 'I had to start from scratch and learn to recognise objects and try to associate them with words.' (p. 81)

Body schema

(27) 'I try to work out what's become of my right arm and leg, the entire right side of my body. I move the fingers of my left hand, feel them, but can't see the fingers of my right hand and somehow I'm not even aware they're there. . . . Sometimes when I'm sitting down I suddenly feel as though my head is the size of a table—every bit as big—while my hands, feet and torso become very small. . . . When I close my eyes, I'm not even sure where my right leg is; for some reasons I used to think (even sensed) it was somewhere above my shoulders, even above my head.' (p. 47)

Memory

(28) 'Sometimes I can't remember what I've eaten for breakfast or dinner that day. My main trouble, the worst symptom, is amnesia and forgetfulness, and that's why I can't remember words.' (p. 84)

Imagery

(29) 'My therapist would mention the word cat or dog and say: "Try to picture to yourself what a dog looks like, what kind of eyes and ears

it has. Can you see it?" But I couldn't visualise a cat, dog or any other creature after I'd been wounded. . . . I tried to remember my mother's and sisters' faces but couldn't form any image of them. But when I was finally sent home and saw my family, I immediately recognised my mother and sisters.' (p. 86–87)

INTERPRETATION: FRACTIONATED COGNITION

Clearly, Z had a complex range of cognitive problems, which Luria interpreted according to his theory. Luria summarises:

- 'The bullet fragment that entered his brain had so devastated his world that he no longer had any sense of space, could not judge relationships between things, and perceived the world as broken into thousands of separate parts.' (Luria, 1975, p. 60)
- 'The bullet that penetrated this patient's brain disrupted the functions of precisely those parts of the cortex that control the analysis, synthesis and organisation of complex associations into a coherent framework.' (p. 97)
- 'He perceived the world as broken into thousands of separate parts.' (p. 60) [This fractionation of cognition for Luria is the result of damage to the tertiary zones where different auditory, visual, and somatosensory information from the association zones is transcoded and integrated.]
- 'It was precisely these "tertiary" sections of the cortex that the bullet fragment had destroyed.' (p. 38)
- 'It appeared he could also remember letters by reciting the alphabet out loud as he did as a child, using a long-established oral-motor skill instead of trying to visualise each letter. This method was possible because it required a faculty that had not been damaged by his injury.' (p. 65)

This illustrates an important therapeutic principle developed by Luria and his collaborators, and demonstrated in this book, namely the compensatory use of intact systems and pathways to substitute for lost skills (Luria, Vinarskaya, Naydin, & Tsvetkova, 1969).

These quotations show that, within the functional systems of his theory, Luria accepted localisation of symptoms and also of brain functions. But for Luria, the functional *systems* had local representation rather than functions.

Present-day neuropsychology and behavioural neurology would classify Z's symptoms in the following ways (the numbers refer to the above quotations):

- Z had an anomic aphasia (1, 2). Subjectively, Z describes his word-finding problems as being due to his memory problems.
- He had a deficit with logical and/or grammatical relations (4). Problems with logico-grammatical operations are for Luria (1973a) part of the syndrome of *semantic* aphasia, due to damage to the parieto-occipital region. (Luria pioneered the notion of disturbances of logico-grammatical operations.)
- Z possibly had a category-specific semantic impairment for body parts (3) together with a general semantic knowledge deficit (5, 6).
- He had a range of reading and writing problems, an unspecified form of dyslexia with symptoms of pure alexia (letter-by-letter reading), additional visuo-spatial impairment (8, 12), and deep dysgraphia (Z was able to write 'automatically') (3, 14).
- Z had at least anarithmetia (a specific calculation deficit) as well as other problems with mathematical operations (acalculia) and possibly also a specific semantic impairment for numbers (15, 17).
- He had a disturbance of body-schema (27), visuo-spatial deficits (18, 22), possibly including right hemineglect (18), simultanagnosia (23, 24), and an impairment of visual imagery (29).
- We speculate but cannot be certain that the reported symptoms of agnosia (25, 26) result from an apperceptive (perceptual) deficit related to Z's visuo-spatial deficits. The memory impairment (28) that is perceived as quite central by Z and considered by Z as underlying his anomia could be loosely related to temporal lobe damage but may also be unspecific with respect to localisation. The deficit of visual imagery reported by Z seems significant, as this disorder has been related to the left temporo-occipital region (Goldenberg, 1987).

As Luria did, present-day neuropsychology would also relate Z's symptoms to left parietal and parieto-occipito-temporal damage. Classic neuropsychology would have done the same and may have described Z's pathology as an 'extended Gerstmann's syndrome' with the core symptoms of anomic aphasia, body-part (finger) agnosia, acalculia, and visuo-spatial deficit (Gerstmann, 1930).

Luria's (and Z's, of course) approach is different, their angle of view is focused on the individual who has to cope with the effects of a brain lesion. On Luria's theory, this left parieto-occipital region is an integral part of the informative system, responsible for the integration of visual, kinaesthetic, and vestibular analysers. Since the area plays an important role in visuo-spatial synthesis, its damage leads to disturbances of spatial relationships and actions in space, which Luria (1980) called apractognosia.

Human spatial perception (Luria, 1980, pp. 172–173):

is always asymmetrical, manifesting obvious lateralisation. In the surrounding space we can distinguish the right and left sides and what lies before, behind, above, and below us; in other words we perceive space by means of a system of basic geometrical coordinates. However, not all of these geometrical coordinates have the same value. Orientation in space essentially always consists of what in external space lies on the right; being related to the dominant right hand, it differs from what lies on the left. These notions of right and left are subsequently designated by words. The subject begins to depend on a complete system of signs in his orientation in space.

Certain linguistic constructions proved to be especially difficult, namely those that reflect logico-grammatical relationships between objects and events. Hence, Z was unable to state whether an elephant is bigger or smaller than a fly or if spring comes before or after winter. Also, expressions with an attributive genitive case such as 'the master's dog' or 'mother's daughter' as well as propositional phrases, were too difficult for him to comprehend. These constructions all require a logical synthesis of all their components into an integral whole. As Z stated, he understood the meaning of individual words but was not able to grasp interrelationships between them.

However, within this shattered world, Z's personality, his identity and his will remained intact. His regulatory, executive (or frontal lobe) system enabled him to get structure into the shambles of his perception and communication, and even to explain his condition to others, with the help of Luria. For both Z and Luria, the little book that is the result of decades of work on the part of Z, is a reflection on the *condition humaine*.

IMPACT OF THE CASE ON NEUROPSYCHOLOGY

One of the important effects of Zasetsky's and Luria's book was that it promoted neuropsychology among psychologists, educators, and in the general public as well. The book (first published in Russian in 1971) was translated into many languages including English, Italian, Spanish, German, and Polish, which reflects its great popularity. The book combines both theoretical as well as practical aspects of neuropsychology and rehabilitation, and demonstrates how the clinical material provided by Z and by Luria's interpretation can contribute to our knowledge of brain function and human cognition in general.

Luria's case description is not limited to the cognitive impact of brain injury but attempts to show how brain damage affects the everyday functional life and personality of the person. In the meantime, we have become more aware of the psycho-social impact of brain damage and cognitive processing impairment. The fractionation of cognition provides us with insights into the representation of cognitive functions in the brain. With Z, Luria illustrates the symbiotic relationship between the academic and clinical faces of neuropsychology. He brings these two faces of neuropsychology together and the book illustrates how they feed off each other. Z's journal gave Luria the opportunity to illustrate his theory of the integration of higher cognitive functions and its application to rehabilitation and present it to a lay readership. Z's shattered mental world provides a powerful illustration of the integrative functions of Luria's tertiary zones.

Syndrome analysis is a complex art. In *The Man with a Shattered World* Luria attempted 'to revive the tradition of romantic science' (Luria, 1979, p. 178). 'Romantic science' certainly is an incongruous concept both within the framework of Soviet (both dialectic and materialistic) psychology and modern cognitive neuropsychology. Today, clinical neuropsychology and neurological/neuropsychological rehabilitation are more concerned than they used to be with the effects of brain injury upon the emotional and psychosocial status of the brain-damaged person and his or her close relatives and friends; they encompass scientific analysis, psychodynamic interpretation, and philosophical evaluation. They are at the same time, both scientific and humane.

REFERENCES

Gerstmann, J. (1930). Zur Symptomatologie der Hirnlösionen im Übergangsgebiet der unteren Parietal- und mittleren Occipitalwindung. *Nervenarzt, 3*, 691–695.

Goldenberg, G. (1987). *Neurologische Grundlagen bildlicher Vorstellungen.* Wien: Springer.

Goldstein, K. (1948). *Language and language disturbances.* New York: Grune & Stratton.

Goldstein, K. (1995). *The organism.* New York: Zone Books.

Luria, A.R. (1968). *The mind of a mnemonist.* New York: Basic Books.

Luria, A.R. (1970). *Traumatic aphasia.* The Hague: Mouton.

Luria, A.R. (1972/1975). *The man with a shattered world.* New York: Basic Books; Harmondsworth: Penguin.

Luria, A.R. (1973a). *The working brain.* Harmondsworth: Penguin.

Luria, A.R. (1973b). *Outline of neuropsychological investigation.* Moscow: Moscow University (in Russian).

Luria, A.R. (1979). *The making of mind: A personal account of Soviet psychology.* Cambridge, MA: Harvard University Press.

Luria, A.R. (1980). *Higher cortical functions in man* (2nd ed.). New York: Basic Books.

Luria, A.R. (1987). *The mind of a mnemonist* (2nd ed.). Cambridge, MA: Harvard University Press.

Luria, A.R., Vinarskaya, E.N., Naydin, V.L., & Tsvetkova, L.S. (1969). Restoration of higher cortical functions. In P. Vinken & G. Bruyn (Eds.), *Handbook of clinical neurology* (Vol. 3). Amsterdam: Elsevier.

Noppeney, U., & Wallesch, C-W. (2000). Language and cognition: Kurt Goldstein's theory of semantics. *Brain and Cognition, 44*, 367–386.

Pribram, K.H. (1978). In memory of Alexander Romanovitsch Luria. *Neuropsychologia, 16*, 137–139.

Sacks, O. (1990). Luria and 'Romantic Science'. In E. Goldberg, (Ed.), *Contemporary neuropsychology and the legacy of Luria.* Hillsdale, NJ: Lawrence Erlbaum Associates Inc.

Van de Veer, R., & Valsiner, J. (1991). *Understanding Vygotsky.* Oxford: Blackwell.

Vygotsky, L.S. (1930/1984). Orudie i znak w razwitii rebionka. In L.S. Vygotsky (Ed.), *Sobranie sochienii. Vol. 6, Nauchnoie issledovania* (pp. 6–90). Moskva: Pedagogika.

NOTE

1. This refers probably to the white matter.

PART TWO

Perception, identification, consciousness

CHAPTER ELEVEN

Pierre Bonnier's (1905) cases of bodily 'aschematie'

Giuseppe Vallar
Department of Psychology, University of Milano-Bicocca, Milano, Italy and IRCCS St. Lucia, Roma, Italy

Costanza Papagno
Department of Psychology, University of Milano-Bicocca, Milano, Italy

> But the Question being here, whether the Idea of Space or Extension, be the same with the idea of Body . . .
> —John Locke, *An essay concerning human understanding*, (4th edition), 1700, Chapter XIII, §23.

BEFORE BONNIER

The general idea that some form of representation or image of the body (or of some aspects of it) is stored in the brain was put forward by the German physiologist Munk (1890), who took the view that the sensorimotor fronto-parietal cortex (*Fühlsphäre*) was the repository of images of movement, which were based on sensations of innervations (perception of active movements of the various parts of the body) and other sensory inputs, such as touch, form, extension, etc. From extirpation experiments in dogs, Munk also suggested that the parietal cortex could be subdivided into discrete areas, each of which was correlated with specific parts of the body—receiving sensations of innervations and other sensory inputs—and stored their images (Critchley, 1953, p. 108; Oldfield & Zangwill, 1941/42; Poeck & Orgass, 1971).

Carl Wernicke (1894, 1906) adopted Munk's ideas, in the context of his classification of psychiatric disorders (see Poeck & Orgass, 1971). Wernicke emphasised the spatial aspect of orientation of the body, and the localisation of somatosensory perception. A number of external inputs (visual, tactile, auditory) and internal inputs (from the muscular activity and the visceral organs) give rise to images of the different body parts, which are stored in memory. These images constitute the *body consciousness* or *somatopsyche*, which should be distinguished from the *consciousness of the external world*, with their psychiatric counterparts being *auto-* or *somatopsychoses* on the one hand and *allopsychoses* on the other.

A case of disordered representation of body parts was described by Deny and Camus (1905). Their female patient reported that:

> I do not feel my limbs any more, I do not feel my head, I do not feel my hair any more. I have to touch myself incessantly to know how I am; it seems to me that all my body has changed, sometimes it is as if it does not exist any more. When I touch an object, I have the sensation that it is not me feeling. I am not how I was any longer. I cannot find myself again, I try to think and *I cannot represent myself* [our italics]. It is horrible this insensitivity, it makes me feel a void.

The patient suffered from a more extensive representational disorder. Based on the patient's introspection, generation of visual images from long-term memory was defective ('I cannot visualise neither the figure of my parents, nor the interior of my house'). The neurological examination was normal, with the exception of a deficit of position sense. She was unable to report the position of body parts with eyes closed. A psychiatric diagnosis, though non-typical, was made: 'a sort of aberrant hypochondria due to the loss of corporeal consciousness'. Deny and Camus (1905) point out that the disorder was selective: neither other neuropsychological deficits (agnosia, apraxia, psychical blindness, or deafness) nor delusions were present and intelligence was preserved.

A similar case (*Afunktion der Somatopsyche*) had been reported by Fœrster (1903). Both Deny and Camus' (1905) and Fœrster's (1903) patients were severely distressed by this disorder.

THE ASCHEMATIA OF PIERRE BONNIER

A biographical sketch

Pierre Bonnier (Figure 11.1) was born in Templeuve (in northern France) in 1861 and discussed his thesis in medicine in Paris in 1890. In 1897 he became assistant in the Clinique Médicale de l'Hôtel-Dieu in Paris, in 1901 president of the Société d'Otologie et de Laryngologie de Paris, in 1902 a member of the Institut Psychologique, and in 1903 of the Société de Neurologie. His list of publications is extensive and his interests concerned mainly the auditory and vestibular systems, and their disorders. In addition to many articles, Bonnier wrote a number of books, including *Vertige* (1893) and *L'Oreille* (1896, five volumes). Bonnier also proposed a therapy based on nasal cauterisations (*centrothérapie*) for the treatment of a variety of diseases. This approach was no longer used after Bonnier's death in 1918.

Figure 11.1   Pierre Bonnier (1861–1918). (Courtesy of the Bibliothèque del'Académie de Médecine, Paris, France.)

The schema and its disorders

Bonnier (1905) introduced the term 'schema' into the neurological literature to denote the internal representation of the body, describing (p. 605) the representation of one's body and some of its disorders with these words:

> ... of schema, topographic configuration, attitude. Because of this trouble some parts of ourselves cease to be represented in our body notion. When they take too much room, there is *hyperschematia*; too little, *hyposchematia*; or a place which is not their right location, *paraschematia*. *The aschematia* is exactly an *anaesthesia confined to the topographic notion*, to the spatial representation, to the distribution, to the form, to the situation, to the attitude.

Bonnier (1905, pp. 605–606) distinguishes the schema and the aschematia from the notion of *cénesthésie* (coenesthesis: the general sense of existence arising from the sum of bodily impressions), and its pathological counterpart *cénesthésiopathie*. Bonnier dismissed this 'terme classique mais impropre' because:

> *common sensations* have no physiological meaning; what all sensations have in common, as far as the question we are interested in is concerned, is the topographic definition, the *notion of space*, of localisation. . . . I then assigned primacy to the spatial notion and I termed *spatial sense* all kinds of sensitivity,

both peripheral and central, contributing to define objective and subjective orientation, the latter being the perception of our position with respect to environmental objects, objectively oriented, of our *attitude*, and of our changes of position and attitude, that is to say of our own movements and displacements.

The *spatial* distinctive feature of the schema, which is concerned with the orientation and position of the body (attitude) and of body parts, also with reference to environmental objects, is further specified by the distinction (p. 606) between:

> two different operations: the sensorial image, providing the perception of a modality of irritation of a peripheral sensation such as sound, light, temperature, consistency etc., and the *definition of the locus of the perceived point*, that is to say the objective localisation of the stimulus, on the periphery of the organism, or at a certain distance, as well as inside the organism.

Here Bonnier mentions Wernicke's (1894) distinction between 'the specific sensory element' (vision, touch, etc.) and 'a myopsychic element' (concerned with the sensation of muscular activity and movement). Bonnier then notes that the process of spatial localisation applies to the different sensory modalities, providing a common medium (pp. 606–607):

> I had distinguished so far the notion of localisation, of topographical distribution, of attitude, of space, where only accommodation, motor adaptation, movement, muscle sensation were seen. I also observed that operations based on sensorial modalities, on analyses specific to each sense, are irreducible and cannot be superimposed, so that a sound, a flavour, a colour cannot share a common measure, while the operations of localisation realise sensorial images, which are absolutely reducible and can be superimposed.

Bonnier then goes on to describe a number of cases showing disorders of the schema. All patients suffered from a peripheral vestibular disease, and no additional neurological deficits were reported. The letters #a, #b, etc. indicate different patients or sections, as in the original text.

Aschematia

Patient #a showed a complete and selective inability to localise sensory stimuli in different modalities, even though they were adequately perceived, and a global disorientation of the body:

> some short critical episodes without impulses, or titubation, or drowsiness, simply consisting in a transient loss of conscious localisation within each sensory domain. A fog appeared in front of her eyes, a noise in her ears, she

perceived contacts without localising them, and kept on walking with no tituba-
tion or deviation, but without feeling that she was walking. Sounds that she
heard perfectly were not localised or exteriorised, however. In one word, it was a
purely sensorial absence, confined to localisation functions and to images of
attitude, without any disorder of her subjective personality.

The patient summarised her deficits with these words: 'During these short
critical episodes . . . I keep feeling everything, but nothing is anywhere and I,
too, am nowhere.'

Patient #i reported a global disorientation of the body and perhaps
depersonalisation:

> One more patient was unable to keep his head still or to be momentarily dis-
> tracted from the object of his vision, due to a noise, a conversation, without
> losing immediately the notion of his own being; he could not know how he
> was oriented in the room where he was, which attitude he had. Then he felt an
> anguish, without vertigo, and he got out of this condition only by shaking
> his head strongly.

Patients #b, #d, and #h (who was also hysterical), reported depersonalisation. For Patient #b:

> very vague vertigo with complete suspension of any notion of his personality.
> He described this condition as we would describe a *petit mal* absence, but he was
> describing it by himself and he noted very carefully that his identity was going
> away and coming back.

Patient #d perhaps also reported defective localisation:

> a short attack of vertigo with total suspension of all psychic personality, per-
> ceiving everything, acting and speaking, but stopping to relate any objective or
> subjective perception to himself

Patient #h:

> her vertigo gave her the feeling that her body was not existing any more and that
> she felt at the same time 'a terrible fear of dying immediately if she started to
> think about it.'

Patient #c suffered from eclampsia during pregnancy, with two episodes
of convulsions and loss of consciousness. The putative aschematia of this
patient is unclear;

> She was carried to the hospital twice, during two pregnancies, completely
> unable to gesture or say any word; a few hours later she regained 'her
> consciousness', she said, and could tell everything about her accident.

Hyperschematia

In section #e patients showing an overestimation of the size of the whole body or of body parts (hyperschematia) are briefly mentioned. Bonnier notes that disorders of this sort, which may shed light on 'the role of spatial perception in the notion of subjectivity and personality' have not been adequately investigated: 'Some patients feel as if they were becoming immense, others are obsessed by the feeling of a constantly open void in front of them' Bonnier also mentions this frequent subjective experience: 'feet for example become hugely longer, risking being run over by cars.'

Patient #g also showed hyperschematia: 'He felt his head becoming huge, immense, lost in the air; his body disappeared and all his being was reduced to his face. I observed clearly two more times this peculiar symptom.'

Paraschematia

Bonnier reports a patient suffering from syphilis in the brainstem:

> a patient presenting with bulbar syphilis who showed, among other symptoms, some very clear crises of angor pectoris; every episode ended with 'the sensation that the painful parts, his heart and the left side of the chest, moved away from their normal site and vanished falling on the left'.

Other disorders

In section #e a patient showing purely spatial hallucinations, with no apparent sensory quality, is described:

> the case of an hallucination confined to the domain of the vestibular nerve, without auditory, visual or tactile sensations. . . . She could not open a window, a door, without the hallucination that something she could not feel, see, hear, was falling strongly on her; meanwhile occasionally she perceived a violent sound.

Patient #f showed an *autoscopic phenomenon*—that is the illusory reduplication of his own body (see the review by Brugger, Regard, & Landis, 1997):

> He had suddenly suffered a short attack of vertigo with space imperception, then he felt as if he was divided into two persons, one keeping the same attitude, and a new one, on the right, looking a little bit outside. Then the two somatic individualities joined, melted and the vertigo disappeared.

Conclusion

Bonnier closed his report stating that:

> it is due to the absence or impairment of topographic definition that external and internal things perceived by the patient lack reality. It is, as I wrote in 1893, the something without some of its parts, the adjective but not the noun, the world without space. It is the meaning of a whole psychological school realised clinically.

Bonnier was aware of the previous theoretical and clinical work of Wernicke (1894) and of the patients studied by Fœrster (1903) and by Deny and Camus (1905, published in the same volume of the *Revue Neurologique*). The deficits of these patients, which, according to Bonnier, provide examples of aschematia, had however been interpreted in the context of a psychiatric disorder, even though Wernicke's account of the processes that underpin the 'somatopsyche' was deeply neurologically based. Bonnier points out also that his views reflect mainly his own work, published in his 1893 book *Vertige*.

An interim comment

The novel elements of Bonnier's report may be summarised in two main points. First, Bonnier suggests the existence of a conscious spatial representation of the body (*schema*), concerned with orientation of the body and of body parts, their volumetric properties, localisation of sensory inputs, and underpinning the very notion of corporeal being.

Secondly, peripheral disorders of the vestibular system, which were found in all reported patients, may bring about disorders of the body schema: a-, hypo-, hyper-, and para-schematia. The inference may be drawn that the vestibular system is deeply concerned with the operation of such a schema. These disorders may occur in the absence of other psychiatric manifestations. Only patient #h was '*hystérique*', in addition to suffering from vertigo.

Revisited over 90 years later, Bonnier's article has two main limitations. First, objective findings, such as the neurological exam, are not provided. Each patient is described only briefly, mentioning his or her subjective symptoms. The report by Deny and Camus (1905) was much more complete in this respect. Furthermore, Bonnier does not provide any information concerning the symptoms, signs and exams on which the diagnosis of a peripheral labyrinthine disorder was based. Taking into consideration the 1905 paper, the possibility should be entertained that Bonnier's patients also suffered from other diseases, including, for example, focal (in the temporo-parietal region?) seizures (patients #a, #b, and #e), or hysteria (patient #i). In the description of patient #h Bonnier mentions that she was also hysterical. A perusal of

Bonnier's bibliography shows however that he was aware of the different diseases that could bring about symptoms such as dizziness. In his book *Vertige* (1893) he drew distinctions between different aetiologies and manifestations of this symptom, including 'labyrinthine, oculomotor, cerebral, cerebellar, epileptic, hysterical and tabetic vertigo'. Furthermore, Bonnier described a vascular brainstem syndrome. In his historical review of the syndromes of the medulla oblongata, Currier (1969, pp. 220–221) interprets 'Bonnier's syndrome' as brought about by a lateral medullary lesion, noting, however, that Bonnier's neurological examination and anatomo-clinical correlation were 'inadequate'. According to DeJong (1979, p. 223) Bonnier's syndrome consists of vertigo, nystagmus, and pallor, often accompanied by contralateral hemiplegia and involvement of some cranial nerves (ninth, tenth, fifth, and third). To summarise, the (admittedly indirect) available information concerning Bonnier's expertise suggests that the diagnoses reported in the 1905 paper were likely to be reliable.

The second limitation of the article is that the neurological basis of the schema is not specified, even though Bonnier's main anatomophysiological reference appears to be to Wernicke's (1894) views.

THE BODY SCHEMA AFTER BONNIER

Arnold Pick

Pick's (1908, 1915, 1922) views on the body schema were essentially based on the ideas of Munk and Wernicke (discussion in Poeck & Orgass, 1971). Using Head and Holmes' (1911) term, Pick suggested the existence of several 'schemata', for the different sensory modalities and for different body parts, with the schemata concerned with the representation of the body surface being particularly relevant. The consciousness of one's own body ('..*Bewußtsein der Körperlichkeit*') is based on these schemata, with a main, though not exclusive role, of the visual image of the body (see discussions of Pick's ideas in Semenza & Delazer—Chapter 15 of the present voume—and in Poeck & Orgass, 1971). In Pick's view, in children the representation of the corporeal self is mainly based on tactile and kinaesthetic sensation; the role of visual sensations becomes gradually more and more relevant, and in adults body representations are mainly visual. This primacy of visual sensations may be related to the important role assigned by Pick to the representations of the body surface. Pick's main empirical contribution to the study of the disorders of body schema is the description of *autotopagnosia* (Pick, 1908, see also the critical discussion by Semenza & Delazer, Chapter 15 of the present volume). Pick also interpreted phantom limb phenomena (1915), and the inability to appreciate the position of body parts (1922) as deficits of the body schema.

Henry Head and British neurology and psychology

The term 'schema' was used by Head and Holmes in their famous and influential paper (1911, pp. 186–189), for the combined standard . . .

> resulting from previous postures and movements . . . against which all sub-sequent changes of posture are measured before they enter consciousness . . . By means of perpetual alterations in position we are always building up a postural model of ourselves which constantly changes. Every new posture or movement is recorded on this plastic schema, and the activity of the cortex brings every fresh group of sensations evoked by altered posture into relation with it. . . . In the same way, recognition of the locality of the stimulated spot demands the reference to another 'schema' . . . This faculty of localisation is evidently associated with the existence of another schema or model of the surface of our bodies . . . Destruction of such 'schemata' by a lesion of the cortex renders impossible all recognition of posture or of the locality of a stimulated spot in the affected part of the body.

Head and Holmes (1911) do not mention Bonnier's (1905) and Wernicke's (1894) papers. They discuss instead the work of Munk, who, in their inter-pretation, regarded 'the cortex as the repository of images of movement'. According to Head and Holmes, Munk's visual image cannot be the postural standard, as 'in cases where all power of recognising postures is lost this visual image remains unchanged'. Head and Holmes concluded that 'the image, whether it be visual or motor, is not the fundamental standard against which all postural changes are measured'. Head and Holmes' criticism reflected, at least in part, a misinterpretation of Munk's view (see the discus-sion in Poeck & Orgass, 1971) and was not entirely empirically grounded, because images of movement can fulfil the function of supplying postural standards (Oldfield & Zangwill, 1941/42). The difference between Head and Holmes' and Munk's teachings may be not irreconcilable (Critchley, 1953, p. 108).

In his constructive theory of remembering, Bartlett (1932) used the term 'schema' to refer to the active organisation of past reactions and experiences. Remembering involves determination by the past, and 'The influence of "schemata" is influence by the past' (p. 202). Bartlett's concept of schema was based on Head and Holmes' views as applied to memory processes. Bartlett also made discerning observations on their postural schema, noting that only in exceptional circumstances, such as 'an unwitting alteration of position', would the measured postural change enter consciousness. 'Every day, many times over, we make accurate motor adjustments in which, if Head is right, the schemata are active, without any awareness at all, so far as the measure of the changing posture is concerned' (Bartlett, 1932, p. 200). He also mentions that Munk (1890) hypothesised a storehouse of individual images or traces of movement. This point was not developed further by Bartlett, but the notion of 'a combined standard' and of a continuously updated 'plastic schema' appears to be more parsimonious in both computational terms and the required storage capacity by the brain.

In the 1940s Pick's (1908) and Head and Holmes' (1911) concepts of body schema and image were used by British neurologists such as Brain (1941) and Roth (1949) to interpret the bodily components of the neglect syndrome, including hemiasomatognosia, anosognosia for hemiplegia, somatopara-phrenia, and tactile (and auditory) allaesthesia or allochiria.[1] Critchley (1953) in his scholarly and influential monograph on *The Parietal Lobes*, has a chapter (VIII: Disorders of the body image) in which Bonnier's terminology is used to classify its different types of distortion from parietal disease or a psychotic type of illness. Critchley (1953, p. 241) points out that aschematia (total asomatognosia or depersonalisation), as well as segmental depersonal-isation, are frequently associated with psychiatric disorders. He also notes that in patients with parietal damage the complaint that the affected limb is unduly heavy or swollen may be considered an hyperschematic disorder. It is worth noticing here that, in his treatment of the higher order disorders of the body image, Critchley does not make reference to Head and Holmes' (1911) concept of body schema (which is discussed in Chapter IV: Disorders of tactile function). Putative 'image' and 'schema' components of bodily repre-sentations have also been distinguished by Paillard, Cole, and Gallagher (see below).

Paul Schilder

In the mid-1930s Schilder (1935) summarised his extensive work on the body image and its disorders in the monograph *The Image and Appearance of the Human Body*. Schilder discussed the body image in its neurophysiological, neuropsychological, psychoanalytic and psychiatric aspects (Part II: The libidinous structure of the body image), as well as its sociological aspects. His views were mainly based on Pick's earlier work (see discussion in Poeck & Orgass, 1971).

Schilder (1933) confirmed and extended Bonnier's (1905) early suggestion of an association between disorders of the body schema and vestibular dysfunction, reporting a number of clinical observations of patients whose visual and somatosensory phenomenal experiences were modulated by the activity of the vestibular system. For instance, after vestibular stimulation a patient suffering from hallucinations produced by belladonna intoxication 'saw the Titanic sinking with many passengers moving on the deck. . . . The face of a woman shows a swollen lip. The jaw disappears' (p. 138). Another patient, a 51-year-old woman studied in 1927, had putative vestibular attacks of a few seconds' duration, with specific somatosensory and visual unilateral symptoms: she reported a variety of abnormalities concerning her left side, which was 'lame', 'burning', 'heavier'; objects in the left visual field were blurred, and she heard the ticking of a watch less on the left side; a one-sided depersonalisation was also present, since 'she can't think on the left side' (pp. 152–153). A patient studied by Hoff and Schilder (see Schilder, 1935, p. 117) felt her extremities had become larger and her neck swollen, under the influence of vestibular irritation. Schilder also mentions hallucinations of being doubled, in vestibular cases (Schilder, 1935, p. 118; see also Bonnier's patient #f).

Jean Lhermitte and French neurology

The French neurologist Jean Lhermitte wrote a number of papers concerned with *L'image corporelle* or *L'image du moi corporel* (1942, 1952; Lhermitte and Tchehrazi 1937). Lhermitte's eclectic views are largely based on the early suggestions by Bonnier (1905) and Schilder (1935), and also by Head and Holmes (1911). As Pick, Lhermitte emphasises the role of the visual component of the body image. He draws a distinction between 'perceptual', based on current sensory inputs, and 'mnestic body images' (Lhermitte, 1942, p. 21). Lhermitte also provides a taxonomy of the pathological derangements of the body image. These include many of the deficits mentioned earlier, such as phantom limb phenomena, anosognosia, asomatognosia, autoscopia, and apraxia. This latter disorder may be explained in terms of a deficit of the body schema, as the organisation of action presupposes the existence of an internal spatial representation of the body (see Lhermitte, Massary, & Kyriaco, 1928, for a clinical study). This interpretation is largely based, as Lhermitte notes, on previous suggestions by Schilder (1935) and van Bogaert (1934).

Lhermitte, who termed the vestibular nerve '*nerf de l'espace*' (1952), repeatedly emphasised the role of the vestibular system in the building up of the internal spatial representation of the body. Confirming Bonnier's observations, Lhermitte (1952) mentions the case of a neurological patient, examined with Bineau and Ducosté, who, after an haemorrhagic stroke in the brainstem, complained of vertigo, and feeling the lower limbs '*en l'air*', above the bed. Lhermitte traces back this distortion of the body image to the damage of the brainstem component of the vestibular system.

In the 1930s and 1940s, French neurologists interpreted unilateral bodily disorders such as 'motor neglect' (Castaigne, Laplane, & Degos, 1970; Heilman, Watson, & Valenstein, 1993; Mark, Heilman, & Watson, 1996), hemiasomatognosia, and somatoparaphrenia, in terms of impairment of the body schema. The right brain-damaged patient of Garcin, Varay, and Hadji-Dimo (1938) did not execute movements using the left limbs, even though no primary motor disorders were present, showed a massive neglect for the left side of his body, and regarded the left hand of the examiner as his own left hand.

THE BODY SCHEMA AND ITS DISORDERS

The concept of body schema or image[2] and their disorders produced by cerebral damage or dysfunction still hold a relevant position in cognitive psychology and human neuropsychology. According to Parsons (1990):

> this expression denotes an abstract internal representation of spatial and physical-mechanical properties of one's body (including muscle, skeleton, organs, and so on). It is based on some combination of past and current information from proprioceptive, kinaesthetic, muscular, articular, postural, tactile, cutaneous, vestibular, equilibrium, visual and auditory senses, as well as from our sense of physical effort and from contact with objects and among our body parts. We likely possess more than one representation of our body.

In the neuropsychological domain the wide popularity of the term reflects, at least in part, the utilisation of the concept to explain, or at best to classify, a variety of deficits as 'disorders of the body schema'. Major comprehensive reviews (Benton & Sivan, 1993; Denes, 1989, 1999; Frederiks, 1969, 1985a; Nielsen, 1946) list under this rubric bilateral disorders, associated with left-sided lesions, and unilateral disorders, more frequently associated with right-sided lesions, and involving the left side of the body.

Bilateral disorders

(1) *Autotopagnosia*: the inability to point on verbal command to one's own body parts (see Semenza & Delazer, Chapter 15 in the present volume).
(2) *Gerstmann's syndrome*: finger agnosia, left–right disorientation, acalculia, agraphia, with the former two deficits reflecting a disorder of the body schema.

Unilateral disorders

(1) *Hemiasomatognosia*: further fractionated (Frederiks, 1969, 1985a) into conscious (loss of the perception of one side of the body) and nonconscious (lack of concern and neglect for one side of the body: personal neglect) component deficits.
(2) *Anosognosia* for motor deficits contralateral to the side of the lesion (hemiparesis, hemiplegia: see Papagno & Vallar, Chapter 12 in the present volume; see also Forde & Wallesch on anosognosia for cortical blindness and Anton's syndrome, Chapter 14 in the present volume),

and related disorders, such as anosodiaphoria (belittling the importance of hemiplegia) and misoplegia (excessive aversion towards the
disabled limb, or 'hatred of paralysis') (Critchley, 1957; 1979, pp. 115–
120), personification of paralysed limbs (Critchley, 1955), somatoparaphrenia (delusional views concerning one side of one's own
body: Gerstmann, 1942).

In his monograph on *The Parietal Lobes*, Critchley (1953, pp. 225–226)
tabulated the distortions of the body image associated with parietal disease,
more frequently on the right side, as follows:

- Unilateral neglect: motor, sensory, visual (see also Marshall &
  Halligan, Chapter 17 in the present volume).
- Lack of concern over the existence of hemiparesis (anosodiaphoria).
- Unawareness of hemiparesis (anosognosia).
- Defective appreciation of the existence of hemiparesis, with
  rationalisation.
- Denial of hemiparesis.
- Denial of hemiparesis with confabulation.
- Loss of awareness of one body-half (which may or may not be para-
  lysed): asomatognosia; hemidepersonalisation.
- Undue heaviness, deadness or lifelessness of one half (hyperschematia).
- Phantom third limb, associated with a hemiparesis.

Other deficits

(1) Asymbolia for pain: the absence of the normal reaction to pain in the
presence of intact elementary sensation (Hécaen & Albert, 1978).
(2) Macro and microsomatognosia: the illusory or hallucinatory perception of one's body parts as disproportionately large or small in size.
(3) Autoscopia: the hallucinatory seeing of one's body image in external
visual space, as in a mirror.
(4) Phantom limb and phantom limb pain phenomena.

While the term 'body schema' has been widely used in clinical neurology,
psychiatry, and neuropsychology, the validity of the theoretical concept has
been questioned, with the main conclusion that the body schema and its
disorders, far from being unitary in nature, fractionate into a number of
discrete disorders, with specific underlying pathological mechanisms and
lesion sites (De Renzi, 1968; Poeck, 1969; Poeck & Orgass, 1971).

In line with these suggestions, Gerstmann's syndrome is an anatomical
syndrome, which, in its pure form, is associated with damage to the left
posterior-inferior parietal region (Denes, 1999). A left parietal lesion is also

the more frequent anatomical correlate of the few published patients with autotopagnosia (Denes, 1999, and Semenza & Delazer, Chapter 15 in the present volume, for reviews).

Anosognosia for hemiplegia and hemiasomatognosia (see Hécaen & Albert, 1978; Roth, 1949, for interpretations in terms of defective body schema or image, and Papagno & Vallar, Chapter 12 in the present volume), and somatoparaphrenia (see recent illustrative case studies in Daprati, Sirigu, Pradat-Diehl, Franck, & Jeannerod, 2000, for an experimental study of a subclinical somatoparaphrenic disorder; Halligan, Marshall, & Wade, 1995) are currently considered as component deficits of the clinical syndrome of left spatial unilateral neglect, the more frequent anatomical correlate of which is damage to the right temporo-parietal junction (Bisiach & Vallar, 2000; Vallar, 1998). Neglect for the left side of the body (personal neglect) is independent of neglect for extra-personal space (Bisiach, Perani, Vallar, & Berti, 1986; Guariglia & Antonucci, 1992) and anosognosia (see Papagno and Vallar, Chapter 12 in the present volume).

The supernumerary phantom limb has been reported after right hemisphere damage or dysfunction in association with other components of the spatial neglect syndrome (Critchley, 1953, p.243; Halligan, Marshall, & Wade, 1993, for a recent case). The misrepresentations of body schema that characterise spontaneous and evoked phantom sensations occur in amputees (reviews in Berlucchi & Aglioti, 1997; Frederiks, 1985b). Defective estimation of the size of body parts (macro and microsomatognosia) may be associated with a variety of neurological diseases, including focal cerebral lesions frequently involving the temporo-parieto-occipital regions, and paroxysmal disorders, such as migraine and epilepsy (Frederiks, 1985a). Autoscopia may occur in association with intoxications and infections, epilepsy, and both diffuse and focal cerebral lesions (Brugger et al., 1997; Frederiks, 1985a). Finally, a variety of distortions of the body schema, including autoscopia, abnormal estimation of the size of body parts, and depersonalisation or derealisation (feeling one's body is not one's own) may occur in psychoses, such as schizophrenia (David, Kemp, Smith, & Fahy, 1996; McGilchrist & Cutting, 1995).

THE LEGACY OF PIERRE BONNIER

Body schema and body image

The terms 'schema' and 'image' refer to representations of the body, which, as their neuropsychological counterparts (see e.g. Sirigu, Grafman, Bressler, & Sunderland, 1991), are far from monolithic (Eilan, Marcel, & Bermúdez, 1995).

Distinctions may be drawn between conscious, as Bonnier's (1905) schema appears to be, and nonconscious, as Head and Holmes' (1911) postural schema, representations. Perceptual, short-term representations provide (conscious and nonconscious) records of the momentary position of the body, of the relative location of body parts, of the space occupied by one's body. Long-term, persisting, representations (again conscious and nonconscious) hold specific (concerning the structure and shape of one's body) and canonical (what bodies look and feel like) information about the body (see an early distinction between 'perceptual' and 'memory' representations in Lhermitte, 1942). Bodily representations include also social and emotional components (see an early discussion in Schilder, 1935), and academically acquired explicit conceptualisations (see Eilan et al., 1995). Bodily representations may differ in the relative contribution by sensory channels to their building up and updating (see early discussions in Head & Holmes, 1911; Munk, 1890; Pick, 1908).

Some of these aspects of bodily representations are captured by the distinction between: (i) a postural body frame or schema, primarily based on proprioceptive inputs and nonconscious subpersonal processes, concerning the local position of the body and of body parts and the organisation of movement (see Head & Holmes, 1911); (ii) the body image, a more global percept or Gestalt, based on exteroceptive multimodal, mainly visual, inputs (Cole & Paillard, 1995; Gallagher, 1995; Gallagher and Cole, 1995; Head & Holmes, 1911, for a distinction between postural and superficial body schemata; Paillard, 1982). According to Gallagher and Cole (1995) the body image consists of a complex set of intentional states, which may involve conscious awareness (perceptions, mental representations, beliefs, attitudes) and whose object is one's own body. The body image would include the subjects' perceptual experience of their own body, their conceptual understanding of the body in general, as well as their emotional attitudes towards their own body. Such a conscious body image, however, may participate in the control of movement under specific circumstances, such as learning of novel motor skills, or when the body schema is impaired. More specifically, Cole & Paillard (1995) suggest that the postural body schema is primarily involved in localisation within sensorimotor bodily space, as assessed, for instance, by pointing to the stimulated spot without visual control. The body image, conversely, would be concerned with verbal localisation in the anatomy of one's body, or on a body diagram. Relevant neuropsychological evidence for such a dissociation has been provided by the case of a patient with a centrally deafferented forearm following a parietal lesion (defective body image, see Paillard, Michel, & Stelmach, 1983) and by patients whose sensory deafferentation is produced by a sensory neuropathy (impaired body schema, see Cole & Paillard, 1995).

Hyperschematia in unilateral spatial neglect

The concept of a disproportionately enlarged spatial representation ('hyper-schematia', using Bonnier's terminology) may be usefully applied to the behaviour of some right hemisphere-damaged patients with left unilateral neglect. In drawing tasks, a few such patients exhibit a paradoxical contral-esional expansion of the drawing, rather than the more frequent defective manifestations (i.e. the more or less complete absence of left-hand details). Figure 11.2 shows the drawing from memory of a daisy by a patient with a right parietal tumour. The left-hand (contralesional) petals are dis-proportionately large. Figure 11.3A shows a clock drawn from memory by a patient with a right temporo-parietal lesion and left unilateral spatial neglect, documented psychometrically. The left-hand hours are displaced to the left in an expanded fashion.

The behaviour illustrated in Figures 11.2 and 11.3, where portions of the neglected side of space are occupied by the patient's contralesionally expanded drawing, which becomes therefore non-symmetrical, in a fashion opposite to the asymmetry produced by contralesional omissions, may be listed under the rubric of productive manifestations of unilateral neglect (Vallar, 2001). This evidence is based on clinical observations (Critchley, 1953, Figure 11.2), or represents a corollary finding in experimental studies assessing the effects of sensory stimulations on neglect (Guariglia, Lippolis, & Pizzamiglio, 1998). With these caveats in mind, these graphic productions may be tentatively interpreted in the context of a putative lateral distortion of the spatial representational medium in patients with left unilateral neglect. This anisometry would consist in a contralesional (left-sided) expansion ('hyperschematia') and in an ipsilesional (right-sided) compression (see Bisiach & Vallar, 2000, for further details).

Figure 11.2   A daisy drawn from memory in a clockwise fashion. (From Critchley, 1953, *The Parietal Lobes*, p. 341, with the permission of Macmillan Publishing Company.)

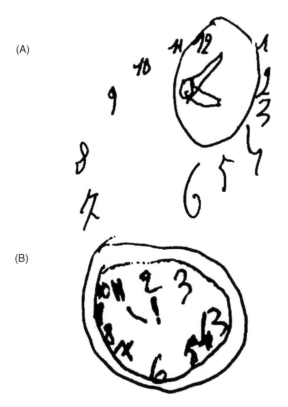

Figure 11.3   A clock drawn from memory in a baseline condition (A), and after transcutaneous electrical stimulation (B). (From Guariglia et al., 1998, and reproduced from *Cortex* with the permission of the publishers Masson.)

The vestibular and other sensory systems and the body schema

Bonnier's observation that all his patients suffered from a peripheral vestibular disease suggested an association between the vestibular system and the body schema. Both Schilder and Jean Lhermitte, as noted earlier, provided clinical evidence in line with this possibility, even though their reports were, as Bonnier's original observations, mainly based on the patient's subjective reports.

Micalizzi (1949) investigated the 'body schema' in patients with a peripheral vestibular disorder, assessing their ability to localise, by pointing, a tactile stimulus in different lateral positions of the trunk. The main result was a lateral displacement of the perceived stimulated position in the half-trunk ipsilateral to the side of the loss. Micalizzi interpreted his results as a pathological expansion of the superficial body schema, but the possible con-founding role of past pointing towards the damaged side should also be considered (see Baloh, 1984).

In the past 15 years, a number of neuropsychological experimental studies, performed with adequate methodology, have shown in right brain-damaged patients that vestibular stimulation affects components of the neglect syn-drome, concerning the left side of the body (reviews in Vallar, 1998; Vallar, Guariglia, & Rusconi, 1997). In four right brain-damaged patients, Cappa, Sterzi, Vallar, and Bisiach (1987) showed that vestibular stimulation not only improved extra-personal, visuo-spatial, unilateral neglect (see Rubens, 1985; Silberpfennig, 1941), but also brought about a temporary recovery from both neglect for the left side of the body (personal neglect or hemiasomatognosia) and anosognosia for left hemiplegia (in two out of four patients). Bisiach, Rusconi, and Vallar (1991) reported the remission of somatoparaphrenic delusions concerning the left side of the body (the patient's belief that her left arm was her mother's) following vestibular stimulation. These observations on anosognosia and somatoparaphrenia were subsequently replicated by other investigators (Ramachandran, 1995; Rode et al., 1992; Vallar, Sterzi, Bottini, Cappa, & Rusconi, 1990).

In right brain-damaged patients, left hemianaesthesia is also improved by vestibular stimulation. In a few left brain-damaged patients with right spatial neglect similar effects on right hemianaesthesia have been found (Vallar, Bottini, Rusconi, & Sterzi, 1993; Vallar et al., 1990). These results suggest that somatosensory deficits contralateral to the side of the hemispheric lesion may have a higher-order, spatial, neglect-related nonsensory component (see discussion in Vallar, 1997). The positive effects of vestibular stimulation extend to left-sided motor deficits, revealing a motor neglect component (Rode et al., 1992; Rode, Perenin, Honoré, & Boisson, 1998).

Other sensory stimulations have similar effects on bodily components of the neglect syndrome. Transcutaneous nervous electrical stimulation modu-lates the severity of contralesional hemianaesthesia in right brain-damaged patients and in left brain-damaged patients with right spatial neglect (Vallar, Rusconi, & Bernardini, 1996). In the domain of extra-personal space, this stimulation also reduced the 'hyperschematic' disproportionate contral-esional expansion of the left-hand side of a clock, drawn by a patient with left neglect (see Figure 11.3A versus 11.3B). The stimulation appears therefore to improve both the more frequent defective ('hyposchematic', borrowing Bonnier's terminology) and these less common productive ('hypersche-matic') behaviours exhibited by patients with left neglect. This provides some indication for the existence of a unitary underlying pathological mechanism.

Optokinetic stimulation, which may be considered functionally equivalent to vestibular stimulation with respect to its perceptual and motor effects (see Bischof, 1974), may improve or worsen the severity of the deficit of position sense in the upper limb of right brain-damaged patients with left spatial neglect (Vallar, Antonucci, Guariglia, & Pizzamiglio, 1993; Vallar, Guariglia, Magnotti, & Pizzamiglio, 1995), affecting a main component of the conscious postural frame or schema, which concerns awareness for the relative position of body parts. Optokinetic stimulation also improves muscle strength in the left hand of right brain-damaged patients with left spatial neglect (Vallar, Guariglia, Nico, & Pizzamiglio, 1997).

The inference, based on neuropsychological evidence from a variety of disorders concerning one side of the body (personal unilateral neglect, anosognosia for hemiplegia, somatoparaphrenia, tactile hemiinattention, motor neglect), that the vestibular system, as well as other sensory channels, participates in the organisation of internal representations of the body, has received converging support from observations in normal subjects. Muscle vibration may generate proprioceptive misinformation, producing illusory changes in one's apparent body orientation and in the relative position of body parts (Goodwin, McCloskey, & Mattews, 1972; Roll, Roll, & Velay, 1991), as well as systematic perceptual distortions. Lackner (1988, p. 284) writes:

> Physically impossible body configurations and dimensions can be represented perceptually. The bizarre sensations that can result, for example, stretching of the nose or shrinking of the waist have no discomfort associated with them. . . . Instead, there is a sense of wonder as the dimensions of the body are perceived to change; as one subject reported: 'Oh my gosh, my nose is a foot long! I feel like Pinocchio'.

Pierre Bonnier would have probably referred to these experimentally induced illusions concerning the size of body parts and their spatial position as manifestations of hyperschematia, hyposchematia, and paraschematia. Revisited nearly one century later, Bonnier's clinical observations, theoretical thoughts, and intuitions seem to have found adequate empirical verification.

ACKNOWLEDGEMENTS

This work has been supported in part by grants from the Consiglio Nazionale delle Ricerche, the Ministero dell'Università e della Ricerca Scientifica e Tecnologica and the Ministero della Sanità. A number of colleagues and friends helped us in the preparation of this chapter. We would like to thank Tony Marcel and Jacques Paillard for providing us with relevant material and for useful discussions, and Chris Code and Claus-W. Wallesch for their suggestions and comments. We are also grateful to Annie Ganansia-Ganem and François Boller for their invaluable help with the biographical information about Pierre Bonnier.

REFERENCES

Baloh, R.W. (1984). *Dizziness, hearing loss and tinnitus: The essentials of neurotology.* Philadelphia: F.A. Davis.

Bartlett, F.C. (1932). *Remembering.* Cambridge: Cambridge University Press.

Benton, A., & Sivan, A.B. (1993). Disturbances of the body schema. In K.M. Heilman & E. Valenstein (Eds.), *Clinical neuropsychology* (3rd ed., pp. 123–136). New York: Oxford University Press.

Berlucchi, G., & Aglioti, S. (1997). The body in the brain: Neural bases of corporeal awareness. *Trends in Neuroscience, 20,* 560–564.

Bischof, N. (1974). Optic-vestibular orientation to the vertical. In H.H. Kornhuber (Ed.), *Handbook of sensory physiology. Vestibular system,* (Vol. 6, Part 2 pp. 155–190). Berlin: Springer.

Bisiach, E., Perani, D., Vallar, G., & Berti, A. (1986). Unilateral neglect: Personal and extrapersonal. *Neuropsychologia, 24,* 759–767.

Bisiach, E., Rusconi, M.L., & Vallar, G. (1991). Remission of somatoparaphrenic delusion through vestibular stimulation. *Neuropsychologia, 29,* 1029–1031.

Bisiach, E., & Vallar, G. (2000). Unilateral neglect in humans. In F. Boller, J. Grafman, & G. Rizzolatti (Eds.), *Handbook of neuropsychology* (2nd., Vol. 1, pp. 459–502). Amsterdam: Elsevier Science, B.V.

Bonnier, P. (1893). *Vertige.* Chartres: Rueff, Imprimerie Durand, Rue Fulbert.

Bonnier, P. (1896). *L'oreille.* Paris: Masson.

Bonnier, P. (1905). L'aschématie. *Revue Neurologique (Paris), 13,* 605–609.

Brain, W.R. (1941). Visual disorientation with special reference to lesions of the right cerebral hemisphere. *Brain, 64,* 244–272.

Brugger, P., Regard, M., & Landis, T. (1997). Illusory reduplication of one's own body: Phenomenology and classification of autoscopic phenomena. *Cognitive Neuropsychiatry, 2,* 19–38.

Cappa, S., Sterzi, R., Vallar, G., & Bisiach, E. (1987). Remission of hemineglect and anosognosia during vestibular stimulation. *Neuropsychologia, 25,* 775–782.

Castaigne, P., Laplane, D., & Degos, J.-D. (1970). Trois cas de négligence motrice par lésion rétro-rolandique. *Revue Neurologique (Paris), 122,* 234–242.

Cole, J., & Paillard, J. (1995). Living without touch and peripheral information about body position and movement: Studies with deafferented subjects. In J.L. Bermudez, A. Marcel, & N. Eilan (Eds.), *The body and the self* (pp. 245–266). Cambridge, MA: MIT Press.

Critchley, M. (1953). *The parietal lobes.* New York: Hafner.

Critchley, M. (1955). Personification of paralysed limbs in hemiplegics. *British Medical Journal, 2,* 284–286.

Critchley, M. (1957). Observations on anosodiaphoria. *L'encéphale, 46,* 541–546.

Critchley, M. (1979). *The divine banquet of the brain and other essays.* New York: Raven Press.

Currier, R.D. (1969). Syndromes of the medulla oblongata. In P.J. Vinken & G.W. Bruyn (Eds.), *Handbook of clinical neurology* (Vol. 2, pp. 217–237). Amsterdam: North-Holland Publishing Co.

Daprati, E., Sirigu, A., Pradat-Diehl, P., Franck, N., & Jeannerod, M. (2000). Recognition of self-produced movements in a case of severe neglect. *Neurocase, 6,* 477–486.

David, A., Kemp, R., Smith, L., & Fahy, T. (1996). Split minds: Multiple personality and schizophrenia. In P.W. Halligan & J.C. Marshall (Eds.), *Method in madness: Case studies in cognitive neuropsychiatry* (pp. 123–146). Hove, UK: Psychology Press.

De Renzi, E. (1968). Sull'utilità del concetto di schema corporeo nella patologia corticale. *Il Lavoro Neuropsichiatrico, 23,* 1395–1406.

DeJong, R.N. (1979). *The neurologic examination* (4 ed.). Philadelphia: Harper and Row.

Denes, G. (1989). Disorders of body awareness and body knowledge. In F. Boller & J. Grafman (Eds.), *Handbook of neuropsychology* (Vol. 2, pp. 207–228). Amsterdam: Elsevier.

Denes, G. (1999). Disorders of body awareness and body knowledge. In G. Denes & L. Piz-zamiglio (Eds.), *Handbook of clinical and experimental neuropsychology* (pp. 497–506). Hove, UK: Psychology Press.

Deny, G., & Camus, P. (1905). Sur une forme d'hypocondrie aberrante due a la perte de la coscience du corps. *Revue Neurologique, 13*, 460–467.

Eilan, N., Marcel, A., & Bermúdez, J.L. (1995). Self-consciousness and the body: An inter-disciplinary introduction. In J.L. Bermudez, A. Marcel, & N. Eilan (Eds.), *The body and the self* (pp. 1–28). Cambridge, MA: MIT Press.

Fœrster, O. (1903). Ein Fall von elementärer allgemeiner Somatopsychose. (Afunktion der Somatopsyche). Ein Beitrag zur Frage der Bedeutung der Somatopsyche für das Wahrneh-mungsvermögen. *Monatsschrift für Psychiatrie und Neurologie, 14*, 189–205.

Frederiks, J.A.M. (1969). Disorders of the body schema. In P.J. Vinken & G.W. Bruyn (Eds.), *Handbook of clinical neurology: Disorders of speech, perception and symbolic behaviour* (Vol. 4, pp. 207–240). Amsterdam: North Holland.

Frederiks, J.A.M. (1985a). Disorders of the body schema. In P.J. Vinken, G.W. Bruyn, H.L. Klawans, & J.A.M. Frederiks (Eds.), *Handbook of clinical neurology: Clinical neuropsychology* (Revised series 1, Vol. 45, pp. 373–393). Amsterdam: Elsevier.

Frederiks, J.A.M. (1985b). Phantom limb and phantom limb pain. In P.J. Vinken, G.W. Bruyn, H.L. Klawans, & J.A.M. Frederiks (Eds.), *Handbook of clinical neurology: Clinical neuropsychology* (Revised series 1, Vol. 45, pp. 395–404). Amsterdam: Elsevier.

Gallagher, S. (1995). Body schema and intentionality. In J.L. Bermúdez, A. Marcel, & N. Eilan (Eds.), *The body and the self* (pp. 225–244). Cambridge, MA: MIT Press.

Gallagher, S., & Cole, J. (1995). Body image and body schema in a deafferented subject. *Journal of Mind and Behavior, 16*, 369–389.

Garcin, R., Varay, A., & Hadji-Dimo. (1938). Document pour servir à l'étude des troubles du schéma corporel (sur quelques phénomènes moteurs, gnosiques et quelques troubles de l'uti-lisation des membres du côté gauche au cours d'un syndrome temporo-pariétal par tumeur, envisagés dans leurs rapports avec l'anosognosie et les troubles du schéma corporel). *Revue Neurologique (Paris), 69*, 498–510.

Gerstmann, J. (1942). Problem of imperception of disease and of impaired body territories with organic lesions. *Archives of Neurology and Psychiatry, 48*, 890–913.

Goodwin, G.M., McCloskey, I., & Mattews, P.B.C. (1972). Proprioceptive illusions induced by muscle vibration: Contribution by muscle spindles to perception? *Science, 175*, 1382–1384.

Guariglia, C., & Antonucci, G. (1992). Personal and extrapersonal space: A case of neglect dissociation. *Neuropsychologia, 30*, 1001–1009.

Guariglia, C., Lippolis, G., & Pizzamiglio, L. (1998). Somatosensory stimulation improves imagery disorders in neglect. *Cortex, 34*, 233–241.

Halligan, P.W., Marshall, J.C., & Wade, D.T. (1993). Three arms: A case study of supernumerary phantom limb after right hemisphere stroke. *Journal of Neurology, Neurosurgery, and Psychiatry, 56*, 159–166.

Halligan, P.W., Marshall, J.C., & Wade, D.T. (1995). Unilateral somatoparaphrenia after right hemisphere stroke: A case description. *Cortex, 31*, 173–182.

Head, H., & Holmes, G. (1911). Sensory disturbances from cerebral lesions. *Brain, 34*, 102–254.

Hécaen, H., & Albert, M.L. (1978). *Human neuropsychology.* New York: John Wiley.

Heilman, K.M., Watson, R.T., & Valenstein, E. (1993). Neglect and related disorders. In K.M. Heilman & E. Valenstein (Eds.), *Clinical neuropsychology* (3rd ed., pp. 279–336). New York: Oxford University Press.

Joanette, Y., & Brouchon, M. (1984). Visual allesthesia in manual pointing: Some evidence for a sensorimotor cerebral organisation. *Brain and Cognition, 3*, 152–165.

Jones, E. (1907). The precise diagnostic value of allochiria. *Brain, 30*, 490–532.

Kawamura, M., Hirayama, K., Shinohara, Y., Watanabe, Y., & Sugishita, M. (1987). Alloaesthesia. *Brain, 110*, 225–236.

Lackner, J.R. (1988). Some proprioceptive influences on the perceptual representation of body shape and orientation. *Brain, 111*, 281–297.

Lhermitte, J. (1942). De l'image corporelle. *Revue Neurologique (Paris), 74*, 20–38.

Lhermitte, J. (1952). L'image corporelle en neurologie. *Schweizer Archiv für Neurologie und Psychiatrie, 69*, 214–236.

Lhermitte, J., Massary, J.D., & Kyriaco. (1928). Le rôle de la pensée spatiale dans l'apraxie. *Revue Neurologique (Paris), 36*, 895–402.

Lhermitte, J., & Tchehrazi, E. (1937). L'image du moi corporel et ses déformations pathologiques. *L'encéphale, 32*, 1–24.

Mark, V.W., Heilman, K.M., & Watson, R. (1996). Motor neglect: What do we mean? *Neurology, 46*, 1492–1493.

McGilchrist, I., & Cutting, J. (1995). Somatic delusions in schizophrenia and the affective psychoses. *British Journal of Psychiatry, 167*, 350–361.

Meador, K.J., Allen, M.E., Adams, R.J., & Loring, D.W. (1991). Allochiria vs Allesthesia. Is there a misperception? *Archives of Neurology, 48*, 546–549.

Micalizzi, F. (1949). Lo schema corporeo in soggetti con funzione labirintica asimmetrica. *Acta Neurologica (Napoli), 4*, 377–406.

Munk, H. (1890). *Über die Functionen der Großhirnrinde* (2nd ed.). Berlin: Hirshwald.

Nielsen, J.M. (1946). *Agnosia, apraxia, and their value in cerebral localisation* (2nd ed.). New York: Hafner.

Obersteiner, H. (1882). On allochiria: A peculiar sensory disorder. *Brain, 4*, 153–163.

Oldfield, R.C., & Zangwill, O.L. (1941/42). Head's concept of the schema and its application in contemporary British psychology. Part I. Head's concept of the schema. *British Journal of Psychology, 32*, 267–286.

Paillard, J. (1982). Le corps et ses languages d'espace. In E. Jeddi (Ed.), *Le corps en psychiâtrie* (pp. 53–69). Paris: Masson.

Paillard, J., Michel, F., & Stelmach, G. (1983). Localisation without content: A tactile analogue of 'blind sight'. *Archives of Neurology, 40*, 548–551.

Parsons, L.M. (1990). Body image. In M.W. Eysenck (Ed.), *The Blackwell dictionary of cognitive psychology* (pp. 46–47). Oxford: Blackwell.

Pick, A. (1908). *Über Störungen der Orientierung am eigenen Körper, Arbeiten aus der deutschen psychiatrischen Universitäts-klinik in Prag* (pp. 1–19). Berlin: Karger.

Pick, A. (1915). Zur Pathologie des Bewußtseins vom eigenen Körper. *Neurologisches Centralblatt, 34*, 257–265.

Pick, A. (1922). Störung der Orientierung am eigenen Körper. Beitrag zur Lehre vom Bewußtsein des eigenen Körpers. *Psychologische Forschung, 1*, 303–318.

Poeck, K. (1969). Modern trends in neuropsychology. In A.L. Benton (Ed.), *Contributions to clinical neuropsychology* (pp. 1–29). Chicago: Aldine.

Poeck, K., & Orgass, B. (1971). The concept of the body schema: A critical review and some experimental results. *Cortex, 7*, 254–277.

Ramachandran, V.S. (1995). Anosognosia in parietal lobe syndrome. *Consciousness and Cognition, 4*, 22–51.

Rode, G., Charles, N., Perenin, M.T., Vighetto, A., Trillet, M., & Aimard, G. (1992). Partial remission of hemiplegia and somatoparaphrenia through vestibular stimulation in a case of unilateral neglect. *Cortex, 28*, 203–208.

Rode, G., Perenin, M.T., Honoré, J., & Boisson, D. (1998). Improvement of the motor deficit of neglect patients through vestibular stimulation: Evidence for a motor neglect component. *Cortex, 34*, 253–261.

Roll, J.P., Roll, R., & Velay, J.-L. (1991). Proprioception as a link between body space and extra-personal space. In J. Paillard (Ed.), *Brain and space* (pp. 112–132). Oxford: Oxford University Press.

Roth, M. (1949). Disorders of the body image caused by lesions of the right parietal lobe. *Brain, 72*, 89–111.

Rubens, A.B. (1985). Caloric stimulation and unilateral visual neglect. *Neurology, 35*, 1019–1024.

Schilder, P. (1933). The vestibular apparatus in neurosis and psychosis. *Journal of Nervous and Mental Disease, 78*, 137–164.

Schilder, P. (1935). *The image and appearance of the human body.* New York: International Universities Press.

Silberpfennig, J. (1941). Contributions to the problem of eye movements.III. Disturbances of ocular movements with pseudohemianopsia in frontal lobe tumors. *Confinia Neurologica, 4*, 1–13.

Sirigu, A., Grafman, J., Bressler, K., & Sunderland, T. (1991). Multiple representations contribute to body knowledge processing: Evidence from a case of autotopagnosia. *Brain, 114*, 629–642.

Vallar, G. (1997). Spatial frames of reference and somatosensory processing: A neuropsychological perspective. *Philosophical Transactions of the Royal Society of London, B352*, 1401–1409.

Vallar, G. (1998). Spatial hemineglect in humans. *Trends in Cognitive Sciences, 2*, 87–97.

Vallar, G. (2001). Extrapersonal visual unilateral spatial neglect and its neuroanatomy. *Neuroimage, 14*, S52–S58.

Vallar, G., Antonucci, G., Guariglia, C., & Pizzamiglio, L. (1993). Deficits of position sense, unilateral neglect, and optokinetic stimulation. *Neuropsychologia, 31*, 1191–1200.

Vallar, G., Bottini, G., Rusconi, M.L., & Sterzi, R. (1993). Exploring somatosensory hemineglect by vestibular stimulation. *Brain, 116*, 71–86.

Vallar, G., Guariglia, C., Magnotti, L., & Pizzamiglio, L. (1995). Optokinetic stimulation affects both vertical and horizontal deficits of position sense in unilateral neglect. *Cortex, 31*, 669–683.

Vallar, G., Guariglia, C., Nico, D., & Pizzamiglio, L. (1997). Motor deficits and optokinetic stimulation in patients with left hemineglect. *Neurology, 49*, 1364–1370.

Vallar, G., Guariglia, C., & Rusconi, M.L. (1997). Modulation of the neglect syndrome by sensory stimulation. In P. Thier & H.-O. Karnath (Eds.), *Parietal lobe contributions to orientation in 3D space* (pp. 555–578). Heidelberg: Springer-Verlag.

Vallar, G., Rusconi, M.L., & Bernardini, B. (1996). Modulation of neglect hemianesthesia by transcutaneous electrical stimulation. *Journal of the International Neuropsychological Society, 2*, 452–459.

Vallar, G., Sterzi, R., Bottini, G., Cappa, S., & Rusconi, M.L. (1990). Temporary remission of left hemianaesthesia after vestibular stimulation. *Cortex, 26*, 123–131.

van Bogaert, L. (1934). Sur la pathologie de l'image de soi. *Annales Médico-psychologiques, 92*, 519–555, 744–759.

Wernicke, C. (1894). *Grundriß der Psychiatrie in klinischen Vorlesungen. Theil I. Psychophysiologie.* Leipzig: Thieme.

Wernicke, C. (1906). *Grundriß der Psychiatrie.* Leipzig: Thieme.

NOTES

1. The terms allaesthesia and allochiria denote the pathological phenomenon whereby sensory stimulations, delivered to the side of the body (tactile stimuli) or presented in the visual half-field or half-space (visual and auditory stimuli) contralateral to the side of the cerebral lesion, are consciously perceived, but referred to the symmetrical position in the ipsilesional side. Allaesthesia is more frequently associated with right-brain damage, involving then a

left-to-right displacement (Critchley, 1953; Joanette & Brouchon, 1984; Jones, 1907; Kawamura, Hirayama, Shinohara, Watanabe, & Sugishita, 1987; Meador, Allen, Adams, & Loring, 1991, for an historical and terminological discussion; Obersteiner, 1882).

2. In the neurological and neuropsychological literature, the term 'body image' (*l'image de soi*, *l'image du corps*) has been frequently used as synonymous with the body schema (*Körperschema*) (Critchley, 1953, p. 225; Roth, 1949; Schilder, 1935, p. 11).

CHAPTER TWELVE

Anosognosia for left hemiplegia: Babinski's (1914) cases

Costanza Papagno
Department of Psychology, University of Milano-Bicocca, Milan, Italy

Giuseppe Vallar
Department of Psychology; University of Milano-Bicocca, Milan, Italy, and IRCCS St. Lucia, Rome, Italy

> Harpastes, my wife's female clown, has remained, as you know, in my house, as an inherited burden. . . . Now this silly woman suddenly became blind. The story sounds incredible, but I assure you that it is true. She does not know that she is blind. She keeps asking her attendant to change her quarters; she says the house is too dark.
>
> —L. A. Seneca, *Epistulae Morales Ad Lucilium*,
> Liber Qvintus, Epistula L.

BEFORE BABINSKI: NON-AWARENESS OF CORTICAL BLINDNESS AND HEMIPLEGIA

Constantin von Monakow (1885): Non-awareness of cortical blindness

Seneca used this story to illustrate the moral problem of awareness of vice. This early description of the phenomenon of unawareness of blindness was later mentioned by Michel de Montaigne (*Essays*, II, XXV), in a chapter primarily concerned with malingering (see discussions by Bisiach & Geminiani, 1991; Critchley, 1953, pp. 256–259). It was only in 1885, however, nearly 2000 years after Seneca's observation, that Constantin von Monakow (professor of neurology at the University of Zürich, Switzerland) reported an association between unawareness of disease and cerebral damage, also

171

drawing attention to the restricted character of the responsible lesion. Von Monakow described a patient with cortical blindness and word deafness who did not see obstacles in front of him, was unable to find the food when he had to eat, did not blink when a fist was shown in front of his eyes, and looked as a blind man. His right pupil showed a reaction to light. The patient, however, did not seem to be aware of his deficit. As Harpastes, he thought that the environment was dark.

> Since the last accident the patient was not aware of his amaurosis. At the beginning he thought he was in a dark humid hole or cellar and strongly screamed for light and fire . . . When he was quiet, he said from time to time that he was old, stupid and weak; never he declared to be blind. (pp. 167–168)
>
> What he saw, either did not reach consciousness, or had for him nothing more than a general meaning. His visual representations were destroyed. In his conversation alone or with people around him, he never made any assertion in relation to vision, as for example about colours or light. Similarly, his blindness never came even minimally to consciousness, while he quietly admitted to be very old, made allusion to his senile incapacity and pointed out that he was at the end of his life. (p. 171)

Von Monakow also noticed that intellectual functions were not disproportionately impaired. The patient remained interested in many things, including his relatives' lives:

> In relation to the psychic behaviour, for the sake of completeness, it has to be said that the patient, in contrast with other forms of intellectual impairment, had an extraordinary interior life until he died. The patient was very interested in many things that were not completely in close connection with him, obviously he worried about his relatives and maintained his involvement with anyone who came in touch with him, so far as this was possible considering his deficit in orientation, and in understanding the world outside. Although the intellectual impairment appeared in a completely astonishing way, it is evident that it never reached inability of judgement, as happens with progressive paralysis. The patient correctly evaluated everyday events, and did not manifest delusional ideas. His memory for past events was still good, according to his relatives, and he had not lost all insight into his psychic impairment. (p. 171)

And moreover:

> The patient showed generally a sufficient organisation of his thinking, he was also able to express himself correctly and what he said was absolutely not always absurd or stupid. He also had aspirations and desires, which were not basically different from those of an old but intellectually unimpaired man. (p. 184)

The lesions responsible for these symptoms were found in the occipital gyri of both sides of the brain and in their connections with peripheral structures. In particular, the cuneus and lobulus lingualis were involved. The temporal areas of the left hemisphere were also damaged.

Von Monakow cited some previous cases of progressive paralysis with similar symptoms, described by Fürstner and Stenger. In those patients, however, the deficit had been transient. In his case the defective visual and acoustical awareness (the patient was also word deaf) was the main neuropsychological disorder, which was stable over time.

Gabriel Anton (1893, 1898): Non-awareness of cortical blindness and of hemiplegia

In 1893 Gabriel Anton (professor of neurology at the University of Graz, Austria) reported the case of a man, H. Wilhelm, who, after a road accident, exhibited a somatosensory impairment, both superficial and deep (he was unable to evaluate the position of his limbs). A confusional state was also present, which prevented a complete examination. Anton briefly mentioned (p. 325) that the patient was not aware of his left-sided paralysis: 'The patient is mildly confused, *he is not aware of his paralysis* (Anton's italics), he thinks to have performed movements with the left arm.' The patient's lesion involved the right cerebral cortex from the temporo-parietal to the occipital area, including the white matter and the optic thalamus.

A few years later, Anton (1899) reported two patients, one with word deafness and another with cortical blindness. According to Anton the latter patient suffered from a *Seelenblindheit* (psychic blindness) for the symptom:

> It was now extremely astonishing, that the patient did not notice her massive and later complete loss of her ability to see. . . . When she was asked directly about her ability to see, she answered in a vague, general way, that it is always so, that one sees better in youth. She assured in a calm and trustful way that she saw the objects that were shown to her, while the everyday examination proved the opposite. . . . The patient was not even aware that there was a reason to be worried or sad about this defect. (p. 93)

Anton noticed that this symptom was relatively frequent in lesions of the occipital cortex. He mentioned Dufour (Anton, 1899, p. 104), a Swiss physician, who thought that patients with hemianopia had also lost the sense of their half-field defect ('hemianopsie nulle'). According to Dufour this symptom could be used to differentiate between central (cortical) and peripheral (ocular, subcortical) damage to the visual pathways. The latter type of lesion brought about 'vision noire' (visual blackness), a deficit of which the patient was aware (see discussion in Levine, 1990).

Anton was not sure that a lesion involving the cuneus and the fissura calcarina was sufficient to produce psychic blindness and discussed this symptom again in another paper (1898). He mentioned two kinds of patients showing unawareness of neurological deficits: (1) patients with a loss of deep (proprioceptive) sensation, with or without paralysis, who tried anyway to walk; and (2) patients with word deafness and cortical blindness. He underlined the similarity of these patients with hysterics. He also pointed out (p. 229) that these individuals are not simply stupid and that the symptom cannot be easily explained with an impairment of intellectual functions. 'These patients are thus, without the presence of a sufficient deterioration, unconsciously paralysed, unconsciously blind or deaf; they are soulblind for these deficits.'

To summarise, Anton made a brief mention of the symptom of *Nicht-bewutsein* (non-awareness) of hemiparesis, but his main interest concerned unawareness of word deafness and of cortical blindness, the latter having come to be known as 'Anton's syndrome' (see Forde & Wallesch, Chapter 14 of this volume). The main points he drew attention to were the possible correlations with somatosensory deficits, and the frequent absence of an intellectual impairment.

Arnold Pick (1898): Non-awareness of hemiplegia

In 1898 (pp. 168–185) Arnold Pick (professor of psychiatry at the University of Prague) described a 31-year-old patient, Adolf W, who, after an acute accident, developed a severe left hemiparesis, of which he was not aware, and a left homonymous hemianopia. No associated somatosensory deficits were present. The patient, reading a newspaper, consistently omitted the first (left-sided) word of each line, showing left neglect dyslexia.

> . . . about three weeks later, it was followed by a left hemiplegia . . . left hemianopia, the cutaneous sensation was not impaired . . . He was completely disoriented in time and place. (pp. 173–174)
>
> . . . that he had no comprehension of his paralysis, he wondered about the fact that he had been dismissed from the army, and he wanted to show how straight he could walk, a sign which persisted from that moment. (p. 175)

A post-mortem examination showed a lesion in the left temporal lobe (three years after the initial observation the patient also developed language disturbances) and in the right optic thalamus. The neuropathological diagnosis was one of chronic diffuse leptomeningitis and of cerebral encephalomalacia of the right thalamus and of the left temporal lobe. The patient had a neurosyphilis.

Pick did more than just observing and reporting the symptom. He

attempted to discuss the aetiology of this loss of comprehension, of awareness of the disease, which he found even more surprising, given that the
paralysed limbs did not show any somatosensory impairment:

> It is worthwhile also to mention that our patient had lost all comprehension,
> even the awareness of his paralysis; this is even more surprising, as the para-
> lysed limbs did not show any sensory impairment; Müller thinks that perhaps
> this state has to be explained in terms of an involvement of the cortical areas; in
> this patient, at least directly, this is not the case; Anton suggests to relate the
> state [of non-awareness] partly to the damage to most of the associative path-
> way, partly to the general atrophy; for this case, the latter explanation is anyway
> much more plausible; but it would be also possible to take into account at the
> same time the situation of the left cerebral hemisphere in terms of Flechsig's
> body sense intention. (p. 179)

Anton's and Pick's clinical reports include three main distinctive features
of non-awareness of hemiplegia:

(1) A general mental deterioration was not a main distinctive feature of
these patients (Anton, 1898) and could not therefore constitute the
main deficit underlying non-awareness. Similarly, in the patient
described by von Monakow (1885), who was unaware of his cortical
blindness, intellectual functions were not disproportionately impaired.
Both Anton's and Pick's patients, however, were confused and
disoriented.

(2) A somatosensory impairment was not necessarily associated with non-
awareness of motor deficits (Pick, 1898) and, as mental deterioration,
could not entirely account for the disorder.

(3) In the two patients described by Anton and Pick unawareness of the
motor deficit concerned the left side of the body. No particular significance was attached to this fact, however. Pick's patient also showed
left neglect dyslexia.

To summarise, at the end of the 19th century unawareness of neurological
deficits was a well-known phenomenon, at least in the German scientific
literature. The cases of two patients showing unawareness of left motor
weakness had been published by two independent investigators (Anton and
Pick), although Anton's report was a brief observation in the context of
papers mainly concerned with unawareness of cortical blindness and
deafness.

Finally, in 1913, one year before Babinski's first report, Hermann Zingerle
from Graz (Austria) described a patient (case 2), with a left hemiplegia, and
complete hemianopia and hemianaesthesia. The patient was well oriented,
showed no dysphasia, was able to use his right hand appropriately, and knew

he was sick. The patient, however, had no attention for the left side of his body and showed obdurate left-sided delusions (a woman was lying in the bed, to the left of the patient's body). He combined this delusional view with erotic joking and sometimes caressed his left arm. The patient was perplexed, and became silent and inattentive, whenever the conversation concerned the left side of his body. He never mentioned his palsy, never drew attention to it, and never showed concern about this handicap. After about two weeks, the patient became aware of the left-sided motor and somatosensory impairments, and of the left side of his body.

BABINSKI

1914

In 1914 the French neurologist Josef François Babinski 1857–1932, (see Figure 12.1), head of the service at *l'Hôpital de la Pitié* in Paris, presented before the *Société de Neurologie de Paris* the cases of two stroke patients showing unawareness of hemiplegia. His communication was specifically devoted to this issue:

> I would like to draw your attention to a mental disorder which I had the opportunity to observe in cerebral hemiplegia, consisting in the fact that the patients ignore or seem to ignore the paralysis which affects them.

Figure 12.1 Josef François Babinski. (Reproduced with permission of the Institut für Geschichte der Medizin der Universität Wien.)

It is clear that I do not consider those cases where intelligence is very diminished, so that the patient can have just a vague notion of his/her impairment.

I would not consider also those cases in which intellectual functions, even though they are not deeply impaired, have been notably involved.

Babinski (1914) mentioned a previous observation by Barat (*Journal de Psychologie Normale et Pathologique*, March–April 1912). A patient with a left hemiplegia and blindness, despite being not intellectually impaired, was not aware of her paralysis. She was, however, mentally confused, totally disoriented in time and space and had visual hallucinations.

Patient #1

One such patient . . . hit by left hemiplegia has largely maintained her intellectual and affective faculties, for many months. She remembered well past events, was willing to talk, expressed herself correctly, her ideas were sensible; she was interested in persons known to her and asked about new people; . . . No hallucinations, delirium, confusional state, confabulation. What did contrast with the apparent preservation of intelligence of this patient was that she seemed to ignore the existence of a nearly complete hemiplegia, which she had been afraid of for many years. Never did she complain about it; never did she even allude to it. If she was asked to move her right arm, she immediately executed the command. If she was asked to move the left one, she stayed still, silent, and behaved as if the question had been put to somebody else.

I should remark that sensation in the paralysed limbs was defective but not abolished; the patient perceived a little passive displacements, and sometimes complained about pain in the left shoulder.

Patient #2

The second patient was similar to the first: no confabulation, no hallucinations, no confusion. At best she was a little overexcited. The housekeeper, who had known the patient for many years, reported that her behaviour had changed a little bit and that she had some strange ideas. Otherwise, the patient's memory was perfect, as was her conversation. She made jokes with her doctor, saying that he had been able to treat all her diseases, but that this time 'his science was powerless'. When she was asked about her present problem, she answered that she had backache, or that she suffered from an old phlebitis (this was indeed the case), but never complained about her upper limb, which was completely inert.

When she was invited to move her left arm, she either did not answer, or simply said 'OK, it's done'. When the possibility of electrotherapy was discussed in front of her, she passed this remark to her doctor, a few days after the consultation: 'Why do they intend to electrify me? I am not paralysed'.

The patient also showed a left anaesthesia and did not seem to perceive passive movements of the upper limb.

Both patients subsequently became demented and died.

Discussion

Babinski suggested a new term to denote the disorder and also mentioned a different, though related, type of impairment:

> It is, I think, permitted to use a neologism to design this state and term it 'anosognosia'.

> I also observed some hemiplegics who, without ignoring the existence of their paralysis, did not seem to attach much importance to it, as if it was a minor disease. A similar condition could be termed 'anosodiaphoria' (adiaphoria, indifference).

Babinski was apparently not aware of the cases previously reported by von Monakow, Anton, Pick, and Zingerle, which were not mentioned in his short communication. He cautiously attempted to interpret his observations:

> We could suppose that this ignorance of the patient, this anosognosia is false; we know that some patients, for coquetry, for self-indulgence, try to dissimulate their impairment, but, in the present case, this dissimulation is completely useless, because the presence of a paralysis cannot escape the attention of anybody. If it is an attempt to dissimulate, the patients' persistence is remarkable, because they have kept on playing the role they had decided to play for months, with no interruption.

> Do we have to admit by contrast that anosognosia is real? I am not able to state this, and it has been impossible for me to interrogate the patients in a sufficient way to be sure about this point. Indeed, in the two cases I have reported, the families considered this pathological condition as fortunate in some way and we were required to avoid any question which could disillusion the patients and disrupt their quietude. If it is real, deficits of sensation apparently play an important role in its genesis.

Finally, Babinski pointed out another main feature of anosognosia—the lateralisation of the deficit: 'In conclusion, I shall remark that the reported patients showed a left hemiplegia. Would anosognosia be specific to lesions occupying the right hemisphere?'

Babinski's report was followed by a discussion, in which the most distinguished French neurologists of the time took part. Apparently, other cases had been observed, but, again, the previous observations of unawareness of neurological deficits made by von Monakow, Anton, and Pick were not mentioned.

Souques briefly reported the case of a colleague who, probably after a stroke, developed a left hemiplegia with total hemianaesthesia. The patient, a very cultivated person, did not *appear* (Souques' italics) to exhibit intellectual deterioration. He was entirely lucid, interested in the newspapers, and his memory was not grossly defective, even though an in-depth examination was not performed. For at least one month the patient did not seem to have any notion of his hemiparesis. Even when the word 'hemiparesis' was mentioned, he did not seem to pay attention. Souques got the impression that the patient had 'a kind of forgetfulness of his left side'. Souques hypothesised that the somatosensory deficit could play a major role in the disorder. Déjérine shared this opinion. Pierre Marie pointed out that this symptom could also appear with different pathologies, such as urinary infections. Henri Meige, in addition to confirming that some patients with hemiplegia exhibit a sort of indifference towards the deficit, remarked that, after strength has recovered in some muscle groups, patients may persist in their inert state and do not execute movements, even though these have become possible again. It seems that nothing can be done to induce the patients to make spontaneous movements: 'Together with the transient impossibility of movement, any memory of function seems to have disappeared; it is as if the paralysed limbs had never existed. The hemiplegic *ignores* them.'

Meige mentioned that 10 years earlier (at the Septième Congrès de Médicine Interne, Paris, 1904) he had proposed the existence of 'motor functional amnesias' in hemiplegic patients, who appear to have forgotten the function of their paralysed limbs. This amnesia interferes with motor rehabilitation. Seneca (*loc. cit.*) had already noted that 'the reason why recovery is difficult is that we do not know we are affected with disease.' Meige concluded his comment, suggesting an interpretation of Babinski's cases in terms of 'anosognosia for motor functional amnesia'.

The final contributor to the discussion was Henry Claude, who suggested a specific sensory deficit, a topographical impairment:

I shall recall some modifications of sensation I observed in a subject ... who had a left hemiplegia with right apraxia. This man, whose intelligence was really well preserved, was unable to localise cutaneous stimuli; when he was pricked, he felt the stimulation, but always localised it in body parts far removed from the stimulated region. I have thought that, in this patient, it was a matter of a disturbance of the topographical representation of the different body parts, which I designated with the term topo-anaesthesia. It is possible that, also in the facts alluded to by Mr Babinski, there is a loss of the representation of the paralysed limb, to which the motor or psychomotor stimuli no longer draw attention.

1918–1924

Four years later, Babinski (1918), in a brief communication, recapitulated the main features of anosognosia stressing the role of the associated deficit of deep sensation (position sense), which, in his view, was likely to be a necessary condition, though not the complete explanation. Babinski provided some details about the patients' behaviour. Patients, when the examiner questioned them as to whether or not they had executed the command of raising the left (plegic) arm, either remained silent or replied 'yes'. Another patient, when the examiner pointed out that he had not fulfilled the order and that the arm was inert, answered: 'It's because it moves less quickly than the other'.

In the following discussion, Pierre Marie argued that there was no specific association between left hemiplegia and anosognosia, which was a manifestation of cerebral hemisyndromes, such as hemianaesthesia and hemianopia, provided the cerebral lesion was extensive enough to disrupt the sensory function concerned with the contralateral side of the body or half-field. Souques reported that in the patient mentioned in the 1914 discussion, anosognosia had disappeared completely in a few weeks, while hemianaesthesia had recovered only in part. According to Henry Meige, the associated somatosensory deficits played a relevant role, but could not entirely explain aspects of anosognosia, such as the indifference or lack of concern about hemiplegia shown by some patients.

In the following years Babinski's observations were confirmed by other French neurologists. Brief reports of anosognosia for left hemiplegia were read before the Société de Neurologie de Paris. Lutenbacher observed a patient with anosognosia for a transient hemiplegia (see Babinski, 1923). Barré, Morin, and Kaiser (1923) reported another patient, who also showed a severe deficit of position sense and allaesthesia, with tactile stimuli delivered to the left upper limb being perceived and reported, but localised in the right upper limb. When the patient's left hand was placed in the preserved right visual half-field and the examiner asked 'Whose is this hand?', the patient replied 'Yours'. Barré et al. (1923) also noted that the patients' behaviour suggested more than a mere unawareness of hemiplegia, but an obdurate resistance to acknowledging the deficit, which was even more puzzling, as intelligence was substantially preserved. Joltrain (1924) reported another patient with anosognosia for left hemiplegia, with no clinical evidence of confusional state, hallucinations, or memory disorders.

To summarise, the clinical observations by Babinski and other French neurologists, published in the *Revue Neurologique* between 1914 and 1924, comprised five main features of unawareness of hemiplegia, in addition to the novel names assigned to the varieties of the disorder (anosognosia and anosodiaphoria):

(1) General mental deterioration, confusional state, impairment of memory functions, or malingering could not explain anosognosia.

(2) Anosognosia for hemiplegia was not a manifestation of a more general unawareness of disease. When she was asked about her present problem, Babinski's (1914) patient #2 answered that she suffered from an old phlebitis, which was indeed the case.

(3) Somatosensory deficits, with particular reference to the associated impairment of position sense, were likely to play an important, though not exclusive, role.

(4) In all the reported patients, anosognosia concerned left hemiplegia, and was therefore associated with damage to the right cerebral hemisphere. No post-mortem pathological evidence concerning the localisation of the right hemisphere lesion was however presented.

(5) The manifestations of the disorder could differ in degree, ranging from *anosognosia* (complete unawareness or denial of hemiplegia) to anosodiaphoria (emotional indifference towards hemiplegia, which could be admitted without concern).

THE LEGACY OF BABINSKI

Babinski's clear, concise, and elegant reports had an enormous impact on the neurological literature, obscuring Pick's (1898) and Anton's (1899) early descriptions, even though anosognosia for hemiplegia is sometimes referred to as Anton-Babinski's syndrome (see Hécaen & Albert, 1978, p. 304). The style of Babinski's papers is very much in line with what we know about Babinski the man. As Critchley (1986, pp. 27–39) wrote: 'All writers make special mention of his taciturnity . . . If the history-taking was brief, not so the clinical examination. . . . Babinski's clinical technique was notable for his thoroughness, simplicity, and lucidity.' A review of the extensive literature on anosognosia is well beyond the aims of this chapter. The interested reader is referred to Critchley (1953), Weinstein and Kahn (1955), Frederiks (1969), Prigatano and Schacter (1991, with special reference to the chapter by Bisiach & Geminiani on anosognosia for hemiplegia), and McGlynn and Schacter (1989). In this concluding section we shall specifically focus on developments based on Babinski's original findings.

In the following years Babinksi's observations were confirmed by many investigators. In series of patients with unilateral brain lesions an association between damage to the right hemisphere and anosognosia for left hemiplegia was found, with some left brain-damaged patients showing anosognosia for right hemiplegia. The frequent association between somatosensory deficits (cutaneous sensation and position sense) and anosognosia was also confirmed (e.g. Cutting, 1978; Nathanson, Bergman, & Gordon, 1952; Von Hagen & Ives, 1937). Studies performed in large series of right brain-damaged patients however provided evidence to the effect that anosognosia for left hemiplegia may occur with no associated deficits in sensation for both touch (Bisiach, Vallar, Perani, Papagno, & Berti, 1986; Cutting, 1978; Willanger, Danielsen, & Ankerhus, 1981a) and position sense (Small & Ellis, 1996; Willanger et al., 1981a), confirming Pick's (1898) early finding. Conversely, patients with left-sided defects for touch and position sense may acknowledge the motor disorder. This pattern suggests that somatosensory deficits are neither a necessary nor a sufficient condition of anosognosia, which, in turn, is also unequivocally double-dissociated from extra-personal visuo-spatial unilateral neglect (Bisiach et al., 1986; Willanger, Danielsen, & Ankerhus, 1981b). Similarly, personal neglect or hemiasomatognosia is an independent disorder, which may occur in isolation, even though its association with anosognosia is frequent (Berti, Làdavas, & Della Corte, 1996; Berti, Làdavas, Stracciari, Giannarelli, & Ossola, 1998; Bisiach et al., 1986; Meador, Loring, Feinberg, Lee, & Nichols, 2000). Anosognosia for hemiplegia cannot therefore be interpreted as a manifestation of a more general disorder of the internal representation (image or schema) of the body (see Critchley, 1953; Gerstmann, 1942; Hécaen & Albert, 1978, pp. 303–307; Nielsen, 1946, pp. 82–85; Roth, 1949; Sandifer, 1946), as Henry Claude had suggested in the 1914 discussion (see also Vallar & Papagno, Chapter 11 of the current volume). Finally, the early clinical observations in individual patients that anosognosia for left hemiplegia may occur in the absence of general intellectual impairment or confusion (e.g. Gilliatt & Pratt, 1952) have been confirmed in series of right brain-damaged patients investigated through psychometric batteries (Berti et al., 1996; Levine, Calvanio, & Rinn, 1991; Small & Ellis, 1996).

Productive manifestations, such as delusional beliefs concerning the left side of the body (somatoparaphrenia, e.g. attributing ownership of the paralysed limb to another person) were reported in association with anosognosia (e.g. Cutting, 1978, for a group study; Gerstmann, 1942; Von Hagen & Ives, 1937, patient #1). The range of manifestations of disordered awareness of hemiplegia increased, including (in addition to Babinski's anosodiaphoria): misoplegia (excessive aversion towards the disabled limb, or 'hatred of paralysis', see Critchley, 1957, 1979, pp. 115–120); personification of paralysed limbs (often in the context of an euphoric pattern the patient has various nicknames for the paralysed limbs, see Critchley, 1955); anosognosic overestimation (the patient's tendency to overestimate the strength of the unaffected side of the body, focusing attention on it, see Frederiks, 1969).

The selectivity of the manifestations of the disorder was unequivocally revealed by observations such as patient #3 of Von Hagen and Ives (1937), who recognised that she was paralysed in the left upper limb, but always denied paralysis of the lower limb (see also Berti et al., 1996). Similarly Anton's (1899) patient Ursula Mercz denied blindness, but was aware of her mild dysphasia. One patient described by Gassel and Williams (1963) was acutely aware of the right hemiplegia, but not of right homonymous hemianopia.

More recently, these findings from studies in patients with permanent unilateral hemispheric damage have been confirmed and extended through a different experimental paradigm, the temporary dysfunction of one cerebral hemisphere produced by intracarotid barbiturate injection (Wada test). Gilmore, Heilman, Schmidt, Fennell, and Quisling (1992) reported that eight patients did not recall their left motor weakness after injection of amytal into their right carotid artery, but recalled their right hemiparesis and aphasia after left-sided injection. The authors concluded that the patients' defective memory for left-sided weakness was due to their never having been aware of it (see also Durkin, Meador, Nichols, Lee, & Loring, 1994). This study, however, differs from the clinical reports mentioned earlier in that awareness of hemiparesis was not assessed *during* hemispheric inactivation and the actual presence of the motor deficit. Adair, Gilmore, Fennel, Gold, and Heilman (1995a), in a subsequent experiment, investigated the role of amnesia versus unawareness of weakness: they found that the vast majority of their subjects questioned during and after right hemisphere anaesthesia demonstrated anosognosia for left hemiparesis in both assessments (24 out of 28 patients, 86%) and concluded that defective recall of left-sided weakness reflected a failure of awareness of disease, rather than a memory disorder. Converging evidence was obtained in a series of 31 patients by Carpenter et al. (1995), who also found that a general memory impairment could not constitute the factor underlying anosognosia for left hemiparesis. In nine patients they assessed awareness for arm weakness during left hemiparesis, finding anosognosia in five cases (related evidence in Adair et al., 1995a; Adair et al., 1995b). Finally, Carpenter et al. (1995) found that three out of the four other patients aware of left weakness following right hemisphere inactivation by amytal could not subsequently recall it, and concluded that the right hemisphere has a specific mnestic function for weakness of the contralateral arm, in addition to the gnostic function.

The specificity of the disorder was also further confirmed. Injection of amytal into the patients' left carotid artery may bring about anosognosia for right weakness, for dysphasia, or for both deficits (Breier et al., 1995). In many patients anosognosia for left hemiplegia is not associated with personal neglect (Adair et al., 1995b). These studies have also shown that anosognosia for left hemiplegia induced by the left-sided amytal injection is not systematically related to factors such as age, general intelligence, hemisphere of seizure focus, or temporal lobe pathology (Adair et al., 1995b; Carpenter et al., 1995).

A detailed discussion of the different explanations proposed to account for the phenomena of anosognosia for hemiplegia and other neurological and cognitive deficits is beyond the aims of this chapter (see McGlynn & Schacter, 1989, for reviews; Prigatano & Schacter, 1991). In addition, Babinski did not offer any explicit interpretation of anosognosia, focusing instead on its clinical presentation. However, noting the absence or presence of other disorders, he cautiously ruled out interpretations in terms of a general cognitive impairment and raised the possibility that somatosensory deficits, with particular reference to the impairment of position sense, played a special role. Critchley's (1986, p. 38) critical remark that Babinski provided only 'simple descriptive accounts' of anosognosic phenomena is not an entirely balanced evaluation of his observations.

These clinical and experimental studies in neurological patients with both unilateral lesions and temporary hemispheric dysfunctions concur to suggest that anosognosia for left hemiplegia is a deficit of a specific right hemisphere-based monitoring function. Explanations in terms of a mode of adaptation to the stress caused by the disease (Schilder, 1935; Weinstein & Kahn, 1955), and of associated somatosensory (proprioceptive) and intellectual impairments (Levine, 1990; Levine et al., 1991) are made unlikely by a number of facts, including the following:

(1) There is a hemispheric asymmetry for anosognosia for hemiplegia, which is more frequent after dysfunction of the right cerebral hemisphere.

(2) In some patients anosognosic phenomena are selective (e.g. unawareness of hemiplegia but not of aphasia and vice versa).

(3) Anosognosia on the one hand, and the putatively associated responsible factors (general cognitive impairment, somatosensory deficits, hemiasomatognosia or personal neglect) on the other, do not necessarily co-occur.

(4) Vestibular stimulation, a manoeuvre which may temporarily improve a number of manifestations of the syndrome of spatial unilateral neglect (review in Vallar, Guariglia, & Rusconi, 1997b; Rossetti & Rode, 2002), including left-sided somatosensory deficits (Vallar, Bottini, Rusconi, & Sterzi, 1993; Vallar, Bottini, Sterzi, Passerini, & Rusconi, 1991; Vallar, Sterzi, Bottini, Cappa, & Rusconi, 1990), also ameliorates anosognosia for left hemiplegia (Cappa, Sterzi, Vallar, & Bisiach, 1987; Rode et al., 1992; Vallar et al., 1990). These observations suggest that the neural processes defective in anosognosia for left motor weakness, and in other aspects of the syndrome of spatial unilateral neglect, are modulated in a similar fashion by specific sensory inputs (see the discussion in Vallar et al., 1997b).

This set of empirical observations supports interpretations in terms of the dysfunction of specific monitoring processes, which may produce anosognosia for neurological disorders such as hemiplegia and hemianopia (see Berti et al., 1996; Berti et al., 1998; Bisiach & Geminiani, 1991). According to a different, though related, view, damage to a 'posterior' (inferior parietal) conscious awareness system (CAS) may bring about anosognosia for perceptual and motor deficits, while disconnections of this CAS from particular input modules may result in specific forms of anosognosia (see Berti et al., 1998 for a critical discussion of the CAS hypothesis; McGlynn & Schacter, 1989). An early neurologically based hypothesis had been put forward by Geschwind (1965), who suggested an interpretation of anosognosic phenomena in terms of disconnection from the speech areas of the left hemisphere: in the case of anosognosia for left hemiplegia, a right–left interhemispheric disconnection. However, manoeuvres such as placing the left arm in the unaffected right half-space, where sensory processing is mainly performed by the left hemisphere, do not consistently induce a remission of anosognosia (Adair et al., 1995a; Adair et al., 1997). Accounts of anosognosia for left hemiplegia in terms of interruption of the flow of information to the left hemisphere do not appear at present to be supported by the available empirical evidence.

A final note about Babinski's observation and its developments concerns a comment made by Henry Meige in the 1914 discussion. Meige, as mentioned earlier, had proposed the existence of *'amnésies motrices fonctionnelles'* in hemiplegic patients, who appear to have forgotten the function of their paralysed limbs and, even after strength has recovered, persist in their inert state and do not execute movements, though these have become possible again. This is an early description of the 'motor neglect' (*'négligence motrice'* in the French neurological literature) component deficit of the neglect syndrome, whereby patients fail to execute movements with the contralesional limbs, though strength is not disproportionately reduced (Castaigne, Laplane, & Degos, 1970; Castaigne, Laplane, & Degos, 1972; Critchley, 1953; Garcin, Varay, & Hadji-Dimo, 1938; Mark, Heilman, & Watson, 1996, for a terminological discussion). Motor neglect, as anosognosia, is more frequent following damage to the right hemisphere (Barbieri & De Renzi, 1989; Coslett & Heilman, 1989).

Heilman and his co-workers (Gold, Adair, Jacobs, & Heilman, 1994, for an empirical verification; Heilman, 1991) proposed an interpretation of anosognosia for hemiplegia as a loss of motor intention. According to their feedforward hypothesis, because patients with anosognosia for hemiplegia do not attempt to move their paretic limbs, there is no expectancy of movement and no mismatch between expectation and actual performance, resulting in unawareness of the motor deficit. Heilman's hypothesis resembles Meige's account in that, according to both views, patients with anosognosia for left motor deficits are reluctant to move their left limbs, due to a higher order, non-primarily motor, disorder: 'motor functional amnesia' in Meige's terminology, defective motor intention according to Heilman and his co-workers.

Three recent studies have shown that the left-sided motor weakness of right brain-damaged patients is temporarily improved by optokinetic (Vallar, Guariglia, Nico, & Pizzamiglio, 1997a) and vestibular (Rode et al., 1992; Rode, Perenin, Honoré, & Boisson, 1998) stimulations, as well as other components of the neglect syndrome (review in Vallar et al., 1997b; Rossetti & Rode, 2002). These results provide empirical support to Meige's early suggestion that a non-primarily motor disorder, which may be provisionally referred to as a manifestation of 'motor neglect' or of a deficit of 'intention' or 'pre-motor' planning, contributes to the left-sided weakness (see also Sterzi et al., 1993, for a similar conclusion drawn on the basis of a community-based epidemiological survey).

In patients in whom the left motor weakness reflects, at least in part, a higher order dysfunction, anosognosia may also be considered as an intrinsic component of their intentional or 'motor neglect' disorder. Seen in this perspective, patients may be unaware of their defective intention to execute movements with the contralesional limbs, rather than of a primary motor deficit *per se*, in the same way as they are unaware of their personal (hemiasomatognosia) or extra-personal (e.g. visuo-spatial) unilateral neglect. As Henry Meige put it in the 1914 discussion, the patients may suffer from '*anosognosie par amnésie motrice fonctionnelle*'. In addition, as Heilman and his colleagues suggest, a defective intention to execute motor acts (or a motor amnesia) would prevent the activation of the motor system, as well as the probing of its normal or disordered (in patients with left motor weakness) function. Accordingly, a primary motor disorder would not be detected by monitoring processes. In other patients, however, in whom the motor neglect component (as revealed, for instance, by sensory stimulation) is comparatively minor, anosognosia for hemiplegia may mainly result from the disordered operation of a system specifically devoted to the monitoring of motor function.

The precise interpretation of anosognosic phenomena remains controversial and a matter of lively theoretical debate and empirical research. The clinical facts perspicaciously detected and so clearly reported by Josef François Babinski are still before us, however, over 80 years later.

ACKNOWLEDGEMENTS

This work has been supported in part by grants from the Consiglio Nazionale delle Ricerche, the Ministero dell'Università e della Ricerca Scientifica e Tecnologica, and the Ministero della Sanità. We are grateful to Claus-W. Wallesch for his suggestions and comments.

REFERENCES

Adair, J.C., Gilmore, R.L., Fennell, E.B., Gold, M., & Heilman, K.M. (1995a). Anosognosia during intracarotid barbiturate anesthesia: Unawareness or amnesia for weakness. *Neurology*, *45*, 241–243.

Adair, J.C., Na, D.L., Schwartz, R.L., Fennell, E.M., Gilmore, R.L., & Heilman, K.M. (1995b). Anosognosia for hemiplegia: Test of the personal neglect hypothesis. *Neurology*, *45*, 2195–2199.

Adair, J.C., Schwartz, R.L., Na, D.L., Fennell, E., Gilmore, R.L., & Heilman, K.M. (1997). Anosognosia: Examining the disconnection hypothesis. *Journal of Neurology, Neurosurgery, and Psychiatry*, *63*, 798–800.

Anton, G. (1893). Beiträge zur klinischen Beurtheilung und zur Localisation der Muskelsinnstörungen im Grosshirne. *Zeitschrift für Heilkunde*, *14*, 313–348.

Anton, G. (1898). Über Herderkrankungen des Gehirnes, welche vom Patienten selbst nicht wahrgenommen werden. *Wiener klinische Wochenschrift*, *11*, 227–229.

Anton, G. (1899). Über die Selbstwahrnehmung der Herderkrankungen des Gehirns durch den Kranken bei Rindenblindheit und Rindentaubheit. *Archiv für Psychiatrie und Nervenkrankheiten*, *32*, 86–127.

Babinski, J. (1914). Contribution à l'étude des troubles mentaux dans l'hémiplégie organique cérébrale. *Revue Neurologique (Paris)*, *27*, 845–848.

Babinski, J. (1918). Anosognosie. *Revue Neurologique (Paris)*, *31*, 365–367.

Babinski, J. (1923). Sur l'anosognosie. *Revue Neurologique (Paris)*, *39*, 731–732.

Barbieri, C., & De Renzi, E. (1989). Patterns of neglect dissociation. *Behavioural Neurology*, *2*, 13–24.

Barré, J. A., Morin, L., & Kaiser. (1923). Etude clinique d'un nouveau cas d'anosognosie. *Revue Neurologique*, *39*, 500–503.

Berti, A., Làdavas, E., & Della Corte, M. (1996). Anosognosia for hemiplegia, neglect dyslexia and drawing neglect: Clinical findings and theoretical considerations. *Journal of the International Neuropsychological Society*, *2*, 426–440.

Berti, A., Làdavas, E., Stracciari, A., Giannarelli, C., & Ossola, A. (1998). Anosognosia for motor impairment and dissociations with patients' evaluation of the disorder: theoretical considerations. *Cognitive Neuropsychiatry*, *3*, 21–44.

Bisiach, E., & Geminiani, G. (1991). Anosognosia related to hemiplegia and hemianopia. In G.P. Prigatano & D.L. Schacter (Eds.), *Awareness of deficit after brain injury* (p.p. 17–39). New York: Oxford University Press.

Bisiach, E., Vallar, G., Perani, D., Papagno, C., & Berti, A. (1986). Unawareness of disease following lesions of the right hemisphere: Anosognosia for hemiplegia and anosognosia for hemianopia. *Neuropsychologia*, *24*, 471–482.

Breier, J.I., Adair, J.C., Gold, M., Fennell, E.B., Gilmore, R.L., & Heilman, K.M. (1995). Dissociation of anosognosia for hemiplegia and aphasia during left hemisphere anesthesia. *Neurology*, *45*, 65–67.

Cappa, S., Sterzi, R., Vallar, G., & Bisiach, E. (1987). Remission of hemineglect and anosognosia during vestibular stimulation. *Neuropsychologia*, *25*, 775–782.

Carpenter, K., Berti, A., Oxbury, S., Molyneux, A.J., Bisiach, E., & Oxbury, J.M. (1995). Awareness of and memory for arm weakness during intracarotid sodium amytal testing. *Brain*, *118*, 243–251.

Castaigne, P., Laplane, D., & Degos, J.-D. (1970). Trois cas de négligence motrice par lésion rétro-rolandique. *Revue Neurologique (Paris)*, *122*, 234–242.

Castaigne, P., Laplane, D., & Degos, J.-D. (1972). Trois cas de négligence motrice par lésion frontale pré-rolandique. *Revue Neurologique (Paris)*, *126*, 5–15.

Coslett, H.B., & Heilman, K.M. (1989). Hemihypokinesia after right hemisphere stroke. *Brain and Cognition*, *9*, 267–278.

Critchley, M. (1953). *The parietal lobes*. New York: Hafner.

Critchley, M. (1955). Personification of paralysed limbs in hemiplegics. *British Medical Journal, 2*, 284–286.

Critchley, M. (1957). Observations on anosodiaphoria. *L'encéphale, 46*, 541–546.

Critchley, M. (1979). *The divine banquet of the brain and other essays*. New York: Raven Press.

Critchley, M. (1986). *The citadel of the senses and other essays*. New York: Raven Press.

Cutting, J. (1978). Study of anosognosia. *Journal of Neurology, Neurosurgery, and Psychiatry, 41*, 548–555.

Durkin, M.W., Meador, K.J., Nichols, M.E., Lee, G.P., & Loring, D.W. (1994). Anosognosia and the intracarotid amobarbital procedure (Wada test). *Neurology, 44*, 978.

Frederiks, J.A.M. (1969). Disorders of the body schema. In P.J. Vinken & G.W. Bruyn (Eds.), *Handbook of clinical neurology. Disorders of speech, perception and symbolic behaviour* (Vol. 4, pp. 207–240). Amsterdam: North Holland.

Garcin, R., Varay, A., & Hadji-Dimo. (1938). Document pour servir à l'étude des troubles du schéma corporel (sur quelques phénomènes moteurs, gnosiques et quelques troubles de l'utilisation des membres du côté gauche au cours d'un syndrome temporo-pariétal par tumeur, envisagés dans leurs rapports avec l'anosognosie et les troubles du schéma corporel). *Revue Neurologique (Paris), 69*, 498–510.

Gassel, M.M., & Williams, D. (1963). Visual function in patients with homonymous hemianopia. Part III. The completion phenomenon; insight and attitude to the defect; and visual functional efficiency. *Brain, 86*, 229–260.

Gerstmann, J. (1942). Problem of imperception of disease and of impaired body territories with organic lesions. *Archives of Neurology and Psychiatry, 48*, 890–913.

Geschwind, N. (1965). Disconnexion syndromes in animals and man. Part II. *Brain, 88*, 585–644.

Gilliatt, R.W., & Pratt, R.T.C. (1952). Disorders of perception and performance in a case of right-sided cerebral thrombosis. *Journal of Neurology, Neurosurgery, and Psychiatry, 15*, 264–271.

Gilmore, R.L., Heilman, K.M., Schmidt, R.P., Fennell, E. M., & Quisling, R. (1992). Anosognosia during Wada testing. *Neurology, 42*, 925–927.

Gold, M., Adair, J.C., Jacobs, D.H., & Heilman, K.M. (1994). Anosognosia for hemiplegia: An electrophysiologic investigation of the feed-forward hypothesis. *Neurology, 44*, 1804–1808.

Hécaen, H., & Albert, M.L. (1978). *Human neuropsychology*. New York: John Wiley.

Heilman, K.M. (1991). Anosognosia: Possible neuropsychological mechanisms. In G.P. Prigatano & D.L. Schacter (Eds.), *Awareness of deficit after brain injury* (pp. 53–62). New York: Oxford University Press.

Joltrain, E. (1924). Un nouveau cas d'anosognosie. *Revue Neurologique, 42*, 638–340.

Levine, D.N. (1990). Unawareness of visual and sensorimotor defects: A hypothesis. *Brain and Cognition, 13*, 233–281.

Levine, D.N., Calvanio, R., & Rinn, W.E. (1991). The pathogenesis of anosognosia for hemiplegia. *Neurology, 41*, 1770–1781.

Mark, V.W., Heilman, K.M., & Watson, R. (1996). Motor neglect: What do we mean? *Neurology, 46*, 1492–1493.

McGlynn, S.M., & Schacter, D.L. (1989). Unawareness of deficits in neuropsychological syndromes. *Journal of Clinical and Experimental Neuropsychology, 11*, 143–205.

Meador, K.J., Loring, D.W., Feinberg, T.E., Lee, G.P., & Nichols, M.E. (2000). Anosognosia and asomatognosia during intracarotid amobarbital inactivation. *Neurology, 55*, 816–820.

Nathanson, M., Bergman, P.S., & Gordon, G.G. (1952). Denial of illness. *Archives of Neurology and Psychiatry, 68*, 380–387.

Nielsen, J.M. (1946). *Agnosia, apraxia, and their value in cerebral localization* (2nd ed.). New York: Hafner.

Pick, A. (1898). *Über allgemeine Gedächtnisschwäche als unmittelbare Folge cerebraler*

Herderkrankung. Beiträge zur Pathologie und Pathologische Anatomie des Centralnervensystems mit Bemerkungen zur normalen Anatomie desselben. Berlin: Karger.

Prigatano, G.P., & Schacter, D.L. (Eds.) (1991). *Awareness of deficit after brain injury: Clinical and theoretical issues.* Oxford: Oxford University Press.

Rode, G., Charles, N., Perenin, M.T., Vighetto, A., Trillet, M., & Aimard, G. (1992). Partial remission of hemiplegia and somatoparaphrenia through vestibular stimulation in a case of unilateral neglect. *Cortex, 28,* 203–208.

Rode, G., Perenin, M.T., Honoré, J., & Boisson, D. (1998). Improvement of the motor deficit of neglect patients through vestibular stimulation: Evidence for a motor neglect component. *Cortex, 34,* 253–261.

Rossetti, Y., & Rode, G. (2002). Reducing spatial neglect by visual and other sensory manipulations: Non-cognitive (physiological) routes to the rehabilitation of a cognitive disorder. In H.-O. Karnath, A.D. Milner, & G. Vallar (Eds.), *The cognitive and neural bases of spatial neglect.* Oxford: Oxford University Press.

Roth, M. (1949). Disorders of the body image caused by lesions of the right parietal lobe. *Brain, 72,* 89–111.

Sandifer, P.H. (1946). Anosognosia and disorders of body scheme. *Brain, 69,* 122–137.

Schilder, P. (1935). *The image and appearance of the human body.* New York: International Universities Press.

Small, M., & Ellis, S. (1996). Denial of hemiplegia: An investigation into the theories of causation. *European Neurology, 36,* 353–363.

Sterzi, R., Bottini, G., Celani, M.G., Righetti, E., Lamassa, M., Ricci, S., & Vallar, G. (1993). Hemianopia, hemianaesthesia, and hemiplegia after left and right hemisphere damage: A hemispheric difference. *Journal of Neurology, Neurosurgery, and Psychiatry, 56,* 308–310.

Vallar, G., Bottini, G., Rusconi, M.L., & Sterzi, R. (1993). Exploring somatosensory hemineglect by vestibular stimulation. *Brain, 116,* 71–86.

Vallar, G., Bottini, G., Sterzi, R., Passerini, D., & Rusconi, M.L. (1991). Hemianesthesia, sensory neglect, and defective access to conscious experience. *Neurology, 41,* 650–652.

Vallar, G., Guariglia, C., Nico, D., & Pizzamiglio, L. (1997a). Motor deficits and optokinetic stimulation in patients with left hemineglect. *Neurology, 49,* 1364–1370.

Vallar, G., Guariglia, C., & Rusconi, M.L. (1997b). Modulation of the neglect syndrome by sensory stimulation. In P. Thier & H.-O. Karnath (Eds.), *Parietal lobe contributions to orientation in 3D space* (pp. 555–578). Heidelberg: Springer-Verlag.

Vallar, G., Sterzi, R., Bottini, G., Cappa, S., & Rusconi, M.L. (1990). Temporary remission of left hemianaesthesia after vestibular stimulation. *Cortex, 26,* 123–131.

Von Hagen, K.O., & Ives, E.R. (1937). Anosognosia (Babinski), imperception of hemiplegia. *Bulletin of the Los Angeles Neurological Society, 2,* 95–103.

von Monakow, C. (1885). Experimentelle und pathologisch-anatomische Untersuchungen über die Beziehungen der sogenannten Sehsphäre zu den infracorticalen Opticuscentren und zum N. opticus. *Archiv für Psychiatrie und Nervenkrankheiten, 16,* 151–199.

Weinstein, E.A., & Kahn, R.L. (1955). *Denial of illness: Symbolic and physiological aspects.* Springfield, IL: Charles C. Thomas.

Willanger, R., Danielsen, U.T., & Ankerhus, J. (1981a). Denial and neglect of hemiparesis in right-sided apoplectic lesions. *Acta Neurologica Scandinavica, 64,* 310–326.

Willanger, R., Danielsen, U.T., & Ankerhus, J. (1981b). Visual neglect in right-sided apoplectic lesions. *Acta Neurologica Scandinavica, 64,* 327–336.

Zingerle, H. (1913). Über Störungen der Wahrnehmung des eigenen Körpers bei organischen Gehirnerkrankungen. *Monatsschrift für Psychiatrie und Neurologie, 34,* 13–36.

CHAPTER THIRTEEN

Friedrich Best's case Z with misidentification of object orientation

Susanne Ferber and Hans-Otto Karnath
Department of Cognitive Neurology, University of Tübingen, Germany

INTRODUCTION

In 1917, the German ophthalmologist Friedrich Best[1] published in *Von Graefe's Archiv für Ophthalmologie* a report on 38 brain-damaged patients with visual field defects due to gunshot wounds or grenade splinters. Working in a field hospital close to the front line, Best saw the patients within days of their being wounded and observed them for the next two to four weeks during the course of their disease. The aim of his study was to describe the neuropathology and symptomatology of hemianopia in full detail. Best basically included patients with retrorolandic lesions affecting the primary visual cortex, the optic radiation, or the lateral geniculate body. His description offers a valuable insight into the attempts to understand the nature of symptoms associated with visual field defects at the beginning of the 20th century.

In the first part of his report, Best explains some problems of measuring the visual field in patients with hemianopia, describes the autopsy findings in selected patients and gives an overview of contemporary theories about the cerebral location of the macula. Best's main focus was the study of disturbances of visual localisation. He viewed the occipital lobes as essential for localising an object in space with respect to the body. Therefore, he expected to find disturbances in line bisection and in pointing tasks. He found that only patients with complete unilateral homonymous hemianopia show the typical bisection error previously described by Axenfeld (1894) and Liepmann and Kalmus (1900) with the longer segment of the line in the unaffected hemifield, whereas patients with incomplete or bilateral visual field cuts bisect lines atypically with the longer segment in the blind hemifield. Additionally, Best was interested in studying visual agnosia (*Seelenblindheit*), agraphia, and alexia. Moreover, he was concerned with the question of whether patients are able to identify several objects simultaneously. In addition, Best tested whether or not reflexive eye movements are affected by visual field defects.

CASE Z

At the end of the section on visual localisation, Best describes one patient in more detail. Case 38, named Z, suffered a gunshot wound through the head 34 days before he was first seen by Best. Z's visual fields could not be precisely determined because he could not maintain fixation. Still, Best estimated that 40° in all directions were spared. Z had no alteration in size perception (dysmetropsia) and no visual hallucinations. While his writing was not affected, the patient was not able to read more than single letters. Z had no visual object agnosia; he easily recognised any stimuli presented to him. However, once Z moved his eyes from the stimulus, it took him a long time to find it again, leading to difficulties in describing the stimuli in more detail. Z had no problems in colour perception, but when two or more colours were presented simultaneously, Z could not recognise them at the same time. When different colours were presented horizontally, he reported only the rightmost colour. When different colours were vertically arranged, Z found only the one at the top. Best made the same observation with stimuli other than colours. Z was always aware of only one of several simultaneously presented items. Best did not use a specific term for these latter observations but one probably has to interpret them as simultanagnosia.

Further, Best conducted some mental imagery tasks. While Z could recall his house or faces of his relatives, he could not remember certain parts of the topography of his home town. Moreover, he was not able to picture in his mind the place where he had been wounded. Best interpreted this deficit as a loss of mental imagery for spatial locations and recent events whereas mental imagery for colours and earlier events was spared.

In another experiment, Best tested for visual and auditory localisation of objects with respect to the body. He presented objects and sounds left, right, above, or below Z's body. The patient was not able to report verbally the location of visual stimuli with respect to his body, and his errors were unsystematic, indicating that he suffered from a complete loss of visual egocentric localisation. Interestingly, he was able to determine verbally the location of sounds with respect to his body and he correctly reported the locations of pressure phosphenes. In contrast, when pointing to objects he usually pointed too low and his gaze accordingly deviated downwards. Moreover, Z was not able to determine the direction of movements of objects.

To summarize, Z had no visual agnosia, no difficulties in size perception, no agraphia, and no disturbances of colour perception, but he was not able to locate objects correctly with respect to his body, he could not determine the direction of movement, and he showed a deficit of mental imagery for spatial locations. Moreover, he suffered from simultanagnosia, optic ataxia, and deficits of exploratory eye movements. Thus, one may cautiously conclude that Z exhibited a combination of symptoms that has been termed 'Balint Syndrome' occurring with bilateral parieto-occipital lesions (Balint, 1909; Rafal, 1997).

Z's object orientation agnosia. In addition to these disturbances, Best made a further, peculiar observation in patient Z. He presented figures, pictures of persons (e.g. the German emperor at that time; see Figure 13.1), and other stimuli either in their canonical upright orientations or rotated through 180°. Z was able to recognise any stimuli presented to him even when they were oriented upside down. In sharp contrast, he was not able to determine the orientations of these stimuli. When Best presented a hand pointing up, down, left, or right, Z could identify the hand but was not able to judge the direction of pointing. Accordingly, when Best presented letters, Z could not differentiate between the letter 'n' and the letter 'u'. Training of the tasks did not improve Z's deficit.

At the fourth day of testing, Z developed a fever. In spite of repeated draining of right-sided abscesses his condition deteriorated. Soon he could no longer move his left arm or leg. Six days later the patient died. According to the autopsy, the point of entry of the projectile affected the upper portion of the left angular gyrus (Figure 13.2). The medial exit of the projectile was in the precuneus. The medial point of entry of the projectile into the right hemisphere was again the precuneus, affecting the parieto-occipital sulcus. The lateral exit of the projectile was slightly above the right angular gyrus in the posterior part of the inferior parietal lobule. Along the path of the bullet through the right hemisphere, an abscess was found that nearly extended to the corpus callosum and the lateral ventricle. In addition, purulent meningitis of the right convexity was discovered.

Figure 13.1   Picture of the German emperor, Wilhelm II, *presented upside down.*

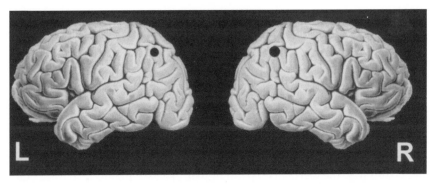

Figure 13.2   Reconstruction of Z's brain lesion according to the autopsy findings.

INTERPRETING Z AND LATER CASES

Although there remain uncertainties concerning the interpretation of the various observations in Z, Best described a clear dissociation in this patient between a preserved knowledge of object identity and an impaired sense of object orientation. Since this classical investigation, six further patients showing the same dissociation have been reported. Solms, Kaplan-Solms, Saling, and Miller (1988) asked a patient (WB) with bifrontal abscesses and episodes of inverted vision to sort letters according to whether they were presented in their upright orientation or inverted through 180°. Although WB could read and identify the letters in both orientations, he incorrectly classified their orientation in 35% of the upright presented and in 82% of the inverted stimuli. A comparable observation was reported from a patient with bilateral parieto-occipital lesions (Robertson, Treisman, Friedman-Hill, & Grabowecky, 1997). The authors presented two letters either upright or inverted. While patient RM correctly named the letters on every trial except one, he incorrectly classified their orientation in 14% of the upright presented and in 64% of the inverted stimuli. Turnbull, Laws, and McCarthy (1995) and Turnbull, Beschin, and Della Sala (1997) reported three further cases. One patient (LG) suffered from multiple strokes emanating from an arterio-venous malformation in the right temporo-parietal region; the other two patients had strokes in the right parietal (NL) and the right temporo-parietal area (SC). When the patients were asked to indicate the canonical upright orientation of those objects that they perfectly identified in any of four possible orientations (0°, −90°, +90°, 180°), the three patients performed 57%, 53%, and 13% incorrect orientation judgements. Karnath, Ferber, and Bülthoff (2000) studied a patient (KB) suffering from an old left frontal lesion and new strokes involving bilaterally the parieto-occipital region. They presented pictures of letters, objects, animals, and faces with unambiguous canonical upright orientations in four different orientations (0°, −90°, +90°,

180°). KB showed no impairment in identifying the stimuli irrespective of their given orientation. In sharp contrast, she was not able to judge the orientation when the stimuli were presented in a non-upright orientation.

Of some of these patients it was reported that they rotated objects by 90° or 180° in copying (Solms et al., 1988; Turnbull et al., 1995, 1997) or in writing with wooden letters (Karnath et al., 2000). Rotational errors in copying tasks were observed in even more patients suffering from cortical lesions but, unfortunately, their knowledge of object orientation and object recognition was not formally compared (Pillon, 1981; Solms, Turnbull, Kaplan-Solms, & Miller, 1998; Turnbull, 1996).

Best (1917) interpreted Z's discrepant ability between determining object orientation and identifying these objects as a kind of 'agnosia' and as evidence that the brain can achieve object recognition without viewer-centred information—i.e. without knowledge of the orientation of the object with respect to the subject. He wrote: 'This case demonstrates that the neural centres for processing the spatial features of visual objects are sharply separated from those centres that process the recognition of all other features of these objects' (p.122). With reference to Z's autopsy, he stated that the centre for processing object orientation is localised in the precuneus and adjacent parts of the superior parietal lobule on the hemisphere's medial surface.

Turnbull et al. (1995, 1997) interpreted the phenomenon quite similarly to Best (1917). The authors likewise assumed an orientation-dependent and an orientation-independent route to object recognition in humans. They argued that this view can be accommodated within the two visual systems account of Milner and Goodale (1995). The latter assumed a ventral and a dorsal stream of processing information about the properties of objects and their spatial locations. While the dorsal stream provides the instantaneous and egocentric features of objects, the ventral stream permits the formation of perceptual and cognitive representations that embody the enduring characteristics of objects. Turnbull and co-workers (1995) interpreted the observation of normal object recognition with an impaired sense of object orientation as an operation mediated via the view-independent ventral stream in the absence of the dorsal stream that carries orientation information. Accordingly, the patients showing this dissociation have been considered as agnosic for object orientation.

The interpretation given by Best and by Turnbull and colleagues corresponds with viewpoint-invariant theories of object recognition. These hold that the mental representations of previously seen objects are stored in object-centred frames of references based on the objects' geometry (Corballis, 1988; Marr & Nishihara, 1978). According to these theories, object recognition does not require mental transformations to align the respective image of an object with a represented view of it. The latter has been assumed by viewpoint-dependent theories of object recognition. These theories hold that the mental representations of previously seen objects are stored in a viewer-centred frame of reference determined by the location of the viewer in relation to the object. Accordingly, objects might be recognised by interpolating between previously seen and stored views (Bülthoff & Edelman, 1992) or by transforming the input and/or the stored view (Shepard & Cooper, 1982; Tarr, 1995).

Support for the notion of a distributed view-based representation of objects in which neurons become tuned to the features present in certain views of an object comes from the study of patient KB (Karnath et al., 2000). The results argue that patients with normal object recognition but with misidentification of object orientation are *not* generally agnosic for object orientation. When KB's abilities to perceive objects' canonical upright versus non-upright orientations were directly contrasted using a forced choice paradigm, the authors found that her knowledge of upright orientation was perfectly preserved but she was not able to judge orientation when the stimuli were presented in a non-upright orientation—i.e. when they were tilted by –90°, +90°, or 180°. These data showed that beyond the obvious discrepancy between the ability to identify objects and to determine their orientation, there was also a discrepancy between the knowledge of upright orientation versus non-upright orientation of objects. Although not systematically tested, observations in the previously studied patients have been reported indicating that these patients, like KB, also were able to gain access to at least some information about objects' canonical upright position.

Thus, it seems that the patients' ability to determine the objects' upright orientation is more robust against neuronal damage than the ability to determine non-upright orientations. This finding of preserved knowledge of upright orientation of objects contradicts Best's (1917) and Turnbull et al.'s (1995, 1997) view of an absence of a neural system that selectively processes orientation information of objects, and argues against their interpretation of a general 'agnosia for object orientation' in these cases. The observation that the patients demonstrate a weakness or inability to determine an object's orientation specifically when that object is presented in a non-upright orientation rather supports the thesis of Perrett, Oram, and Ashbridge (1998) that one does not need mental rotation to recognise familiar objects in non-canonical orientations. Perrett and colleagues proposed that objects are represented by neurons tuned to view, orientation, and size and that the number of tuned neurons for a particular orientation depends on the amount of experience with it. Since most natural objects are oriented in a gravity-based upright orientation we can assume that many more neurons are recruited to code an object in that orientation. Karnath and co-workers (2000) argued that this numerical bias is sufficient to explain why the patients with impaired sense of object orientation were not generally agnosic for object orientation but rather showed a dissociation between their knowledge of objects' canonical upright orientation and their ability to perceive objects' orientation in non-upright positions. A larger number of neurons tuned for upright orientation would predict that the perception of objects' canonical upright orientation is more robust against neuronal damage or may recover earlier than knowledge of other orientations.

Our ability to recognise objects from many viewpoints is remarkable. The questions of how object recognition copes with changes in view, scale, and orientation and how such processes are represented in the human brain are relevant to various fields of cognitive neuroscience. To conclude, it seems that Best's observation of a dissociation between normal object recognition but impaired sense of object orientation in a patient with bilateral parietal lesions (Best, 1917) opened a new field in human neuropsychology that promises to contribute helpful new insights to our understanding of the neurobiological and the cognitive mechanisms of object recognition.

REFERENCES

Axenfeld, D. (1894). Eine einfache Methode Hemianopsie zu constatiren. *Neurologisches Centralblatt, 13*, 437–439.

Bálint, R. (1909). Seelenlähmung des 'Schauens', optische Ataxie, räumliche Störung der Aufmerksamkeit. *Monatsschrift für Psychiatrie und Neurologie, 25*, 51–81.

Best, F. (1917). Hemianopsie und Seelenblindheit bei Hirnverletzungen. *v. Graefes Archiv für Ophthalmologie, 93*, 49–150.

Bülthoff, H.H, & Edelman, S. (1992). Psychophysical support for a 2-D view interpolation theory of object recognition. *Proceedings of the National Academy of Science, 89*, 60–64.

Corballis, M.C. (1998). Recognition of disoriented shapes. *Psychological Review, 95*, 115–123.

Karnath, H-O., Ferber, S., & Bülthoff, H.H. (2000). Neuronal representation of object orientation. *Neuropsychologia, 38*, 1235–1241.

Liepmann, H., & Kalmus, E. (1900). Ueber eine Augenmassstörung bei Hemianopikern. *Berliner Klinische Wochenschrift, 38*, 838–842.

Marr, D., & Nishihara, H.K. (1978). Representation and recognition of the spatial organisation of three-dimensional shapes. *Proceedings of the Royal Society of London, B200*, 269–294.

Milner, A.D., & Goodale, M.A. (1995). *The visual brain in action.* Oxford: Oxford University Press.

Perrett, D.I., Oram, M.W., & Ashbridge, E. (1998). Evidence accumulation in cell populations responsive to faces: An account of generalisation of recognition without mental transformations. *Cognition, 67*, 111–145.

Pillon, B. (1981). Troubles visuo-constructifs et methodes de compensation: Resultats de 85 patients atteints de lesions cerebrales. *Neuropsychologia, 19*, 375–383.

Rafall, R.D. (1997). Balint syndrome. In T.E. Feinberg & M.J. Farah (Eds.), *Behavioral neurology and neuropsychology.* New York: McGraw-Hill.

Robertson, L., Treisman, A., Friedman-Hill, S., & Grabowecky, M. (1997). The interaction of spatial and object pathways: Evidence from Balint's syndrome. *Journal of Cognitive Neuroscience, 9*, 295–317.

Shepard, R.N., & Cooper, L.A. (1982). *Mental images and their transformations.* Cambridge, MA: MIT Press.

Solms, M., Kaplan-Solms, K., Saling, M., & Miller, P. (1988). Inverted vision after frontal lobe disease. *Cortex, 24*, 499–509.

Solms, M., Turnbull, O.H., Kaplan-Solms, K., & Miller, P. (1998). Rotated drawing: The range of performance and anatomical correlates in a series of 16 patients. *Brain and Cognition*, *38*, 358–368.

Tarr, M.J. (1995). Rotating objects to recognise them: A case study on the role of viewpoint dependency in the recognition of three-dimensional objects. *Psychonomic Bulletin and Review*, *2*, 55–82.

Turnbull, O.H. (1996). Rotated drawing and object recognition. *Brain and Cognition*, *32*, 120–124.

Turnbull, O.H., Beschin, N., & Della Sala, S. (1997). Agnosia for object orientation: Implications for theories of object recognition. *Neuropsychologia*, *35*, 153–163.

Turnbull, O.H., Laws, K.R., & McCarthy R.A. (1995). Object recognition without knowledge of object orientation. *Cortex*, *31*, 387–395.

NOTE

1. Friedrich Best was born in 1871 in Wermelskirchen, Germany. He received his degree in medicine from the University of Heidelberg in 1894 and wrote his habilitation thesis in Giessen about a type of corneal opacity in 1900. Best expressed wide scientific interests, publishing articles on pathological anatomy, neuropathology, neuroophthalmology, and sensory physiology. In 1901 he discovered a new stain which differentiated retinal rods and cones, named 'Best's carmine'. In 1905, while working as a senior physician in Giessen, Best published a paper about an autosomal dominant, slowly progressive, macular degeneration which still bears his name ('Best disease'). Only recently, in 1992, the gene locus for Best's macular degeneration was discovered. Best moved to Dresden in 1906 and became the head of the Department of Ophthalmology at the Friedrichsstätter Hospital. After World War II, he moved to Marsberg and started an ophthalmological practice. He finally retired in 1960 at the age of 89 and died on 6 June 1965.

CHAPTER FOURTEEN

'Mind-blind for blindness': A psychological review of Anton's syndrome

Emer M.E. Forde
Neuroscience Research Institute, University of Aston, Birmingham, UK

Claus-W. Wallesch
Department of Neurology, Otto-von-Guericke University, Magdeburg, Germany

INTRODUCTION

Towards the end of the 19th century, a German neurologist, Gabriel Anton (1899), drew attention to the growing number of reports of patients that appeared to be unaware of profound cognitive impairments:

> It is a common, but rarely discussed, medical experience that focal brain lesions, and resulting disturbances of function, are perceived, acknowledged and judged very differently by different patients ... There are a great number of disorders originating in the CNS, especially with focal brain pathology, which are hardly noticed by the patients, little attention is paid to them, they are continuously forgotten after suspiciously short intervals, and they have little impact on thought and affect. Frequently, these massive disturbances of thinking, speaking, perception and movements are not attended to and do not enter the consciousness of the affected person. I do not refer here to diseases in which the ability to perceive and evaluate is lost due to severe reduction or loss of psychological function as a result of severe dementia or disorders of consciousness. (pp. 86–87).

The patients Anton was referring to were not suffering from degenerative diseases that can cloud awareness (such as Alzheimer's disease), but appeared to have selective disorders of awareness for very debilitating cognitive and physical impairments. For example, he quoted an earlier report (by Janet) of a girl who 'asked for advice for a "most annoying" numbness in the right

199

hand following a trauma; the examination, however, revealed a complete anaesthesia of the left half of the body which the patient did not notice and did not complain about' (p. 88). Anton also noted that although some patients vehemently denied their impairments, others verbally acknowledged them when they were brought to their attention. However, even in the latter cases, the patients showed little concern for the consequences of their deficit: 'Loss of movement, especially unilateral paresis of the body, is little perceived and attended to, when simultaneously the afferent pathways—i.e. those for skin, muscle and joint sensations—are severed. Occasionally, such patients have some knowledge, especially when the deficit is brought to their attention; but in a short time this information vanishes from consciousness, the patients "forget themselves", try to walk and fall' (p. 87). Anton argued that: 'it is a psychologically plausible experience that the body side from which no signal and no impulse comes in becomes indifferent and less represented in consciousness' (p. 87).

In his paper, Anton (1899) described three patients who appeared to be unaware of their debilitating cognitive impairments. Two were unaware of their deafness and the other of her blindness. The focus of this chapter is on Anton's syndrome (i.e. unawareness of blindness) but there have now been reports of patients with deficits in awareness, or 'anosognosia', for many different kinds of impairment, including hemiplegia, memory loss, aphasia, and social/behavioural problems (see McGlynn & Schacter, 1989, for a comprehensive review). Patients who were unaware of their blindness had been described earlier by Anton (1893), Von Monakow (1885), Dejerine and Vialet (1893), Rossolimo (1896), and Lunz (1897) (cited in Redlich & Dorsey, 1945), although Anton's (1899) case is the most well known and the syndrome bears his name. In the following section we provide a direct translation of Anton's (1899) report of the patient who was unaware of her blindness (see also David, Owen, & Förstl, 1993). We also provide translations of Anton's (1899) reports of two other patients who were unaware of their deafness, although our discussion will focus primarily on contemporary theories of unawareness of blindness.

TRANSLATION OF ANTON'S (1899) CASE

Ursula Mercz., a 56-year-old seamstress, was treated from 30 November 1894 to 29 May 1895 in the Graz Hospital for Nervous Diseases. Case history revealed that Mercz had frequently suffered from vertigo and headache, that she had changed mentally over the past four years and that she had been completely unable to work for the last two years (p. 92). . . . Conversation soon revealed that the patient could not (or only with difficulty) access various words, especially object names, and she tended to use descriptions. She immediately realised that she had used the wrong words and this realisation, in addition to her difficulty in finding the desired word, led to expressions of anger. She could express spontaneous thoughts best and was much more impaired when talking about memories and descriptions that the physician demanded from her. Here she often asked for cues and to be left in peace.

At times, a minimal field of vision could be detected, although this finding could change to complete amaurosis on the same day. In early January, she could occasionally, indistinctly, see objects and recognise them (e.g. a circle drawn on a blackboard, a triangle, scissors, and a red ribbon). This state soon deteriorated to complete blindness, with normal pupillary reaction and fundoscopy.

From then on, the patient could not discriminate between light and darkness, perceive close or distant objects, and sudden movements towards her or flashes of light did not lead to a lid reaction. Gaze was unfocused and there was no fixation.

It was highly peculiar that the patient did not notice this severe and later complete loss of vision. The otherwise complaining patient was almost unaffected by this loss. When objects were presented for naming, she immediately palpated them—obviously from years of habit—and did not even try to look at them. When objects were presented further away or palpation precluded, she named purely by guessing. It appeared that—as with other people blind for years—she had some practice in guessing. Her language abilities were sufficient to support this. When asked directly about her visual ability, she replied vaguely in rather general terms 'this is not unusual, you see better when you are young'. She stated calmly and candidly that she saw objects that were presented to her, although the almost daily examination proved the opposite. She also claimed to see objects when nothing was presented.

The patient did not consciously realise her visual loss and it gave her no cause for further thought, reasoning, grief, or stress. This was at a time when word-finding problems caused obvious distress (pp. 92—93).

. . . When requested, she was able to draw a circle and other figures in the air or cut them from paper with scissors. Visual images could be retrieved from memory. She could describe—as far as her language competence allowed—her region of origin, her house, her household animals, their size, and their colour. Her weeping on this occasion seemed a normal emotion. She recognised people by hearing and by touch but she never attempted to form a visual image of them . . . The patient died after long coma (29 May, 1895) (p. 94).

Additional spatial problems shown by Ursula Mercz

Another peculiar symptom was her lack of spatial orientation. The patient cannot find her way in the room in which she had been living for several weeks.[1] She does not find the glass that was always placed in the same location next to her, does not know where her bedside table or her night-stool etc. are. When asked where the door, the window, or the patient's dining table are she gives the wrong directions. In addition, auditory perceptions that had clearly been perceived could not be localised. She could hear a watch ticking from a distance of about 35 cm but located it close to her ear. Frequently she gives the wrong side for sounds that she perceives. In addition, she cannot state with certainty which side of the bed the examiner, who is speaking loudly, stands. If the rim of the bed is struck and the patient receives tactile perceptions, she can orient quite quickly. The distinction of right and left is frequently wrong despite lengthy deliberation. On several dates, when given five trials she erred twice.

It has to be noted that the patient can localise tactile and pain sensations on her own body quite well. She is reasonably proficient when requested to touch her own nose, mouth, ear, knee etc. She is easily able to detect the respective positions of her limbs and, when the limbs on one side of the body are passively moved, she can copy this with the contralateral limbs without gross errors in movement (pp. 93–94).

Pathological findings in Anton's report

The brain as a whole was not grossly atrophic although the vessel walls were massively thickened and rugged. The dura was thickened and bilaterally adhered to the lateral side of the occipital lobe so that brain substance was ripped off when the dura was lifted. The regions of adherence were almost bilaterally symmetrical. Below, the brain substance was markedly shrunk and the gyri shrivelled.

On the left side there was a crown (coin) sized focal lesion which damaged the first and second occipital convolution and reached to the angular gyrus. A horizontal section through this lesion revealed that the white matter below was transformed into a cyst that included a large part of the white matter of the angular gyrus and reached the lateral wall of the posterior horn. The posterior horn was considerably enlarged and bulged posteriorly and laterally so that its wall came as close as 2 mm to the lateral cortex in several places, obviously resulting from massive loss of white matter (p. 94).

. . . The surface lesion on the right lateral occipital lobe was symmetrical and a little broader. A transverse section perpendicular to this surface lesion revealed similar findings as on the left side: a wedge-shaped lesion in the white matter of the occipital lobe. This reached to the lateral wall of the posterior horn causing particular damage to the angular gyrus and also to the first and second occipital gyri (p. 95).

. . . Besides the externally visible destruction of the first and second occipital convolutions and of the posterior angular gyrus on the convex surface of the occipital lobe, much of the pathways connecting the occipital lobe with the other brain lobes were destroyed. This affected the regional fibres of the arcuate fasciculus and the still largely unexplored connections to the frontal lobe (fasciculus fronto-occipitalis). The pathways that interconnect the cortical areas of the occipital lobe, especially the perpendicular and transverse occipital bundles, were similarly affected. The short cortical connections, the fibriae propriae, were preserved better. In addition, the connections from the thalamus and the lateral geniculate body were totally disconnected in their superior parts. This was partly caused by a large superior lesion and partly by a smaller lesion in the posterior temporal gyrus. In the same area, these two lesions also destroyed the larger parts of the inferior longitudinal bundle, which is progressively degenerated and atrophic.

The central end station of the visual pathways—i.e. the cuneus and the calcarine fissure—was generally intact, but on the way there the optic tract was severed and destroyed, so that in this cortical area the optic radiation was degenerated. This centre was thus disconnected from the periphery. Finally, a large lesion of the posterior part of the corpus callosum destroyed the forceps corporis callosi and resulted in degeneration of its fibres . . . consequently the occipital lobes lost their interconnection (pp. 101–102).

. . . With respect to subcortical structures, the posterior thalami and the lateral geniculate nucleus were markedly atrophic bilaterally. On the other hand, the optic tract was microscopically normal. The medial parts of the occipital brain tended to be preserved best (p. 102).

. . . The described lesions did not destroy the region that is accepted as the most central station of the cerebral cortex for the optic radiation, namely the medial aspect of the occipital lobe. However, this cortex was severed from the peripheral stations of the optic system above and below the ventricle (p. 103).

Consideration of the case

The symptom that we must emphasise in consideration of the following case was the fact that the patient was not conscious of her blindness. Mercz was mind-blind for her blindness, i.e. she did not mentally evaluate this severe deficit in brain function, whereas she was deeply concerned by the occasional lack of words (p. 104).

. . . I do not agree with a number of respected authors (Dufour and Friedrich Mueller) that patients with unilateral cortical lesions do not perceive or do not become aware of their visual deficit (p. 105) . . . Dufour emphasised that patients with a unilateral visual field deficit would also lose the perception of the lack of this visual field (hemianopsie nulle) (p. 104)

. . . On the basis of my own research and from the literature, I conclude that the lesion of the cuneus and the calcarine fissure as such do not suffice for the resulting hemianopia to remain 'unconscious'. The concomitant cortical lesion affects both the objective as well as some subjective sensory perceptions; also those mental processes that are based on these perceptions lose continuous impulse and update. On the other hand, many patients can rely on other resources to detect the visual field loss and arrive at knowledge of, and insight into, the problem. The patient retains the opportunity and capability to compare perceptions to the right and left. In addition, at least remnants of the ability to compare his previous and present condition are usually preserved, and a comparison with unimpaired people could possibly prompt the recognition and awareness of the deficit. Memory and ability need not be especially impaired (in these cases) (p. 105). . . . Thus I was able to find a very clear awareness of the visual deficit in a number of hemianopic patients . . . On the other hand, the literature contains other cases which emphasise that the patient was entirely unaware of his visual field loss. As an example, I quote the very instructive case of cortical blindness of Foerster, who was anatomically analysed by H. Sachs. The case description emphasises that 'he also lacked the awareness of the lost visual field defect'. Anatomical examination revealed a bilateral, not entirely symmetrical, softening that affected not only the region of the cuneus and lingual gyrus but also the entire white matter layers median and below the ventricle, including the large collateral sulcus and the bulk of the inferior longitudinal bundle below the ventricle wall. It can be concluded that additional lesions are required in order that a central loss of a sensory function remains latent, inaccessible and outside awareness for the patient (pp. 105–106).

. . . It seems possible that the cortical areas that are disconnected from the periphery can be activated from other cortical regions. Especially in the case of Mercz, microscopic inspection revealed a number of shorter and longer association pathways, which could transmit excitations from, for example, the temporal lobe to the (basically intact) visual centre. It cannot be decided on the basis of this case, whether the patient erroneously, though confidently and without any doubt, judged these excitations as sensory perceptions and thus named objects that she did not see (and that occasionally were not presented at all). Furthermore, that the intact subcortical visual and auditory capacities—the major factor in lower animals—can precipitate dark sensations that mask the loss of conscious cortical sensory perceptions remains a possibility (p. 122).

Mind-blind for deafness: Case 1

Johnann Fuchs, aged 64 years, was previously employed as a coachman . . . Many years ago he suffered a severe head injury that left him deaf and psychologically altered. He was admitted to the Graz Hospital for medical assessment on 11 November 1897 in an agitated and talkative state. He was orientated . . . and on occasions gave adequate reports of his life situation. However, his train of thoughts was disrupted and he could not hold a topic in conversation. It was immediately apparent that he did not react to sounds, calls, or even loud noises close to his ear. He does not show any attempt to listen or to understand conversation or questions from the examiner. He does not react to questions or exhibit any reaction to answers or to his surroundings. He is much more accessible by gesture. When his ear is pointed at, or a listening gesture made, he always states that he hears the bells of his hometown . . . or hears people named Steffelbauer and Eiser, who shout into his ear, and he frequently complains about their calls . . . On one occasion he reports to hear 'The devil shall take you, the thunderstorm shall slay you'. He also hears 'gruesome songs' being sung . . . [Anton then describes word finding difficulties, circumscriptions, paraphasias and garbled utterances.]

Frequently, communication by writing is possible, and he repeatedly states that he can write in German and Latin and has read many books. His reading errors are interesting. Thus, he reads 'geboren' (born) for gefallen (fallen), and 'achtungsvoll' (full of respect) for antwort (answer). . . . Many words, however, especially numbers, are read correctly. When asked in writing about his deafness he denies it vigorously. 'He is not deaf, he can hear well and heard Steffelbauer talking' . . . When by writing or by gesture the patient's attention is focused, his auditory hallucinations occur with increasing strength. We never succeeded in drawing his attention to real auditory events. . . . Before he starts reading or writing, he seems to ward off the distracting voices from the right ear. He generally seems to hallucinate more on the right ear . . . It was remarkable that the patient had both ears plugged with cotton wool and covered with bandages. . . . Innumerable times he repeats 'plug ears', 'keep warm' (pp. 89–90).

. . . In this case, the patient's behaviour towards the acquired auditory impairment is evidence that the most central organs of perception are disabled and partially destroyed. Not only were the low-level components of auditory perception lost, but also any evoked train of thoughts destroyed by the disease. The patient himself seems to have lost the memory that he could hear before, and that mouth movements of his companions previously corresponded to language; an observation that will probably never be made with the peripherally deaf (p. 92).

Mind-blind for deafness: Case 2

Juliane Hochrieser, a 69-year-old mountain farmer, was brought for psychiatric treatment because of severe confusion and agitation. . . . Within weeks she was more orientated. It was quickly established that she could not understand spoken language and did not even react to it by turning her head or by a response. Similarly, she did not respond to loud clapping, calling or loud noises close to her ears. . . . In addition, her spontaneous speech was, and remained, peculiarly disturbed. Frequently she chose the wrong words to describe her thoughts. [Anton then describes phonemic paraphasia and other symptoms associated with Wernicke's aphasia.]

. . . The patient recognises people visually and named most common objects that were visually presented. She correctly describes tactile perceptions and bodily sensations . . . Concerning her auditory perceptions, she never reacted to acoustic stimuli, such as clapping, whistling, calling etc. Although generally a complainer, she never complained about this defect and remained completely indifferent to it. . . . In conversation she never realised that she neither heard nor understood the questions that were asked. Her responses were only the continuation of her respective train of thoughts. She was repeatedly asked in writing whether she heard and she always replied candidly and without affect that she heard well. . . . It is remarkable that, despite this severe hearing impairment, she frequently realised that she produced wrong words and tried to correct them (pp. 106–107).

. . . It was remarkable that the patient did not realise her sensory deficit i.e. her complete deafness. Her condition was distinct from mind-deafness as she did not react at all to auditory stimuli and did not perceive such sensory stimuli. She did not only behave like someone absolutely deaf, but also like someone who had never heard. Not only did she lack auditory perceptions, she did not miss them, which distinguishes her from the peripherally deaf (p. 115).

The right hemisphere was generally small and only mildly atrophic. There was a regional softening of the first and upper second temporal convolution. This softening destroyed the projections of the superior temporal lobe. Similar, but less extensive, lesions were found in the left hemisphere (p. 108). . . . Analogous to bilateral occipital lesions, bilateral lesions of the temporal lobes seem to have resulted in patient Hochrieser's inability to realise her bilateral deafness. In a sense she was mind-deaf for her deafness (p. 119).

CASE INSIGHTS

Anton's (1899) description of the patient who was unaware of her blindness provided new insights into the organisation and biological basis of conscious awareness. First, Anton demonstrated that a patient could be fully aware of one problem (her word finding) but not of another (her blindness), indicating that awareness may fractionate. He also challenged the prevailing view that damage to the occipital lobes not only caused visual problems but also impaired awareness of these deficits. Instead, Anton suggested that unawareness of blindness arose because (a) the occipital lobes were disconnected from the rest of the brain and/or (b) patients had visual experiences as a result of visual processing in subcortical pathways and consequently rejected the idea that they were completely blind. In addition, Anton noted that awareness of blindness could be inferred by comparing previous and current visual experience, if the patient's general intellectual abilities were intact. We discuss similar contemporary ideas in the next section.

Anton's patients who were unaware of their deafness have received relatively little attention in the literature. However, Anton made two particularly interesting observations that may provide important clues to the nature of the underlying impairment in these patients. First, one patient had very vivid hallucinations of people talking to him and it is possible that the vividness of this internally generated speech contributed to his belief that he could hear. We explore the idea that internally and externally generated images may be confused in Anton's syndrome in the next section. The second interesting point is Anton's observation that one of the patients behaved 'like somebody who had never heard' (p. 115). A striking number of the reports of anosognosic patients mention that these patients not only appear unaware of their problems, but also remain indifferent to them when they are informed that they are blind, deaf, etc. It seems like they have lost any memory of what it was like to see (or hear or move their limbs) and do not fully comprehend the consequences of their disorder. Again, we return to this point later in the chapter.

DISCUSSION OF CONTEMPORARY VIEWS OF ANTON'S SYNDROME

Anton's case report of Ursula Mercz who was 'mind-blind for her blindness', raises a number of important psychological and philosophical questions. How do we *know* that we can see? Can this form of self-knowledge, or 'conscious awareness', be constructed directly from physical brain matter? If so, what mechanisms mediate 'conscious awareness' and how do they break down following brain injury? Can 'conscious awareness' be located in a particular brain region (which has been damaged in these patients)? How could Ursula Mercz be aware of one problem (word finding) but not of another (her blindness)? Can 'conscious awareness' fractionate? Patients with selective impairments in reading, object recognition, and language production have provided us with invaluable insights into the organisation of the neuronal systems mediating these cognitive abilities. But can patients with impairments in 'conscious awareness' inform us about the neuronal systems underpinning this elusive and uniquely human capacity? A number of leading philosophers and psychologists argue that they can (Churchland, 1986; Dennett, 1991; Eilan, Marcel, & Bermúdez, 1995; Johnson, 1991; Marcel & Bisiach, 1988; Milner & Rugg, 1992; Schacter & Prigatano, 1991). For example, Schacter and Prigatano (1991) suggested that anosognosic patients can not only provide new insights into the cognitive components and brain systems involved in awareness, but the neuropsychological theories developed to explain these findings may be applied to 'motivated denial', which has hitherto been investigated within a psychoanalytic framework. Marcel (1993, 1994) argued that the 'reflexive consciousness' required to know that '*I* can see' or '*I* can no longer see' is so closely related to the concept of 'self' that studies of patients with Anton's syndrome may provide new insights into the nature of selfhood. Similarly, Kihlstrom and Tobias (1991) suggested that these studies could bring us 'one step closer to uncovering the biological basis of consciousness and the experience of selfhood that is the essence of human nature' (p. 219).

However, the optimism concerning the contribution that studies of anosognosic patients can make to our understanding of the functional organisation and anatomical substrates of 'self-awareness' or 'conscious awareness' is not universally shared. For example, Chalmers (1996) suggested that 'conscious experience' is so fundamentally different from anything physical that it will be governed by its own 'psychophysical' laws. Others have offered a more psychodynamic, rather than neuropsychological, explanation for anosognosia and suggested that it reflects a motivated, psychological coping strategy such as 'psychological denial' or 'organic repression' (Schilder, 1935; Weinstein & Kahn, 1955). Furthermore, others have suggested that, even if Anton's syndrome is not denial in the psychodynamic sense of the term, it might reflect general intellectual problems (e.g. in the latter stages of dementia) rather than a selective deficit in the neuronal systems mediating 'conscious awareness' (Levine, 1990). In the remainder of this chapter, we review a number of contemporary influential theories and assess whether Anton's syndrome reflects (a) motivated denial, (b) general intellectual impairments, (c) deficits in visual monitoring, (d) impoverished visual input, and (e) deficits in source monitoring. Our discussion focuses on psychological explanations of Anton's syndrome although we mention the anatomical correlates when they are particularly relevant (for more detail on the neuroanatomical damage associated with Anton's syndrome, see McGlynn & Schacter, 1989).

Motivated denial

Around the turn of the century, Sigmund Freud suggested that memories, thoughts, and perceptions may not reach conscious awareness for psychological, rather than neuropsychological, reasons. He suggested that psychological defence mechanisms, such as repression or projection, may 'block' unpleasant thoughts or memories from consciousness and a number of authors have suggested that these defence mechanisms can account for Anton's syndrome. For example, Schilder (1935) suggested that patients with Anton's syndrome may show 'organic repression' and Stengel and Steele (1946) reported an interesting case of a patient with Anton's syndrome who 'projected' his impairments on to other (imaginary) patients. Stengel and Steele's (1946) patient had a varicose ulcer in his leg (which he was aware of) and was blind. When asked if anything was wrong with him the patient replied, 'I have a sore leg . . . I am quite all right, the only thing that is the matter is the left foot'. When asked specifically if he could see and hear he replied 'I can see and hear all right'. When asked if there were any other patients in the room, he replied incorrectly that there were. He said 'one is a bad walker and the one next to me could not see. He cannot see if you give him a match'. The last comment was particularly interesting because a few minutes earlier the patient had been unable to light a cigarette because he could not see the match.[2] On another occasion the patient announced 'there is one good thing I have got; my eyes never bothered me', characteristic of Freud's concept of 'reaction formation' where a person represses unpleasant information and then ardently professes the opposite. Thus, there is some evidence that, although patients may verbally deny their impairments, their behaviour reveals that it has been processed at some level. Interestingly, there are other cases where patients may verbally acknowledge their impairment (e.g. their hemiplegia), yet at a behavioural level they seem unaware of it (e.g. they try to get up and walk).

More recently, Lewis (1991) suggested that it is not only patients with neurological damage who deny their problems, but at some time in our lives, we all distort reality to suit our own wishes or to protect ourselves from something painful. This distortion of reality, however, is not necessarily a conscious attempt to deceive but can be 'outside' our conscious awareness. Lewis (1991) proposed that, although some patients may deny cognitive or physical impairments for psychological reasons, others could be genuinely unaware of their impairments as a result of their brain damage disrupting the neuronal systems mediating conscious awareness. The challenge, therefore, is to develop criteria for distinguishing between these two classes of patient. Lewis (1991) suggested that there may be at least three ways to differentiate between organic and psychological denial: (1) organic denial will have a shorter time course and is rarely a chronic disorder (McDaniel & McDaniel, 1991); (2) organic denial will be accompanied by other cognitive impairments and associated brain damage; (3) patients with organic denial often appear indifferent to their impairments whereas patients with psychological denial are more likely to become distressed or angry when questioned about their problems.

However, even if Anton's syndrome is not a form of motivated denial it could reflect a general impairment in intellect, memory, or reasoning, rather than a selective impairment to some form of 'awareness machinery'. We review this hypothesis in the next section.

Confounding and generalised intellectual impairments

Levine (1990) suggested that awareness of blindness is acquired through a qualitatively different process than awareness of seeing. He argued that awareness of blindness is not awareness of a sensation, and, consequently, the knowledge that one is blind must be inferred through a process of hypothesis testing and inference. Normally if we find ourselves in a situation in which we cannot see we assume that the light is inadequate. Consequently, Levine (1990) argued that someone who suddenly becomes blind (e.g. following a stroke) will immediately, and quite sensibly, conclude that the lights are off or it is a dark night. Consistent with this, patients often blame their poor performance on visual tasks on the lighting (see Table 14.1). However, blind patients who retain their general intellectual abilities will soon be able to infer they are blind (e.g. if they are told it is mid-day and they can feel the sun on their face). Levine (1990) proposed that patients who lose their general intellectual abilities (e.g. problem solving, reasoning), in addition to their sight, would no longer have the prerequisite cognitive skills to correctly interpret their visual problems. He also suggested that blindness does not necessarily leave patients in a 'black world', but that auditory and tactile stimuli, or even suggestion from others, may be able to evoke visual images that are subsequently misinterpreted as real visual percepts (see the 'Source monitoring' section later for further discussion of this view).

According to this view, Anton's syndrome emerges in blind patients who have additional cognitive deficits in reasoning, memory, or attention. One interesting proposal outlined by Levine was that deficits in spatial attention might lead to Anton's syndrome in blind patients. He suggested that spatial problems might preclude blind patients integrating their visual experiences

TABLE 14.1

Examples of responses from patients with Anton's syndrome when informed that what they reported to see was inaccurate

---

'This is not unusual, you see better when you are young' (Anton, 1899).

'Oh. I see you all right. It's quite dark, but I see you' (Case 1, Redlich & Dorsey, 1945).

He insisted he could see and when pressed further retorted 'I don't care if I can't see' (Case 2, Redlich & Dorsey, 1945).

'It's a little dark'. 'I don't see as well as I did before, but I can see all right. I need new glasses'. 'I'm tired". "This is not a bright day' (Case 6, Redlich & Dorsey, 1945).

'The left eye is not good; the right eye is all right. I have been idle for a year'.

'There is one good thing I have got; my eyes never bothered me' (Stengel & Steele, 1946).

'No I can see it, I just have a headache' (McDaniel & McDaniel, 1991).

---

within a spatially coherent world. Consequently, they would remain unaware of their blindness. Interestingly, Anton (1899) reported that Ursula Mercz had problems localising objects and sounds in addition to her blindness. However, as Levine (1990) acknowledged, this hypothesis does not capture the full extent of the problem in Anton's syndrome (e.g. patients' apparent indifference when informed that they are blind). In addition, there are cases of blind patients with spatial problems who do not show Anton's syndrome (Angelergues, 1960, cited in Levine, 1990). Levine, therefore, proposed that deficits in memory (associated with temporal lobe damage) and reasoning (associated with frontal lobe damage), in association with blindness, were the primary factors causing Anton's syndrome. Note that according to this model there is no specialised neuronal system dedicated to mediating conscious awareness. Rather, awareness depends on the ability to remember facts, to reason, and to draw inferences.

Consistent with Levine's view, a number of studies have shown that patients with Anton's syndrome have several cognitive deficits and in many cases it co-occurs with the profound and global impairments associated with dementia (Feinberg et al., 1994; McGlynn & Schacter, in press; Michon et al., 1994; Starkstein et al., 1995). In particular, patients are often disorientated in time and place, they perform poorly on tests of general intellectual ability, they confabulate responses to questions about visual stimuli, and they have memory problems (Fisher, 1989; Raney & Nielsen, 1942; Redlich & Bonvicini, 1908; Redlich & Dorsey, 1945). However, McDaniel and McDaniel (1991) argued that generalised intellectual decline was not a necessary precondition for Anton's syndrome (see also Stuss, 1991; Stuss & Benson, 1986) and they reported a case of a patient who was well-orientated to time and place, had a normal digit span, normal language comprehension and naming, intact ability to perform calculations, showed good constructional ability, and yet denied her visual problems. The patient did, however, perform poorly on tests of frontal/executive skills and recent and remote memory. McDaniel and McDaniel's (1991) patient is particularly interesting because it is one of the few reports of Anton's syndrome in a case of peripheral blindness rather than cortical blindness. The patient had no visual acuity or light perception in the right eye and she did not respond to visual threat. Visual acuity, extraocular movements and a direct light pupillary response were normal in her left eye. She denied her right-sided blindness and confabulated responses. For example, when asked to count the number of fingers in front of her she guessed and, when informed that she was incorrect, she blamed her poor performance on a headache, the lighting, or the angle of the bed. However, two weeks after her operation the vision in her right eye improved. Her short-term memory also improved, she confabulated less, and began to acknowledge that she had some visual problems. A month later, the confabulation, denial of illness, and memory problems had significantly improved.

Since these impairments resolved concurrently, McDaniel and McDaniel suggested that 'confabulation is a requisite accompaniment to Anton's syndrome regardless of the site of visual system damage . . . interaction of a memory deficit with the inability to critically self monitor responses due to frontal dysfunction was sufficient to produce denial of blindness secondary to a peripheral lesion' (p. 104) (see also Fisher, 1989).

A number of studies on patients with Alzheimer's disease have also suggested that frontal lobe dysfunction is a critical contributing factor in anosognosia (although these studies have not been confined to patients with Anton's syndrome). Michon et al. (1994) showed that the degree of anosognosia correlated significantly with performance on executive (frontal) tasks, such as the Wisconsin card sorting task and verbal fluency. Starkstein et al. (1993) found a significant difference on 'frontal' tasks, but not on memory tasks, between patients with and without anosognosia. Consistent with these neuropsychological tests, Starkstein et al. (1995) demonstrated that patients with anosognosia had reduced blood flow in the right frontal lobe. The idea that the frontal lobes play a special role in 'conscious awareness' is not a new one. Burdach (1819) referred to the frontal lobes as the 'special workshop of the thinking process' and Gall (1810) believed that they were the neural substrate of human intellect (cited in Rylander, 1932). Numerous studies have shown that following frontal lobe damage, patients appear to lack insight into their problems and they are likely to provide bizarre and inappropriate responses to questions about their impairments (Burgess & Shallice, 1996a, 1996b; Shallice, 1988; Stuss, 1991, 1992; Stuss & Benson, 1986). However, patients with frontal lobe damage tend to have global impairments in awareness; they are not only unaware of their cognitive impairments, but also of their social and behavioural problems. In contrast to this, there are several reports of patients with Anton's syndrome who are aware of other debilitating cognitive deficits (Anton, 1899; Bisiach et al., 1986). For example, Anton's patient, Ursula Mercz, complained about her word-finding problem, yet remained oblivious to her blindness. Similarly, his patient Juliane Hochreiser was unaware of her deafness but aware of mistakes in speech production. In a group study, Bisiach et al. (1986) reported that from 10 patients with anosognosia for hemianopia only 4 were also unaware of their hemiplegia. The other 6 were aware of their hemiplegia. Consequently, Bisiach et al. (1986) argued that conscious awareness of a particular cognitive domain (say, visual perception) is not mediated by a unitary, 'central' monitoring system (e.g. located in the frontal lobes), but is decentralised and mediated by that particular cognitive system. Young and De Haan (1992) reported an even more selective impairment in a patient who showed a dissociation within the domain of visual/perceptual processing: she was aware of her hemianopia but not of her prosopagnosia. Despite the fact that she could recognise less than 25% of the faces shown to her, she maintained that her face recognition was 'as good as before'. Young and De Haan (1992) suggested that she was not only unaware of her prosopagnosia, but seemed 'to have lost all knowledge of what it was like to have the relevant ability'. This observation is similar to Anton's remark that the cortically deaf patient 'behaved as if she had never heard'.

These latter studies suggest that, although many of the patients with Anton's syndrome do have additional cognitive impairments, unawareness of visual problems can emerge in: (a) patients who do not have global intellectual deterioration (McDaniel & McDaniel, 1991); and (b) patients with intact awareness for other cognitive impairments (Anton, 1899; Bisiach et al., 1986; Young & De Haan, 1992). Anton's syndrome, therefore, does not necessarily depend on global intellectual deterioration, frontal lobe pathology, or impaired memory, although it remains possible that frontal lobe pathology, for example, may be sufficient to cause Anton's syndrome in a blind person.

Visual monitoring

One theme running through a number of contemporary explanations of Anton's syndrome is that the fundamental problem is in 'monitoring' visual experience. There are two main variants of this hypothesis. The first is that we have one 'central' monitoring system for all perceptions, thoughts, and behaviour. For example, McGlynn and Schacter (1989) suggested that we have a centralised 'conscious awareness system' (CAS), located in the inferior parietal lobes, which receives input from different cognitive systems (e.g. visual perception, memory) when they are actively processing information. They argued that this system would be responsible for monitoring modality-specific information whereas a functionally independent executive system, located in the frontal lobes, would be responsible for monitoring and integrating information from several modalities in more complex cognitive tasks. According to this account, Anton's syndrome results from damage to the connection between the visual processing system and CAS. Damage to CAS would result in unawareness for all sensory and motor impairments (e.g. visual deficits, motor problems) and damage to the frontal/executive system would result in unawareness of more complex behaviours (e.g. problem solving, social behaviour). Patients with damage to a central monitor could therefore be differentiated from patients with a disconnection between this monitor and a modality-specific processing system on the basis of their behaviour.

Thus, one view is that Anton's syndrome results from a disconnection between the visual processing system and a central monitor that mediates awareness. The alternative variant of the 'impaired monitoring' account of Anton's syndrome is that it reflects damage to a modality-specific 'visual monitor'. For example, Bisiach et al. (1986) argued that 'unawareness of the failure of a particular function betrays a disorder at the highest levels of organisation of *that* function'. Heilman (1991) also argued that Anton's syndrome could arise from damage to a visual monitor, perhaps located in visual association cortex. However, Heilman (1991) also suggested that it could arise from damage to pathways between the visual monitor and areas mediating speech production. Under these conditions the patient would be unable to verbally report what they saw, and consequently, the language areas would confabulate a response (see also Gazzaniga, 1970).

Impoverished visual input

Anton (1899) suggested that unawareness of blindness may emerge because 'intact sub-cortical visual and auditory capacities . . . precipitate dark sensations that mask the loss of conscious cortical sensory perceptions' (p. 122). More recently, Heilman (1991) reiterated this idea. He suggested that Anton's syndrome might emerge in patients who were cortically blind but had intact subcortical visual pathways that allowed some visual experience. Since patients were experiencing some visual input, they would deny that they were blind. Paradoxically, this idea is similar to contemporary views of blindsight, which some have argued is the reverse of Anton's syndrome (Marcel, 1993). Blindsight patients claim not to see but demonstrate some ability to access visual information (perhaps as a result of subcortical processing); patients with Anton's syndrome claim to see (perhaps as a result of subcortical processing), but cannot correctly access any visual information.

Goldberg and Barr (1991) also suggested that Anton's syndrome may emerge in patients who had severely impoverished visual input leading to impaired cortical representations of the visual world. According to their model, conscious awareness of visual problems depends on a comparison between expected visual experience and actual visual experience and they suggested that, in patients with Anton's syndrome, the 'monitor' that compares expected and actual visual experience may be impaired (see also discussion in the previous subsection). Goldberg and Barr (1991) also suggested that, if a patient's visual experience was so impoverished that an internal representation of the world could not be formed, the patient would not be able to compare expected with actual visual experience. Furthermore, they proposed that 'if the damage to internal representations in the given modality is profound, a situation may arise that the patient loses not only the precision of internal representations of sensory objects—the whole sensory dimension of the multi(sensory) dimensional image of the world is lost. This situation may not only result in the loss of knowledge of *what* the subject is supposed to see/hear in a particular situation but also in the loss of knowledge *that* he is supposed to see/hear. The internal experiential knowledge base for the concept of seeing/hearing is destroyed, and the patient loses the ability to appreciate the loss of the whole sensory modality' (p. 169). This is consistent with the observation that many patients with Anton's syndrome (and other forms of anosognosia) are unconcerned about their blindness and appear to have lost any appreciation of what it was like to see (Anton, 1899). Goldberg and Barr (1991) predicted that this degree of damage to the internal representation of the visual world should be associated with impairments to visual memory, visual imaging, and dreaming. There are, however, patients with Anton's syndrome who have no problems in visual imagery (Redlich & Bonvicini, 1908; Stengel & Steele, 1946) and indeed others have suggested that the fundamental problem in Anton's syndrome might be confusion between internally generated visual images and externally driven visual percepts (Goldberg, Mullbacher, & Nowak, 1995; Heilman, 1991; Johnson, 1991). We discuss this hypothesis in some detail in the next section.

One final point to note here is the idea that impoverished visual input can cause vivid but sham visual experiences is consistent with contemporary views of visual hallucinations in blind hemifields and Charles Bonnet syndrome[3] (Ball, 1991; Halligan, Marshall, & Ramachandran, 1994; Kölmel, 1985; Schultz & Melzack, 1991). Patients with Charles Bonnet syndrome provide an interesting contrast to patients with Anton's syndrome because, although both report vivid visual 'hallucinations', the former are aware, or can be convinced, that their visual experiences are not genuine percepts. One prominent explanation for the visual hallucinations associated with Charles Bonnet syndrome is that the lack of sensory input leads to 'disinhibition' or 'release' of stored visual/perceptual traces (Kölmel, 1985; Scheibel & Scheibel, 1962; West, 1975). Schultz and Melzack (1991) drew an analogy between the sham visual experiences associated with Charles Bonnet syndrome and phantom limb phenomena. They suggested that, when sensory visual input is impoverished, the visual cortex might be activated by preserved 'arousal' systems, such as the reticular formation, or by pathological hyperactivity of cortical neurons in the damaged areas. One could speculate that the visual experiences reported by patients with Anton's syndrome arise via similar mechanisms, and studies comparing the type of visual images reported by patients with Anton's and Charles Bonnet syndrome would be an interesting avenue for future research. However, there are a number of important differences between these two groups of patients. For example, patients with Charles Bonnet syndrome sometimes report rather fantastic and unnatural hallucinations, whereas patients with Anton's syndrome typically report plausible visual experiences often only in response to questions. The critical difference in relation to this chapter is, however, that patients with Charles Bonnet syndrome are aware that the visual hallucinations they experience are not genuine visual percepts. Consequently, systematic comparisons between these patient groups might provide interesting clues about the cognitive components and anatomical substrates of 'conscious awareness'. One possibility is that patients with Anton's syndrome can no longer determine the 'source' of their visual experience (i.e. whether it is internally or externally generated), and we discuss this idea in more detail in the next section.

Source monitoring

Johnson (1991) argued that because we can normally perceive visual scenes and generate our own visual images, we need to continually engage in a process of 'reality testing'—i.e. we need to assess whether what we 'see' is really 'out there' or if it is an image that we have generated internally. She proposed that we can normally discriminate between visual percepts and visual images because the former usually have more perceptual detail and are encoded in a certain place and time. She also suggested that, although internally derived images tend to have less visual information (e.g. about colour and size), we may have access to more information about the cognitive processes involved in activating the image. So, for example, Johnson suggested that a perceptually rich visual scene, combined with little information about the cognitive procedures involved in activating the scene, would be judged as an externally derived visual percept. In contrast, a visual scene with more information about the cognitive processes involved in establishing the image, but less perceptual detail, would be more likely to be judged as an internally generated visual image. This theory predicts that Anton's syndrome could arise when patients cannot engage in reality testing: for example, when the amount of visual information available in imagined and perceived visual scenes is too similar. This could arise when patients have either unusually good visual imagery or degraded visual/perceptual information. Consistent with this prediction, Johnson et al. (1979) showed that subjects (with no neurological damage) who were good imagers were more likely to confuse images and perceptions. Also consistent with the idea that patients with Anton's syndrome are misidentifying imagery and perception, Suzuki, Endo, Yamadori, and Fujii (1997) reported a case of a cortically blind patient who showed left spatial neglect in her responses to what she 'saw'. When asked to draw a clock from memory she only drew the numbers on the right side (a classic indication of unilateral spatial neglect). In addition, when asked to count the number of people or objects on her right and left side, she always reported 'seeing' more objects on the right and sometimes conceded that things on the left were blurred. Given that the confabulatory responses in this totally blind patient had a spatial quality, it seems unlikely that accounts stressing 'motivated denial' or generalised confusion are sufficient to account for all cases. The tendency of Suzuki et al.'s (1997) patient to report seeing objects on the right side of space suggests that she is basing her responses on a mental image that has spatial properties. Although these studies support the hypothesis that patients with Anton's syndrome cannot determine the source of their visual experience, Johnson's (1991) source misidentification account cannot explain other important characteristics of the syndrome. For example, it cannot explain why patients often confabulate unlikely scenarios or why they appear unconcerned when told that they are blind.

CONCLUDING REMARKS

We have used the term 'unawareness' rather generally in this review to refer to a patient's inability to know that he/she cannot see. However, we have also noted that *unawareness* of deficit does not fully capture the nature of the impairment, because many patients are not only unaware but also appear to be *indifferent* when told that they are blind. A number of authors noted that patients acted as if they had never seen and did not appear to be concerned about the consequences of their condition. Babinski (1914, cited in Bisiach & Geminiani, 1991) drew attention to this distinction and referred to the indifference as 'anosodiaphoria' rather than 'anosognosia', although in contemporary studies these are rarely differentiated. Consequently, it is possible that Anton's syndrome could arise from impairments in either of these abilities (i.e. knowing that . . ., comprehending the consequences of . . .). Thus, there may be two functionally independent forms of Anton's syndrome: (1) unawareness of perceptual loss; and (2) unawareness of the consequences of perceptual loss. Future work that systematically compares patients' knowledge of their impairments to their understanding of the subsequent consequences would help tease apart the relative importance of these two factors (see also McGlynn & Schacter, 1989). Furthermore, we suggest that future studies need to experimentally investigate patients' explicit and implicit knowledge about their impairments. This is important because some patients in the literature appear to have no conscious or unconscious (explicit or implicit) access to the knowledge that they are blind. In contrast, the behaviour of other patients suggests some level of insight into their impairment (e.g. the patient described by Stengel & Steele, 1946, who 'projected' his blindness onto another imaginary patient).

In addition to distinctions between patients' knowledge and understanding of their impairments and the level at which their impairments are processed, we suggest that future studies need to distinguish between unawareness of complete blindness (Anton, 1899) and hemianopia (Bisiach et al., 1986; McDaniel & McDaniel, 1991). It is possible, and in our opinion likely, that different factors will contribute to the unawareness of visual deficit in these two cases. The former is obviously a more profound deficit in unawareness because the patient cannot see at all; in the latter case, the patient can process some visual information and 'perceptual closure' may help mask their hemianopia (McGlynn & Schacter, 1989; Walker & Mattingley, 1997; Warrington, 1962).

In this chapter, we have reviewed a somewhat disparate set of accounts of Anton's syndrome and, while some progress has been made in developing more fully articulated models, few have been experimentally tested. In addition, many of the models (though not all, see Goldberg & Barr, 1991) are designed to account for *the* fundamental problem. Our view is that Anton's syndrome will comprise a collection of patients with functionally and anatomically separate impairments. The proposal that these patients can provide us with new insights into the functional architecture and biological basis of 'conscious awareness' and 'the experience of selfhood that is the essence of human nature' (Kihlstrom & Tobias, 1991) remains an exciting prospect but the veracity of these claims will depend on more systematic and empirical analyses of the neurological cases.

REFERENCES

Anton, G. (1899). Ueber die Selbstwahrnehmung der Herderkrankungen des Gehirns durch den Kranken bei Rindenblindheit und Rindentaubheit. *Archiv für Psychiatrie, 32*, 86–127.

Babinski, J. (1914). Contribution à l'étude des troubles mentaux dans l'hémiplégia organique cébérale (anosognosie). *Revue Neurologique (Paris), 22*, 845–884.

Ball, C.J. (1991). The vascular origins of Charles Bonnet syndrome: Four cases and a review of the pathogenic mechanisms. *International Journal of Geriatric Psychiatry, 6*, 673–679.

Bisiach, E., & Geminiani, G. (1991). Anosognosia related to hemiplegia and hemianopia. In G. Prigatano, & D. Schacter (Eds.), *Awareness of deficit after brain injury: Clinical and theoretical issues*. Oxford: Oxford University Press.

Bisiach, E., Vallar, G., Perani, D., Papagno, C., & Berti, A. (1986). Unawareness of disease following lesions of the right hemisphere: Anosognosia for hemiplegia and anosognosia for hemianopia. *Neuropsychologia, 24*, 471–482.

Burgess, P., & Shallice, T. (1996a). Confabulation and the control of recollection. *Memory, 4(4)*, 359–411.

Burgess, P., & Shallice, T. (1996b). Bizarre responses, rule detection, and frontal lobe lesions. *Cortex, 32*, 241–259.

Chalmers, D. (1996). The puzzle of conscious experience. *Scientific American, 275*, 62–68.

Churchland, P.S. (1986). *Neurophilosophy: Towards a unified science of the mind/brain*. Cambridge, MA: MIT Press.

David, A., Owen, A.M., & Förstl, H. (1993). An annotated summary and translation of 'On the self-awareness of focal brain diseases by the patient in cortical blindness and cortical deafness' by Gabriel Anton (1899). *Cognitive Neuropsychology, 10(3)*, 263–272.

Dennett, D.C. (1991). *Consciousness explained*. Boston: Little Brown.

Eilan, N., Marcel, A., & Bermúdez, J.L. (1995). *The body and the self*. Cambridge, MA: MIT Press.

Feinberg, T.E., & Roane, D.M. (1997). Anosognosia, completion and confabulation: The neutral–personal dichotomy. *Neurocase, 3*, 73–85.

Feinberg, T.E., Roane, D.M., Kwan, P.C., Schindler, R.J., et al. (1994). Anosognosia and visuoverbal confabulation. *Archives of Neurology, 51(5)*, 468–473.

Fisher, C.M. (1989). Neurological fragments, 2: Remarks on anosognosia, confabulation, memory and other topics; and an appendix on self observation. *Neurology, 39*, 127–132.

Gazzaniga, M.S. (1970). *The bisected brain.* New York: Appleton.

Goldberg, E., & Barr, W.B. (1991). Three possible mechanisms of unawareness of deficit. In G. Prigatano, & D. Schacter (Eds.), *Awareness of deficit after brain injury: Clinical and theoretical issues.* Oxford: Oxford University Press.

Goldberg, G., Mullbacher, W., & Nowak, A. (1995). Imagery without perception: A case of anosognosia for cortical blindness. Special issue: The neuropsychology of mental imagery. *Neuropsychologia, 33(11),* 1373–1382.

Halligan, P.W., Marshall, J.C., & Ramachandran, V.S. (1994). Ghosts in the machine: A case description of visual and haptic hallucinations after right hemisphere stroke. *Cognitive Neuropsychology, 11 (4),* 459–477.

Heilman, K. (1991). Anosognosia: Possible neuropsychological mechanisms. In G. Prigatano, & D. Schacter (Eds.), *Awareness of deficit after brain injury: Clinical and theoretical issues.* Oxford: Oxford University Press.

Johnson, M. (1991). Reality monitoring: Evidence from confabulation in organic brain disease patients. In G. Prigatano & D. Schacter (Eds.), *Awareness of deficit after brain injury: Clinical and theoretical issues.* Oxford: Oxford University Press.

Johnson, M.K., Raye, C.L., Wang, A.Y., & Taylor, T.H. (1979). Fact and fantasy: The roles of accuracy and variability in confusing imaginations with perceptual experiences. *Journal of Experimental Psychology: Human Learning and Memory, 5,* 229–240.

Kihlstrom, J.F., & Tobias, B.A. (1991). Anosognosia, consciousness and the self. In G. Prigatano & D. Schacter (Eds.), *Awareness of deficit after brain injury: Clinical and theoretical issues.* Oxford: Oxford University Press.

Kölmel, H.W. (1985). Complex visual hallucinations in the hemianopic field. *Journal of Neurology, Neurosurgery, and Psychiatry, 48,* 29–38.

Levine, D. (1990). Unawareness of visual and sensorimotor defects: A hypothesis. *Brain and Cognition, 13,* 233–281.

Lewis, L. (1991). Role of psychological factors in disordered awareness. In G. Prigatano & D. Schacter (Eds.), *Awareness of deficit after brain injury: Clinical and theoretical issues.* Oxford: Oxford University Press.

Marcel, A. (1993). Slippage in the unity of consciousness. In *Experimental and theoretical studies of consciousness, Ciba Foundation Symposium, 174,* 168–186.

Marcel, A. (1994). Objectivity, simulation and the unity of consciousness. *Proceeding of the British Academy, 83,* 79–88.

Marcel, A. & Bisiach, E. (Eds.). (1988). *Consciousness in contemporary science.* Oxford: Oxford University Press.

McDaniel, K., & McDaniel, L.D. (1991). Anton's syndrome in a patient with post-traumatic optic neuropathy and bilateral contusions. *Archives of Neurology, 48,* 101–105.

McGlynn, S.M., & Schacter, D.L. (1989). Unawareness of deficits in neuropsychological syndromes. *Journal of Clinical and Experimental Neuropsychology, 11,* 143–205.

McGlynn, S.M., & Schacter, D.L. (in press). The neuropsychology of insight: Impaired awareness of deficits in a psychiatric context.

Michon, A., Deweer, B., Pillon, B., Agid, Y., et al. (1994). Relation of anosognosia to frontal lobe dysfunction in Alzheimer's disease. *Journal of Neurology, Neurosurgery, and Psychiatry, 57(7),* 805–809.

Milner, A.D., & Rugg, M.D. (1992). *The neuropsychology of consciousness.* London: Academic Press Limited.

Neisser, U. (1976). *Cognition and reality.* San Francisco: W.H. Freeman and Company.

Prigatano, G., & Schacter, D. (1991). *Awareness of deficit after brain injury: Clinical and theoretical issues.* Oxford: Oxford University Press.

Raney, A.A., & Nielsen, J.M. (1942). Denial of blindness (Anton's syndrome): Two clinical cases. *Bulletin of the Los Angeles Neurological Society, 7,* 150–151.

Redlich, E., & Bonvicini, G. (1908). Über mangelnde Wahrnehmung (Autoanästhesie) der Blindheit bei cerebralen Erkrankungen. *Neurologisches Centralblatt, 20*, 945–951.

Redlich, F.C., & Dorsey, J.F. (1945). Denial of blindness by patients with cerebral disease. *Archives of Neurology and Psychiatry, 53*, 407–417.

Rylander, G. (1932). Personality changes after operations on the frontal lobes. *Acta Psychiatrica et Neurologica Scandanavia*, Supplement No. 20.

Schacter, D., & Prigatano, G. (1991). Forms of unawareness. In G. Prigatano & D. Schacter (Eds.), *Awareness of deficit after brain injury: Clinical and theoretical issues*. Oxford: Oxford University Press.

Scheibel, M.E., & Scheibel, A.B. (1962). Hallucinations and the brain stem reticular core. In J. West (Ed.), *Hallucinations*. New York: Grune and Stratton.

Schilder, P (1935). *The image and the appearance of the human body*. London: Kegan, Paul, Trench, Truber, and Co.

Schultz, G., & Melzack, R. (1991). The Charles Bonnet syndrome, 'phantom visual images'. *Perception, 20*, 809–825.

Shallice, T. (1988). *From neuropsychology to mental structure*. Cambridge: Cambridge University Press.

Starkstein, S.E. Fedoroff, J.P., Price, T.R., Leiguarda, R., & Robinson, R.G. (1993). Neuropsychological deficits in patients with anosognosia. *Neuropsychiatry, Neuropsychology and Behavioural Neurology, 6(1)*, 43–48.

Starkstein, S.E., Vazquez, S., Migliorelli, R., Teson, A., et al. (1995). A single-photon emission computed tomographic study of anosognosia in Alzheimer's disease. *Archives of Neurology, 52(4)*, 415–420.

Stengel, E., & Steele, G.D.F. (1946). Unawareness of physical disability. *British Journal of Psychiatry, 92*, 379–388.

Stuss, D.T. (1991). Disturbances of self-awareness after frontal system damage. In G. Prigatano & D. Schacter (Eds.), *Awareness of deficit after brain injury: Clinical and theoretical issues*. Oxford: Oxford University Press.

Stuss, D.T. (1992). Biological and psychological development of executive functions. *Brain and Cognition, 32*, 8–23.

Stuss, D.T., & Benson, D.F. (1986). *The frontal lobes*. New York: Raven Press.

Suzuki, K., Endo, M., Yamadori, A., & Fujii, T. (1997). Hemispatial neglect in the visual hallucination of a patient with Anton's syndrome. *European Neurology, 37*, 63–64.

Von Monakow, A. (1885). Experimentelle und pathologischanatomisch Untersuchungen über die Beziehungen der sogenanten Sehspare zu den infracorticalen Opticuscentren und zum Nervus opticus. *Archiv für Psychiatrie. 16*, 151–199.

Walker, R., & Mattingley, J.B. (1997). Ghosts in the machine? Pathological visual completion phenomena in the damaged brain. *Neurocase, 3(5)*, 313–335.

Warrington, E.W. (1962). The completion of visual forms across hemianopic visual field defects. *Journal of Neurology, Neurosurgery, and Psychiatry, 25*, 208–217.

Weinstein, E.A., & Kahn, R.L. (1955). *Denial of illness: Symbolic and physiological aspects*. Springfield, IL: Charles C. Thomas.

West, L.J. (1975). A clinical and theoretical overview of hallucinatory phenomena. In R.K. Siegel & L.J. West (Eds.), *Hallucinations: Behaviour experience and theory*. New York: John Wiley.

Young, A.W., & De Haan, E.H.F. (1992). Face recognition and awareness after brain injury. In A.D. Milner & M.D. Rugg (Eds.), *The neuropsychology of consciousness*. London: Academic Press Limited.

NOTES

1. Anton (1899) changes between the past and present tense on a number of occasions throughout the paper.

2. We note that there are interesting parallels between this patient and patients who have been described as having reduplicative paramnesia. For example, Weinstein and Kahn (1955) reported a case of a patient who denied that she was ill, but insisted (incorrectly) that she had a son called Willie who was recovering from an illness. For a more detailed discussion of the links between Anton's syndrome and reduplicative paramnesia, see Feinberg and Roane (1997).

3. The defining characteristics of this syndrome include: (1) vivid visual hallucinations; (2) no disorientation or intellectual decline; (3) co-existing normal visual perception; (4) no bizarre sensations or associated emotional distress; (5) knowledge that visual hallucinations are not real percepts; and (6) cessation of the hallucinations when the eyes are closed (Schultz & Melzack, 1991).

CHAPTER FIFTEEN

Pick's cases on body representation (1908, 1915, 1922): A retrospective assessment

Carlo Semenza
Department of Psychology B.R.A.I.N., Neuroscience Centre, University of Trieste, Italy

Margarete Delazer
University Hospital for Neurology, Innsbruck, Austria

INTRODUCTION

Arnold Pick, the eminent Prague neurologist, first provided a number of case descriptions of patients showing difficulties in a variety of tasks implying awareness, recognition, naming, and pointing to body parts (Pick, 1908, 1915, 1922). This work has been widely quoted and is considered a milestone in the history of neuropsychological research on bodily representation (Denes, 1989; Poeck & Orgass, 1971; Semenza, 2001). The meaning of Pick's findings, however, seems to have been, in large measure, misinterpreted by following authors and some of their implications seem to have escaped Pick himself.

Pick described four cases at some length. Unfortunately the level of detail in the description of each patient's performance across tasks is very variable. In most instances Pick did not go beyond the anecdotal level and very rarely matched modern standards of reporting. It is thus very difficult for the modern reader to draw firm conclusions on the disturbances Pick might have observed.

The current chapter will show, after a careful reconsideration, that, in contrast to most claims (exceptions will, however, be mentioned), Pick's main discoveries were rather inadequate in answering basic questions about bodily representation. Some of Pick's observations, however, anticipated descriptions of phenomena whose full meaning has been appreciated only in recent times. Indeed, if properly considered, Pick's findings would have brought an earlier understanding of category and modality-specific aphasic disorders.

EARLY VIEWS AND CLINICAL FINDINGS BY PICK'S PREDECESSORS AND CONTEMPORARIES

Exhaustive critical reviews on earlier studies on bodily representation are available, with different emphasis on clinical observations (Schilder, 1935; Denes, 1989; Poeck & Orgass, 1971; Semenza, 2001), psychophysiological findings, and philosophical theories (Gallagher, 1986; Bermudez et al., 1995). The key works and concepts are however few, and will be reported here before introducing more modern and appropriate studies.

By the end of the 19th century the awareness of the body was generally understood as being based on diffuse sensory impressions from the viscera, muscles, joints, and skin, that were subsumed under the term 'coenestesia'. Bonnier (1893, 1905), in relation to the observation of patients with laby-rinthine vertigo who described experiencing their own body as larger, smaller, distorted, or without limits, first introduced the term 'body schema', supposedly disturbed in such conditions. This theoretical construct implied, besides sensory impressions, the existence, in the awareness of the body, of a certain, ill-defined, spatial quality. No mention was made of a possible neural substrate.

At about the same time, however, Munk (1890) suggested, after cortical extirpation experiments in dogs, the parietal lobe as the site where images of single body parts would be located. These images would result from the reactivation of former sensations stored in the sensorymotor cortex and allow the process of maintaining a correct body orientation despite changes in sensory information and continuous active and passive movements. The process of building these images would develop in early life from reflex and locomotor movements.

Munk's theory was later adopted and expanded by Wernicke (1900), who postulated the existence of a point-to-point association between the single cells in the sensorymotor cortex and the receptor elements of any sense organ, including the skin. He then assumed that any sensory impulse is charged with a certain quality, varying according to the location of the stimulated receptor elements. The sensorymotor cortex would thus receive from any receptor element a specific 'local sign', enabling the individual to build up by experience stable spatial images corresponding to the distribution of the receptor elements in the body. Oddly enough, Wernicke, one of the founders of neuropsychology, did not bother with neurological syndromes related to bodily representation and applied these concepts to the study of psychoses.

Head and Holmes (1911/1912) approached the problem of bodily representation by distinguishing two basic theoretical constructs corresponding to two different functions: the 'postural schema' and the 'superficial schema'. The two functions could be disturbed separately. The 'postural schema' is the function comparing, at the preconscious level, the position at any moment with the immediately preceding one. 'Every new posture or movement is recorded on this plastic schema, and the activity of the cortex brings every fresh group of sensations evoked by altered posture into relation with it.' The 'superficial schema' subserves, instead, the patient's ability to localise the exact position of a spot stimulated on the surface of the body. The separability of the two functions would be demonstrated by the dissociation shown in one of their patients who could not tell the position of his hand, while he could always localise stimulated spots correctly. In elaborating their views, Head and Holmes go on to sketch the distinction between 'schema' and 'image', whereby 'schema' is the term reserved for the preconscious process and 'image' is used once information has entered consciousness.

PICK'S FINDINGS: AUTHENTIC AUTO/SOMATOTOPAGNOSIA?

The first question addressed in the present chapter is whether or not Pick observed a genuine disturbance to a bodily representation[1] (a disturbance in the function he called 'autotopagraphia'). There are no convincing data supporting such a conclusion. Described patients could not, indeed, point to body parts on verbal command,[2] neither on themselves nor on another person (although patient FZ seemed better on another person). The following instance concerns patient FZ, the only patient described in some detail (Pick, 1922, p. 305):

Examiner: Wo haben Sie die Augen? *(Where do you have your eyes?)*
    [Looks as if searching in his hand, starts to be tearful.]
Examiner: Wo sind die Augen? *(Where are the eyes?)*
FZ: Ich sehe sie nicht. *(I do not see them).*
Examiner: Sie sehen mich doch! *(But you see me!)*
FZ: Ja. *(Yes.)*
    [Eyes are covered with a screen.]
Examiner: Wo haben Sie jetzt die Augen? *(Where do you have your eyes now?)*
FZ: Ich sehe jetzt nichts. *(Now I cannot see anything.)*
Examiner: Wo sind die Augen? *(Where are the eyes?)*
FZ: Ich weiß nicht, wo sie sind. *(I do not know where they are.)*

TABLE 15.1
A summary of Pick's cases

	Case 1	Case 2	Case 3	Case 4
Patient	55-year-old woman; worker in a printing press	Franz Z; 67 year-old-man; shop servant	63-year-old woman	25-year-old woman
Described in	Pick (1908)	Pick (1922)	Pick (1922)	Pick (1922)
Neurological background	Dementia	For 1.5 years weakness of legs; right side hemiparesis; atrophy of the white matter; hydrocephalus intern., no focal lesions	Severe dementia	For 3 days status epilepticus; test 2 days later
Neuropsychological background	Visual problems,; memory problems; no apraxia; problems in right–left orientation, poor localisation of tactile stimulation	Apraxia; memory problems; confabulations; optic ataxia (problems in grasping objects); Problems in right–left orientation; signs of extinction (tactile stimulation)	Peculiar and severe language problems; memory problems; lacking recognition of environment	Dazed and disoriented; lack of memory for recent past; transient amaurosis
Language problems	No	No	Yes	No
Comprehension of names of body parts	Yes	Yes	Not clear	Yes
Touching body parts on own body—verbal command	Not possible	Not possible	Not possible, but fluctuating deficit	Partially correct
Verification-Matching spoken word and body part	Yes	Yes	Not reported	Not reported

Touching body parts on other person	Not possible	Not possible	Not reported	Not reported
Touching body parts on a drawing	Yes (only head tested)	Yes (only eyes and ears tested)	Not reported	Not reported
Pick's explanation	Disturbance in the visual image of the body (*optisches Vorstellungsbild*). In adults the visual image substitutes the prevailing tactile and kinaesthetic image of the child	Disturbance in visual image	→	→
Interesting phenomena	She is looking for body parts outside the body (hands or ears on table). Fluctuating deficit; problem is more pronounced for the parts of the head than for other body parts	Tactile anomia; better performance on picture; Extinction on tactile stimulation		

However, there is no evidence that the patients' difficulties were confined to bodily locations (a summary of Pick's findings is given in Table 15.1). This sort of disturbance can then be, at best, classified as one of those cases, first reported by De Renzi and Scotti (1970), where the patient's deficit lies in isolating single parts within complex objects. All patients suffered from a very severe functional pathology, sustained by widely diffuse lesions, and many confusing factors may have determined the patients' performance, among which problems with visual recognition, reaching, language, and attention (see the opinion expressed by Poeck & Orgass in their 1971 paper). Case 3, for instance, a 63-year-old woman affected by severe dementia, showed peculiar language problems (Pick, 1922, p. 316):

Examiner: Wo waren Sie gestern? *(Where have you been yesterday?)*
Patient: Gestern war ich heute. No gestern war ich unten. Ich weiß nicht wo das dort Mutter unten. *(Yesterday I was today. Yesterday I was down. I don't know where this there mother down.)*
Examiner: Waren Sie im Garten? *(Have you been in the garden?)*
Patient: Ich war dort niemals fortwährend. *(I was there never always.)*
Examiner: Wer ist das? *(Who is that?)*
Patient: Ich auch noch auch solche bin unten. *(I also still also such am down.)*
Examiner: Wo haben Sie die Augen? *(Where do you have your eyes?)*
    [Patient points correctly.]
Examiner: Nase? *(Nose?)*
Patient: Das weiß ich nicht. Das ist ja nichts anderes. *(I don't know. This is nothing different.)*
Examiner: Mund? (Mouth?)
    [Patient points to the nose.]
Examiner: Ohr? *(Ear?)*
Patient: Ohr, wenn es lernt, so reißt es ab. *(Ear, if it learns, it tears off.)*

Confabulation concerning location of body parts is one of the most striking features in at least two of the patients. For instance, they looked for their own body parts on the bed, on the table, or in the waistcoat of the examiner. However, whether confabulations did or did not extend to other objects and domains is nowhere mentioned. FZ could not point to objects in different positions (Pick, 1922, p. 308).

    [A watch is held 25 cm from his face at the height of his eyes. He looks at it, grasps wide behind, with the hand in the air. Asked whether he sees it, he says no. Glass named correctly.]
Examiner: Nehmen Sie es! *(Take it!)*
    [Gropes wide behind, gropes slowly closer. Pipe named correctly.]
Examiner: Nehmen Sie sie! *(Take it!)*
    [Grasps in the air wide behind, does not fixate at all, looks around.]

Pick did not yet doubt body-specificity for the phenomena he was observing. He followed Munk and Wernicke: somatognosic orientation would develop by experience on the basis of tactile and kinaesthetic engrams in the first years of life. According to Pick, a 'visual image' would instead prevail in the adult. A disturbance of such image ('*optisches Vorstellungsbild*') he saw as an explanation for his patients' symptoms. Pick also spoke of '*Bewußtsein der Körperlichkeit*'—an expression that might be translated as 'awareness of the body' or 'awareness of having a body'. He thought that his 1908 patient was somehow better at pointing to locations at the back of the body and therefore not perceived by vision. This suggested the idea of a dissociation between visual and non-visual thinking.

PICK'S MOST IMPORTANT FINDINGS ON BODY PART KNOWLEDGE

In 1908 Pick mentioned the fact that in some patients (not included in the four cases reported in Table 15.1) the comprehension of the names of body parts seemed to be more clearly compromised than the comprehension of the names of objects. He also briefly described a patient who showed the reverse dissociation. This aphasic patient understood the names of his body parts particularly well in comparison with those of objects. No details are given to support such conclusions, but Pick seems to be rather clear about the veridicality of these effects. Pick was thus well aware of the idea that body parts constitute a special word category in the brain. This early observation of the special linguistic status of the names of body parts was confirmed in modern time by Goodglass, Klein, Carey, and Jones (1966). They showed that the comprehension of body part names was frequently selectively impaired in Wernicke's aphasia. The same phenomenon was particularly evident in a patient described by Yamadori and Albert (1973). Other dissociations concerning body part names were reported by Goodglass, Wingfield, Hyde, and Therkauf (1986) and Dennis (1976). The effects concerning body part names were among the first instances of the category-specific aphasic disorders that have raised enormous interest in the past three decades. Pick's role in the discovery of the phenomenon was, however, never clearly acknowledged.

The last but not least of Pick's (1922) interesting findings seems also to have passed unnoticed. FZ, Pick's most extensively described patient, showed, in fact, a consistent dissociation between naming in the visual modality and naming in the tactile modality, with a clear disadvantage in the latter case. Unfortunately, Pick did not pursue a convincing demonstration of the phenomenon. However, as regards immediate and correct naming of the same objects on visual presentation, FZ is reported to have been unable to name, blindfolded and on tactile presentation, a handkerchief, a ring, a bottle, a spoon, a key, and a watch. The possibility that an elementary tactile deficit or an agnosic deficit alone might have determined the symptomatology is unlikely, because FZ showed recognition ability, for example by putting the ring on his own finger.

Tactile anomia, the symptom that Pick seems to have discovered, has been described in modern times by Geschwind (1965a, 1965b). However, Geschwind's description mainly concerned the case where tactile anomia appears to be limited to the material presented to the left hand, an easily demonstrable correlate of callosal lesions that has a convincing explanation in neuroanatomical terms. Geschwind's report of the more problematic (and interesting) bilateral tactile anomia was as anecdotal as Pick's one. Only in 1978 was a bilateral tactile anomia described and discussed in detail by Beauvois, Saillant, Meininger, and Lhermitte.

MODERN NEUROPSYCHOLOGICAL STUDIES

The meaning of Pick's work may be better evaluated in the context of relevant modern studies on autotopagnosia. This term is still used for designating what appears to be a genuine disturbance of bodily representation, consisting of the inability to locate body parts on command. A group study and three single case studies are reported in the literature.

Group study (Semenza & Goodglass, 1985)

In 1985 Semenza and Goodglass set up an investigation aimed at obtaining information specific to knowledge and awareness of body parts. The issue was whether neuropsychological patients committed errors in indicating body parts that were not explicable on the basis of linguistic, visual, and motor deficits, and could then be appropriately accounted for in terms of a disturbed representation of the body. A battery of converging tasks that could control for confounding factors such as language disorders was then constructed. The selection of the subjects therefore excluded patients with reaching disorders, spatial disorientation, and visual agnosia, along with patients with problems of vigilance. Patients with right hemisphere lesions were required to point to body parts on their right side, in order to partial out the possible effect of unilateral spatial neglect.

The results revealed that, indeed, a number of left hemisphere patients (right hemisphere patients scored at ceiling) made errors based on conceptual confusions even in non-verbal tasks (e.g. joint for joint, eye for ear, etc.). A typical error of this sort, for example, is the patient who has been touched on the elbow by the examiner, while she/he kept eyes closed, indicating the knee on a whole-body drawing. These errors, the number of which largely exceeded chance level, may only be attributed to a genuine disturbance of bodily representation. This representation seems to be 'modality neutral', because no significant difference was found between localisation on one's own body and on a full-size drawing.

While, in general, verbal tasks were performed more poorly, a number of patients made significantly more errors in non-verbal tasks, thus ruling out the possibility (never fully excluded before) that aphasia is the only factor that would account for the errors. Of interest as regards speculation on the content of the disturbed representation was the fact that errors correlated negatively with the frequency of the names of single body parts (this was in two linguistically independent groups—American and Italian). While it is no surprise that this happened in verbal tasks, the significant correlation found in non-verbal tasks seems again revealing about the content of the representation.

Semenza and Goodglass (1985) could not single out in their population an individual patient with an isolated body-specific disturbance; however, they prepared the framework for the proper observation of single case studies. Interestingly, their battery of tasks produced results substantially similar to those of adult aphasic patients when administered to young children (Lucca, Semenza, & Sgaramella, 1991), where all main effects and types of errors were replicated.

Single case studies

Case JPB (Ogden, 1985)

The first case convincingly featuring the inability to locate body parts on command as an isolated deficit was described in 1985 by Ogden. The patient, JPB, affected by a metastatic carcinoma in the left parietal lobe, had no nominal aphasia and could name body parts when they were pointed to by someone else, could understand complex verbal instructions, and could correctly describe the functions of named body parts. Watching the examiner while pointing to body parts on another person on verbal command he was able to comment correctly whether the examiner pointed to the correct part (plus showing at least a good auditory comprehension of body part names). He successfully pointed to items of clothing named by the examiner on himself and the examiner. He was also able to point to parts of objects, plants, and animals on command. In contrast, JPB could not perform the following tasks:

(1) Pointing to or touching body parts named by the examiner on himself, the examiner, three dolls, and a photograph of a man.
(2) With the eyes closed, touching body parts on himself to the examiner's verbal command.

(3) Pointing to parts of the body on himself that the examiner pointed to on herself.

(4) Pointing to those parts of his own body that corresponded with numbered body parts on a picture of a naked man facing frontward and facing backward.

He could draw a reasonably accurate stick picture of a man. When asked where the foot would go he pointed to the arm, drew a stick and said 'It would go here on the end on the leg'. He was also shown a model of a face with removable ears, eyes, nose, mouth, hat, and spectacles. After removing the parts while he watched, the experimenter asked him to pick up each part, name it, and slot it into the face in the correct position. He named all the parts correctly as he picked them up, but put the ears where the eyes should go, the eyes where the ears should go, the mouth on the top of the head where the hat should go, and the nose in the correct place. He said that he did not realise the face looked strange until this point.

Case IS (Semenza, 1988)

In this study a more extended analysis of error types, similar to that proposed by Semenza and Goodglass (1985), was performed.

The patient, IS, was affected by a metastatic melanoma in the left parieto-occipital (angular) area. A very mild nominal aphasia was evident where naming body parts was not worse than naming other categories. Auditory comprehension was good. Agraphia, acalculia, fingeragnosia (more severe on non-verbal conditions), right–left disorientation, and ideomotor apraxia were present.

The ability to localise body parts was also tested with the Semenza and Goodglass (1985) battery. The classification of errors was made according to Semenza and Goodglass's criteria and it was used to permit an easy matching with the results of their group study. The error totals were therefore grouped into three categories:

- *Conceptual.* Different types of errors were grouped under this label: joint substituted for joint, eye–ear–nose substitution or toe–thumb substitution.
- *Contiguity.* Same limb as stimulus or face–head response for a face–head stimulus. This group basically includes errors that reflect misreaching.
- *Random.* Neither of above.

Eye–ear substitutions were classified as 'conceptual' despite the anatomical contiguity of these body parts for two reasons. First, they also share a conceptual relation as structures specially built for sensory reception and are learned in childhood as such. Secondly, their prominence on the head allows one to judge the patient's pointing as unambiguously unlikely to result from motor inaccuracy. IS, however, made few of these errors.

IS gave a response to all orders. Of the 52 errors she made 23 could be classified as conceptual, 20 as contiguity, and only 9 as random. Considering IS's performance it was safe to conclude that it was by no means determined by chance. Most errors were of the conceptual type and it seems reasonable to argue that contiguity errors are also unlikely to have been determined by motor inaccuracy rather than made on the basis of a conceptual confusion. This is suggested by the fact that IS did not show reaching disorders in other domains and from the performance on the isolated part conditions where motor inaccuracy could not explain contiguity choices. It is to be noted that the non-verbal stimulus conditions produced even more errors than did the verbal conditions.

Additional tests concerning body parts were given to IS. In one she had to watch while the examiner pointed to the full-size drawing of a human figure on verbal command and to comment on whether the examiner pointed to the correct part. She performed correctly on this test. Another test asked for information about the functional ('What is the mouth for?') and spatial ('Where is the mouth with respect to nose?') nature of body parts. She was relatively accurate in giving 'functional' information while in three out of five cases she did not seem to understand questions concerning relative locations of body parts. Unfortunately, no attempt was made at that time to better understand the reasons for this latter difficulty.

In contrast with her difficulties with body parts, IS was quick and accurate when asked to show on herself where items of clothing should be worn, including items neither she nor the examiner were actually wearing, like gloves or necktie. She also performed perfectly in a variety of verbal and non-verbal conditions requiring the localisation of parts of complex objects.

Case DLS (Sirigu, Grafman, Blessler, & Sunderland 1991)

This study was focused on the spatial aspects of the patient's deficit in order to distinguish the spatial representation from other components of the overall bodily representation.

Patient DLS received a diagnosis of probable dementia of Alzheimer's type. She was mildly amnesic, had ideational and constructional apraxia, agraphia, acalculia, fingeragnosia, and right–left confusion.

Her naming of body parts indicated by the examiner on the patient's body with the eyes closed or open, was relatively spared. The ability to localise body parts was tested using verbal and non-verbal instructions. In the verbal conditions the patient was asked to point to a body part named by the examiner on her own body (eyes closed and/or open), on the examiner's body, and on a doll's body. In non-verbal conditions the patient had to touch the examiner's body on the same part that the examiner touched the patient's body with the eyes closed/open. DLS's performance was poor in all these conditions, especially in non-verbal ones.

In the analysis of the errors the observed proportions for each type of error (contiguity, functional substitutions, or random) were carefully evaluated against the probability of occurrence by chance. Contiguity errors were overwhelmingly above chance in contrast to random errors that were rather few. Functional substitutions ('conceptual errors') appeared to be above chance only in the verbal conditions while in the non-verbal conditions their number was what would be expected if the pointing responses were performed at chance. It is, however, difficult to conclude with Sirigu et al. that DLS was relatively immune to conceptual disturbances in non-verbal tasks just on the basis of the reported data. The non-verbal tasks were much easier and less likely to produce conceptual errors than, for instance, those administered to patient IS: in the only difficult one, where the patient had to keep her eyes closed, more functional substitution errors indeed seemed to appear.

DLS's performance was near perfect in pointing to parts of objects, and in defining the functions of body parts, but she failed completely in defining verbally their locations. This disturbance was extremely severe because she failed also when the task was administered in a much simpler form—i.e. using a two-choice forced recognition probe task ('Is the wrist next to the forearm?').

Sirigu et al. (1991) then raised the question as to whether any spatial information could be coded using a body map as a reference system. A set of tasks was prepared to address this issue. DLS was therefore requested to point to a body part or to a small object attached at the same location. Two types of instructions, verbal and non-verbal, were used. The patient either had to point to the object named by the examiner (verbal), or was requested to point on the examiner's body to the same object that had been touched by the examiner on the patient's body (non-verbal; note that both the examiner and patient had identical objects attached to the same parts of their bodies). This was contrasted with the same tasks performed with the body parts as targets without any object being present on anyone's body. The results were consistent with the previous results in that a large number of errors were made when body parts were used as targets. However, when the targets were objects attached to the same body parts, the patient was virtually perfect.

DISCUSSION: TOWARDS A COGNITIVE, NEUROPSYCHOLOGY-BASED THEORY OF BODILY REPRESENTATION

Having described Pick's findings and modern neuropsychological works on autotopagnosia, it seems worthwhile to explore their meaning as regards a neuropsychological-based theory of bodily representation. The aim of a cognitive theory of bodily representation would be to specify the content and the format of the representation(s) and the processes that such representations would undergo in relevant tasks.

Despite an over-abundant literature (see, for a review, Denes, 1989; Semenza 2001), relevant observations are indeed scarce and tentative answers are available to a limited number of questions. The following questions seem to be the most important ones:

(1) What sort of representation mediates voluntary localisation of one's body parts? And voluntary generation of body parts images? In other words, what sort of information (e.g. spatial, topological, structural, functional, propositional etc.) constitutes the object of one's body consciousness in the localisation tasks?

(2) How independent is the storage and processing of this representation from the representation of other possible contents of consciousness, in particular that of complex objects? Is there a brain location specifically supporting the processing of the representation of the human body? Is there a specifically devoted module? Would this representation work in the same way in locating one's body parts and the body parts of another human being (or of a bi/tridimensional human figure)?

(3) Is there a peculiar quality distinguishing the representation of the body, at this level, from the representation of complex objects, including animal bodies?

The answers to these questions imply the observation of neuropsychological cases that are indeed very rare. Before the relevant observations can be made, however, an analysis of the task of locating body parts has to be performed and an appropriate testing apparatus has to be built. As we have seen, this has indeed been a very recent enterprise despite much speculation and the personal interest that leading figures in the (neuro)psychological field took in the topic. Arnold Pick, himself, could make the following statement in his paper: 'The abundance of speculation and theoretical constructs in the doctrine of the loss of awareness of the body . . . is inversely proportional to factual observations: leaving aside symptoms demonstrated by psychoastenic and hysterical subjects, which can hardly be considered as reliable cases, there remains very little.' Pick's words, indeed, seem to indicate, unintentionally, why the field has remained underdeveloped for several decades before and since. This reason is not the lack of factual observations, as Pick seemed to think, nor, in principle, the abundance of speculations and theoretical constructs. The true reason is that the theorisation did not start with a theory of tasks involving body knowledge and awareness, or about the mental representation(s) that could mediate such tasks. Theoretical constructs and speculation started, instead, straight from the observation of some clinical facts. It was then thought that such facts could be better understood as disturbances involving a no better specified construct called 'body schema'. Once the term became popular, a great variety of symptoms were considered to concern 'body schema' and were then used to prove the validity of the theoretical concept. As Poeck and Orgass (1971) later argued, this is a classical case of petitio principii, in that one hypothesis served to explain another hypothesis and vice versa.

The kind of theory that one wanted to test had therefore to be made explicit. As Semenza and Goodglass (1985) observed, there are in principle two classes of theories that can be put forward about bodily representation. The first class of theories would bear upon a content largely determined by sensory factors. The amount of information stored for each body part would be proportional to the amount of somatosensory receptors, and, perhaps, the precision and selectivity of muscular innervation, in a fashion resembling the cellular representation in the primary cortical areas (the 'homunculus sensorius' and the 'homunculus motorius'). Alternatively, with the content determined mainly on the basis of visuo-spatial information, the representation could be construed as a prototypical platonic image or a canonical 3D image of the body. Errors in body part localisation supporting this first class of theories should relate, for example, to axial versus peripheral or to proximal versus distal localisation of targets or else be caused by poor space control with errors either contiguous to the target or randomly distributed. The second class of theories would have, instead, a higher order, conceptual/semantic content. Errors in localisation, according to this type of theory, would depend upon factors such as similarity of function, operativity (in the Piagetian sense), or word frequency of the target. Errors may follow similar determinant rules, whether committed on one's own body, on a drawing, or on isolated pictures of body parts.

Experimental investigations to test the theoretical hypotheses and their general validity without prejudice have never been carried out, with the exception of those reported in the preceding section. A main feature, together with incorrect procedures, was that prior to Semenza and Goodglass's study (1985), no attention was devoted to tasks apt to capture information specific to body knowledge and awareness. The detection of theoretically relevant patients was thus impossible. Note that single cases of isolated disturbances related to the body were not necessary to answer most of the main questions

TABLE 15.2
Relevant tasks

Stimulus	Example	Response
Group A: Pointing		
Verbal command	'Show me the nose'	Pointing to self
		Pointing to other person
		Pointing to drawing (full size)
		Pointing to drawing (single parts)
Non-verbal command	Examiner touches self	Pointing to self
	Examiner touches the patient (eyes closed)	Pointing to other person
		Pointing to drawing (full size)
	Shows a picture of isolated parts	Pointing to drawing (single parts)
Group B: Verification	'Am I touching the nose?'	Yes/no (verbal or non-verbal indication)
Group C: Construction	From pieces of puppets etc.	
A + B + C	Also on parts of complex objects (and animals)	
Group D: Description		
Structural description	'Is the mouth above or below the nose?'	
	'Is the wrist next to the forearm?'	
Functional description	'What is the mouth for?'	
	'Is the mouth for eating?'	

(apart from the independence of neural implementation). The condition for success proved to be, indeed, the building of a battery of converging tasks that could eliminate confounding factors. Procedures had to be designed, bearing on body part awareness, tapping specific factors independent of language, level of consciousness, memory, intelligence, and spatial orientation. Aphasia and non-linguistic disorders such as unilateral spatial neglect, visual agnosia, and reaching problems could easily interfere with a brain-damaged patient's response and understanding of the task. Human body specificity had also to be demonstrated with a preservation in the performance concerning the bodies of animals and complex objects. The practical outcome of these theoretical considerations may be synthesised in the form of a minimal list of tasks, such as that appearing in Table 15.2, that should be given in a modern study. Guidelines to a proper diagnosis of a genuine disorder of bodily representation that should rightly be called 'autotopagnosia' are given in Table 15.3.

TABLE 15.3
What should be called autotopagnosia?

Conditions required to call 'Agnosia' a given symptom complex:

(1) (Modality) specificity of the defect.
(2) Intact sensory and motor pathways.
(3) No problems with language, attention, intelligence, object reaching etc. interfering with stimulus perception and response.

Then autotopagnosics should:

(1) Show their deficit only for body parts: thus they should be able to recognise and point to objects and parts of objects.
(2) Show their deficit also on non-verbal command. [If only for verbal commands the disorder must be aphasic in nature; if then found to be body-part-specific the deficit is akin to category-specific aphasias: difficulty in accessing body part meaning from phonological form?]

Consider also the following minor problem (pointed out by Gerstmann, 1942, and Poeck & Orgass, 1971): autotopagnosia should in principle refer to difficulties with one's own body and not with the body of other persons or drawings of a body. This dissociation however has never been reported. As will be described later all genuine cases perform in the same way in all conditions. As Gerstmann (1942) pointed out, the correct name for such a disturbance should be 'somatotopagnosia', a term that, however, was never used earlier.

CONCLUSION

The conclusion of this retrospective study on Pick's papers on bodily knowledge and representation may be viewed as an answer to the following two questions: (1) Did Pick describe genuine disturbances to a bodily representation? (2) Did Pick's finding have any relevance for a theory of the organisation of lexical semantics?

The answer to the first question is probably not. It is really hard to tell what Pick might have observed: he certainly did not demonstrate body specificity for the disturbances he described, nor did he demonstrate independence from language. He also did not partial out confounding factors. However, he started to put together a theory and to show the way forward for modern researchers. In his view the content of bodily representation was mostly based on the sensation coming from single organs. A visual content would prevail in the adult. Since Pick's 'body image' the modern current knowledge may be summarised as follows. A mental module exists, in the left parietal lobe foremost, working not only on the basis of visuo-spatial knowledge. This knowledge, in fact, seems to be organised, with respect to proportions, by integration with functional (semantic) knowledge. This module does not process information about objects.

The answer to the second question is surprisingly positive. Indeed Pick's work provided an early description of phenomena that were appreciated much later, like category- and modality-specific aphasias. Indeed in the past two decades the discussion and rediscovery of these phenomena has contributed significantly to modern conceptualisation about the lexicons and their representation in the brain.

REFERENCES

Beauvois, M.F., Saillant, B., Meininger, V., & Lhermitte, F. (1978) Bilateral tactile aphasia: A tacto-verbal dysfunction. *Brain, 101*, 381–401.

Bermudez, J.L., Marcel, A.J., & Eilan, N. (1995). *The Body and the self.* Lond: MIT Press.

Bonnier, P. (1893). *Vertige.* Chartres: Rueff, Imprimerie Durand, Rue Fulbert.

Bonnier, P. (1905). L'aschematie. *Revue Neurologie, 13*, 605–609.

Denes, G. (1989). Disorders of body awareness and body knowledge. In F. Boller & J. Grafman (Eds.), *Handbook of neuropsychology* (Vol. 2, pp. 207–227). Amsterdam and London: Elsevier Publishers.

Dennis, M. (1976). Dissociated naming and locating of body parts after anterior temporal lobe resection: An experimental case study. *Brain and Language, 3*, 147–163.

De Renzi E., & Scotti G. (1970). Autotopagnosia: Fiction or reality? Report of a case. *Archives of Neurology (Chicago), 23*, 221–227.

Gallagher, S. (1986). Body image and body schema: A conceptual clarification. *The Journal of Mind and Behaviour, 7(4)*, 541–554.

Gerstman, J. (1942). Problems of imperception of disease and of impaired body territories with organic lesions: Relations to body schema and its disorders. *Archives of Neurology and Psychiatry, 48*, 890–913.

Geschwind, N. (1965a). Disconnexion syndromes in animals and man. *Brain, 88*, 237–294.

Geschwind, N. (1965b). Disconnexion syndromes in animals and man. *Brain, 88*, 585–644.

Goodglass, H., Klein, B., Carey, P., & Jones, K.J. (1966). Specific semantic categories in aphasia. *Cortex, 2*, 74–89.

Goodglass, H., Wingfield, A., Hyde, M.R., & Therkauf, J. C. (1986). Category specific dissociations in naming and recognition by aphasic patients. *Cortex, 22*, 87–102.

Head, H., & Holmes, G. (1911/12). Sensory disturbances from cerebral lesions. *Brain, 34*, 102–254.

Lucca A., Semenza C., & Sgaramella T.M. (1991). The ability in localising body parts in children. In A. Lucca & F. Cristante (Eds.), *Modelli log-lineari nella ricerca psicologica.* Padova: UPSEL.

Munk, H. (1890). *Über die Funktion der Großhirnrinde, 2. Auflage.* Berlin: Aug. Hirschwald.

Ogden, J.A. (1985). Occurrence in a patient without nominal aphasia and with an intact ability to point to parts of animals and objects. *Brain, 108*, 1009–1022.

Pick, A. (1908). *Über Störungen der Orientierung am eigenen Körper. Arbeiten aus der deutschen psychiatrischen Universitäts-Klinik in Prag.* Berlin: Karger.

Pick, A. (1915). Zur Pathologie des Bewußtseins vom eigenen Körper. *Neurologisches Centralblatt,* 34, 257–265.

Pick, A. (1922). Störung der Orientierung am eigenen Körper. *Psychologische Forschung, 1*, 303–318.

Poeck, K., & Orgass, B. (1971). The concept of the body schema: A critical review and some experimental results. *Cortex, 7*, 254–277.

Schilder, P. (1935). *The image and the appearance of the human body.* New York: International Universities Press.

Semenza, C. (1988). Impairment in localisation of body parts following brain damage. *Cortex, 24*, 443–449.

Semenza, C. (2001). Disorders of body representation. In R.S. Berndt (Ed.), *Handbook of neuropsychology* (Vol. 3, pp. 285–303). Amsterdam: Elsevier Science BV.

Semenza, C., Goodglass H. (1985). Localisation of body parts in brain-injured subjects. *Neuropsychologia, 23(2)*, 161–175.

Sirigu, A., Grafman, J., Blessler, K., & Sunderland T. (1991). Multiple representations contribute to body knowledge processing. Evidence from a case of autotopagnosia. *Brain, 114*, 629–642.

Wernicke, C. (1900). *Grundriß der Psychiatrie in klinischen Vorlesungen*. Leipzig: Thieme.

Yamadori, A. & Albert, M.L. (1973). Word category aphasia. *Cortex, 9*, 112–125.

NOTES

1. The term 'autotopagnosia', generally used up to our times in designating such disturbance, is often credited to Pick but nowhere does it appear in the papers considered here.
2. Non-verbal commands were not given.

CHAPTER SIXTEEN

Delusional misidentifications: History and contemporary theory

Hadyn D. Ellis
School of Psychology, Cardiff University, UK

INTRODUCTION

The way in which facial information conveying people's identity is processed by the mind/brain has long been the subject of serious scientific enquiry. How the process can become blocked or distorted by brain injury has provided valuable insights into the underlying mechanisms of this all-important socio-biological process, and what I want to discuss in this chapter are some conditions often but not invariably associated with psychopathology that have recently been seen to provide equally significant data. The value of such information in helping us understand normal information processing is the substance of the newly coined area of cognitive neuropsychiatry (David, 1993; Ellis, 1991). Some of the specific advantages for modelling face recognition were recently rehearsed by me in a paper demonstrating the two-way process of using models of cognitive process to understand pathological states and, where necessary, taking observations from cases where these are aberrant to modify those models (Ellis, 1998). Here, however, I want to concentrate on the aberrant processes themselves.

During the period 1923–1932 three papers by French psychiatrists were published that each described a different form of what we now term delusional misidentification syndromes (DMI). These seminal studies have had an impact upon the ideas of psychiatrists, psychologists, philosophers, and neurologists concerning the nature of belief in general and, more specifically, the ways in which person recognition is mediated.

The three papers concern:

(1) *The Capgras Delusion*: The belief that others, often close to the patient, have been replaced by doubles (Capgras & Reboul-Lachaux, 1923—'L'illusion des "sosies" dans un délire systématisé chronique').

(2) *The Frégoli Delusion*: The belief that significant people disguise themselves as strangers in order to influence the patient (Courbon & Fail, 1927—'Syndrome d'"illusion de Frégoli" et schizophrénie').

(3) *Intermetamorphosis*: The experience of seeing others immediately physically transform into another person (Courbon & Tusques, 1932—'Illusions d'inter-métamorphose et de charme').

Translations of the three key DMI papers are to be found in Ellis, Whitley, and Luauté (1994). Here I shall summarise the key parts of these papers and offer a brief commentary on each of them. I shall also introduce each paper by offering a little biographical detail on the principal authors.

JOSEPH CAPGRAS (1873–1950)

Capgras, though renowned for his writings on the 'curious little syndrome' that now bears his name, was better known in his day for his more substantial work with Sérieux on trying to understand the basis for mental disorders rather than merely describing them. Indeed, this philosophy was also held by Kahlbaum, a 19th-century German psychiatrist (Lanczik, 1892). Kahlbaum (1866), in fact, had briefly described a case where the patient believed others to have been replaced by doubles, but it was not until the publication in 1923 by Capgras and his assistant Reboul-Lachaux that the phenomenon was extensively described and analysed. The *'illusion de sosies'* was the term they used, *'sosie'* meaning double in French, derived from Plautus' play, 'Amphytrion' in which the god Mercury assumes the appearance of Sosie, the servant of Amphytrion.

Luauté (1986) has explored the influences of Capgras' thinking at some length. Here we should simply record that the philosopher/psychologists Ribot (1905) and Bergson (1911) were each probably influential in shaping the way he originally interpreted the *'illusion de sosies'*. Ribot had emphasised the role of affective aspects of the mind, while Bergson had contributed the notion of dual recognition: an automatic feeling of familiarity; and the more cognitively based identification by matching to stored representation. I shall elaborate these influences in the following theoretical discussion. At this juncture, it is worth recording that in his subsequent papers describing cases of delusional misidentification (Capgras & Carrette, 1924; Capgras, Lucchini, & Schiff, 1924), the psychoanalytically oriented influences of Capgras' colleagues became much more prominent in his thinking; and for many decades afterwards this type of explanation dominated theoretical approaches to the delusional misidentification syndromes.

MME M

Capgras and Reboul-Lachaux described the case of Mme M, who for some years had been displaying a series of delusions in which everyone in her family, as well as others, had been transformed into doubles.

Mme M was 53 years old at the time of the report. She had been married for 25 years and lived with her husband and their one surviving daughter (four children died in infancy). For many years she had expressed the belief that her husband had been replaced by a double. She also evinced delusions of grandeur, *inter alia* believing herself to be the granddaughter of Princess Eugénie, and that she had been abducted by her apparent parents. At other times Mme M complained of being persecuted by people who, she thought, had taken both her money and her children. Furthermore, she insisted that these same people were behind the various substitutions of people she knew, including doubles of herself.

When her husband disappeared to be replaced by a double, Mme M requested a divorce: 'If this person is my husband,' she asserted, 'he is more than unrecognisable, he is a completely transformed person.' Eventually, everyone in Mme M's society was believed to have been replaced by doubles and the originals either murdered or incarcerated in subterranean vaults. Her distress was compounded by the belief that the police, to whom she made complaints, were themselves impostors. Of course, all the doctors and nurses as well as fellow patients, had also been replaced, some many times, as doubles themselves were replaced by other doubles. (She claimed, for example, some 2000 doubles of her daughter had appeared to her over a 4-year period.)

According to Capgras and Reboul-Lachaux, Mme M's delusions of doubles were largely persecutory in nature and may have arisen in response to the grief at losing her other children. This, they argued, could have led to feelings of strangeness that, in turn, may have masked any normal feelings of familiarity that normally accompany face perception: 'With her, the delusion of doubles is not therefore really a sensory delusion, but rather the conclusion of an emotional judgement . . . [it is] created by the logic of feelings'. This assessment by Capgras and Reboul-Lachaux has proved to be remarkably accurate, as I shall discuss later. Unfortunately, as I mentioned earlier, Capgras quickly abandoned that particular approach to DMI in order to pursue more psychoanalytically inspired ideas (de Pauw, 1994).

One other feature of Mme M's case history worth highlighting was her belief that she could discern small physical differences between the double and the original person: 'a little mark on the ear . . . a thinner face . . . a longer moustache . . . different colour eyes. . .'. Such claims are not at all uncommonly observed in patients with Capgras syndrome and probably serve to help them to rationalise their bizarre beliefs and to sustain their confabulations.

THE CAPGRAS DELUSION

The '*illusion de sosies*' soon became known as Capgras Syndrome or the Capgras Delusion. Unfortunately, the immediate theoretical ideas offered by Capgras to explain Mme M's complex symptoms were quickly forgotten: instead, his subsequent views emphasising psychodynamic origins of the syndrome, particularly Oedipal feelings, began to dominate ideas, first in France and then elsewhere. But it is clear from his first paper on the subject that, originally, he conceptualised the disorder in a quasi-neurological way. He used the word 'agnosia', for example, and, without mentioning him by name, invoked Bergson's (1911) dichotomy between a feeling of familiarity and full identification to explain the patient's responses to recognising others yet being unable to believe that they were truly who they seemed. This approach to the Capgras Delusion was periodically dusted off and reasserted (e.g. Derombies, 1935) but was not fully explored until, in a theoretical paper, Andy Young and I (Ellis & Young, 1990) suggested that the Capgras Delusion is the mirror image of prosopagnosia (i.e. the neurological condition resulting in profound inability to recognise faces [Ellis, 1975; Meadows, 1974). What we meant by this requires some explanation.

Some prosopagnosics reveal covert face recognition (Bauer, 1984; Bruyer et al., 1983; Young & De Haan, 1992). That is, when shown previously familiar faces whom they cannot consciously recognise they may, nonetheless, reveal a normal increased autonomic activity compared with that elicited by faces never encountered before; or they may display an inhibition in learning incorrect face–name pairs compared with correct pairs. It is not entirely certain why or how such covert activity occurs, but one explanation offered by Bauer (1984) has certain attractions in general if not in its anatomical specifics. He argued that there are two routes to recognition: a ventral route connecting visual cortex to temporal lobe and limbic structures via the inferior longitudinal fasciculus that produces overt recognition; and a dorsal route between the same centres that passes closer to parietal structures and that may convey affective information or signal some sort of significance in the stimulus. As I said, since these particular anatomical routes may not necessarily be correct (Breen, Caine, & Coltheart, 2000); it is probably safer at this stage simply to refer to them as route one and route two (Ellis, 1998). Some prosopagnosics, while clearly having damage to or disconnection at some point along route one, nonetheless may receive some information, albeit unconsciously, via route two.

Ellis and Young (1990) suggested that in the Capgras Delusion the reverse may be true: an intact route one coupled with an impaired or disconnected route two. As Ellis and Young (1990) pointed out, if this hypothesis is true, patients with Capgras Delusion should not show the usual raised autonomic activity to familiar compared with unfamiliar faces (cf. Ellis, Young, & Koenken, 1993; Tranel, Fowles, & Damasio, 1985). In other words, they have a disorder that is the mirror image of that seen in some prosopagnosics. This is depicted in Figure 16.1.

This prediction received empirical support from two independent studies. Ellis, Young, Quayle, and de Pauw (1997) presented five Capgras Delusion patients with a random series of familiar and unfamiliar faces and, as predicted, found no difference in skin conductance responses (SCRs) to these two types of stimuli. Normal subjects and psychiatric controls, however, revealed the typically larger SCRs to familiar faces. Following the same hypothesis, Hirstein and Ramachandran (1997) made exactly the same observations in a patient with neurological damage following a car accident who revealed Capgras Delusion for both famous and personally familiar faces. Interestingly, he did not experience the belief that his parents were impostors

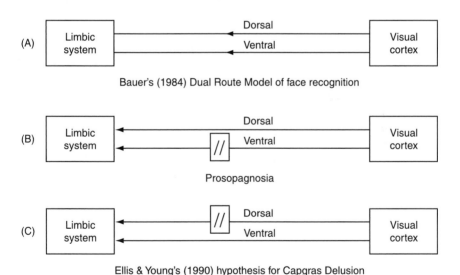

Figure 16.1   (A) Schematic account of Bauer's (1984) Dual Route Model of face recognition. The ventral route conveys identity information and the dorsal route carries information about a face's significance. (B) Applied to covert recognition phenomena in prosopagnosia the Dual Route Model suggests that the dorsal route may operate even in the absence of ventral route information, giving rise to increased SCRs to previously familiar faces. (C) Ellis and Young (1990) originally accepted Bauer's anatomical scheme and applied it to Capgras Delusion phenomena: they suggested that the ventral route may be intact but the dorsal route may be disconnected (i.e. the mirror image of prosopagnosia). Later they pointed out that their suggestion is not dependent upon Bauer's specific anatomical pathways.

when speaking to them on the phone: it seems a face-specific condition. Moreover, the delusion can occur for objects, independently of faces (Anderson, 1988; Ellis, de Pauw, Young, & Kolkiewicz, 1996).

As Ellis and de Pauw (1994) pointed out, the second route may be described as signalling affective significance but, equally, it could transmit what Bergson (1911) inferred to be a necessary accompanying sense of familiarity. Mandler (1980) later argued that, normally, recognition may involve the convergence of two independent processes—familiarity and identification. If someone receives only the latter type of information, then it is conceivable that he or she may conclude that something is wrong with the person—the appearance may not have changed but some indefinable quality is missing, *ergo* they confabulate that it is a double, robot, or whatever (Ellis & Shepherd, 1992). This analysis, of course, is not very different from that originally proposed by Capgras and Reboul-Lachaux (1923).

For the final erroneous conclusion to occur, however, another system malfunction may have to be posited. Not everyone who receives such a faulty or anomalous experience data will conclude that someone has been substituted by a double. Following the work of Benson and Stuss (1990) on the role of the prefrontal cortex in reduplicative paramnesia, Ellis and Young (1996) suggest that delusion misidentification, too, may require the conjunction of a perceptual/cognitive disorder coupled with a malfunctioning attribution or decision-making system that produces the confabulated explanation. According to this argument, either alone will not produce a delusion of misidentification, but the combination of both may be necessary.

Some authorities have emphasised the selective nature of the Capgras Delusion. Berson (1983), for example, argued that no organic lesion could damage recognition only for the faces of specific individuals. Ellis and Young (1990) countered the criticism by arguing that, perhaps, only faces with emotional significance (i.e. family, friends, etc.) normally elicit strong signals from both recognition routes; and, thus, usually only these people are thought to have been substituted. It is also clear from the case of Mme M, however, that virtually anyone within purview could appear to be a double. Moreover, for her the doubles themselves could spawn countless doubles—which is uncommon but not unique (Todd, Dewhurst, & Wallis, 1981, also reported a case of multiple doubles). Silva, Leong, Weinstock, and Ferrari (1991) reported cases of Capgras Delusion where politicians and other famous people rather than just intimates seemed to have been substituted; again, this is rare but it does show that the delusion is not confined to people with whom patients are intimate. As suggested, it may be that some faces evoke strong affective/familiarity feelings and the absence of these following a functional deficit in route two may give rise to delusions.

It would be remiss of me not to include at least some discussion of Capgras' later theoretical position on his syndrome. As I indicated earlier, there is every reason to believe that he assumed the ideas of his colleagues and allowed Freudian theory to supplant that of Bergson (Luauté, 1986). Freud (1911/1958), in fact, believed all delusions sprang from repressed homosexual impulses—which is somewhat different, of course, from Capgras' and Carrette's (1924) notion of Oedipal conflict. Nonetheless, for a considerable period, psychodynamic interpretations of the Capgras Delusion were in the ascendant (Brochado, 1936; Coleman, 1933; Murray, 1936). Indeed, there has been little or no diminution in the volume of published work predicated on the psychodynamic approach (e.g. Berson, 1983; Enoch & Trethowan, 1991). These largely revolve around the idea that such patients develop ambivalent feelings towards certain individuals and subsequently resolve the conflict by 'splitting' them into positive (i.e. the true individual) and negative (i.e. double, robot, etc.) personae. It is difficult to see how this explanation can be considered universal: it fails to explain how the delusion can apply to individuals for whom patients form no obvious ambivalent feeling; nor can it account for the increasingly large number of cases where the Capgras Delusion is transient and clearly attributable to one of a number of toxic or metabolic states (Ellis & de Pauw, 1994).

Indeed, it would take some effort to apply such psychodynamic concepts as those recently in circulation to the original case described by Capgras and Reboul-Lachaux. As I have mentioned, Mme M duplicated not only her immediate family but hospital staff and patients as well. Moreover, she insisted that there were doubles of the doubles, running sometimes in thousands. Are we to believe that she had ambivalent feelings to all of these, including the doubles themselves?

What makes the delusion described by Capgras and his colleagues so important in the history of psychiatry is that it is the most common of all the delusions of misidentification. Its incidence has proved difficult to quantify in any definitive way, with estimates varying from 1% to 5.3% of psychiatric patients and an unknown proportion of neurological patients. It is not uncommon among dementing patients at some point in their symptom development (Forstl et al., 1994).

A suggestion by Malloy, Cimino, and Westlake (1992) that it may be necessary to distinguish primary from secondary Capgras Delusions, which may help resolve some of the theoretical and clinical difficulties thrown up in the almost 80 years since the delusion was first detailed. Indeed, further work by Fleminger and Burns (1992) implies that there may be an inverse relationship between the presence of persecutory beliefs preceding delusional misidentification and the degree of organic involvement. Such fine-grain meta-analyses could provide useful future insights into resolving some diagnostic and therapeutic issues stimulated by Joseph Capgras' original observations but it seems unlikely that the fundamental, underlying mechanisms will alter from case to case even if clinical outcomes are variable.

Before leaving the topic of the Capgras Delusion I should mention recent theoretical work by Breen et al. (2000), described and extended by Ellis and Lewis (2001). These papers illustrate the power of the cognitive neuropsychiatric approach—a view endorsed in a recent review by Halligan and David (2001).

Now I shall turn to the other major misidentification delusions; here the work of Courbon is significant. Like Capgras before him, Courbon eventually became head of psychiatry at the Ste Anne Hospital in Paris, where he also helped to found the Department of Neurosurgery. For many years he was the secretary general to the Société Médico-Psychologique. Doubtless he was influenced somewhat by his father-in-law, Paul Sollier (1861–1933), who was a professor of psychology in Brussels from 1897 until his death. Sollier wrote two books on memory and one entitled *Les phénomenes d'autoscopie* (1903). Courbon worked with him on a later edition of another book concerning the semiology of mental illness in which Capgras' work on the '*illusion de sosies*' is acknowledged.

Courbon co-authored two papers, one on the Frégoli Delusion (Courbon & Fail, 1927) and the other on intermetamorphosis (Courbon & Tusques, 1932). Each of these papers introduced new DMIs to the scientific community and, therefore, rank alongside the arguably more seminal paper of Capgras and Reboul-Lachaux.

COURBON AND FAIL'S CASE OF FRÉGOLI DELUSION

Courbon and Fail (1927) described the case of a 27-year-old single woman, for whom they did not provide a name. She was described as a coarse-featured woman who had lived by taking a succession of menial jobs and sleeping in hostels. Despite her lifestyle, her overriding passion was the theatre and she thought of herself as somewhat refined.

The patient presented with persecutory delusions, chief of which was the belief that the most famous actresses of the day, Robine and Sarah Bernhardt, for some years had been pursuing her disguised as other people. They could also take over her thoughts and make her do things against her will, such as masturbate. (This, apparently, was mainly the work of Robine who used the patient's distress to create an attractive dark line around her own eyes.) The actresses could enter the bodies of others so that neighbours and passers-by, while not looking any different, might well, in fact, be one of the patient's tormentors. Her doctor at times was invaded either by her dead father or by the doctor who had treated her as a baby.

Courbon and Fail discussed the patient's symptoms within the then still novel classification of schizophrenia, which they discussed in terms of mental degeneration. They carefully differentiated the delusion from Capgras' doubles syndrome. There is no confusion of physical appearance in the Frégoli Delusion: instead, the original patient of Courbon and Fail, as well as those described subsequently, insist that their tormentors either disguise themselves as others or can actually invade their bodies. It is worth introducing a caveat at this point: although in all published cases there is a strong persecutory theme to the Frégoli Delusion in at least one case (Sadler & Quayle, personal communication), the patient believed a family were disguising themselves in order to keep a benign eye on her while she was in a Cardiff hospital. For this patient the belief that others were able to disguise themselves in this way was an obvious comfort.

Courbon and Fail's identification of the Frégoli Delusion was the first published record of the disorder. Its essential feature is that the patients usually believe persecutors etc. can disguise themselves in the form of others usually in order to tempt, torment, or otherwise bother them. This phenomenon reminded Courbon and Fail of the skills of Léopoldo Frégoli, the Italian actor, long famous in France for his ability on stage to transform himself into various people. It is important, perhaps, that they chose to give the delusion his name because, whereas Frégoli adopted various methods to achieve physical transformations during his stage act, the Frégoli Delusion involves little apparent change in outward appearance. Patients believe that the persecutors have successfully invaded the body of others and it is, therefore, psychological substitution rather than a corporeal one. De Pauw, Szulecka, and Poltock (1987) described a patient with the Frégoli Delusion whose symptoms were similar to those of Courbon and Fail's patient. Mrs C, a 66-year-old widow, believed her cousin, by whom many years earlier she had had a child, together with a lady friend, were disguising themselves as all sorts of people using beards, wigs, and other means of changing their appearance and even their outer sexual identity. 'It's like an actor and actress preparing for different scenes,' she said, which could be interpreted as both psychological and physical change. However, when I subsequently asked her more closely about the nature of the changes it became evident that Mrs C simply reported that she could see through the disguise. This is different from the false recognitions sometimes described in the psychiatric literature.

Because of the ambiguity in Courbon and Fail's case description of the Frégoli Delusion, for some patients there has been some confusion in the literature as to the appropriate diagnosis. The most common interpretation is that in the Frégoli Delusion there is no physical similarity between the persecutor and the person in which he or she hides.

In their original paper, Courbon and Fail did talk about apparent physical and psychological changes, but it may be more useful, nosologically, to stick to the latter criterion.

The final French neuropsychiatric pioneer I want to mention is Tusques. Throughout his long career Tusques was both psychiatrist and biologist, holding chairs in history, pathology, neurology, and psychiatry. Eventually he settled at the University of Nantes where he was in charge of psychiatry, psychology, and sociology. In short, Tusques was something of a polymath who published a great deal on numerous topics, culminating in his 1978 article where he proposed a dynamic model of neuronal functioning to explain variations in psychiatric symptoms. In this work can be found echoes of his interaction with Courbon 46 years earlier, but he did not pursue specifically the phenomenon of intermetamorphosis following the single collaboration.

COURBON AND TUSQUES' CASE OF INTERMETAMORPHOSIS

Courbon and Tusques (1932) reported the case of Sylvie G, a 49-year-old married woman initially diagnosed as being both depressed and paranoid. Over an eight-year period Sylvie G displayed a range of related delusions involving objects, animals, and people. 'They have changed my hens, they've put two old ones in place of two young ones, they had large combs instead of small ones,' she claimed. On another occasion she remarked that '. . . I have seen women change into men, young women into old men . . .'. She saw many people who resembled her son and her aunt. An impostor son was identified as such because his feet were not large enough and his shoes were too clean. Her husband could take on the appearance of a neighbour—'In a second my husband is taller, smaller or younger.' One day, whilst he was transformed into someone else, the electrical supply in the house failed and the husband, an electrician by trade, immediately 'reappeared' to reconnect the supply.

Courbon and Tusques offered the term 'intermetamorphosis' to describe the illusion whereby things/people suddenly changed into something or someone else. They vaguely alluded to the *jamais vu* and *déja vu* phenomena to reinforce their idea that Sylvie G may have experienced strange sensations that, in turn, could have corrupted her perceptions. They further suggested that in her depressed state sensory impressions may not have integrated so easily with stored representations. This idea was reprised much later by Ellis and Young (1990) in their theoretical analysis of intermetamorphosis, to which I shall return later.

The paper by Courbon and Tusques outlining the case of Sylvie G is extremely interesting. The particular intermetamorphosis delusion, however, is quite rare. In fact the next case, published by Malliaros, Kossovitsa, and Christodoulou, did not come to light until 1978, some 46 years after it was first reported. Bick (1986) detailed another case; and shortly afterwards in a single paper Young, Ellis, Szulecka, and de Pauw (1990) described three more cases of intermetamorphosis. This implies, perhaps, that the long absence of reported cases may have been due either to diagnostic inefficiencies or to the transient nature of the symptoms. In other words, intermetamorphosis may well be an unusual psychiatric symptom but it may not be quite as rare as was once thought.

Returning to the original case, the phenomena reported by Sylvie G are quite bizarre. When, for example, she saw her husband virtually transformed before her into the appearance of others, she noted that his grey eyes and his hand with an amputated finger remained unchanged. As I mentioned, with the people who appeared exactly like her son she was compelled to look at their feet to see if they were large and wore dirty shoes: if not she concluded they were not him. These small islands of accuracy are themselves interesting but were not commented upon either by Courbon and Tusques or by later commentators, including Ellis and Young (1990), who proposed a cognitive explanation involving a malfunctioning face recognition system to explain intermetamorphosis. Courbon and Tusques did suggest, however, that their patient attended excessively to details at the expense of the whole. This may be characteristic of many patients with schizophrenia (Bemporad, 1967), but hardly explains the perceptions of Sylvie G. Why her husband should change his appearance to look like a neighbour or other people should look like her son requires more elaborate explanation than the suggestion that she was simply attending to details.

Sylvie G also reported that two of her chickens had become old and that her coat had been replaced by one that was worn and ripped. This aspect of her illness is reminiscent of many reports by patients with Capgras Delusion for people and for objects. Anderson (1988), for example, reported the case of a man who believed his tools had been stolen and replaced by older, more worn substitutes. Staton, Brumback, and Wilson (1982), following their description of a neurological patient who had both reduplicative paramnesia and the Capgras Delusion, suggested that he was unable to update memories—which must be a normal function in information processing. Thus he could be said to be comparing faces, objects, and places not with recent experiences of them but with more temporally distant representations. If that mechanism were the basis for reduplication phenomena then things would certainly appear older, more worn, etc.

It is conceivable that the phenomenon of intermetamorphosis may be related to the delusion of paraprosopia sometimes described in patients with schizophrenia. This refers to the perception that before their eyes people's faces appear to become distorted, usually in some unpleasant way (Grüsser & Landis, 1991). Patients have also been described who perceive photographs of faces to change, and Peter Williams and I recently examined a psychotic man who displayed what may be termed 'autoparaprosopia'—i.e. he saw similar unpleasant distortions of his own face in a mirror.

Grüsser and Landis (1991) reported a case of a young woman who not only described the faces of others changing instantaneously to look like Dracula but also sometimes thought all faces looked 'empty and dead'. Similar observations have sometimes been made by prosopagnosic patients who have perceived faces to be blank or all alike (Ellis, 1975). Courbon and Tusques' patient, in fact, did report what may be termed a mirror paraprosopia; people's faces sometimes appeared to change physically without appearing to be someone else known to her.

Finally, the hypoemotionalilty of the patient mentioned by Courbon and Tusques is noteworthy. This symptom has subsequently rarely, if ever, been referred to but, conceivably, it may have played a crucial role in the development of Sylvie G's delusion. It is, perhaps, interesting to note that the prosopagnosic patient described by Bauer (1984) was also hypoemotional for visual stimuli. He displayed covert (autonomic) face recognition while gaining no apparent conscious sense of familiarity from faces. Interestingly, Courbon and Tusques alluded to Capgras' original explanation for his eponymous delusion where 'emotional judgement' was cited as a constituent in the recognition process. Unfortunately, there is no record of the follow-up work on 'intuition' as a factor in misidentifications that Courbon and Tusques promised in their paper. Any relationship between hypoemotionality and the delusion misidentification syndromes, of course, will need much more extensive investigation: it is sufficient to record here that the relevant comments of Courbon and Tusques have been ignored without any obvious rationale.

OVERVIEW

Cases involving the delusions concerning the identity of others provide an interesting set of phenomena on the nature of person perception. These cases have been unsuccessfully examined from psychodynamic perspectives but more recently the theoretical emphasis has been cognitive neuropsychiatric (Ellis, 1998; Ellis & de Pauw, 1994; Ellis & Young, 1990; Halligan & David, 2001). As with cognitive neuropsychology, this approach attempts to explain case symptoms within a framework of normal cognitive processing and uses information-flow models to do so: when, however, the models are inadequate they are adapted to fit the data for brain-damaged patients. Similarly, cognitive neuropsychiatry takes the same approach. As has been commented, cases of the Frégoli Delusion and intermetamorphosis may be interpreted within conventional models of face recognition (Ellis, 1998; Ellis & Young, 1990) but the Capgras Delusion is less easily accommodated. Ellis (1998) has suggested that the models, therefore, need to be modified and a good deal of empirical and theoretical work is needed to ensure that the comprehensive account of face recognition can be given that incorporates data from normals, prosopagnosics; and those cases revealing different forms of DMI.

REFERENCES

Anderson, D.N. (1988). The delusion of inanimate doubles. *British Journal of Psychiatry, 153,* 694–699.

Bauer, R.M. (1984). Autonomic recognition of names and faces in prosopagnosia: A neurological application of the Guilty Knowledge Test. *Neuropsychologia, 20,* 457–465.

Bemporad, J.R. (1967). Perceptual disorders in schizophrenia. *American Journal of Psychiatry, 123,* 971–976.

Benson, D.F., & Stuss, D.T. (1990). Frontal lobe influences on delusions: A clinical perspective. *Schizophrenic Bulletin, 16,* 403–411.

Bergson, H. (1911). *Matter and memory.* London: George Allen and Unwin (translated by N.M. Paul & W. Scott Palmer).

Berson, R.J. (1983). Capgras syndrome. *American Journal of Psychiatry, 140,* 969–978.

Bick, P.A. (1986). The syndrome of intermetamorphosis. *Biblioteca Psychiatrica, 164,* 131–135.

Breen, N., Caine, D., & Coltheart, M. (2000). Models of face recognition and delusional misidentification: A critical review. *Cognitive Neuropsychology, 17,* 55–71.

Brochado, A. (1936). Le syndrome de Capgras. *Annales Médico-Psychologiques, 15,* 706–727.

Bruyer, R., Lattere, G., Seron, X., Feyereisen, P., Strypstein, E., Pierrard, E., & Rectem, D. (1983). A case of prosopagnosia with some preserved covert remembrance of familiar faces. *Brain and Cognition, 2,* 257–284.

Capgras, J., & Carrette, P. (1924). Illusion de sosie et complexe d'Oedipe. *Annales Médico-Psychologiques, 132,* 48–68.

Capgras, J., Lucchini, P., & Schiff, P. (1924). Du sentiment d'éstrangeté a l'illusion des sosies. *Bulletin de la Société Clinique et Médecine Mentale, 12,* 210–217.

Capgras, J., & Reboul-Lachaux, J. (1923). L'illusion des 'sosies' dans un délire systématisé chronique. *Bulletin de la Société Clinique et Médecine Mentale, 11,* 6–16.

Coleman, S.M. (1933). Misidentification and nonrecognition. *Journal of Mental Science, 79,* 42–51.

Courbon, P., & Fail, G. (1927). Syndrome d'"illusion de Frégoli' et schizophrénie. *Bulletin de la Société Clinique et Médecine Mentale.*

Courbon, P., & Tusques, J. (1932). Illusion d'intermétamorphose et de charme. *Annales Médico Psychologiques, 90,* 401–405.

David, A.S. (1993). Cognitive neuropsychiatry? *Psychological Medicine, 23,* 1–5.

de Pauw, K.W. (1994). Psychodynamic approaches to the Capgras Delusion: A critical historical review. *Psychopathology, 27,* 154–160.

de Pauw, K.W., Szulecka, K., & Poltock, T.L. (1987). Frégoli syndrome after cerebral infarction. *Journal of Nervous and Mental Diseases, 175,* 433–438.

Derombies, M. (1935). L'illusion de sosies, forme particulière de la méconnaisance systématique. *These de Paris* (Jouve and Co.).

Ellis, H.D. (1975). Recognising faces. *British Journal of Psychology, 61,* 409–426.

Ellis, H.D. (1991). *The cognitive neuropsychiatric origins of the Capgras Delusion.* Paper presented at the International Symposium on the Neuropsychology of Schizophrenia, Institute of Psychiatry, London.

Ellis, H.D. (1998). Cognitive neuropsychiatry and delusional misidentification syndromes: An exemplary vindication of the new discipline. *Cognitive Neuropsychiatry, 3,* 81–90.

Ellis, H.D., & de Pauw, K.W. (1994). The cognitive neuropsychiatric origins of the Capgras Delusion. In A. David & J. Cutting (Eds.), *Cognitive neuropsychology of schizophrenia.* Hove, UK: Lawrence Erlbaum Associates Ltd.

Ellis, H.D., & Lewis, M.B. (2001). Capgras Delusion: A window on face recognition. *Trends in Cognitive Science, 5,* 149–156.

Ellis, H.D., Quayle, A.H., de Pauw, K.W., Young, A.W., & Kolkiewicz, L.A. (1996). Delusional misidentification of inanimate objects: Cognitive deficits in two cases. *Cognitive Neuropsychiatry*, *1*, 27–40.

Ellis, H.D., & Shepherd, J.W. (1992). Face memory: Theory and practice. In M. Gruneberg & P.E. Morris (Eds.), *Aspects of memory, Volume 1*. London: Routledge.

Ellis, H.D., Whitley, J., & Luauté, J.-P. (1994). Delusional misidentifications: The three original papers on the Capgras, Frégoli and intermetamorphosis delusions. *History of Psychiatry*, *5*, 117–146.

Ellis, H.D., & Young, A.W. (1990). Accounting for delusional misidentification. *British Journal of Psychiatry*, *152*, 239–248.

Ellis, H.D., & Young, A.W. (1996). Problems of person perception in schizophrenia. In C. Pantelis, H.E. Nelson, & T.R.E. Thomas (Eds.), *Schizophrenia: A neuropsychological perspective*. Chichester, UK: Wiley

Ellis, H.D., Young, A.W., & Koenken, G. (1993). Covert face recognition without prosopagnosia. *Behavioural Neurology*, *6*, 27–32.

Ellis, H.D., Young, A.W., Quayle, A.W., & de Pauw, K.W. (1997). Reduced autonomic responses to faces in Capgras Delusion. *Proceedings of the Royal Society, London (B)*, *264*, 1085–1092.

Enoch, M.D., & Trethowan, W. (1991). *Uncommon psychiatric syndromes (third edition)*. Oxford: Butterworth-Heinemann.

Fleminger, S., & Burns, A. (1992). The delusion misidentification syndromes in patients with and without evidence of organic cerebral disorder: A structural review of case reports. *Biological Psychiatry*, *32*, 22–32.

Forstl, H., Besthorn, C., Burns, A., GeigerKabisch, C., Levy, R., & Sattel, A. (1994). Delusional misidentification in Alzheimer's disease: A summary of clinical and biological aspects. *Psychopathology*, *27*, 194–199.

Freud, S. (1958). Psychoanalytic notes on an autobiographical account of a case of paranoia (dementia paranoids). Published in the 1991 *Standard edition of the complete works of Sigmund Freud, Volume 12*. London: Hogarth.

Grüsser, O.J., & Landis, T. (1991). *Visual agnosias and other disturbances of visual perception and cognition (Volume 12 of Vision and visual dysfunction)*. London: Macmillan Press.

Halligan, P.W., & David, A.S. (2001). Cognitive neuropsychiatry: Towards a scientific psychopathology. *Nature Reviews: Neuroscience*, *2*, 209–215.

Hirstein, W., & Ramachandran, V.S. (1997). Capgras syndrome: A novel probe for understanding the neural representation of the identity and familiarity of persons. *Proceedings of the Royal Society, London (B)*, *264*, 437–444.

Kahlbaum, K.L. (1866). Die sinnesdelirien. *Allgemeine Zeitschrift für Psychiatrie*, *23*, 56–78.

Lanczik, M. (1892). Karl Ludwig Kahlbaum (1829–1899) and the emergence of psychopathological and nosological research in German psychiatry. *History of Psychiatry*, *3*, 53–58.

Luauté, J.-P. (1986). Joseph Capgras and his syndrome. *Biblioteca Psychiatry*, *164*, 9–21.

Malliaros, D.E., Kossouitsa, H.T. & Christodoulou, G.N. (1978). Organic contributors to the intermetamorphosis syndrome. *American Journal of Psychiatry*, *135*, 985–987.

Malloy, P., Cimino, C., & Westlake, R. (1992). Different diagnosis of primary and secondary Capgras delusions. *Neuropsychiatry, Neuropsychology, and Behavioural Science*, *5*, 83–96.

Mandler, G. (1980). Recognising: The judgement of previous occurrence. *Psychological Review*, *76*, 252–271.

Meadows, J.C. (1974). The anatomical basis of prosopagnosia. *Journal of Neurology, Neurosurgery and Psychiatry*, *38*, 489–501.

Murray, J.R. (1936). A case of Capgras' syndrome in the male. *Journal of Mental Science*, *72*, 63–66.

Ribot, T. (1905). *La Logique des Sentiments*. Paris: Alcan.

Silva, J.A., Leong, G.B., Weinstock, R., & Ferrari, M.M. (1991). *Misidentified political figures*.

Paper presented to the 43rd annual meeting of the American Academy of Forensic Science, Anaheim, California.

Staton, R.D., Brumback, R.A., & Wilson, H. (1982). Reduplicative paramnesia: A disconnection syndrome of memory. *Cortex*, *18*, 23–36.

Sollier, P. (1903). *Les phénomenes d'autoscopie*. Paris: Alcan.

Todd, J., Dewhurst, K., & Wallis, G. (1981). The syndrome of Capgras. *British Journal of Psychiatry*, *139*, 319–327.

Tranel, D., Fowles, D.C., & Damasio, R. (1985). Electro-dermal discrimination of familiar and unfamiliar faces: A methodology. *Psychophysiology*, *22*, 403–408.

Young, A.W., Ellis, H.D., Szulecka, J.K., & de Pauw, K.W. (1990). Face processing impairments and delusional misidentification. *Behavioural Neurology*, *3*, 153–168.

Young, A.W. & De Haan, E.H.F. (1992). Face recognition and awareness after brain injury. In D. Milner & M.D. Rugg (Eds.), *The neuropsychology of consciousness* (pp. 69–90). London: Academic Press.

CHAPTER SEVENTEEN

Whoever would have imagined it? Bisiach and Luzzatti (1978) on representational neglect in patients IG and NV

John C. Marshall
Neuropsychology Unit, University Department of Clinical Neurology, Radcliffe Infirmary, Oxford, UK

Peter W. Halligan
School of Psychology, Cardiff University, UK

CLASSIC OBSERVATIONS

In 1978, Edoardo Bisiach and Claudio Luzzatti published a brief note in *Cortex*. They described two patients (IG and NV) with right hemisphere lesions who showed left neglect of imagined scenes or, more precisely, of real scenes but conjured up from memory. This deficit was in addition to the patients' expected neglect of the left side of visually presented arrays. The idea that half a visual array could be ignored is bizarre enough. That half a *subjective* image could be neglected almost defies reason itself. In a short time, this little note became justly famous, and has subsequently provoked a huge experimental literature on (to quote the title of Bisiach and Luzzatti's paper), 'unilateral neglect of representational space'. It seems to be widely believed that Bisiach and Luzzatti (1978) were the first students to describe imaginal (or 'representational') neglect, an impression that is not dispelled by the fact that their paper's only reference is Karl Pribram's 1971 book on *Languages of the Brain*.

The real story is, of course, considerably more interesting than any mere discovery.

A LITTLE HISTORY

By 1978, unilateral visual neglect (née unilateral spatial agnosia) had become a 'textbook' neuropsychological disorder. Hécaen and Albert (1978) traced the study of 'unilateral visual inattention' back to the seminal studies of Poppelreuter (1917) on the consequences of penetrating missile injury in World War I. And they credit Brain (1941) with driving home the point that 'neglect of one side of space was related to right hemisphere lesions' (p. 217). Hécaen and Albert (1978) also stress Brain's discovery of how severe the condition could be: Brain's patients, they write, 'completely ignored everything on their left and behaved as if this part of space did not exist' (p. 217).

The relevant patients of Brain (1941) had massive lesions of the right parietal lobe. And the disorder that Brain himself emphasised was 'characterised by an inability to follow familiar routes owing to a tendency to take turnings to the right instead of to the left' (p. 246). Although the data that Brain (1941) presents are somewhat sparse (by current standards), he is clear that his patients did *not* necessarily suffer from 'an inability to describe familiar routes' (p. 257). The problem only arises, writes Brain, when the patients must physically traverse a route. Case 4 gets 'lost' when going from his bedroom to the sitting-room, but 'experienced no difficulty in visualising the correct route' (p. 258). Indeed, it is this dissociation (action versus verbalisation of visualisation) that leads Brain to distinguish these patients with 'neglect of the left half of external space' or 'inattention to the left half of external space' from patients who suffered 'loss of topographical memory' per se, and including therefore 'an inability to describe familiar routes' (p. 257).

Case 5 of Brain (1941) is a little more ambiguous. When asked to describe routes (within her house or outside) verbally she correctly included the relevant landmarks, but almost always said 'right' when the actual turnings were left: 'This mistake extended even to No. 5's description of her route from the underground station to her home' (Brain, 1941, p. 263). Has Brain (1941) then described 'unilateral neglect of left representational space'? He *has* reported a pronounced tendency for the patient to *say* 'turn right' when the correct route involves 'turn left' at a particular point, but he has *not* reported that his patients with neglect fail to mention more landmarks on the left of the imagined path than they do landmarks on the right. The answer to whether Brain should be credited with the discovery of representational neglect is thus yes and no. Critchley (1953) reported a further four cases who either turned right instead of left or said 'right' instead of 'left' when following or describing a route. But he interprets these patients under the rubric 'loss of topographical sense' (p. 336), not under the designation 'Neglect of one half of external space (or imperception for one half of external space)' (p. 339).

It is nonetheless important to note that verbal route description had firmly entered the set of testing procedures deployed with neglect patients as early as 1941 (in addition to its use in the investigation of patients with topographical memory disorder). Case 1 of Paterson and Zangwill (1944) 'could describe his ward and routes followed in routine hospital life with tolerable accuracy' (p. 343) at a time post-trauma (a penetrating wound of the right parieto-occipital area) when the left side of complex figures was neglected on copying. A year later, Paterson and Zangwill (1945) take the position of Brain (1941) as standard. Cases of 'visual disorientation (with or without left-sided visual agnosia)', they write, 'may retain the capacity to describe oft-traversed routes and scenes with which the patient was acquainted before his illness' (p. 192).

But their own case of 'topographical disorientation' after a penetrating lesion of the right parietal lobe (Paterson & Zangwill, 1945) starts to take them in a slightly different direction. This 34-year-old man had left homonymous hemianopia, with only very slight weakness of the left arm. Nonetheless, the patient failed to make use of this arm despite adequate power (motor neglect) and there was also marked 'agnosia for the left half of external visual space' (p. 194). He would turn right wherever possible, neglected the left side of pictures and books 'despite the fact that his attention was constantly being drawn to the oversight' (p. 195) by the examiners. When playing draughts (checkers), he 'neglected the left side of the board and when his attention was drawn to the pieces on this side he recognised them but immediately thereafter forgot them' (p. 195).

More crucial to the present discussion, the patient showed topographical agnosia, failing to recognise well-known buildings and geographical landmarks in his home town of Edinburgh. He also showed topographical disorientation for routes that he had previously known well. The patient was asked to draw a sketch map of Princes Street (Edinburgh's main thoroughfare). He oriented his sketch horizontally, beginning at the right-hand side of the page, which he labelled the 'West End'. Does this suggest that the patient lived in the New Town (objective north), and hence had the West End on his right when walking to Princes Street (objective south of the New Town)? If we interpret the drawing itself as an imaginary journey from the West End to the centre, the patient neglected to include any of the five streets that lead off on the 'left', while including two intersections that lead off 'rightwards'. (This task was repeated two weeks later. The patient produced a similar drawing but now labelled right as east and left as west!)

We here use 'left' and 'right' to mean left and right of the principal axis of the drawing (a horizontal Princes Street) when traversing that axis from right-to-left of the page. With respect to the page itself, there is 'bottom' neglect: That is, streets 'lower' than Princes Street on the page are omitted or transposed into 'upper' space. It makes more sense, however, to think of the patient's performance as showing left neglect along an imagined (and then drawn) horizontal route (although it is not totally clear that this is how the authors interpreted the patient's map drawings).

What did Paterson and Zangwill *not* ask the patient to do? They did not ask him to draw Princes Street starting from the *left* side of the page (Waverley Station) and moving towards the West End (if ego is 'seeing' the layout from the vantage point of the New Town). Only this manipulation would begin to demonstrate *conclusively* whether the patient was showing 'bottom' neglect or 'left' neglect. If with this new starting point on the left the patient produced the same drawing as before, the diagnosis would be 'bottom' neglect. But if, *per contra*, he now drew in the five streets on the *right* (from the new vantage point) while neglecting to put in any streets on the left. . . . then Bisiach and Luzzatti (1978) would have had a true predecessor. (A third drawing of Princes Street by the patient was vertically oriented on the page and hence once more does not resolve the issue without further experimental manipulation of the starting point.) It is also, of course, unfortunate that the patient was asked to *draw* rather than verbally describe: his performance could thus be interpreted as a lateralised motor output disorder (as seen in all classical accounts of, e.g., clock drawing). A tantalising glimpse of just how close Paterson and Zangwill (1945) were to the current notion of 'imaginal' neglect comes when they ask the patient 'to describe the order and sequence of the principal streets and buildings in various parts of Edinburgh with which he was well acquainted' (p. 204). These investigations include a description of 'going along Princes Street from East to West' (p. 204). The patient reports the Castle (which is now on the 'left'!), and transposes a street on the right from this viewpoint over onto the ('left') Castle side. Is the patient now paradoxically showing right neglect? One waits with baited breath. . . . but no, Paterson and Zangwill do *not* ask the patient to make the imaginary journey from west to east. Too little information is given to draw any conclusions. So close and yet so far. Princes Street is the wrong experimental material. There are more shops on one side of the street, but the smaller number of landmarks on the other side are visually and cognitively more prominent. The Castle and the Scott Monument are, it would seem, difficult for a Scot to neglect from any vantage point.

But despite the weakness of their data with respect to neglect, Paterson and Zangwill (1945) do conclude with respect to the more general issue of topographical disorientation that: 'ideational representation suffers in much the same way as topographical perception and is a function of a specific inability to maintain a coherent scheme or frame of reference in the visual sphere' (p. 208). In cases of neglect, *per contra*, the usual pattern is that described by McFie, Piercy, and Zangwill (1950). Their Case 3 suffered a large tumour in the right fronto-parietal region. The patient could give a good verbal description of 'the general topography of the neighbourhood' (p. 186) and 'was able to describe the layout of his house accurately but unable to represent it coherently as a ground plan' (p. 174) by drawing. In addition to problems with drawing and copying, the patient showed 'pronounced neglect of the left half of visual space' (p. 174) in reading and describing pictures.

By contrast, the case of Denny-Brown, Meyer, and Horenstein (1952) seems to show that both imaginal neglect (of scenes encountered post-stroke) and visuo-spatial neglect can be found in the context of good route-following. Their patient was a 55-year-old woman with a mild left hemiparesis and left inferior homonymous quadrantonopia after right parietal stroke. Left neglect was apparent on reading, writing, and drawing tasks. She also had great difficulty in recognising and naming the objects on the left side of Poppelreuter's composite figure. Her 'orientation in space' was nonetheless good: 'She had no difficulty in finding her way around the ward, and never approached the wrong bed, even if taken by a devious route into the ward kitchen and allowed to return to her room. She was able to recall her way even if both left and right turns had to be negotiated' (p. 438).

Verbal description of locales was assessed two months after she left hospital. The patient was requested 'to recall as much about the ward as she could' (p. 438). We note that this task presupposes that, as seems true of this patient's performance, some new spatial information had been learned post-stroke; it is *not* the same task as describing scenes known from before the brain damage. The results are not too surprising (but nonetheless important to have documented): 'She began by describing all the patients and the windows which had been on her right, mentioning them from right to left' (*within* the space to the right of her bed, presumably). 'She made no mention of the patients on the left until pressed and then was able to recall 2 out of 5' (pp. 438–439). Likewise, 'when asked about the corridor from the ward she mentioned the rooms and the nurses' desk on her right but only mentioned the staircase and the rooms on the left when asked "what did you pass on your left?"' (p. 439). It is nonetheless difficult to call this pattern imaginal neglect, in the sense of Bisiach and Luzzatti (1978) when (one presumes) the patient's left neglect made her less likely to have acquired *and* overlearned information about who and what was on her left in the ward and adjoining locales. It would seem that Denny-Brown et al. (1952) were not mentally ready to discover imaginal neglect because they were already convinced that neglect was due to 'loss of spatial summation of contralateral sensation' (p. 469). This account is clearly antithetical to the notion that a more central representational deficit might be implicated in neglect.

Later cases from pre-1978 confirm and in one case significantly extend these findings. Of critical importance, Case 10 of Ettlinger, Warrington, and Zangwill (1957) showed left neglect on a range of drawing and copying tasks, and on the verbal report of *previously known* locales: 'When asked to describe the ground floor of her house from the vantage point of the front door, the patient tended to omit rooms situated on her left-hand side' (p. 353). We *cannot* tell from this report whether the memory of the left-hand side in some canonical sense (e.g. defined with respect to ego entering the front door) has been lost. It is possible that the 'left' from the earlier vantage point (front door) might have re-emerged in memory (or conscious awareness) if the patient had been asked to describe her house from the back door looking towards the front. The 'missing' rooms on the left would now be on the right, and the rooms previously described on the right would now be on the left. This manipulation remained for Bisiach and Luzzatti (1978) to investigate. They were, it seems, the first scholars to realise the full importance of the fact that what is left depends upon where the observer is looking (or imagining he/she is looking). But, in one sense, imaginal neglect had already been described with reasonable adequacy by Denny-Brown et al. (1952) and was undoubtedly reported by Ettlinger et al. (1957). In short, textbooks of the 1960s onwards *should* have told how severe visual neglect could be found without (apparent) imaginal neglect of routes and scenes at least (Brain, 1941). And of how left visual neglect *is* sometimes found in association with left imaginal neglect (Ettlinger et al., 1957). That, in a more general sense, Zingerle (1913) had argued that neglect was a representational disorder, rather than a lateralised impairment of sensation, oculo-motor praxis, or attention seems to have gone unrecognised until 1987. His contribution was revived by Bisiach and Berti (1987) in a paper that also argued for the use of Zingerle's term 'dyschiria' rather than the by now conventional designation of 'neglect'.

ITALIAN SPACES

And so (at last!) to Bisiach and Luzzatti (1978). The first advantage that Bisiach and Luzzatti possessed over earlier students of imaginal (representational) neglect is that they were (indeed still are) Italian. Italy is a land of piazzas, and the Piazza del Duomo in Milan is a particularly magnificent example. Palaces, shops, arcades, monuments, and side streets surround the great Cathedral. Any respectable Milanese would have spent significant time in the Piazza, watching the pigeons, shopping, wandering, sitting, eating gelato, drinking espresso, entering and leaving the Duomo for Mass, gossiping with friends, and simply being. Wherever you stand, in whichever direction you look, there is a rich and variegated visual environment. The Piazza del Duomo could have been specifically built as apparatus for the study of imaginal neglect.

Figure 17.1 illustrates the long-standing acquaintance of the Bisiach family with (one side of) the Piazza. The Luzzatti family likewise had a strong connection with (the other side of) the Piazza. From 1930 to 1938, Claudio Luzzatti's mother and grandmother ran the Libreria dello Stato (a state-owned bookstore selling official government publications). This libreria was under the Galleria, on the other side of the piazza to the musical

Figure 17.1   Bisiach's Piazza

establishment of Leandro Bisiach. The Luzzatti family's association with the bookstore (and any other state employment) ended, at least for seven years, when in the autumn of 1938 the government enacted laws depriving them (and 57,000 other loyal citizens) of their civil rights (see Stille, 1992, for a moving account of the fascist years).

Bisiach and Luzzatti (1978) described two Milanese patients with right hemisphere stroke who presented with left hemianopia and left hemiparesis. The two patients are stated to have unilateral left neglect on the basis of their performance on one (somewhat non-standard) task: They were asked to touch thirteen dots 'composing a symmetrical pattern' (p. 129). Each patient had difficulty in touching those on the left: The first patient only did so after some hesitation, the second patient never succeeded with the left half of the stimulus despite prompting by the examiner.

Bisiach and Luzzatti's interest lies elsewhere. Prior studies of neglect, they claim, 'have generally disregarded the question of whether the phenomenon is only manifest in the egocentrical perspective of the physical environment (including one's own body) or evident in representational space as well' (p. 129). We have seen, in the previous section, that this claim is simply not true. What is more important than issues of priority is that Bisiach and Luzzatti realised that 'an answer to this question would somehow contribute to the understanding of the nature of unilateral neglect' (p. 129). Although prior researchers *had* tested for imaginal neglect, they seem not to have registered that the issue had any particular significance either for the interpretation of neglect or for the cognitive structure of imagery, or of retrieval from visual memory.

Bisiach and Luzzatti did the right study because they realised that there were theoretical considerations at stake. They accordingly asked their patients 'to describe a familiar place, the Piazza del Duomo in Milan, according to definite perspectives' (p. 129). Note the plural. 'First (a), they were requested to imagine themselves looking at the front of the cathedral from the opposite side of the square; then the reverse perspective (b) had to be described—i.e. the perspective seen from the front doors of the cathedral' (p. 129). The overhead map that the authors provide with numbered buildings and streets corresponding to the patients' recall makes the point. Figure 17.2, taken from Banich (1997), shows the results in a particularly clear fashion. From vantage point (A) the patients reported a reasonable number of items on the right and few or none on the left. From vantage point (B), the patients again reported items on the right from that new perspective and few or none on the left. Information about what is on both sides of the Piazza is clearly stored in long-term memory (and is accessible), but only the items on the right *from a given perspective* can be retrieved. As Meador, Loring, Bowers, and Heilman (1987) express it in a later replication and extension of these results, 'the engrams for left-sided visuo-spatial memories in neglect

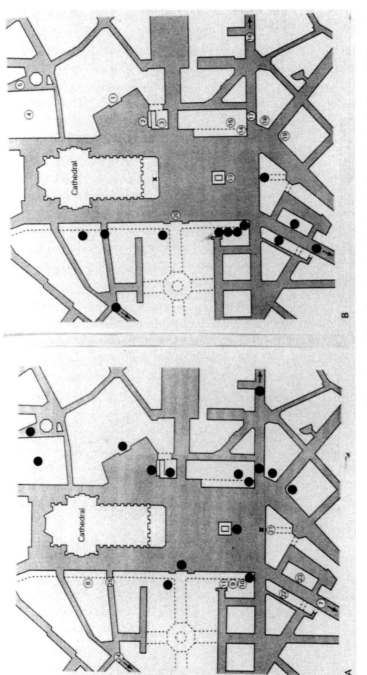

Figure 17.2 Maps indicating which structures were reported by patients with hemineglect when they imagined standing in the Piazza del Duomo in Milan, Italy. The landmarks that the patients described are designated by filled circles. (A) The landmarks mentioned by patients when they imagined themselves facing the cathedral. These landmarks are situated mainly on the right. (B) The landmarks mentioned when the patients imagined themselves standing on the steps of the cathedral and facing away from it. Once again mainly the landmarks on the right are mentioned. These individuals' memory for the square is intact because they mentioned most of the square's major landmarks across the two imagined positions. (Note: Adapted from M.T. Banich, 1997, *Neuropsychology*, pp. 261–262.)

syndrome are not destroyed, but rather fail to be activated' (p. 522). In this latter study, that interpretation was supported by the fact that performance on reporting imaginal scenes was modulated by the patient turning his head: More items could be reported from the left side of an imagined scene when the patient turned his head to the left than when he turned it to the right (Meador et al., 1987).

But back to Milan. Despite knowing the importance of their observations, Bisiach and Luzzatti give very little theoretical interpretation of their data. The descriptions, they think, are 'per se sufficiently eloquent' (p. 132). One is inclined to agree (and especially so after struggling to understand what the patient of Paterson & Zangwill, 1945, was actually doing). Bisiach and Luzzatti had demonstrated unambiguous left imaginal neglect *from two opposite (imaginal) vantage points*. The descriptions requested from the patients were 'static' snapshots: Say what you would see from position X when looking toward Y. They do not explicitly involve a route (along Princes Street, say, or an analogous Milanese Via) and hence avoid some of the complications that attend upon topographical impairment (see Riddoch & Humphreys, 1989). Such anyway seems to be how this seminal paper of Bisiach and Luzzatti has been interpreted. There can be no doubt that route description is sometimes, but not invariably, impaired in neglect (Bisiach, Brouchon, Poncet, & Rusconi, 1993; Brain, 1941), but the problem with dynamic routes is that ambiguity can arise when reporting landmarks. Imagine, for example, that one is pointing due north. There is a street to the right (east) and a prominent landmark also on the right but slightly further north. That landmark is right of the original position of ego, but left of ego after one has taken the right (east) turning. The investigator cannot always be sure with dynamic route descriptions of where the patient is (in imagination) when he/she mentions a particular landmark: cannot indeed be sure that the patient is 'anywhere' in a true (albeit imaginal) *spatial* sense. The point that the data of Bisiach and Luzzatti (1978) are *not* route descriptions is reinforced by further results (rarely mentioned in secondary sources) from Patient 2. In addition to his descriptions of the Piazza del Duomo, this patient was asked to describe his working-room ('where he had spent most of his life', p. 129) from a position behind and then a position in front of his desk. The pattern of results is very similar to that obtained about the Piazza, although prompting does provoke the patient into describing a few objects on the left of a particular vantage point.

The very short discussion that Bisiach and Luzzatti provided states that 'unilateral neglect cannot be reduced to a disorder confined to the input–output machinery of the organism interacting with its physical environment' (p. 132). In addition, they state, 'it seems to affect mental events whose occurrence is not contingent upon actual stimulation from the outside or actions of the organism on his environment' (p. 132). So far so good. Bisiach and Luzzatti have clearly made their case, *and* have realised some of the import of what they have demonstrated. And they do speculate (albeit just a little) about the putative deeper consequences of their results.

Their findings, they claim, 'support the view that the mechanisms underlying the mental representation of the environment are topologically structured in the sense that the processes by which a visual image is conjured up by the mind may split between the two cerebral hemispheres, like the projection of a real scene onto the visual areas of the two sides of the brain' (p. 132). For *this* claim about the topology of mental images, they provide *no* evidence at all (although their findings would not necessarily contradict such an account). If this (we assert, unsupported) conjecture was correct, it might, the authors claim, 'be argued that even stimulus-unbounded properties of the mind such as those at issue here have *extension . . .*' (p. 133). And now we see why the reference to Pribram (1971) has crept in: Pribram's 'holographic model' of mental representations does *not* map the extension of external objects and spaces into analogous spatially congruent extensions within the brain. Bisiach and Luzzatti accordingly suspect that they have falsified a general model of brain organisation (the holographic metaphor) that was quite popular throughout the 1970s (and has, to some degree, been revived in the connectionist 1980s and 1990s).

Bisiach and Luzzatti initially followed up their 1978 paper by investigating a new task—or rather an old task that had not been previously used with neglect patients: aperture viewing (see Morgan, Findlay, & Watt, 1982, for review). Bisiach, Luzzatti, and Perani (1979) showed patients with left neglect (after right hemisphere damage) two cloud-like shapes that had to be judged same or different. The catch was that each shape was viewed through a small slit. Each pair of shapes passed successively behind this narrow slit, either left-to-right or right-to-left. The full object had accordingly to be reconstructed in short-term memory and stored for comparison with the shape of the next object in the pair. Irrespective of whether the shapes were moved leftward or rightward behind the aperture, the patients with neglect were significantly less accurate in detecting differences on the left side of the shapes. Because these differences were on the left side of images that had, of necessity, to be 'mentally reconstructed', Bisiach et al. (1979) conclude that 'a representational disorder plays a primary role in unilateral neglect' (p. 616).

With some justification, Bisiach et al. (1979) argue that it is difficult to see how this deficit with central aperture viewing could be interpreted as consequent upon an over-powerful 'orienting response' to right external space (Heilman & Watson, 1977). They also repeat their 1978 claim that Pribram's holographic model will have difficulty accounting for representational neglect. And more crucially, they begin to engage with Zenon Pylyshyn's earlier critique of 'misuses of the phenomenological concept of "image" as an explanatory construct in psychological theories' (p. 615). In particular, they quote the remark of Pylyshyn (1973) that visual representations (in the sense of imagined views) are 'much closer to being a description of a scene than a picture of it' (p. 615). But against Pylyshyn's position, they reiterate the kind of *visuo-spatial* claims that characterised the discussion in Bisiach and Luzzatti (1978). Bisiach et al. (1979) continue to insist that 'our findings suggest that the spatial attributes of representations cannot be accounted for solely in terms of propositional retrieval: Their *left* side fades in consequence of *right* hemisphere impairment, so that their spatial schema appears to be mapped across the brain' (p. 615). This last sentence is not entirely unambiguous. Should the stress fall on 'their spatial schema appears to be mapped across the brain' (but perhaps is *not* actually so mapped at the level of neuronal instantiation)? Or do the authors truly believe that the spatial schema *is* mapped across the brain: that the left side of an imagined or reconstructed object, from a given vantage point, *is* represented in the right hemisphere, and the right side in the left hemisphere?

Two years later we are back to the cathedral square in Milan. The original experiment of Bisiach and Luzzatti (1978) is convincingly replicated on a larger sample of patients with left neglect (Bisiach, Capitani, Luzzatti, & Perani, 1981). In addition, three control groups are employed: healthy people, and patients without neglect but with right hemisphere damage, with and without a left hemianopia. All three control groups show conclusively that there are no intrinsic differences in the number of reported landmarks (etc.) between the two (imagined) viewing perspectives. But the 15 patients with left visual neglect (as assessed by a conventional cancellation task) show the strong asymmetry favouring items from the right (on each of the two perspectives) that had been previously found in the two patients of Bisiach and Luzzatti (1978). In addition, the effect is shown to be highly modifiable by cuing. Thus when the patients with left neglect were explicitly asked 'to describe the *right* and then the *left* side of the square, according to the first perspective' and then 'the *left* and then the *right* side according to the second' (Bisiach et al., 1981, p. 548), there were no statistically significant differences in the number of items reported from each side.

One might have thought that this cuing effect would be most plausibly regarded as attentional. That is, that from a given vantage point, the representation of imagined space is intact, but only the right half is attentionally scanned unless an explicit instruction to report the left is given. Yet Bisiach et al. (1981) explicitly *reject* this interpretation. Rather, they suggest that it is the side of the 'visuo-spatial scratch pad' (Baddeley & Lieberman, 1980) that deals with left space that is 'inoperative' (p. 549). It is, they write, 'safer and more parsimonious to hypothesise that full awareness of a representation is nothing over and above the display of some information within a spatio-temporal structure, like the "scratch pad", somewhere in the brain' (p. 549).

And where is that 'somewhere'? 'The best candidate', Bisiach et al. (1981) claim, 'seems to be the association cortex of the parieto-temporo-occipital junction' (p. 549). And they continue to believe that, like 'real' space, 'imaginal space is topologically structured across the two hemispheres' (p. 549). Despite this claim, they are firm that 'It is not implied, of course, that similar spatial properties characterise the form in which the information needed for a representation is stored in a neural network' (p. 549). Nonetheless, damage to the *right* parieto-temporo-occipital junction perturbs the overt representation of *left* space both when there is and when there is not an actual visual stimulus in the visual field. It is as if the projections of mental images decussate at an imaginary optic chiasm in a manner similar to the projection of the lateral visual fields to the contralateral cerebral hemisphere.

WHERE NEXT?

We should perhaps step back a little at this point. In particular, we should inquire whether Bisiach and Luzzatti (1978 and subsequently) have drawn too strong an analogy between the structure of genuine visual input and of visual imagery.

There is, for example, compelling evidence that the patients of Bisiach and Luzzatti (1978) could *not* (in all instances) have been describing what they would see from the two opposite vantage points in the Piazza. If you are in the square and facing the front of the Cathedral (perspective *A*), you *cannot* actually see (e.g.) the Archiepiscopal Palace (4 on Figure 17.2) or the Via delle Ore (5 on Figure 17.2). Direct perception of them would be blocked by other buildings. Likewise, from the opposite perspective (*B*), looking out at the square 'from the front doors of the Cathedral', you cannot actually see La Rinascente (8 on Figure 17.2): It would be behind you. There is even an *overt* example of this phenomenon given in Patient 2's description of his workroom from the perspective of 'sitting at the desk' (but not commented upon by Bisiach and Luzzatti). The patient's *first* remark is 'Behind me there is a book-case' (Bisiach & Luzzatti, 1978, p. 131). Unless the patient has eyes in the back of his head, this is not a description of what he would see when sitting at his desk. In fact, a very substantial number of the landmarks reported by the patients in Bisiach and Luzzatti (1978) *cannot* be seen from the vantage points purportedly adopted, assuming that the patients (in their imagination) have their feet on the ground, that they do not turn around, or otherwise move. The items could, of course, be seen from a helicopter hovering overhead, or indeed from ordinary inspection of ordinary (overhead) maps: maps such as those that Bisiach and Luzzatti (1978) include in their paper in order to describe the results in an understandable way. We were thus not surprised to learn that Bisiach and Luzzatti had spent 'many hours of discussion on how to interpret the descriptions given by the patients' (personal communication from Claudio Luzzatti, 23 March 1999).

The point we are making can be seen in a *reductio ad absurdum* fashion in the imagery tasks used by Halsband, Gruhn, and Ettlinger (1985) and by Barbut and Gazzaniga (1987). Halsband et al. (1985) asked their neglect patients to list the countries bordering on West Germany, and to name a country 'lying at each of the compass points (N, S, W, and E in that order) when viewed from West Germany' (p. 178). They term an impairment on these tests 'conceptual neglect', but do not discuss *how* such neglect comes about other than to remark that 'some attentional factor' can interact with representational space. Barbut and Gazzaniga (1987) asked their patient with left neglect to imagine himself in New York, facing California, and to name the states before him. Even in a helicopter, it is difficult to *see* Montana or Oregon from the George Washington Bridge in New York City (but easy to read the relevant information from a map of the USA). The point we are making is explicitly acknowledged (but not further discussed) in a study by Bartolomeo, D'Erme, and Gainotti (1994). These authors employ three tasks. One is the now traditional Piazza test (albeit transposed to Rome). But the second task requests the patients to 'list the countries they "saw" while imagining a geopolitical map of Europe' (p. 1711). And task three was to 'list the towns they "saw" on the western coast of Italy from a vantage point on the eastern coast of Sardinia (disregarding that it is actually impossible to see anything from that distance)' (p. 1711). In one study, that of Rode and Perenin (1994), the patients with neglect were explicitly required 'to evoke mentally the map of France ... with a vertical axis linking Perpignan to Lille.'! (Rode & Perenin, 1994, p. 869). The patients then named as many towns as they could on each side of this axis, first 'looking' from south to north, and then 'looking' from north to south (see also Rode, Perenin, & Boisson, 1995). These papers from Rode and colleagues are also of interest in showing that a temporary remission of imaginal neglect can result from vestibular stimulation and by adaptation to a prismatic shift of the visual field to the right (Rode & Perenin, 1994; Rode, Rossetti, & Boisson, 2001), just as with both techniques perceptual neglect may be so ameliorated.

In short, what price the hypothesis that 'imaginal space is topologically structured across the two hemispheres' (Bisiach et al., 1981, p. 549) when in many studies of representational neglect even real vision in the right visual field could not provide as a static snapshot what the patients describe in the right spatial field? Rather, the patients of Bisiach and Luzzatti (1978 et seq.) seem to be reporting what they *know* is where (and they may, or may not, be conjuring up a mental image of an ordinary commercial map). Indeed, the situation may have yet another dimension: the patients may have been reporting what they know *had been* where. Luzzatti writes (personal communication, 23 March 1999): 'Both Edoardo's father and my mother made essential contributions to the analysis of the descriptions of the piazza for the group study (Bisiach et al., 1981). Their wonderful memory for names and places allowed us to identify and allocate descriptions of items, recalled by the patients, but which had disappeared from the square decades previously.'

If the patients are indeed reporting what they know is (or was) where, the possibility arises that the memorial code is as much verbal as visual. And that point, of course, was the starting place for Pylyshyn's original claim that the medium of imagination constructs representations that are more like descriptions of scenes than pictures thereof (Pylyshyn, 1973). Even a conventional map is not much like a picture, if by picture one means a representational painting or a photograph: think of that notorious, but so useful, map of the London Underground. But irrespective of the validity of Pylyshyn's position, it seems very surprising that in no paper on imaginal neglect of which we are aware has the experimenter actually asked the patients what *they* thought they were doing during the imaginal task(s). One accordingly cannot be sure that the patients were *not* imagining themselves moving across the piazza, turning into side streets, and so on. It is as if the behaviourist horror of introspection had been overcome to the extent of asking subjects to report content (the landmarks themselves) but not process (how the subjects thought they retrieved the landmarks). Even the study of content itself 'could benefit from analysis of the path followed during the description of familiar views: from left-to-right; right-to-left; jumping irregularly from here to there' (Luzzatti, personal communication, 23 March 1999).

Nonetheless, the existence of representational left neglect (in some sense) is not in question, although the condition is found in only a small subset of patients with visuo-spatial neglect (Bartolomeo, D'Erme, & Gainotti, 1994). Likewise, during inactivation by intracarotid amobarbital of the right hemisphere of 10 subjects who showed left neglect on a cancellation task, only one showed additional left neglect of a remembered room (Manoach, O'Connor, & Weintraub, 1996). The typical patient with left neglect seems, then, to have 'spared awareness for the left side of internal visual images' (Anderson, 1993, p. 213), although it is doubtful whether the notion of 'typical' neglect has much content. And we are accordingly left with the fact that *some* patients do indeed manifest both representational and visuo-spatial neglect. For students of neglect whose patients do not have access to a convenient Italian Piazza or Parisian Place (Lhermitte, Cambier, & Elghozi, 1981), the o'clock test of Grossi, Angelini, Pecchinenda, and Pizzamiglio (1993) is an excellent tool for eliciting lateralised imaginal deficits. Subjects are asked to imagine pairs of traditional clock faces each with an hour hand and a minute hand indicating different times on each of the members of a pair (e.g. 7.30 and 11.30 on the left of the clockface, or 5.30 and 1.30 on the right of the clock-face). The patient must then state on which member of each pair of clock settings (e.g. 5.30 and 1.30) the two hands display the larger angle between them. In the two examples given, the answers are 11.30 and 1.30. Patients with left neglect find the task easier when the relevant hand(s) is/are in right space on the clockface.

But even more surprising than the (occasional) co-occurrence of imaginal and perceptual neglect is the fact that a very small number of patients seem to show imaginal neglect without visuo-spatial neglect (as assessed by conventional tasks). The patient reported by Guariglia, Padovani, Pantano, and Pizzamiglio (1993) had no signs of personal, peripersonal, or extrapersonal neglect at a time when he had severe problems in reporting items from the left side (from two opposite vantage points) of familiar piazzas. As in the earlier report of Bisiach et al. (1981), the patient of Guariglia et al. (1993) also misplaced landmarks from the left to the right side of a piazza. It is important to note that this patient did *not* have a general impairment of imagery. He performed normally on tasks requiring the generation and manipulation of images of the weight and colour of objects; mental paper-unfolding tasks were done well, and there was no impairment on the aperture test (Bisiach et al., 1979). Site of lesion was right frontal and anterior temporal; no parietal involvement was found on either computerised tomography (CT) or single-photon emission tomography (SPECT). The authors summarise their patient's deficit as a failure that emerges only when 'he had to attend to details and position them with respect to the internal spatial coordinates' (Guariglia et al., 1993, p. 237). A brief case report by Peru and Zapparoli (1999) likewise described florid imaginal neglect without evidence of perceptual neglect.

'Pure' imaginal neglect is nonetheless very rare: No subject in the sample of 30 patients with right brain damage reported by Bartolomeo et al. (1994) showed *isolated* representational neglect on first testing. There was, however, one patient (number 26) who originally presented with both visuospatial and representational neglect, but in whom only the latter deficit remained 8 months later. Bartolomeo et al. accordingly suggest that the 'uncommon finding of isolated representational neglect in single patients after recovery from visuo-spatial neglect' (p. 1714) might arise because 'in imaginal tasks, subjects do not use those compensatory strategies that they learned to use during exploration of the external world' (p. 1714). This explanation might also hold for the patient of Guariglia et al. (1993) who was first tested 16 months after his stroke, and for patient MN of Coslett (1997) who was tested two years after her stroke. But the argument from differential recovery put forward by Bartolomeo et al. (1994) somewhat suggests that representational neglect in association with visuo-spatial neglect should be considerably more common than they themselves found. In many published accounts of neglect, including Bartolomeo et al. (1994), many of the patients are tested within one or two weeks of their stroke. But no imaginal neglect is seen in most of these patients.

One further case seems to argue against the specific position of Bartolomeo et al. (1994). Beschin, Cocchini, Della Sala, and Logie (1997) reported a patient who sustained a large right parietal infarct. Surprisingly, there was no informal evidence of visuo-spatial ('perceptual') or personal neglect even immediately after the stroke or on formal testing a few weeks later. Nonetheless, there was persistent unilateral neglect 'limited to visual imagery' (p. 3) in the context of severe visual extinction on bilateral confrontation. The authors point out that visual extinction and visuo-spatial neglect (as conventionally assessed) are known to be doubly dissociable. Hence they feel confident in regarding their patient as manifesting 'pure' imaginal neglect. Certainly, the impairment is extremely striking when assessed by reports of familiar piazzas and maps of Italy 'based on mental images processed and stored in long-term memory before the lesion' (p. 14). The patient was also extremely poor at a spatial imagery task originally devised by Brooks (1967) that involves newly acquired information. In this task, 'the subject is asked to imagine placing consecutive numbers in consecutive squares of a four by four matrix' (p. 16). The instructions are thus of the form 'up 2, right 3 . . .', and the response is 'verbatim vocal recall of the series of directions and numbers' (p. 16). Although both stimulus and response are verbal, the relevant task representations are regarded as reliant in the main on visuo-spatial working memory. A further case of acute representational neglect without perceptual neglect was reported by Ortigue et al. (2001). There was no visual (or tactile or auditory) extinction; drawing and verbal description of objects and animals from memory was intact. A right thalamic lesion was seen on MRI. The case is of particular interest because representational neglect was tested in both viewer-centred (egocentric) and environment- (or object-) centred (allocentric) reference frames. In viewer-centred coordinates (describing and drawing the Place Neuve in Geneva from four different vantage points; listing the towns that could be seen from Evian in France when looking out over Lake Geneva towards Lausanne in Switzerland) the patient showed severe left representational neglect. But when he was 'asked to draw and describe a map-like representation of the Place Neuve without requiring any specific vantage point', as one might give information to a tourist, performance showed no neglect. Likewise, he could report verbally the names of 19 Swiss cities between Geneva and Villeneuve, cities at opposite ends of Lake Geneva (with Lausanne in the middle). Again, there is no representational neglect on this allocentric task.

At present, then, it does seem as if 'at least two related but isolatable visuo-spatial representations are computed from visual input' (Coslett, 1997, p. 1169). One of these is 'an on-line, real time spatial representation' (p. 1169), while the other is a more cognitive, 'relatively long-lasting egocentric visuo-spatial representation' (Coslett, 1997, p. 1169). Double dissociation between on-line neglect and imaginal neglect can occur when either one of these systems is impaired with preservation of the other. Similarly, with representational (imaginal) neglect, viewer-centred neglect can be observed in the absence of environment-centred neglect (Ortigue et al., 2001). Whether the reverse dissociation exists remains to be determined. Just how complex some of these dissociations can be is demonstrated by Beschin, Basso, and Della Sala (2000). Their patient had a lesion of both left parieto-occipital cortex and the right thalamus. He presented with right personal neglect and right peripersonal neglect, including right neglect dyslexia. But he also showed *left* representational neglect on imagery tasks.

ENVOI

Finally, we should reconsider the very notion of 'representational' neglect. To which theoretical domains do the data we have discussed here speak, and what do they imply about the neuronal substrate of spatial representation?

It should be stressed that the more appropriate (albeit cumbersome) term is probably 'imaginal neglect with verbal output'. Bisiach and Luzzatti (1978) achieved their breakthrough by virtue of two methodological tools: they found just the right 'stimulus' for which it was plausible that long-term memory might hold two (or more) perspectives; and they asked their patients to give *verbal* descriptions from a particular 'line of sight', not to draw the Piazza. Consider how this differs from a traditional test of 'representational' neglect—clock drawing. First, in order (even potentially) to achieve a true analogue of the Piazza del Duomo effect one would need transparent clocks (but with opaque hands) that were as frequently seen from behind as in front! Second, clock *drawing* would need to be replaced by some form of clock description (as in Grossi et al., 1993).

But we have never seen (or heard of anyone else who has seen) a neglect patient who did not *say* (in more informal language than we use here) that most normal clocks have 12 numbers, equidistantly placed around a circular circumference. Or that normal people have two arms, eyes, legs (etc.), distributed symmetrically about the midsagittal plane. Despite this knowledge, drawings that fail to include the 'left' are diagnostic of visual neglect (Halligan & Marshall, 1994). Is the structure of the human body and of a conventional clock too overlearned in semantic memory to be verbally neglected? Or is the Piazza del Duomo (and related locales) a radically different type of stimulus, requiring attention to objects and their position in a space through which the observer may move (Courtney, Petit, Maisog, Ungerleider, & Haxby, 1998; Ghaem et al., 1997; Maguire, Burgess, Donnett, Frackowiak, Frith, & O'Keefe, 1998)?

On the other hand, there are similarities between neglect on drawing and imaginal neglect. In both domains, there is neglect of the left in the sense of omissions, and there can be transposition of items from the left to the right (visual and imaginal allochiria). Imaginal allochiria was reported by Bisiach et al. (1981) and in the pure case of neglect restricted to visual imagery described by Guariglia et al. (1993). Halligan, Marshall, and Wade (1992a) discuss visual allochiria on copying tasks, and it is well known that left-to-right transpositions often take place when neglect patients are asked to locate cities or states on a map. Case 35253 of Battersby, Bender, Pollack, and Kahn (1956) shows the latter effect very clearly: the patient places California on the east coast of the USA, close to the Canadian border. We have also shown that it is possible for a patient to give an accurate verbal description of a scene (objects and their location) learned *after* temporo-parietal brain damage, but nevertheless make left-to-right transpositions when drawing the scene a few moments later (Halligan, Marshall, & Wade, 1992b). Output by the mouth and by the right hand are thus not necessarily equivalent despite the fact that both response modes are controlled primarily by the left hemisphere.

Which aspects of the neural substrate of visual imagery that are impaired in neglect remains controversial, as indeed does the more general issue of whether primary visual cortex is necessary to sustain visual imagery (Bartolomeo, 2002; Chatterjee & Southwood, 1995). The two patients with pure imaginal neglect after cortical damage have a right frontal and anterior temporal lesion (Guariglia et al., 1993) and a right parietal lobe lesion (Beschin et al., 1997), respectively. The patient of Ortigue et al. (2001) has a right thalamic lesion. All these lesion types are common in patients with visuo-spatial neglect with and without imaginal neglect. It may also be pertinent to remember that the case of Guariglia et al. (1993) did *not* have a visual field deficit and did *not* have any generalised mental imagery disorder for colour, weight, or shape. Normal visual fields and normal non-spatial visual imagery were also seen in the patient of Ortigue et al. (2001). The long-running controversy about whether retinotopic areas mediate mental images of single complex objects (Are the hind legs of a kangaroo shorter than the front legs?) may thus be of limited relevance to the study of neglect (Roland & Gulyás, 1994). That is, failure to generate visual imagery per se (Goldenberg, 1998; Grossi, Modafferi, Pelosi, & Trojano, 1989) is *not* the core problem in imaginal neglect after right hemisphere lesion. Rather, the global representation of scenes that the neglect patient can construct 'does not suffice to place specific (local) items correctly within the overall space' (Marshall & Halligan, 1993, p. 194). This account is consistent with Kosslyn's computational account of how the right hemisphere may be better equipped for the accurate positioning of imaged objects in a scene, due to an underlying specialisation for coordinate spatial scaling (Kosslyn, 1987). On the other hand, Rode et al. (1999) have shown that representational neglect can be ameliorated by adaptation to rightward displacing optical prisms: can the 'imaginal field' be displaced in the same fashion as the visual field?

But the issue raised by the original descriptions of imaginal neglect (Bisiach & Luzzatti, 1978; Bisiach et al., 1981)—whether the left side of the representational map is degraded, or whether the attentional system fails to scan the left side of a normal internal representation—remains undecided. Likewise, the question of precisely how to frame the distinction between pictorial/analogue and propositional/digital representations is still open. For example, Bisiach (personal communication, 27 July 1998) writes: 'I cannot agree with your claim that imagining what you cannot really see from a given vantage point supports the contention that mental representations are more like descriptions than pictures.' Bisiach and Berti (1989) had earlier raised this problem in connection with those neglect patients who draw all 12 numbers along the right hemicircumference of a clockface. Such examples, they claim, show 'how optical rules alone cannot wholly capture the essence' (Bisiach & Berti, 1989, p. 150) of the representational medium over which neglect is expressed. In part, the problem involves 'what we mean by pictures' (Bisiach, personal communication, 27 July 1998). Similarly, Luzzatti (personal communication, 23 March 1999) writes: 'The first problem is to discover how topographical visual images are stored. The storage of the 'representational space' of well-known views seems not to be fully realistic: I know that La Rinascente cannot be seen from the entrance of the Cathedral but that does not hinder me from seeing it clearly when scanning my stored visual representation. If I had to describe it, however, I would certainly say (from this vantage point) that it is ROUND THE CORNER on my right-hand side.' (When describing the Place Neuve from particular vantage points, the patient of Ortigue et al., 2001 was explicitly instructed that he must not, in his imagination, walk around the square.) As the challenges we have discussed imply, one definition of a classic paper is that the questions it raises continue to be of concern 20 (or more) years later. Bisiach and Luzzatti (1978) meets that criterion without even an imagined shadow of a doubt.

Yet what the community of scientists considers a classic paper does not always correspond with the evaluation of the authors of those 'classic' papers. We will accordingly let Edoardo Bisiach himself have the last word (for the moment). Bisiach writes (personal communication, 27 July, 1998):

> When the paper that eventually appeared as Bisiach and Luzzatti (1978) was originally written, I had the preconceived belief that unilateral neglect was of course a representational disorder. The research with cloud-like shapes moving behind a vertical slit was done in order to find out whether this task could *improve* neglect (not reveal its presence at the representational level). I thought it was unnecessary to make this point in the introduction to our 1979 paper (Bisiach, Luzzatti and Peroni, 1979): that was, I am afraid, a slightly Orwellian adjustment. The Piazza del Duomo test, was originally simply added to the experiment with cloud-like shapes (Bisiach, Luzzatti and Perani, 1979) as a collateral test for imaginal neglect, and I must acknowledge that it was only the insistence of Ennio De Renzi (the Editor of *Cortex* at that time) that convinced me to publish the first two observations on the Piazza del Duomo effect

separately as a short Note. In fact I thought that those observations were rather unimportant per se, although greatly important in their implications for the analogue/propositional debate of which, at that time, I had insufficient knowledge. This explains the lack of citations, except for the cursory mention of Pribram's book. It is interesting to note here that in 1985 I met Messerli at the World Congress of Neurology in Hamburg. He told me that several years before the publication of our 1978 paper he had collected many similar observations with the Place Neuve in Geneva. Indeed, he then sent me his material. It was fascinating, but despite my repeated insistence he never published it and I subsequently had to cite his results as 'personal communication'. The reason why he had not published his observations—he told me at that time—was that he took them for granted! This is exactly what I did, and I should add that to a very large extent I never changed my mind on this issue in the following years and, therefore, I am still surprised by the popularity of our 1978 paper, towards which I must confess to having mixed feelings.'

It would, however, be a pity to end on a negative note. The word after the last word will accordingly belong to Claudio Luzzatti: 'I remember the feeling we were working on something sensible and worthy of an extended research project' (Luzzatti, personal communication, 23 March, 1999).

ACKNOWLEDGEMENTS

The work of J.C.M. and P.W.H. is supported by the Medical Research Council (UK). We are also deeply grateful to Edoardo Bisiach and Claudio Luzzatti for help with this chapter that only they could provide.

REFERENCES

Anderson, B. (1993). Spared awareness for the left side of internal visual images in patients with left-sided extrapersonal neglect. *Neurology, 43*, 213–216.

Baddeley, A.D., & Lieberman, K. (1980). Spatial working memory. In R. Nickerson (Ed.), *Attention and performance VIII*. Hillsdale, NJ: Lawrence Erlbaum Associates Inc.

Banich, M.T. (1997). *Neuropsychology: The neural bases of mental function*. New York: Houghton Mifflin.

Barbut, D., & Gazzaniga, M.S. (1987). Disturbances in conceptual space involving language and speech. *Brain, 110*, 1487–1496.

Bartolomeo, P. (2002). The relationship between visual perception and visual mental imagery: A reappraisal of the neuropsychological evidence. *Cortex, 38*, 357–378.

Bartolomeo, P., D'Erme, P., & Gainotti, G. (1994). The relationship between visuo-spatial and representational neglect. *Neurology, 44*, 1710–1714.

Battersby, S., Bender, M.B., Pollack, M., & Kahn, R.L. (1956). Unilateral 'spatial agnosia' ('inattention') in patients with cerebral lesions. *Brain, 79*, 68–93.

Beschin, N., Basso, A., & Della Sala, S. (2000). Perceiving left and imagining right: Dissociation in neglect. *Cortex, 36*, 401–414.

Beschin, N., Cocchini, G., Della Sala, S., & Logie, R.H. (1997). What the eyes perceive, the brain ignores: A case of pure unilateral representational neglect. *Cortex, 33*, 3–26.

Bisiach, E., & Berti, A. (1987). Dyschiria: An attempt at its systematic explanation. In M. Jeannerod (Ed.), *Neurophysiological and neuropsychological aspects of spatial neglect*. North-Holland: Elsevier Science Publishers BV.

Bisiach, E., & Berti, A. (1989). Unilateral misrepresentation of distributed information: Paradoxes and puzzles. In J.W. Brown (Ed.), *Neuropsychology of visual perception*. London: Lawrence Erlbaum Associates Ltd.

Bisiach, E., Brouchon, M., Poncet, M., & Rusconi, M.L. (1993). Unilateral neglect in route description. *Neuropsychologia, 31*, 1255–1262.

Bisiach, E., Capitani, E., Luzzatti, C., & Perani, D. (1981). Brain and conscious representation of outside reality. *Neuropsychologia, 19*, 543–551.

Bisiach, E., & Luzzatti, C. (1978). Unilateral neglect of representational space. *Cortex, 14*, 129–133.

Bisiach, E., Luzzatti, C., & Perani, D. (1979). Unilateral neglect, representational schema and consciousness. *Brain, 102*, 609–618.

Brain, W.R. (1941). Visual disorientation with special reference to lesions of the right cerebral hemisphere. *Brain, 64*, 244–272.

Brooks, L.R. (1967). The suppression of visualisation by reading. *Quarterly Journal of Experimental Psychology, 19*, 289–299.

Chatterjee, A., & Southwood, M.H. (1995). Cortical blindness and visual imagery. *Neurology, 45*, 2189–2195.

Coslett, H.B. (1997). Neglect in vision and visual imagery: A double dissociation. *Brain, 120*, 1163–1171.

Courtney, S.M., Petit, L., Maisog, J.M., Ungerleider, L.G., & Haxby, J.V. (1998). An area specialised for spatial working memory in human frontal cortex. *Science, 279*, 1347–1351.

Critchley, M. (1953). *The parietal lobes*. London: E. Arnold.

Denny-Brown, D., Meyer, J.S., & Horenstein, S. (1952). The significance of perceptual rivalry resulting from parietal lesion. *Brain, 75*, 432–471.

Ettlinger, G., Warrington, E., & Zangwill, O.L. (1957). A further study of visuo-spatial agnosia. *Brain, 80*, 335–361.

Ghaem, O., Mellet, E., Crivello, F., Tzourio, N., Mazoyer, B., Berthoz, A., & Denis, M. (1997). Mental navigation along memorised routes activates the hippocampus, precuneus, and insula. *NeuroReport, 8*, 739–744.

Goldenberg, G. (1998). Is there a common substrate for visual recognition and visual imagery? *Neurocase, 4*, 141–147.

Grossi, D., Angelini, R., Pecchinenda, A., & Pizzamiglio, L. (1993). Left imaginal neglect in heminattention: Experimental study with the o'clock test. *Behavioural Neurology, 6*, 155–158.

Grossi, D., Modafferi, A., Pelosi, L., & Trojano, L. (1989). On the different roles of the cerebral hemispheres in mental imagery: The 'o'clock test' in two clinical cases. *Brain and Cognition, 10*, 18–27.

Guariglia, C., Padovani, A., Pantano, P., & Pizzamiglio, L. (1993). Unilateral neglect restricted to visual imagery. *Nature, 364*, 235–237.

Halligan, P.W., & Marshall, J.C. (1994). Completion in visuo-spatial neglect: A case study. *Cortex, 30*, 685–694.

Halligan, P.W., Marshall, J.C., & Wade, D.T. (1992a). Left on the right: Allochiria in a case of left visuo-spatial neglect. *Journal of Neurology, Neurosurgery, and Psychiatry, 55*, 717–719.

Halligan, P.W., Marshall, J.C., & Wade, D.T. (1992b). Contrapositioning in a case of visual neglect. *Neuropsychological Rehabilitation, 2*, 125–135.

Halsband, U., Gruhn, S., & Ettlinger, G. (1985). Unilateral spatial neglect and defective performance in one half of space. *International Journal of Neuroscience, 28*, 173–195.

Hécaen, H., & Albert, M.L. (1978). *Human neuropsychology*. New York: John Wiley.

Heilman, K.M., & Watson, R.T. (1977). The neglect syndrome: A unilateral defect of the orienting response. In S. Harnad, R.W. Doty, L. Goldstein, J. Jaynes, & G. Krauthamer (Eds.), *Lateralisation in the nervous system*. New York: Academic Press.

Kosslyn, S.M. (1987). Seeing and imagining in the cerebral hemispheres: A computational approach. *Psychological Review, 94*, 148–175.

Lhermitte, F., Cambier, J., & Elghozi, D. (1981). Thalamic control of lateralised hemispheric function. In C. Loeb (Ed.), *Studies in cerebrovascular disease*. Milan: Masson.

Manoach, D.S., O'Connor, M., & Weintraub, S. (1996). Absence of neglect for mental representations during the intracarotid amobarbital procedure. *Archives of Neurology, 53*, 333–336.

Maguire, E.A., Burgess, N., Donnett, J.G., Frackowiak, R.S.J., Frith, C.D., & O'Keefe, J. (1998). Knowing where and getting there: A human navigation network. *Science, 280*, 921–924.

Marshall, J.C., & Halligan, P.W. (1993). Imagine only the half of it. *Nature, 364*, 193–194.

McFie, J., Piercy, M.F., & Zangwill, O.L. (1950). Visuo-spatial agnosia associated with lesions of the right cerebral hemisphere. *Brain, 73*, 167–190.

Meador, K.J., Loring, D.W., Bowers, D., & Heilman, K.M. (1987). Remote memory and neglect syndrome. *Neurology, 37*, 522–526.

Morgan, M.J., Findlay, J.M., & Watt, R.J. (1982). Aperture viewing: A review and a synthesis. *Quarterly Journal of Experimental Psychology, 34A*, 211–233.

Ortigue, S., Viaud-Delmon, I., Annoni, J.-M., Landis, T., Michel, C., Blanke, O., Vuilleumier, P., & Mayer, E. (2001). Pure representational neglect after right thalamic lesion. *Annals of Neurology, 50*, 401–404.

Paterson, A., & Zangwill, O.L. (1944). Disorders of visual space perception associated with lesions of the right cerebral hemisphere. *Brain, 67*, 331–358.

Paterson, A., & Zangwill, O.L. (1945). A case of topographical disorientation associated with a unilateral cerebral lesion. *Brain, 68*, 188–210.

Peru, A., & Zapparoli, P. (1999). Case report: A new case of representational neglect. *Italian Journal of Neurological Sciences, 20*, 243–246.

Poppelreuter, W. (1917). *Die psychischen Schadigungen durch Kopfschuss im Kriege 1914/1916*. Leipzig: Voss.

Pribram, K.H. (1971). *Languages of the brain*. Englewood Cliffs, NJ: Prentice-Hall.

Pylyshyn, Z.W. (1973). What the mind's eye tells the mind's brain: A critique of mental imagery. *Psychological Bulletin, 80*, 1–24.

Riddoch, M.J., & Humphreys, G.W. (1989). Finding the way around topographical impairments. In J.W. Brown (Ed.), *Neuropsychology of visual perception*. London: Lawrence Erlbaum Associates Ltd.

Rode, G., & Perenin, M.T. (1994). Temporary remission of representational hemineglect through vestibular stimulation. *NeuroReport, 5*, 869–872.

Rode, G., Perenin, M.T., & Boisson, D. (1995). Neglect of the representational space: Demonstration by mental evocation of the map of France. *Revue Neurologique, 151*, 161–164.

Rode, G., Rossetti, Y., & Boisson, D. (2001). Prism adaptation improves representational neglect. *Neuropsychologia, 39*, 1250–1254.

Rode, G., Rossetti, Y., Li, L., & Boisson, D. (1999). Improvement of mental imagery after prism exposure in neglect: A case study. *Behavioural Neurology, 11*, 251–258.

Roland, P.E., & Gulyás, B. (1994). Visual imagery and visual representation. *TINS, 17*, 281–287.

Stille, A. (1992). *Benevolence and betrayal: Five Italian Jewish families under fascism*. London: Jonathan Cape.

Zingerle, H. (1913). Ueber Stoerungen der Wahruehmung des eigenen Koerpers bei organischen Gehirnerkrankungen. *Monatschrift für Psychiatrie und Neurologie, 34*, 13–36.

CHAPTER EIGHTEEN

Goldstein and Gelb's Case Schn.: A classic case in neuropsychology?

Georg Goldenberg
Bogenhausen Hospital, Munich, Germany

> Er ist ein interessanter Kasus. Subjekt Woyzeck, er kriegt Zulage.
>
> He is an interesting case. Subject Woyzeck, he gets extra pay!
> Georg Büchner, *Woyzeck*

JOHANN SCHNEIDER

On 26 October 1914, the 23-year-old mineworker Johann Schneider was called up as a musketeer to the German army. On 4 June 1915 he was wounded by mine-splinters. He received two wounds on the occiput and was unconscious for 4 days. After healing from the wounds he suffered from vegetative and emotional lability, bradycardia, headache, and feelings of insecurity when standing or walking. On neurological examination he had no nystagmus, but produced jerks of the head and eyes when looking to the right. He missed his nose when he was asked to touch it with the left index finger. His mental capacities appeared normal apart from a slight reduction of the ability to memorise auditorily presented digits. He complained of rapid fatigue and of blurring of vision after prolonged reading.

He was transferred to the brain injury department of the military hospital in Frankfurt for rehabilitation. There he learned the profession of a 'porte-feuiller' manufacturing wallets and pencil cases from pieces of leather. He had some difficulties in the beginning but soon mastered the job and worked very precisely, albeit slowly.

Johann Schneider had been lucky. Even if vegetative instability and fatigue were there to stay, they were not too high a price to be paid for escaping from a cruel and foolish war which was to rage for another three years. Was he afraid that the price might be considered too low and that he might be sent back to the battlefield? The director of the department, Professor Goldstein, together with a psychologist, Adhemar Gelb, were examining visual functions of their patients with a tachistocope. Four months after admission to the department it was Schneider's turn to be examined.

This examination was the starting point of a long-lasting collaboration between Schneider, Goldstein, and Gelb. Together they created and elaborated 'Case Schn'. In the course of repeated examinations Schn. displayed alexia, form agnosia, loss of movement vision, loss of visual imagery, tactile agnosia, loss of body schema, loss of position sense, acalculia, and loss of abstract reasoning. Case Schn. thus became a vivid and comprehensive illustration of Goldstein and Gelb's ideas about the influence of brain damage on perception and reasoning.

Johann Schneider learned to be Case Schn. as eagerly as he had learned to be a portefeullier. Goldstein and Gelb were enthusiastic about him. Their enthusiasm led them to invent fantastic embellishments and swept away any doubts about their credibility. Summing up their results they wrote (Goldstein & Gelb, 1918): 'That much is sure: there is not a single result speaking against our assumptions; all findings without exception can be explained by them (p. 137). The apparently perfect accordance of Schn.'s symptoms with Goldstein and Gelb's theoretical assumptions evoked the scepticism of contemporary clinicians. In his obituary to Kurt Goldstein, Hans-Lukas Teuber (Teuber, 1966) wrote that Schn. 'to some of us seemed more like the platonic idea of a brain-injured patient than a patient himself' (p. 306).

CASE SCHN.

Apart from increased fatigue after reading, Schn. did not spontaneously complain of any visual deficiencies, nor was he visually handicapped in his daily life. He performed well at visually exacting work. He moved freely in the hospital and in the town of Frankfurt where he had never been before. However, he did display striking abnormalities when visual functions were examined. On perimetry, there was a concentric narrowing of visual fields of both eyes, leaving a 'tunnel' of about 20 degrees. When simple geometrical figures, line-drawings of objects, letters, or words were displayed tachistoscopicly for 1½ to 2 seconds (sic!), Schn. was unable to recognise them. He claimed to see only 'black dots', 'irregular circles', or 'confusion'. He needed repeated exposures for a total time of 5 to 10 seconds before eventually recognising the stimuli. When stimuli were presented normally his recognition latencies were of the same order. They were filled by conspicuous movements of either the head or the hand.

The education of Schn.

Goldstein and Gelb were well aware that the complete failure of tachisto-copic recognition was contradicted by the absence of any visual handicap outside the testing situation: 'The patient's performance in the tachistocopic experiment is much worse than that of patients who display conspicuous optic-agnostic disturbances already with ordinary (permanent) presentation of stimuli' (p. 17). 'He did not display any disturbance at all on normal examination with familiar objects' (p. 107). 'It was quite conspicuous how relatively well our patient could orient in the surroundings, even when depending on vision only' (p. 107).

The authors made this very discrepancy the starting point of their theory. Their basic idea was that Schn. lacked any visual experience of forms (or, respectively 'Gestalt') but that he compensated this deficit by tracing visually presented forms with movements of either the head or the fingers, eventually recognising the form by kinaesthetic feedback.

The first person who had to be convinced of this theory was Schn.: it took Goldstein and Gelb much time and devotion to teach Schn. to provide self-observation compatible with their theory.

> In a way we had to educate him. (p. 52)

> About two to three months after starting our examinations he remarked one day that he now had realised what was deficient: his vision was different than before. The examiner's questions had drawn his attention to the change. Until then he had believed that the slowing of reading and other optical performances was a sequel of his general impairment (the patient mentioned 'fatigue', 'headache', and 'vertigo'), but now he believed that he must *see* differently from before. (p. 50)

> Once he had understood what he ought to tell us, his statements became different and quite usable. (p. 52)

Goldstein and Gelb repeatedly stress that even after having learned to describe it properly, Schn. considered his way of perceiving completely nor-mal. Concerning the tracing of forms by movements of head and hand they state: 'When his attention was drawn to these movements, he knew about them, but for a long time he did not yet know that recognition by movement is something exceptional. He spoke of these movements as being something obviously normal' (p. 50). Goldstein and Gelb reemphasised Schn.'s belief in the normality of his vision when reporting his loss of movement vision: 'When our examinations and questions revealed to the patient that he did not see movements, he was unable to get an idea of what it is like to have a normal optical impression of movement' (p. 94). The inability to imagine normal vision is mysterious as Schneider had seen normally for 24 years. Apparently, Schn. had no recollection of Schneider's life-long visual experience.

In their first monograph on Schn., Goldstein and Gelb (1918) explored four symptoms: alexia, form agnosia, loss of movement vision, and loss of visual imagery.

Alexia

Schn. did not recognise any letters or words with tachistocopic exposure for 1½ to 2 seconds. When reading was examined with normal presentation he correctly read even unfamiliar and long words but it took him 10 minutes and more to read one word. During that time his head and the right index singer would move, apparently tracing letters in the air. Schn. did not, however, directly trace the written letters: 'He let his hand in its momentary position and . . . moved the finger within a narrow frame as if he would write each letter at the same place' (p. 18). When the experimenter fixated the fingers of Schn.'s right hand, he would move his head. Movements of the head were preferred spontaneously when Schn. read print rather than script.

Goldstein and Gelb emphasised that Schn.'s reading movements were closely tied to his habitual motor programmes for writing. Thus, he could read script only if the letters were formed exactly in the same way as he himself used to write them. Minor variations of non-defining features of a letter were sufficient to make letters unrecognisable. For reading print Schn. did not employ finger movements but moved his head only. In this way he could read Latin as well as gothic letters. Apparently, his head but not his hand was able to disregard the distracting ornaments of printed gothic letters for finding out their defining features. However, 'head movements could not evoke experiences which were senseful, habitual and useful for understanding of mirror writing' (p. 31). In this case, Schn. accompanied his head movements by moving the left hand which apparently had a motor habit of writing from right to left. We are not told whether and how Schn. could cope with mirror print.

Goldstein and Gelb did not control whether the rigid motor habits that limited recognition of script were present in his tracing movements or in his actual writing. Inspection of their own paper might have taught them that this was not the case (see Figure 18.1).

Form agnosia

Schn. was said to have lost any visual experience of form, but to compensate this loss by tracing movements of the head or the hand which then permitted deduction of the form from kinaesthetic feedback. Because of the unusual efficiency of this compensation, the true nature of his deficit became apparent only during explicit examinations of visual functions.

A   B   C   D   E

Figure 18.1   A, B: Schn. was said to be able to read the L shown in A but not that in B, because only the former corresponded to his habitual way of handwriting (Goldstein & Gelb, 1918, p. 27). C: Schn. used to trace printed letters with the head only. He was asked to replicate his head movements with the finger, and the movement was recorded (p. 82). His tracing of the gothic L has much more resemblance with the L shown in B than with the one which allegedly corresponded to his way of handwriting. D: In the same paper there is a reproduction of a curriculum vitae written by Schneider (p. 119). It contains a capital L. Note the variation of the basic horizontal line. Schn.'s motor programs of handwriting were much less rigid than proposed by the dependence of recognition on minor details E: Schn.'s tracing of the gothic letter V (p. 82). There is hardly any formal similarity between the model and the trace. Schn. must have recognised the identity of the letter before producing the tracing movement.

It took Schn. 6 seconds to identify a triangle from repeated tachistocopic presentations. After a first presentation of 1 second he saw only 'a big dot'. After another 1½ seconds he recognised one line going obliquely upwards, 1½ seconds later a second line going obliquely downwards, and after another 2 seconds he realised that the figure was a triangle. With free presentation of pictures 'from children's painting books, picture books, etc.' he needed 'at least 5 to 10 seconds, but usually up to 30 seconds or more' for recognition. During that time he made tracing movements of the head, but 'he traced only those parts of the picture which correspond to simple geometrical formations, (p. 39). For pictures which did not contain any familiar geometrical formation, he made no tracing movements at all: 'The fact that the patient could identify simple geometrical figures only with the help of appropriate movements but could describe without movements, albeit somewhat slowly, the gross contents of large pictures rich on details, will certainly appear rather strange to some readers' (p. 42).

Goldstein and Gelb argue that in these cases Schn. actually perceived nothing but 'dots of different colour and different size' but guessed the identity of the objects without the necessity to recognise the specific form of the coloured dots. The protocols of his examinations do not fit well with this explanation. Confronted with 'Meinhold's picture "Springtime" he described: 'A lawn . . . and there is water . . . and there is a mill' (p. 40).

The same painter's picture 'Winter' gave rise to the following dialogue between Schn. and the examiner:

'It is all with snow (why?) instead of leaves all is white . . . there is also deer and a food-trough (what is that light spot?) that might be a path leading out of the forest' (p. 40).

He was shown a picture of a tailor's workshop. 'The patient says: there are persons (about 10 seconds pause) they are tailors (on questioning he says that he has recognised the cutter by his scissors) . . . they are sitting on the tailor's table . . . a coat is hanging on the wall' (p. 40).

It is very unlikely indeed that Schneider could deduce a mill, deer, a food-trough, scissors, and a hanging coat from 'formless dots'. Perhaps Goldstein and Gelb felt that the examples are hardly convincing of a complete loss of form vision. They add:

> The real characteristic features of his statements are expressed only very imperfectly by these transcriptions. They miss the specific behaviour of the patient, which gave the impression that he suddenly detected the details on the picture, similar to situations where we are left to guessing rather than to distinct vision. (p. 41)

Presumably this is the impression that any layperson would try to give when asked to behave as if being visually agnosic. Schn. was cooperating well indeed.

Schn. was willing but not cunning. Goldstein and Gelb confronted him with optical illusions like that of Müller-Lyer where contextual cues make two lines of the same length appear different. Schn. must have realised that they expected him to be insensitive to these illusions. He fulfilled the expectations but exaggerated: rather than believing both lines to be of equal length, he considered the one that appeared shorter to be longer, thus betraying that he had sensed the illusion. How else would he come to believe that there was any difference at all? Goldstein and Gelb did not note the fallacy. Their cunningness was clouded by enthusiasm.

Goldstein's and Gelb's explanatory versatility was challenged by Schn.'s superior performance of tasks that should be impossible to solve for a person without any form vision. Asked to copy pictures (see Figure 18.2),

> the patient provided drawings that could raise the suspicion that he copied like a normal, gifted person. His optical impressions were of such a nature as to make it impossible to render them by drawing. The drawings had been achieved by copying only ostensibly. In reality, he had first traced the pictures, in this way experiencing their form, and had then drawn them spontaneously. (p. 121)

Schn. was able to mark the centre of a circle very exactly:

> When he was given a black-on-white circle of 6 cm diameter, he made a movement of the head and 'recognised' the circle. Now he started to make concentric circling movements of the head which became smaller and smaller, until

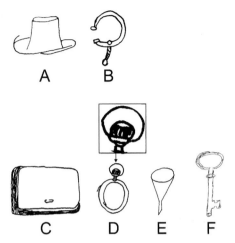

A   B

C   D   E   F

Figure 18.2   A, B: Drawing from memory of a hat and a table-clasp (Goldstein & Gelb, 1918, p. 120). It is hard to believe that Schn. had lost all internal optical representations. C to E: Copies of drawings (p. 121; obviously a bag, a watch, and a funnel). Goldstein and Gelb argue that Schn. had not actually copied the model, but had recognised it by tracing and then reproduced it 'spontaneously'. Note the details of the watch-case. Is it possible that a person who can neither copy nor imagine the visual appearance of objects has drawn them? F: Drawing of a tactually explored key (Goldstein & Gelb, 1919, p. 43). Schn. recognised the key neither from palpation nor from his own drawing. Apparently the compensatory mechanisms which usually allowed him to recognise drawing of objects (see, for example, explanation for good copying!) failed in this particular experiment. Remember that his favourite and most effective compensatory mechanism was kinaesthetic feedback from tracing movements. One may ask why this did not work for palpation of objects.

> eventually, after 3 to 5 circles, he marked the point. This was placed quite well: in the horizontal direction it deviated to the right by 1 mm, and in the vertical direction upwards by ½ mm. (p. 125)

To scale head movements with an exactitude of ½ mm and to transfer the position of the head with the same exactitude to a hand-held pen would indeed suggest a feast of visuomotor coordination.

Loss of movement vision

As with the other symptoms, Schn. neither spontaneously complained of any change of movement vision nor were there any signs of defective appreciation of movement in his behaviour. The symptom was detected only when Schn. was explicitly tested for his visual impression of movements.

> If a fast downward movement of the extended index finger was made before the eyes of the patient, he said, 'now it is above' when the hand was above and

'now it is below' when it was below. On the question of whether he had not seen something between above and below he constantly responded 'no' and stated that the hand had appeared first above and then below. When the movement was made slower and he was asked to fixate on the hand, one could note a continous tracking movement of the eyes, but the patient did not see the movement. Between the start and the end position he only saw single isolated positions. (p. 92).

Once the symptom was detected, Schn. was eager to provide further evidence for its reality.

After the patient's attention had been directed to this disturbance, he reported peculiar observations from his ordinary life that had obviously been caused by the loss of a movement impression . . . Once when going for a walk with his sister-in-law, she left the house first and he followed her at a distance of about 20 metres. He then had the impression of seeing that his sister-in-law stopped ('*stehenblieb*') and remained still, and he was astonished not to catch up with her; 'the distance did not get shorter'. (pp. 94–95)

Schn. did his best to imagine what it is like to see no movements but did not consider that in the experiments he had always recognised changes of position, albeit without noting the interpolated movement. He should have noted that the position of his sister-in-law relative to the street and the houses had changed while he was trying to catch up with her. And, of course, one may ask how he could perceive a stop without having perceived the motion that stopped!

Loss of visual imagery

In contrast to the peculiarities of visual recognition, loss of visual imagery was a symptom that Schn. himself reported had changed from the time before his injury: 'He reports that as a schoolboy he had modelled his teacher from clay very well: his schoolfellows could also. He would be unable to do so now, because he could not represent anything internally' (p. 116). Mental visual images were not degraded or weak but completely absent: 'We admonished the patient to consider whether there could not sometimes occur some, even very vague or fragmented, image. The patient repeated with certainty that he had no optical representation at all' (p. 117).

Schn.'s claim that he would be unable to create a representation of visually perceived objects was contradicted by his drawings of objects from memory, which appeared to be completely normal (see Figure 18.2). For Goldstein and Gelb, however, this only proved 'how great the independence of drawing from visual imagery can be' (p. 121). When asked for verbal descriptions of the visual appearance of objects he usually refused to answer saying that he could not imagine them. Only sometimes did he mention some visual properties, which, however, were commonplace enough to be retrieved from verbally overlearned knowledge rather than from visual imagery. For example, when asked to describe a lion Schn. answered: It has a yellow fur . . . the male has hair on the neck, the female is fierce' (p. 114).

This part of the examination process appeared consistent and convincing, but when the medical records were reviewed it turned out that consistency had been achieved by suppression of conflicting evidence (see below).

Loss of body schema and tactile agnosia

Schn. was dismissed from the military hospital in 1918 but returned for a further stay in 1919 and then attended the hospital regularly for follow-up examinations. From 1919 to 1932 a number of papers on Case Schn. by different authors were edited by Goldstein and Gelb in a series of "Psycho-logical Analyses of Cases of Brain-Pathology" (Goldstein & Gelb, 1919; Benary, 1922; Mäki, 1928; Hochheimer, 1932). During this time Schn. developed disturbances that had not been mentioned at all in the first publi-cation. The first and most spectacular of them was an inability to localise where he was being touched on his body (Goldstein & Gelb, 1919). Similar to his inability to recognise visually presented objects without tracing move-ments, he became unable to localise touch without producing 'touch-jerks' ('*Tastzuckungen*') of the touched body part. Asked to localise touch: 'one could see that the movements first affected the whole body, and then concen-trated more and more on the examined extremity, until eventually there were only jerks of the touched location' (p. 14).

Schn. had similar difficulties selecting the appropriate body part for movements on command, particularly with eyes closed:

> When asked to move a certain extremity he first appeared completely helpless. He repeated the request verbally, then one could note that he made movements of the whole body (head, neck, legs, etc.); gradually the movements con-centrated more and more in the target extremity until at last only this one remained. (p. 57)

Schn. hardly ever recognised objects by touch. He could make quite detailed drawings of tactually unidentified objects but remained unable to recognise them (see Figure 18.2).

As was the case for his visual symptoms, the disorders of touch and of motor control did not affect his behaviour outside the testing situation:

> In contrast to his extraordinary awkwardness in executing determined, but objectively simple movements, the patient performs a large number of apparently complicated movement sequences in daily life quite promptly . . .

For example, he reached safely, without looking, into his pocket, took out his handkerchief and took it to his nose. With eyes closed he could quite quickly take out a match from a matchbox and light a candle. (p. 64)

Loss of position sense

Having conquered touch and motor control the loss of 'Gestalt' perception attacked the sense of equilibrium:

> The patient arrived at making statements about the position of his whole body only indirectly. His behaviour when lying on the sofa was characteristic: He moved the whole body and tried to find out which body part pressed most strongly against the surroundings. From feeling most pressure on the back and the buttocks he concluded that these parts touched and that consequently he must be in an approximately horizontal position. When he was standing he concluded from pressure on the sole and the characteristic sensations in the knee that he was in an upright position ... He did not note any difference between a vertical position and a 30 degree inclination; from the pressure to feet and legs he concluded that he was upright for both of them. (p. 53)

Outside the testing situation this dramatic loss of position sense did not lead to any postural imbalance.

Acalculia

Presumably paralleling the further development and elaboration of Goldstein and Gelb's ideas about the impact of brain injury on abstract reasoning (Gelb, 1937; Goldstein, 1934/1995; Harrington, 1996) Schn.'s symptoms transgressed the limits of motor and sensory functions to invade his intellect: He turned out to be unable to understand basic arithmetic concepts. He solved arithmetical problems with the help of finger-counting and other primitive strategies: 'If you ask the patient what is more, 7 or 4, he starts reciting the number series "1, 2, 3, 4" and then says: "7 is more, because it comes later; it has not appeared until now"' (Gelb, 1937, p. 227).

Loss of abstract reasoning

The same lack of conceptual understanding marked his language and thinking. He was unable to abstract from the literal meaning of words for understanding metaphor and humour. The following dialogue about rabbits (Schneider used to raise rabbits) was cited by Hochheimer (1932) to illustrate Schn.'s clinging to the literal and concrete meaning of words:

H: It's funny that in the winter rabbits do not freeze in their fur. Humans freeze so much in theirs.

Schn: They don't have one.

H: But there is a saying 'he has a thick fur' (German for 'he is thick-skinned').

Schn: That's not true. That has nothing to do with the fur. This refers to the receptivity of their mind. (p. 29)

He was assessed to be completely incapable of any conceptual reasoning beyond automatised verbal associations:

H: Where do the waves on the water come from?

Schn. . . . 'the wind rustles': from the wind.

H: What does that mean: 'the wind rustles'?

Schn: Waves . . . 'the waves murmur, the wind rustles' (this being recited with a completely empty facial expression).

H: What is this?

Schn: This must be a poem. I do not know myself how that came to my mind. How should I explain? What should I say? Waves! Where do the waves come from? And then it came: 'the waves murmur, the wind rustles'. Therefore: from the wind! (pp. 13–14)

Hochheimer adds: 'This peculiar behaviour made the impression of a medium in a trance. It was produced by Schn. like from an automatically triggered gramophone record. And he himself did not really know what was spoken out of him' (p. 14).

We will return to this peculiar behaviour in a later part of the chapter. At this point we may summarise that Schn. was indeed more like a platonic idea of a patient than a real patient (Teuber, 1966). What may have appeared to a naive observer as a puzzling collection of disparate symptoms constituted for Goldstein, Gelb and their followers a coherent illustration of the idea that brain damage affects the ability to create a holistic 'Gestalt' out of the diversity and fragmentation of perception and thought.

KURT GOLDSTEIN AND ADHEMAR GELB

Why did Goldstein and Gelb believe Schn.'s symptoms to be real? Their experience with other brain-damaged patients and a minimum of critical reasoning should have been sufficient to evoke their doubts. Obviously they strongly wanted Schn. to embody the case they wanted to demonstrate. It is hard to resist the nagging suspicion that this 'classic' case is indeed a case of scientific fraud. There is, however, a strong argument against deliberate faking of the case report by Goldstein and Gelb. If they had wanted to cheat they would have done better: They would have eliminated its obvious inconsistencies and fallacies to make the report internally consistent. Two experienced authors did not control whether the illustrations corresponded to the text (see Figure 18.1). Two philosophically educated scientists did not realise that 'to stop' means to end a motion (see the 'Loss of movement vision' section). A professor of neurology did not realise the consequences that a complete loss of equilibrium sense must have on standing and walking. Their minds must have been clouded. They were clouded by the enthusiasm of proving the truth of an all-embracing theory of the human mind and its reaction to brain damage (Gelb, 1937; Goldstein, 1934/1995; Harrington 1996).

At their time Goldstein and Gelb were not the only ones whose minds were clouded by a belief in all-embracing theories. They may have suppressed conflicting evidence (see below) and they may have violated logic for constraining reality to conform with their faith. Others used infinitely more brutal means for forcing reality to theories that were vastly less reasonable than those of Goldstein and Gelb.

Goldstein and Gelb were Jews. In 1933 both lost their professorships. Goldstein was denounced by an assistant who complained that he had leftist sympathies in addition to being Jewish. He disappeared for a week during which he was held in a basement and flogged with sand-filled rubber hoses. He was released after signing a statement that he would leave Germany forever (Teuber, 1966). He emigrated to Holland and then to New York, where, arriving at the age of 56, he succeeded in starting a new career that made him a founding father of modern neuropsychology. Gelb left Germany in 1934. He and his family suffered from economic deprivation and misery. He tried to obtain a professorship at the University of Stockholm but died from tuberculosis in 1936 at the age of 48 years (Bergius, 1963).

EBERHARD BAY AND RICHARD JUNG

In 1942 and 1944 two German neurologists, Richard Jung and Eberhard Bay, visited and re-examined Schneider. For that purpose they also admitted him to the ward for several days. Bay also gained access to the original medical records. Both concluded that Schn.'s symptoms were faked. They published their reports only in 1949 (Bay, Lauenstein, & Cibis, 1949; Jung, 1949). We hope that neither the authors nor the readers of these reports considered the sceptical re-evaluation of Goldstein and Gelb's scientific *chef d'oevre* as support for the reluctance of post-war German universities to reintegrate Jewish emigrants (Pfeiffer, 1998).

Jung and Bay relate many anecdotes illustrating the normality of Schneider's visual perceptual abilities. Head movements were absent outside of testing situations. He could read letters subtending a visual angle of less than 1°, far below the discriminatory exactitude of head movements. He shaved and combed his hair with the help of a mirror which replicates and thus makes useless tracing movement of the head. He recognised doctors and medical assistants from a distance of 20 metres even when meeting them outside the hospital in civilian clothes. When an air-alert forced them to rapidly leave the examination room, he took his bag without hesitation from the cupboard where it lay beside a second, visually very similar bag. The following episode is instructive not only about Schneider's vision but also about his character (see below): 'Schn. stands in conversation with another patient who is filling his pipe. Some tobacco falls down. Schn. reaches for it, catches the falling tobacco and puts it back in the pipe again' (Bay et al., 1949, p. 87).

During testing Schn. behaved in the same way as described by Goldstein and Gelb. However, both examiners noted that the amplitude of his head movements transgressed the magnitude of the traced details and that the direction of movements frequently bore little similarity to the allegedly traced features. Jung describes Schn's reading: 'He is reading all sorts of text correctly. Reading is accompanied by head movements which after the first few words run mechanically. Neither their number nor their direction have any recognisable relationship to the letters, syllables, and words read' (p. 357).

Bay duped Schn. He provoked 'touch-jerks' by touching Schn.'s ear. Schn. performed movements of the whole head to confirm that the ear had been touched. Bay presented a picture repeatedly with constant exposition time but told Schn. that exposition time was first increasing and then decreasing. The completeness of Schn's report increased and decreased in tight correlation with the pretended variations of exposure time.

In the medical records Bay found a composition of Schneider's dating from May 1916, describing a walk to the palm-garden in Frankfurt:

> What I have seen there is all splendid and beautiful, and I hardly find words to describe it. Nearest to my heart is the beautiful flower terrace at the entrance, and then the marvelous building from which plants, shrubs, and trees are looking out, and where I always stop to admire. From there I proceed to the flower and planthouses which offer innumerable beautiful flowers for inspection. Then I go into the surroundings of the garden. I arrive at the rock grotto which stands there very artificially with its walking-passages. Close to the grotto there is a large pond where I have seen many fishes. The pond is traversed by a bridge without piers which is suspended only by strong steel cables. The steel cables are fixed to the rock . . . After a while I start my way back home, taking with me the sights and the splendour of the beautiful, magnificent palm-garden. (p. 87)

Being part of the medical records this document cannot have escaped the attention of Goldstein and Gelb. They obviously preferred not to include it in their publication for fear of casting serious doubts upon their assertion that Schn.'s genuine visual experience was restricted to 'formless dots' and that he had no mental visual images.

JOHANN SCHNEIDER AND SCHN.

Schneider left the military hospital in 1918 with a 70% pension for 'mind-blindness and cerebellar disturbances'. He settled in a little village near Frankfurt, worked as a portefeullier, married, and had children but continued to attend the hospital, being examined as Case Schn. In 1931 he opened a grocery store of his own. In 1937 he applied for augmentation of the pension, but the justification of his claim was called into question as he was observed to serve the clients in his shop without any noticeable visual handicap. He was re-examined by the neurologist and ophthalmologist of the pension board who found his symptoms credible enough to award him a 80% pension for 'mindblindness and traumatic cerebral weakness'. This remained his only means of subsistence when in 1944 his house was bombed and he had to give up the grocery store. Good luck returned after the war. He was elected mayor of his little village and fulfilled this office to the satisfaction of his fellow-citizens at least until 1949 when for the last time he was the subject of two publications (Bay et al., 1949; Jung, 1949).

Johann Schneider benefited substantially from being case Schn., and Bay and Jung noted repeatedly that he produced visual symptoms when he suspected observation by critical examiners, but not when believing he was unobserved. There are, however, reasons to consider malingering insufficient to explain Schn.'s behaviour during testing.

Schneider and Schn. were two different personalities. Schneider, the person outside the testing situation, was unequivocally described as being a most aimable man, always friendly and helpful, open-minded and interested, humorous, and with wit and talents beyond his educational level.

> Who comes closer to him, loves him: his colleagues, the doctors who treat him, his neighbours and relatives. (Hochheimer, 1932, p. 7)

> He attracts attention by his friendly and helpful manner. So, for example, he supports a blind fellow patient in every way. He prepares food for him, leads him to the air-raid shelter when there is an alarm etc. Also in other situations he helps without request whenever he can. (Bay et al., 1949, p. 79)

Schneider had a sense of humour and irony:

> We had not met for a long period of time. I explained to S. that this was due to overwork. S, laughing: 'Well, you want to become professor too quickly'. (Hochheimer, 1932, p. 7)

In his language he used metaphor appropriately:

> I am pleased to hear that you are fine and I wish you the best for your further vacation. I hope to be able to recognise you when you come back to

Frankfurt, or will the splendid weather and the sunny days change you into a negro? It must be wonderful to relax in a deserted wilderness away from the hubbub of the big city, but, as I infer from your letter, you will soon exchange this paradise for the city rush again (p. 5, from a letter written to Dr. Hochheimer).

His compassion with other creatures could be read from his vivid mimical expression:

Another time S told me of his roasted rabbit. I asked whether he had killed the rabbit himself. S: No, I cannot do that. I once tried. My wife said: Kill that rabbit, and I tried. But then my wife said: 'Go away, go away, your nose is completely pale'. I did not want to hurt the rabbit and so it escaped from my hands and cried.

S's physiognomic behaviour accompanying this part of his speech was quite appropriate. (p. 7)

When Schneider turned into Schn., his manner changed:

During examinations Schn. displays a completely different behaviour. From the beginning of any—particularly optical—examination he is visibly tense, the otherwise good rapport with him deteriorates markedly. He now makes all statements after careful reflection with an exalted, theatratically lecturing prosody and similarily fixed facial expression and gesturing (Bay et al., 1949, p. 79).

Presumably Bay intended this description to endorse the suspicion of malingering. However, Hochheimer, who did not distrust Schn.'s symptoms, gave a very similar description of the metamorphosis that took place when examinations started: 'The easy running falters; the otherwise cheerful and warm face suddenly becomes tortured and tense. The human resonance of his speech prosody turns into a taciturn behaviour, defensive and unsteady: the "human being" S turns into "patient"' (p. 12).

Schneider and Schn. were two different personalities. Schneider was an amiable, open-minded, vivid human being. Schn., by contrast, was a freak: speaking with an exalted, monotonous voice, shaking all over the body, exploring the world around him like an alien, he resembled a strange automaton more than a human being. In his last lectures Gelb (1937) mentioned that kinematographic records had been made of Schn. I have a suspicion that Schn. appeared on them like a grotesque victim of omnipotent hypnosis, a favourite subject of German movies of that time.

We do not know whether the extra pay for being a case was Schneider's only motive for turning into Schn., but we may conclude that this extra pay was not earned easily.

A CLASSIC CASE IN NEUROPSYCHOLOGY?

Goldstein and Gelb's first monograph, though not the subsequent papers, has remained a citation classic in neuropsychology. The reason for this survival is that several of the symptoms that they claimed to find in Schn. were indeed detected in later patients. Form agnosia (e.g., Benson & Greenberg, 1969; Landis, Graves, Benson, & Hebben, 1982; Milner, 1997; Milner et al., 1991), loss of movement vision (Zeki, 1991; Zihl, Von Cramon, & Mai, 1983), and loss of visual imagery (see Goldenberg, 1993, 1998 for reviews) have credibly been documented to exist as sequels of brain damage, but on closer reading the differences between the clinical features of later patients and Schn. confirm the unreality of Schn.'s symptoms.

The anecdote of Schn. catching the falling tobacco is reminiscent of DF, a patient with severe form agnosia. DF can exploit visual information about size and orientation of objects for accurate grasping but not for conscious perception (Milner et al., 1991). DF's preserved visual processing subserves exclusively motor actions directed towards the object. Thus, the accuracy of her grasp breaks down when she is asked to pantomime grasping immediately after presentation of the object or a few centimetres beside the visible object (Goodale et al., 1994). She can use preserved motor reactions for self-cuing about single properties of a given object. For example, when asked to discriminate a square block from a rectangular one she may initiate reaches towards both objects and make a decision based on kinaesthetic feedback about the anticipatory grip size. She even attained above chance accuracy for copying the orientation of lines by imagining the motor act of tracing the line with the finger (Milner, 1997). These achievements are remarkable but far away from Schn.'s reading by head or finger movements or from his perfect copies of line-drawings, and of course preserved visuo-motor coordination cannot account for Schn.'s verbal description of his visual impressions in the palm-garden.

Landis et al. (1982) documented a form-agnosic patient who used writing with the finger as a strategy for reading. Differently from Schn., however, he used the same strategy for cuing himself in naming from auditorily presented definitions suggesting that the strategy served lexical retrieval rather than visual analysis, and he did not display the curious dependence of finger writing on minor visual details of the letter, which was so conspicuous in Schn.

Schn.'s story of the sudden stop of his sister-in-law has little in common with the real complaints of a lady in whom bilateral temporo-ocipital lesions had caused a loss of movement vision:

> She had difficulty, for example, in pouring tea or coffee into a cup because the fluid appeared to be frozen, like a glacier. In addition, she could not stop pouring at the right time since she was unable to perceive the movement in the cup (or a pot) when the fluid rose. Furthermore the patient complained of

difficulties in following a dialogue because she could not see the movements of the face and, expecially, the mouth of the speaker. In a room where more than two other people were walking she felt very insecure and unwell, and usually left the room immediately, because 'people were suddenly here or there but I have not seen them moving'. The patient experienced the same problem but to an even more marked extent in crowded streets or places, which she therefore avoided as much as possible. She could not cross the street because of her inability to judge the speed of a car. (Zihl, Von Cramon, Mai, & Schmid, 1991, p. 315).

Even the inability to compare the size of two numbers other than by counting has been reliably documented in later patients (Butterworth, 1999). As a consequence of the complete absence of number sense these patients had severe difficulties with the commercial transactions of basic daily life as well as with even the most simple arithmetical operations. None of them would have dared to open a grocery store at a time when there was not even to possibility of taking refuge in electronic calculators. In fact, one patient, who had been a market trader and had lost his number sense after a stroke, had to give up his business.

It does not matter for the validity of Goldstein and Gelb's report whether Schneider had suffered any substantial brain damage at all and whether it had left any lasting neuropsychological disturbances. There are indications that this was the case. He suffered from fatigue and vegetative instability. Hochheimer, Jung, and Bay agree in noting that even outside the testing situation Schneider was somewhat slow, that he could do no more than one thing at a time, and that his reasoning sometimes appeared to be circumstantial and inflexible. These subtle symptoms afflicted Schneider. They would not suffice for making him a classic case. The classic case was Schn., and Schn.'s symptoms had at best a loose relationship to the real consequences of Schneider's brain damage.

If a case report is considered to be classic only if later papers have confirmed and expanded its findings, Case Schn. does not merit inclusion in this collection of classic cases. The fact that Case Schn. is still cited in papers on visual agnosia is rather a paradoxical effect of the inaccessibility, length, and (for non-German-speaking readers) incomprehensibility of the original papers. Presumably, few of the authors who cite them have read them.

There may be other ways in which Schn. is a 'classic case'. He influenced the development of ideas not only in neuropsychology but also in general psychology and philosophy (Merleau-Ponty, 1945; van Orden et al., 2000), and he has an important message about the nature of neuropsychological research. We are reminded that neuropsychology is a human science in more than one sense. It is concerned with the architecture and the biological foundation of the human mind, and it draws its evidence from interactions between human beings acting as scientists or cases. Both, scientists and cases, are embedded in and influenced by the society they live in. Germany between the wars was imbued with beliefs in universal theories that pretended to replace 'mechanistic' dissections by 'holistic' insights into the essence of nature and soul (Harrington, 1996). Enthusiasm for their version of such a theory must have induced Goldstein and Gelb to fabricate case Schn. Schneider was willing to assume his part in that scenario. He illustrated not only the symptoms that the theory predicted but also the presumption that holistic insight into the essence of experience is itself the highest mental faculty of man. His peculiar behaviour during testing looks like a demonstration of the mechanistic 'machine man' whom holistic theories predicted would result from loss of this faculty.

ACKNOWLEDGEMENT

I want to thank Klaus Willmes and Dieter Heller for biographical information about Adhemar Gelb.

REFERENCES

Bay, E., Lauenstein, O., & Cibis, P. (1949). Ein Beitrag zur Frage der Seelenblindheit: der Fall Schn. von Gelb und Goldstein. *Psychiatrie, Neurologie und medizinische Psychologie, 1*, 73–91.

Benary, W. (1922). Studien zur Untersuchung der Intelligenz bei einem Fall von Seelenblindheit. *Psychologische Forschung, 2*, 209–292.

Benson, D.F., & Greenberg, J.P. (1969). Visual form agnosia: A specific defect in visual discrimination. *Archives of Neurology, 20*, 82–89.

Bergius, R. (1963). Zum 75. Geburtstag von Adhemar Gelb. *Psychologische Beiträge, 7*, 360–369.

Butterworth, B. (1999). *The mathematical brain*. London: Macmillan.

Gelb, A. (1937). Zur medizinischen Psychologie und philosophischen Anthropologie. *Acta Psychologica, 3*, 193–271.

Goldenberg, G. (1993). The neural basis of mental imagery. *Bailliere's Clinical Neurology, 2*, 265–286.

Goldenberg, G. (1998). Is there a common substrate for visual recognition and visual imagery? *Neurocase, 4*, 141–148.

Goldstein, K. (1934/1995). *The organism: A holistic approach to biology derived from pathological data in man*. New York: Zone Books.

Goldstein, K., & Gelb, A. (1918). Psychologische Analysen hirnpathologischer Fälle auf Grund von Untersuchungen Hirnverletzter: I. Abhandlung. Zur Psychologie des optischen Wahrnehmungs- und Erkennungsvorganges. *Zeitschrift für die gesamte Neurologie und Psychiatrie, 41*, 1–142.

Goldstein, K., & Gelb, A. (1919). Über den Einfluss des vollständigen Verlustes des optischen Vorstellungsvermögens auf das taktile Erkennen. Zugleich ein Beitrag zur Psychologie der taktilen Raumwahrnehmung und der Bewegungsvorstellungen. *Zeitschrift für Psychologie, 83*, 1–94.

Goodale, M.A., Jakobson, L.S., & Keillor, J.M. (1994). Differences in the visual control of pantomimed and natural grasping movements. *Neuropsychologia, 32*, 1159–1178.

Harrington, A. (1996). *Reenchanted science: Holism in German culture from Wilhelm II to Hitler*. Princeton, NJ: Princeton University Press.

Hochheimer, W. (1932). Analyse eines 'Seelenblinden' von der Sprache aus. Ein Beitrag zur Frage nach der Bedeutung der Sprache für das Verhalten zur Umwelt. *Psychologische Forschung*, *16*, 1–69.

Jung, R. (1949). Über eine Nachuntersuchung des Falles Schn. von Goldstein und Gelb. *Psychiatrie, Neurologie und medizinische Psychologie*, *1*, 353–362.

Landis, T., Graves, R., Benson, D.F., & Hebben, N. (1982). Visual recognition through kinaesthetic mediation. *Psychological Medicine*, *12*, 515–531.

Mäki, N. (1928). Natürliche Bewegungstendenzen der rechten und linken Hand und ihr Einfluss auf das Zeichnen und den Erkennungsvorgang. (Auf Grund von Untersuchungen am 'Seelenblinden' Schn.). *Psychologische Forschung*, *10*, 1–19.

Merleau-Ponty, M. (1945/1997). *Phénoménologie de la perception*. Paris: Gallimard.

Milner, A.D. (1997). Vision without knowledge. *Philosophical Transactions of the Royal Society of London, B*, *352*, 1249–1256.

Milner, A.D., Perrett, D.I., Johnston, R.S., Benson, P.J., Jordan, T.R., Heeley, D.W., Bettucci, D., Mortara, F., Mutani, R., Terazzi, E., & Davidson, D.L.W. (1991). Perception and action in 'visual form agnosia'. *Brain*, *114*, 405–428.

Pfeiffer, J. (1998). Die Vertreibung deutscher Neuropathologen 1933–1939. *Nervenarzt*, *69*, 99–109.

Teuber, H.L. (1966). Kurt Goldstein's role in the development of neuropsychology. *Neuropsychologia*, *4*, 299–310.

Van Orden, G.C., & Jansen op de Haar, M.A. (2000). Schneider's apraxia and the strained relation between experience and description. *Philosophical Psychology*, *13*, 247–259.

Zeki, S. (1991). Cerebral akinetopsia (visual motion blindness). *Brain*, *114*, 811–824.

Zihl, J., Von Cramon, D., & Mai, N. (1983). Selective disturbance of movement vision after bilateral brain damage. *Brain*, *106*, 313–340.

Zihl, J., Von Cramon, D., Mai, N., & Schmid, C. (1991). Disturbance of movement vision after bilateral posterior brain damage: Further evidence and follow-up observations. *Brain*, *114*, 2235–2252.

CHAPTER NINETEEN

The case studies of Gilles de la Tourette

Nellie Georgiou-Karistianis and John L. Bradshaw
Neuropsychology Research Unit, Psychology Department, Monash University, Clayton, Victoria, Australia

INTRODUCTION

Born in the kitchen of his uncle's home in the small village of St. Gervais les Trois Clochers, George Albert Edouard Brutus Gilles de la Tourette (1857–1904), like George Huntington and James Parkinson, was brought up in a family of doctors. His love of the 'haunted' town of Loudun, his ancestral home, strongly influenced his researches. Tourette was a French neurologist at the Salpêtrière Hospital in Charcot's department in 1884, and in 1886 became his registrar. He was a man of great talent, subject to extraordinary activities and overexcitement. He wrote many books, research articles, communications, and historical papers in the fields of both neurology and psychiatry, including hysteria and hypnosis. In his later life, a young paranoid woman, confined to a mental hospital, shot Tourette three times in a consulting room. One of the bullets hit him in the head, and although it was removed he never really fully recovered (Stevens, 1971). Depressive episodes and mania manifested in his later years, and reports suggest that he most likely died from syphilis in 1904 (Guilly, 1982).

This chapter begins with a review of George Gilles de la Tourette's important historical accounts (and especially the case descriptions in his 1885 publication) of the disorder that bears his name. The next section will document today's account of the symptomatology, neuropsychology, heredity, and neuropathology of Tourette's syndrome (TS), and the concluding section will demonstrate Tourette's extraordinary accuracy and precision in his original descriptions of this condition; his early accounts have made a significant and important contribution to medical science, neuropsychology in particular, and to our knowledge of the disorder today.

HISTORICAL ACCOUNT OF GILLES DE LA TOURETTE'S SYNDROME

One of the earliest accounts of the condition was made in the infamous Renaissance manual on witch-hunting, the *Malleus Maleficarum*, written by two Dominican monks, Heinrich Kramer and Jakob Sprenger (1489, cited in Lohr & Wisniewski, 1987) who describe (on p. 191):

> A sober priest without any eccentricity . . . no sign of madness or any immoderate action [who was said to be possessed of the devil] . . . When he passed any church, and genuflected in honour of the Glorious Virgin, the devil made him thrust his tongue far out of his mouth; and when he was asked whether he could not restrain himself from doing this, he answered: 'I cannot help myself at all, for so he used all my limbs and organs, my neck, my tongue and my lungs, whenever he pleases, causing me to speak or to cry out; and I hear the words, as if they were spoken by myself but I am altogether unable to restrain them and when I engage in prayer he attacks me more violently thrusting out my tongue.'

The first clear medical description of what is today clinically known as TS was made by Itard (1825, cited in Comings, 1990), a French physician, who reported the case of a French noblewoman, the Marquise de Dampierre, who developed persistent body tics, barking sounds, and uncontrollable utterances of obscenities. He describes (p. 7):

> Madame de D . . . at the age of seven was afflicted by convulsive movements of the hand and arms . . . After each spasm, the movements of the hand became more regular and better controlled until a convulsive movement would again interrupt her work. It soon became clear that these movements were indeed involuntary . . . in nature . . . involved the shoulders, the neck, and the face, and resulted in contortions and extraordinary grimaces.

Tourette, in 1884, published a paper which examined the compulsive movement disorders then known as *saut du Maine, latah de Malaisie*, and *myriachit de Sibérie*. The 'jumpers' of Maine were described by George Beard in 1880. 'Jumpers' were people who responded immediately to commands, were both echolalic (i.e. repeating another's words or sounds) and echopraxic (i.e. repeating another's movements), but generally quite modest and in good health. Beard asserted that the disorder was hereditary, it manifested in childhood, and it rarely afflicted women. The second disorder, *latah*, was described by O'Brien in 1883. He described patients as impulsive, subject to striking out at objects and uttering involuntary obscenities, who were also echolalic and echopraxic. The third disorder, *miryachit*, had been reported by Hammond in 1884, and the disorder was described by officers of an American ship sent to Siberia, of which the steward had shown some very bizarre behaviours (Finger, 1994), Hammond wrote:

> It seems that he was afflicted with a peculiar mental or nervous disease, which forced him to imitate everything suddenly presented to his senses. Thus, when the captain slapped the paddle-box suddenly in the presence of the steward, the latter instantly gave it a similar thump; or if any noise were made suddenly, he seemed compelled against his will to imitate it instantly, and with remarkable accuracy (p. 191, cited in Finger, 1994).

Tourette (1884) reported that jumping, *latah*, and *miryachit* were identical disorders and that he had seen a case of a seemingly related movement disorder when working with Charcot. It is these original descriptions that led Tourette to study this condition. Today, as Tourette correctly pointed out, they are not viewed as separate disorders but are generally viewed as symptoms of the disorder.

Tourette reported, in his classic 1885 paper, nine cases, whereby the characteristic features of all involved the presence of involuntary, rapid, purposeless jerks of facial and limb muscles, which were accompanied by bizarre vocalisations, such as barks, grunts, and/or random swearing or cursing. On the basis of two classic papers (1884, 1885) he has generally been acknowledged as the first clinician to define both clinical characteristics and evolutionary aspects of tic disorders. Tourette, however, did not see the need to distinguish TS from conditions such as *latah* and *myriachit*. (The disorder was also called *maladie des tics compulsifs, et dégénérés, mimische Krampfneurose*, and *myospasmosa impulsiva* [Tourette, 1885]). Based on nine patients, six of whom were his, Tourette proposed that the symptoms observed should constitute a new disease category, which should be separate from the choreas (Shapiro, Shapiro, Young, & Feinberg, 1988).

GILLES DE LA TOURETTE'S EARLY CASE DESCRIPTIONS

The following section will describe each of the nine patients reported in Tourette's 1885 paper.

The first, the Marquise de Dampierre, was seen by both Itard (see above) and Charcot. Her symptoms were characterised by convulsions of the hands, arms, shoulders, neck, and face which manifested at 7 years and persisted throughout puberty, but at 17 she experienced remission that lasted for a period of 18 to 20 months. The symptoms then returned, including coprolalia (i.e. uttering socially inappropriate or obscene words), and persisted throughout her life. She lived to be 86 years old.

The symptoms of Tourette's second patient, a male, began at 16 years with the onset of rapid movements of the right leg and left side. At 17, he began to utter 'hm' and 'ouah' and soon developed echolalia and coprolalia, this latter condition disappearing at 20 years. Movements of the upper limb and tongue protrusion persisted throughout the remainder of his life.

Tourette's third patient was also a male, and onset of symptoms began at 9 years with rapid flexions and extensions of the head and neck; facial grimaces and movements of the shoulders and arms developed thereafter. Movements entailed rapid bouts of running, getting down on knees and then rising. At the age of 14 coprolalia developed; echopraxia and echolalia were also noted.

Tourette's fourth patient was a male in whom symptoms began at 8 or 9 years of age consisting of movements of the face, trunk, and limbs. Echolalia, clicking of the teeth, biting the tongue (no coprolalia), and complex jumping movements were noted.

Tourette's fifth patient, also a male, at 8 years developed twitches of the face, followed by arm and leg movements. Complex knee bends and jumps, including lip biting (no coprolalia) were also evident.

The sixth patient, also male, manifested facial grimaces at 7 years of age, followed by twitches all over the body, and although there was no evidence of coprolalia, a strident cry of 'ouh! ouh!' was reported.

Tourette's seventh patient was again a male. Symptoms began at 8 or 9 and included eye blinking followed by contortions of the body that soon led to a different style of walking. The patient's aunt was said to suffer from similar symptoms, and the aunt of the mother was reported to have had chorea. If brushed accidentally he would jump.

The eighth patient, a female, developed symptoms at 9 years. Movements of the face and limbs, a guttural sound, coprolalia, echolalia, and echopraxia were reported.

The ninth patient, a male, manifested symptoms at 14 years, consisting of rapid movements of the arms and legs. The movements were described as fits or convulsions, with the patient turning around and around, falling, biting his tongue, but not ever losing consciousness. He would also repeat his own words or the same syllables of the same word, and in the evenings he would utter obscenities.

In his 1885 paper, Tourette made a number of very important and insightful observations. He asserted that the disease was more likely to affect males than females, and the range of symptom onset was between 6 to 16 years. He also wrote that uncoordinated movements, as well as twitches, tend to be the first symptoms to develop, which generally start in the face, or upper extremities. There is shaking of the arms, fingers flex and extend, shoulders flinch, and the head, as a whole, may swing from side to side or forward and backward. The face may grimace, the tongue tends to protrude from the mouth, the eyes squint, and the teeth grind. After some time, the lower extremities may become involved; the contractions can affect all the limbs and can lead to jumping, knee bending, and stamping the feet. These movements appear suddenly and tend to be executed quite rapidly. He also noted that the more global movements tend to be separated by longer intervals, with considerable variability among patients, whereas limited bouts of movements tend to recur within a few minutes. He also ascertained that stress and/or discomfort could aggravate the movements, whereas during sleep they disappeared (Shapiro et al., 1988).

Tourette considered tics and grimaces to be the first category of symptoms. In the second category he included vocal symptoms, such as grunting sounds and echolalia. In the third category he placed coprolalia, and ascertained that it accompanied the movements in some of his patients, but not all. Tourette also emphasised that patients were often highly intelligent, conscious of their state, and their acts were not those of the insane. He found no evidence of epilepsy, and reported that sensory perception, physical health, and life expectancy were normal. Since two, out of nine, patients had family members with tics, Tourette suggested that hereditary factors may play a contributing role in the aetiology of the condition. Indeed, it has been suggested that several renowned historical figures, including Prince Condé, a member of the court of Louis XIV, and Dr Samuel Johnson, the prominent 18th-century literary figure (Singer & Walkup, 1991), were afflicted with the syndrome. He ascertained that the disorder could be observed in a diversity of countries and climates, and that social or professional status had no relevance to its aetiology. Toward the end of his paper he asserted that there may be spontaneous periods of remission, although the symptoms never disappear completely. Tourette was, however, very sceptical about the effectiveness of treatment, and in 1885 described (as translated by Goetz & Klawans, 1982, p. 14:

> The treatment for this singular condition is still to be discovered. By reading our observations, one sees clearly that curative attempts have thus far been unsuccessful; all central nervous system sedatives have failed. The only treatment that has seemed to help the symptoms and has been associated with periods of remission has been isolation combined with various treatments: iron preparations, hydrotherapy, etc. . . . Perhaps these treatments can slow the natural progression of the disease, especially in patients who are treated early. In any case, we do not feel that we have a definite treatment for this condition.

Charcot honoured his devoted student by naming the disorder after him soon after his 1885 publication. After Tourette's publication, Charcot made a number of important observations in three lectures that were published in an Italian medical journal by Melotti in 1885. Charcot disagreed with Tourette that jumping Frenchman, *latah*, and *myriachit* were identical to the condition described in his 1885 publication. He observed that coprolalia was not observed in jumping Frenchman nor in *myriachit*, though it was observed in *latah*. Charcot also commented on Tourette's overemphasis of echolalia and echopraxia (Shapiro et al., 1988).

In an 1899 publication, Tourette revised some of his original ideas. He stated that the disease was likely to occur in both sexes equally, whereas previously he had stated that the condition was more likely to manifest in males. (While TS manifests more in males, more females may exhibit pure obsessive compulsive disorder, or OCD; about half of TS sufferers have comorbid OCD, which may express itself as an alternative manifestation of a common gene causative for TS and OCD; Devinsky & Geller, 1992). He also revised his original classification of movements as motor incoordination; he now agreed that the movements were systematic and coordinated, an observation made by Guinon in 1886. The most significant revision, however, concerned the mental status of the patient and the abnormal mental disorders observed in the family background. In his 1899 paper, Tourette stated that there was always a nervous condition in the family and the patient almost always suffered from various anxieties, fantasies, and fears— a statement in contrast to his earlier suggestion that the illness was not psychiatric. In regard to coprolalia, Tourette was convinced that there was an irresistible psychic impulsion that made patients utter obscenities. He also considered echolalia to be a psychic stigma, but acknowledged that it was less frequent among patients than he had previously thought. It is somewhat unfortunate that Tourette revised his original evaluation regarding the mental status of these patients, instead of heeding his earlier astute observations about how well they function in society, apart from the tic symptomatology which can at times be quite debilitating (Shapiro et al., 1988).

By the beginning of the 20th century, in line with the development of psychoanalytic theory generally, it was thought that psychic factors were of major significance to the predisposition to TS (Meige & Feindel, 1902, cited in Devinsky & Geller, 1992), and controversy regarding the nature and origin of tics followed for quite a number of years. The uncontrollable sexual impulses, cursing, and aggressive unsociable behaviour were thought to be a consequence of a disturbance in the psyche's capacity to repress the forbidden (Ferenczi, 1921, cited in Devinsky & Geller, 1992). These speculations, based on clinical observations without any empirical support, were applied to the aetiology of tics and TS. However, it was not until Seignot (1961) and Caprini and Melotti (1961) discovered that dopamine antagonists, in particular haloperidol, were efficacious in the treatment of TS, that research into pharmacological and neurochemical aspects of the disorder unfolded (Devinsky & Geller, 1992). It is generally accepted today that TS is the consequence of a chemical imbalance in the brain involving various neurotransmitters (Petersen et al., 1993; Singer et al., 1993).

GENERAL SYMPTOMATOLOGY OF TOURETTE'S SYNDROME AS WE KNOW IT TODAY

The initial symptom of TS, as we know it today, is usually a tic, most commonly involving the eyes. Tics may involve virtually any voluntary muscle in the body, and are usually expressed as a sudden, brief, rapid, hyperactive involuntary contraction of that muscle (clonic tics); they can occasionally be expressed as sustained movements (dystonic or tonic tics). Motor and vocal tics can be classified as either simple or complex; however, this classification can be at times somewhat arbitrary. Simple motor tics include eye blinking, facial grimace, head or neck jerk, forced staring, shoulder shrug and contractions of abdominal muscles. Simple vocal tics may consist of coughing, throat clearing, grunting, clicking, snorting, and shrieking. Complex motor tics include facial expressions, grooming behaviours, touching, smelling a particular object and/or body part, and aggressive actions towards oneself or others. Tics differ however from voluntary movement due to absence of prior EEG negativity (i.e. a *Bereitschaftspotential*); this negativity is seen for similar movements produced voluntarily by the same patients (Obeso, Rothwell, & Marsden, 1981). However, there is a suggestion that they may occur with tics preceded by strong urges to move, over the lateral premotor area (Karp, Porter, Toro, & Hallett, 1996). Complex vocal tics consist of words and phrases that are often repeated; symptoms include palilalia (i.e. compulsive repetition of one's own sounds or words), echolalia, echopraxia, and coprolalia (Comings, 1995; Devinsky & Geller, 1992; Singer & Walkup, 1991; Wallesch, 1990).

Symptom onset usually occurs between 2 and 15 years of age (mean age 7 years) in more than 90% of patients. Simple vocal tics usually constitute the original manifestation in 15–30% of cases, and begin within 3 years of onset in most others (Leckman et al., 1997; Lees, 1985; Shapiro, Shapiro, Bruun, & Sweet, 1978). Ludlow et al. (1982) compared the speech production of TS and normal control subjects and reported that during connected speech even normal subjects produced extraneous movements of larynx and articulators. The authors argue that the majority of vocal tics in TS tend to also have their origin in normal behaviour; however, verbal and coprolalic tics were very uncommon in the controls. They concluded that tics have a similar quality to that seen in transcortical aphasia (i.e. an increase in non-purposeful stereotypic behaviour as well as a suppression of purposive propositional language formation). Generally, speech remains intact; it is the pragmatics of speech that are affected in TS.

The range of tic symptoms varies enormously from individual to individual; they vary in type and severity, often occur in bouts, and are regularly exacerbated by stress, anxiety, and fatigue, while focused concentration can alleviate them (Bruun & Budman, 1992).

TS has been reported to occur in all socio-economic classes, races, and countries worldwide (Cardoso, Veado, & Oliveira, 1996; Micheli et al., 1995). It is thought to have a prevalence rate of about 0.3 to 0.5 per 1000 (Devinsky & Geller, 1992); however, some authors suggest that the prevalence is as high as 1 to 10 per 1000 (Shapiro et al., 1988).

Tics may be observed in other neurological disorders, such as Huntington's disease, dystonia musculorum deformans, athetosis, hemiballismus, and neuroacanthocytosis. However, according to Jancovic (1997), tics, as observed in TS, should be differentiated from other hyperkinetic movement disorders on the following basis: (a) the occurrence of an unusual sensation and an urge to move prior to the tic; (b) the ability to voluntarily suppress the tic for variable periods; and (c) their occurrence during all stages of sleep.

Patients with TS may suffer from a number of co-morbid symptoms. The relationship between TS and attention deficit hyperactivity disorder (ADHD) has been studied in great detail by Comings and Comings (1987, 1988). They argue that symptoms of ADHD tend to precede the onset of tics by an average of 2.5 years, reaching a maximum severity at about 10 years of age, and then gradually receding during adolescence and adulthood; however, subtle cognitive deficits may still prevail. There is a general consensus in the literature that 60% of TS patients have co-morbid ADHD, and that males tend to be most commonly affected (Channon, Flynn, & Robertson, 1992; Nee, Caine, Polinsky, Eldridge, & Ebert, 1980; Singer & Walkup, 1991; Shapiro et al., 1988; Shytle, Silver, & Sanberg, 1996). Clinically, except for the tics, TS and ADHD, according to Comings and Comings (1993), are very similar; both are associated with a range of behavioural problems, and both show the same higher frequency of behavioural disorders in relatives (Biederman, Newcorn, & Sprich, 1991; Faraone, Biederman, Keenan, & Tsuang, 1991; Leckman et al., 1997). Epidemiological studies have found a relatively high frequency of ADHD among TS children (Caine et al., 1988, who found a prevalence of 3 cases per 10,000 among school age). Of the 41 probands who met diagnostic criteria for TS, 11 carried the additional diagnosis of ADHD; this represents a considerable increase in the usual frequency of ADHD found in the general population.

Obsessive compulsive disorder (OCD) may also be genetically related to TS (Lombroso et al., 1995; Pauls, Alsobrook, Goodman, Rasmussen, & Leckman, 1995; Pauls & Leckman, 1986). Singer and Rosenberg (1989) found that more than 40% of TS patients in the 6–10 year age group had OCD behaviours. Generally, however, it has been well established that co-morbid OCD symptoms may exist in around 50% of TS sufferers and tend to be most prominent in females (Shytle et al., 1996). They tend to manifest later than tic symptoms and to persist in adulthood (Comings, 1990; Comings & Comings, 1985, 1987; Devinsky & Geller, 1992). Patients often describe both tics and compulsions as a need to perform an action/behaviour until a feeling of tension is relieved, or until it "feels just right" (Comings, 1995).

Other associated or comorbid behavioural problems that have been given less attention, include conduct disorders, aggressiveness, depression, panic attacks and anxiety, phobias, mania, withdrawal, self-injury, inappropriate sexual behaviours, sleep problems, learning difficulties, and dyslexia (Comings, 1987; Hagin & Kugler, 1988; Robertson, 1989; Robertson, Trimble, & Lees, 1988; Singer, Allen, Brown, Salam, & Hahn, 1990; Singer & Rosenberg, 1989). Moreover, Robertson, Channon, Baker, and Flynn (1993) have observed that TS patients tend to be significantly more depressed and anxious than normal controls.

According to the DSM-IV (American Psychiatric Association, 1994, p. 106), the criteria for the diagnosis of TS are as follows: (a) both multiple motor and one or more vocal tics must have been present at some time during the illness, although not necessarily concurrently; (b) the tics occur many times a day (usually in bouts), nearly every day or intermittently throughout a period of more that 1 year; (c) the anatomic location, number, frequency, complexity, and severity of tics change over time; (d) onset before age 21; and (e) occurrence not exclusively during psychoactive substance intoxication or known central nervous system disease, such as Huntington's chorea and postviral encephalitis.

THE NEUROPSYCHOLOGY OF GILLES DE LA TOURETTE'S SYNDROME

The cognitive changes observed in TS seem to be subtle in nature rather than global. Children with TS often have learning difficulties at school and require, at times, special care and treatment. Some problems appear to be directly related to the TS symptoms themselves, such as the tics, which may cause disruption to other class members and/or interfere with school work (Walkup, Scahill, & Riddle, 1995). At least 50% of children with TS may, as we saw earlier, satisfy the diagnostic criteria for attention deficit disorder (poor attention span, difficulty concentrating, distractibility, impulsivity) with hyperactivity (fidgety movements, ceaseless activity). The attention deficit of these children may originate in early pre-school years and tends to precede the onset of tics. The attention deficit worsens with tic severity and is thought to reflect the underlying psychobiological dysfunctions involving inhibition in TS (Cohen, Leckman, & Shaywitz, 1985). In tasks requiring the inhibition of more natural and practised responses, children with TS *together with* co-morbid disorders showed a pronounced and generalised deficit compared to controls. The same deficit was not found for TS children *without* co-morbidity (Sheppard, 1999). In a local–global task, requiring the detection of target stimuli at either the local or global hierarchical level, no performance anomalies were found for TS children relative to controls in their ability to maintain and shift attention between hierarchical levels; however, the TS children did not show the *advantage* shown by controls for detecting stimuli at the global level relative to the local level (Sheppard, 1999). In a task examining the ability to effectively allocate attention over time, TS children showed a prolonged 'attentional blink'. They required a larger interval between the first and second targets to effectively detect the presence of the second (Sheppard, 1999). These results suggest a deficit in the ability to allocate attention over time in TS children.

In adult TS sufferers impaired visuo-perceptual performance, reduced visual motor skills, and short attention span, including distractibility, have also been noted. There seem to be consistent deficits in accurate copying of geometrical designs, such as the Rey Osterrieth Complex Figure; there is also evidence of deficits in finger tapping and motor coordination, for example with the Purdue Pegboard Task, though these problems could possibly stem from the difficulties with visuomotor integration. However, on the other hand, there is less persuasive or consistent evidence for visuospatial or visuoperceptual deficits (Bradshaw, 2001).

Georgiou et al. (1995b) report that adult TS patients, compared with controls, were more reliant on external visual cues to execute (rather than to initiate) a motor programme; in consequence, with limited visual guidance their movements progressively slowed with each successive element in the response cycle. Moreover, if no advance information was provided before each successive move, movement execution was slower than that of controls. This finding was also reported in children with TS (Sheppard et al., 2000). It may be the case that TS patients (like Huntington's and Parkinson's disease patients) have difficulties in internally cuing their movements. TS patients may require more time to plan and programme each next submovement, and under such circumstances may require external cues to direct attention effectively when cues are limited. Clinically, TS patients have also been reported to experience problems in sequencing movements and in planning movements in advance (Channon et al., 1992).

Singer and Walkup (1991) suggest that TS patients may have neuropsychological problems specific to deficits in executive functions, in terms of impairments in the capacity to plan and sequence complex behaviours, and to organise and sustain goal-directed activities. However, there is a debate as to whether or not there is a general deficit in the performance of executive function tasks involving set and attention (Schultz, Carter, Scahill, & Leckman, 1999). Channon et al. (1992) administered a wide range of clinical and experimental measures of attention to a group of adult TS patients and their controls. Attention deficits were clearly noted in the TS group on several of the more complex tasks, such as Serial Addition, Block Sequence Span (forward), the Trail Making Test, joining ascending sequences, and a Letter

Cancellation task. However, given that this and other studies have shown that TS patients have normal IQ levels (Pauls & Leckman, 1986), the authors argue that the attention deficits observed may represent a selective deficit rather than an overall global impairment. Indeed on various vibro-tactile experimental procedures we report that TS patients are impaired in holding attention at a given location (Georgiou, Bradshaw & Phillips, 1998; Georgiou, Bradshaw, Phillips, & Chiu, 1996). In a cost–benefit paradigm, using valid, neutral and invalid precues, we report that TS adults show no deficits in the ability to orient attention (Howells, Georgiou-Karistianis, & Bradshaw, 1999). In another experiment we report that although TS adults were slower in responding to spatially congruent and incongruent visual stimuli, they were not any more disadvantaged by incongruent spatial relationships and by the imposed need to change cognitive set (Georgiou et al., 1995a). Overall, we argue that the impairments in TS resemble a more subtle deficit with respect to both cognition and movement. This is in keeping with the fact that the disorder involves a chemical imbalance of neurotransmitters rather than of structural damage as seen in other more debilitating disorders, such as Huntington's and Parkinson's disease, which are prone to more severe motor and cognitive impairments. The behavioural deficits observed in TS seem to suggest frontal-BG disturbances (Georgiou et al., 1995a,1996).

Despite the neuropsychological deficits reported above, many TS sufferers tend to excel in various domains, such as art, music, literature, etc. Indeed, Sacks (1986) describes 'Witty Ticcy Ray', a remarkable musician with an equally remarkable intellect, who would have scarcely survived had he not been a weekend jazz drummer of real virtuosity.

HEREDITARY FACTORS OF GILLES DE LA TOURETTE'S SYNDROME

In his original monograph in 1885 Tourette suggested that hereditary factors may play a role in the manifestation of TS, and recent accounts have confirmed this. Based on segregation analyses of family data and twin studies, current findings support a sex-influenced, autosomal dominant role of inheritance (Curtis, Robertson, & Gurling, 1992; Eapen, Pauls, & Robertson, 1993; Kurlan et al., 1986; Pauls & Leckman, 1986; Pauls et al., 1990; Pauls, Raymond, Stevenson, & Leckman, 1991). The concordance rate for TS among monozygotic twins is greater than 50% while in dizygotic twins it is about 10% (Price, Pauls, & Caine, 1984). If co-twins with chronic motor tic disorder are included, the overall concordance, for both monozygotic twins (75%) and dizygotic twins (30%), is substantially higher. Differences in concordance between monozygotic and dizygotic twin pairs indicates that genetic factors play an important role in the aetiology of TS and related co-morbid conditions (Leckman & Cohen, 1995). Other studies have indicated that first-degree family members of TS probands are at a higher risk of developing TS, chronic motor tic disorder, and/or OCD than unrelated individuals (Pauls, Raymond, & Robertson, 1991). Genetic linkage studies have also shown that while more than 60% of the autosomal genome has been examined, there has been little success in identifying the chromosomal location of the putative TS gene or genes (Pakstis et al., 1991; Pauls et al., 1990). The problem with linkage studies, however, is that they lack power due to inaccuracies or misdiagnoses that may occur within the sample. The role of sexhormones may also play a modulating role given the increased prevalence of males over females (3:1), despite the fact that autosomal dominant transmission has been implicated (Devinsky & Geller, 1992). In order to determine whether there is an associated sex-associated difference in the transmission of TS behaviours, Lichter, Jackson, and Schachter (1995) sought to ascertain whether gender of the affected parent influences childhood TS phenotype. Maternal transmission of TS was found to be related to greater motor tic complexity and more frequent non-interfering rituals, whereas paternal transmission was associated with increased frequency of rituals, earlier onset of vocal tics, and more prominent ADHD behaviours. The authors conclude that the findings are consistent with genomic imprinting in TS. Moreover, epigenetic (i.e. environmental) factors, such as vulnerability to toxins, prenatal stress, psycho-social stress, exposure to thermal stress, and exposure to androgenic steroids (Leckman & Peterson, 1993), may also operate to mediate the expression of TS (Comings, MacMurray, Johnson, Dietz, & Muhleman, 1995; Kurlan, 1994; Palumbo, Maughan, & Kurlan, 1997).

There is general consensus in the literature that TS may be transmitted as an autosomal dominant gene disorder with incomplete penetrance (Comings, Comings, Devor, & Cloninger, 1984; Curtis et al., 1992; Devor, 1984; Eapen et al., 1993; Pauls & Leckman, 1986). More recently, however, a semirecessive-semidominant and oligogenetic mode of inheritance has been proposed (Comings, 1990, 1995; Comings & Comings, 1992; Comings, Comings, & Knell, 1989); that is, more than one gene may be involved in the aetiology of TS. The gene may be present in a double dose (i.e. semirecessive), but can also produce some symptoms in single doses (i.e. semidominant), and both major genes and minor modifying genes may be implicated (i.e. oligogenetic). Comings (1995) proposed that the genes are not specific to a given disorder but rather can cause disturbances in the balance of serotonin and DA; this may lead to an increased susceptibility to a wider range of impulsive, compulsive, affective, anxiety, and related disorders. Brett, Curtis, Robertson, and Gurling (1995) conducted segregation analyses to ascertain whether genes encoding proteins in the catecholamine pathways may contribute to the genetic aetiology of TS. The authors found that polymorphic markers at or near the D1, D2, D3, D4, and D5 neuroreceptor gene loci, as well as the genes encoding DA beta hydroxylase, tyrosinase, and tyrosine hydroxylase, do not play a role in the aetiology of TS.

THE NEUROPATHOLOGY OF GILLES DE LA TOURETTE'S SYNDROME

Considerable evidence has implicated the basal ganglia (BG), and related cortical and thalamic structures, in the neuropathology of TS (Chappell, Leckman, Pauls, & Cohen, 1990). Positron emission tomography (PET) studies have demonstrated that there is decreased regional metabolic activity in the frontal, cingulate, and insular cortices in TS patients (Chase et al., 1984; Chase, Geoffrey, Gillespie, & Burrows, 1986). George et al. (1992) have shown elevated right frontal rCBF in unmedicated TS patients as compared to normal controls. Moreover, the authors confirmed that activity in the frontal region was not significantly different between subgroups of TS patients with and without OCD.

Magnetic resonance imaging (MRI) studies (Petersen et al., 1993; Singer et al., 1993) have reported that the putamen and globus pallidus (i.e. lentiform nucleus) in the *left* hemisphere of TS sufferers is *reduced* in volume as compared with the situation in the control group. These abnormal asymmetries suggest that the BG in TS patients do not have the volumetric asymmetry (i.e. left greater than right) seen in normal controls. Furthermore, Hyde et al. (1995) more recently have shown a significant reduction in *right caudate volume*, and in *left lateral ventricular volume*, as well as a loss of the normal lateral ventricular asymmetry in monozygotic twins discordant for the severity of TS; six, out of ten, severely affected twins had a right ventricle larger than the left. Volumetric and metabolic studies of brain regions in TS have however proved conflicting (Robertson & Yakeley, 1996).

It is well established that TS may be caused by a chemical imbalance that may be associated with increased levels of dopamine within the lentiform nucleus (globus pallidus and putamen) of the BG (Graybiel, 1990; Lombroso, Mack, Scahill, King, & Leckman, 1992; Parent, 1986; Shapiro et al., 1989; Shapiro & Shapiro, 1988). In addition, TS may be associated with disturbances of other neurotransmitter systems that are also involved in the frontal-subcortical circuits; these include serotonin, norepinephrine, noradrenaline, GABA, and acetylcholine (Devinsky & Geller, 1992; Devor, 1990). Indeed, preliminary post-mortem brain studies in TS have shown that serotonin, and related compounds tryptophan and 5-hydroxindoleacetic acid, may be substantially reduced in BG structures (Anderson et al., 1992). Other evidence has focused attention on the endogenous opioid peptide projections from the striatum to the pallidum and substantia nigra (Chappell, Leckman, Pauls, & Cohen, 1990; Haber, Kowall, Vonsattel, Bird, & Richardson, 1986). Because TS is often thought to be transmitted through autosomal dominant inheritance, males and females should be equally at risk. Given, however, that males are three times more likely to develop TS than females, this has led to the suggestion that androgenic steroids may be implicated in the development of TS (Leckman et al., 1987).

CONCLUDING REMARKS: HOW ACCURATE WAS GILLES DE LA TOURETTE IN HIS ORIGINAL DESCRIPTIONS OF THE CONDITION?

Tourette's early 1885 descriptions of the condition have made an important and significant contribution to today's understanding of the disorder. His original reports are very much in accord with our general understanding and knowledge of the condition today. Common to all nine case studies reported in his 1885 publication, is the presence of involuntary, rapid, purposeless jerks of facial and limb musculature, which were accompanied by bizarre vocal actions known today as palilalia, coprolalia, echolalia, and echopraxia. Tourette recognised that these actions were not present in every patient, nor were they all present at once, though they may appear sooner or later. In fact it has been well established in the literature that coprolalia is present in less than one-third of diagnosed TS patients (Comings & Comings, 1993). In addition to the motor and vocal tics, Tourette also noted that: the disorder had a childhood onset; it affected more males than females (despite his later revision of this observation); it was hereditary; tics were usually the first symptom that tended to manifest in the face or upper extremity; the symptoms waxed and waned spontaneously; the tics were made worse by stress; and it was not progressive. He also correctly distinguished tics from other similar disorders, in that the movements were short-lived, extremely quick and abrupt, intermittent, and never continuous. He also noted that intelligence was relatively normal and that many individuals were highly creative and skilled. Indeed in one study, Georgiou, Bradshaw, Phillips, Cunnington, and Rogers (1997) showed that TS patients demonstrated performance superiorities in a graphics tablet task consisting of rapid movements toward circular visual targets. 'Witty Ticcy Ray', as described by Sacks (1986), was a remarkable musician with an amazing talent: 'a weekend jazz drummer of real virtuosity, famous for his sudden and wild extemporisations, which would instantly arise from a tic or a compulsive hitting of a drum and would instantly be made the nucleus of a wild and wonderful improvisation, so that the "sudden intruder" would be turned to a brilliant advantage' (p. 94).

It may be the case that the TS, ADHD, and OCD gene or genes, in low doses or penetrance in the community, may even facilitate aspects of behaviour, and so may persist in the genome. Jensen et al. (1997) also note the potentially adaptive nature, in ADHD, of characteristics of inattention, motoric hyperactivity and impulsivity, in certain natural environments of our hunter-gatherer past, especially during times of shortage, when an 'ice-age readiness to respond' to every new emergency would doubtless have been advantageous.

The clinical descriptions of Tourette's 1885 accounts are almost identical to the condition as we know it today. Tourette was undoubtedly a man of great wisdom and insight who has made a significant contribution to the disorder that now bears his name.

REFERENCES

American Psychiatric Association. (1994). *Diagnostic and Statistical Manual of Mental Disorders* (4th Ed.). Washington DC: American Psychiatric Press.

Anderson, G.M., Polack, E.S., Chatterjee, D., Leckman, J.F., Riddle, M.A., & Cohen, D.J. (1992). Post-mortem analysis of subcortical monoanines and aminoacids in Tourette syndrome. In T.N. Chase, A.J. Friedhoff, & D.J. Cohen (Eds.), *Tourette syndrome: Genetic, neurobiology, and treatment* (pp. 253–262). New York: Raven Press.

Biederman, J., Newcorn, J., & Sprich, S. (1991). Co-morbidity of attention deficit hyperactivity disorder with conduct, depressive, anxiety and other disorders. *American Journal of Psychiatry, 148(5)*, 546–577.

Bradshaw, J.L. (2001). *Developmental disorders of the frontostriatal system: Neuropsychological, neuropsychiatric, and evolutionary perspectives.* Hove, UK: Psychology Press.

Brett, P.M., Curtis, D., Robertson, M.M., & Gurling, H.M.D. (1995). The genetic susceptibility to Gilles de la Tourette syndrome in a large multiple affected British kindred: Linkage analysis excludes a role for the genes coding for dopamine D1, D2, D3, D4, D5 receptors, dopamine beta hydroxylase, tyrosinase, and tyrosine hydroxylase. *Biological Psychiatry, 37*, 533–540.

Bruun, R.D., & Budman, C.L. (1992). The natural history of Tourette syndrome. In T.N. Chase, A.J. Friedhoff, & D.J. Cohen (Eds.), *Tourette syndrome: Genetics, neurobiology and treatment* (pp. 1–5). New York: Raven Press.

Caine, E.D., McBride, M.C., Chiverton, P., Bamford, K.A., Rediess, S., & Shiao, J. (1988). Tourette's syndrome in Monroe county school children. *Neurology, 38*, 472–475.

Caprini, G., & Melotti, V. (1961). Un grave sindrome ticcosa guarita con haloperidol. *Riv Sper Freniatr Med Leg Alienazioni Ment, 85*, 191–196.

Cardoso, F., Veado, C.C.M., & de Oliveira, J.T. (1996). A Brazilian cohort of patients with Tourette's syndrome. *Journal of Neurology, Neurosurgery and Psychiatry, 60*, 209–212.

Channon, S., Flynn, D., & Robertson, M.M. (1992). Attention deficits in Gilles de la Tourette syndrome. *Neuropsychiatry, Neuropsychology, and Behavioral Neurology, 5*, 170–177.

Chappell, P., Leckman, J.F., Pauls, D., & Cohen, D.J. (1990). Biochemical and genetic studies of Tourette's syndrome: Implications for treatment and future research. In S. Deutsch, A. Weizmar, & R. Weizmar (Eds.), *Application of basic neuroscience to child psychiatry* (pp. 241–260). New York: Plenum.

Chase, T.N., Foster, N.L., Fedio, P., Brooks, R., Mansi, L., Kessler, R., & Di Chiro, G. (1984). Gilles de la Tourette syndrome: Studies with the Fluorine 18-labeled fluorodeoxyglucose positron emission tomographic method. *Annals of Neurology, 15*, Suppl. 175.

Chase, T.N., Geoffrey, V., Gillespie, M., & Burrows, G.H. (1986). Structural and functional studies of Gilles de la Tourette syndrome. *Revue Neurologique, 142*, 851–855.

Cohen D.J., Leckman, J.F., & Shaywitz, B.A. (1985). The Tourette syndrome and other tics. In D. Shaffer, A.A. Erhardt, & L.L. Greenhill (Eds.), *The clinical guide to child psychiatry*. New York: Free Press.

Comings, D.E. (1987). A controlled study of Tourette syndrome. VII. Summary: A common genetic disorder causing disinhibition of the limbic system. *American Journal of Human Genetics, 41*, 839–866.

Comings, D.E. (1990). *Tourette syndrome and human behaviour*. Duarte, CA: Hope Press.

Comings, D.E. (1995). Tourette's syndrome: A behavioral spectrum disorder. In W.J. Weiner & A.E. Lang (Eds.), *Behavioral neurology of movement disorders: Advances in neurology* (pp. 293–303). New York: Raven Press.

Comings, D.E., & Comings, B.G. (1985). Tourette syndrome: Clinical and psychological aspects of 250 cases. *American Journal of Human Genetics, 37*, 435–450.

Comings, D.E., & Comings, B.G. (1987). A controlled study of Tourette syndrome. I. Attention-deficit disorder, learning disorders, and school problems. II. Conduct. *American Journal of Human Genetics, 41*, 701–760.

Comings, D.E. & Comings, B.G. (1988). Tourette's syndrome and attention deficit disorder. In D.J. Cohen & R.D. Bruun (Eds.), *Tourette's syndrome and tic disorders: Clinical understanding and treatment* (pp. 120–135). New York: John Wiley.

Comings, D.E., & Comings, B.G. (1992). Alternative hypotheses on the inheritance of Tourette syndrome. *Advances in Neurology, 58*, 189–199.

Comings, D.E., & Comings, B.G. (1993). Co-morbid behavioural disorders. In R. Kurlan (Ed.), *Tourette syndrome and related disorders* (pp. 111–147). New York: Marcel Dekker.

Comings, D.E., Comings, B.G., Devor, E.J., & Cloninger, C.R. (1984). Detection of a major gene for Gilles de la Tourette syndrome. *American Journal of Human Genetics, 36*, 586–600.

Comings, D.E., Comings, B.G., & Knell, E. (1989). Hypothesis: Homozygosity in Tourette syndrome. *American Journal of Medical Genetics, 34*, 413–421.

Comings, D.E., MacMurray, J., Johnson, P., Dietz, G., & Muhleman, D. (1995). Dopamine D2 receptor gene (DRD2) haplotypes and the defence style questionnaire in substance abuse, Tourette syndrome, and controls. *Biological Psychiatry, 37*, 798–805.

Curtis, D., Robertson, M.M., & Gurling, H.M.D. (1992). Autosomal dominant gene transmission in a large kindred with Gilles de la Tourette Syndrome. *British Journal of Psychiatry, 160*, 845–849.

Devinsky, O., & Geller, B.D. (1992). Gilles de la Tourette's syndrome. In A.B. Joseph & R.R. Young (Eds.), *Movement disorders in neurology and neuropsychiatry* (pp. 471–478). Oxford: Blackwell Scientific Publications.

Devor, E.J. (1984). Brief communication: Complex segregation analysis of Gilles de la Tourette syndrome: Further evidence for a major locus mode of transmission. *American Journal of Human Genetics, 36*, 704–709.

Devor, E.J. (1990). Untying the Gordian knot: The genetics of Tourette syndrome. *The Journal of Nervous and Mental Disease, 178*, 669–679.

Eapen, V., Pauls, D.L., & Robertson, M.M. (1993). Evidence for autosomal dominant transmission in Tourette's syndrome. *British Journal of Psychiatry, 162*, 593–596.

Faraone, S.V., Biederman, J., Keenan, K., & Tsuang, M.T. (1991). Separation of DSM-III attention deficit disorder and conduct disorder—evidence from a family-genetic study of American child psychiatric patients. *Psychological Medicine, 21*, 109–121.

Finger, S. (1994). *Origins of neuroscience: A history of explorations into brain function*. New York: Oxford University Press.

George, M.S., Trimble, M.R., Costa, D.C., Robertson, M.M., Ring, H.A., & Ell, P.J. (1992). Elevated frontal cerebral blood flow in Gilles de la Tourette syndrome: A 99Tcm-HMPAO SPECT study. *Psychiatry Research, 45*, 143–151.

Georgiou, N., Bradshaw, J.L., & Phillips, J.G. (1998). Directed attention in Gilles de la Tourette syndrome. *Behavioural Neurology, 11*, 85–91.

Georgiou, N., Bradshaw, J.L., Phillips, J.G., Bradshaw, J.A., & Chiu, E. (1995a). The Simon effect and attention deficits in Gilles de la Tourette's syndrome and Huntington's disease. *Brain, 118*, 1305–1318.

Georgiou, N., Bradshaw, J.L., Phillips, J.G., Bradshaw, J.A., & Chiu, E. (1995b). Advance information and movement sequencing in Gilles de la Tourette's syndrome. *Journal of Neurology, Neurosurgery, and Psychiatry, 58,* 184–191.

Georgiou, N., Bradshaw, J.L., Phillips, J.G., & Chiu, E. (1996). The effect of Huntington's disease and Gilles de la Tourette's syndrome on the ability to hold and shift attention. *Neuropsychologia, 34,* 843–851.

Georgiou, N., Bradshaw, J.L., Phillips, J.G., Cunnington, R., & Rogers, M. (1997). Functional asymmetries in the movement kinematics of patients with Tourette's syndrome. *Journal of Neurology, Neurosurgery and Psychiatry, 63,* 188–195.

Gilles de la Tourette, G. (1884). Jumping, latah, myriachit. *Archives de Neurologie, 8,* 68–84.

Gilles de la Tourette, G. (1885). Etude sur une affection nerveuse caractérisée par de l'incoordination motrice accompagnée d'écholalie et de copoalalie (jumping latah, myriachit). *Archives de Neurologie, 9,* 19–42, 158–200.

Goetz, C.G., & Klawans, H.L. (1982). Gilles de la Tourette on Tourette syndrome. In A.J. Friedhoff, & T.N. Chase (Eds.), *Gilles de la Tourette syndrome* (pp. 1–16). New York: Raven Press.

Graybiel, A.M. (1990). Neurotransmitters and neuromodulators in the basal ganglia. *Trends in Neurosciences, 13,* 244–254.

Guilly, P. (1982). Gilles de la Tourette. In F.C. Rose & W.F. Bynum (Eds.), *Historical aspects of the neurosciences* (pp. 397–413). New York: Raven Press.

Haber, S.N., Kowall, N.W., Vonsattel, J.P., Bird, E.D., & Richardson, E.P. (1986). Gilles de la Tourette's syndrome: A post-mortem neuropathological and immunohistochemical study. *Journal of the Neurological Sciences, 75,* 225.

Hagin, R.A., & Kugler, J. (1988). School problems associated with Tourette's syndrome. In D.J. Cohen, R.D. Bruun, & J.F. Leckman (Eds.), *Tourette's syndrome and tic disorders* (pp. 223–236). New York: John Wiley.

Howells, D., Georgiou-Karistianis, N., & Bradshaw, J.L. (1999). The ability to orient attention in Gilles de la Tourette syndrome. *Behavioural Neurology, 11,* 205–209.

Hyde, T.M., Stacey, M.E., Coppola, R., Handel, S.F., Rickler, K.C., & Weinberger, D.R. (1995). Cerebral morphometric abnormalities in Tourette's syndrome: A quantitative MRI study of monozygotic twins. *Neurology, 45,* 1176–1182.

Jancovic, J. (1997). Pathophysiology and clinical assessment of motor symptoms in Parkinson's disease. In W.C. Koller (Ed.), *Handbook of Parkinson's disease* (pp. 99–126). New York: Marcel Dekker.

Jensen, P.S., Mrazek, D., Knapp, P.K., Steinberg, L., Pfeffer, C., Schowalker, J., & Shapiro, T. (1997). Evolution and revolution in clued psychiatry: ADHD as a disorder of adaptation. *Journal of the American Academy of Child and Adolescent Psychiatry, 36,* 1672–1679.

Karp, B.I., Porter, S., Toro, C., & Hallett, M. (1996). Simple motor tics may be preceded by a premotor potential. *Journal of Neurology, Neurosurgery, and Psychiatry, 61,* 103–106.

Kurlan, R. (1994). Hypothesis II: Tourette's syndrome is part of a clinical spectrum that includes normal brain development. *Archives of Neurology, 51,* 1145–1150.

Kurlan, R., Behr, J., Medved, L., Shoulson, I., Pauls, D., Kidd, J.R., & Kidd, K.K. (1986). Familial Tourette syndrome: Report of a large pedigree and potential for linkage analysis. *Neurology, 36,* 772–776.

Leckman, J.F., & Cohen, D.J. (1995). Tic disorders. In M. Rutter, E. Taylor, & L. Hersov (Eds.), *Child and adolescent psychiatry: Modern approaches* (pp. 455–466). Oxford: Blackwell Science.

Leckman, J.F., & Peterson, B.S. (1993). The pathogenesis of Tourette's syndrome: Epigenetic factors active in early CNS development. *Biological Psychiatry, 34,* 425–427.

Leckman, J.F., Peterson, B.S., Anderson, G.M., Arnsten, A.F.T., Pauls, D.L., & Cohen, D.J. (1997). Pathogenesis of Tourette's syndrome. *Journal of Child Psychology and Psychiatry, 38(1),* 119–142.

Leckman, J.F., Price, R.A., Walkup, J.T., Ort, S.I., Pauls, D.L., & Cohen, D.J. (1987). Letter to the editor: Nongenetic factors in Gilles de la Tourette's syndrome. *Archives of General Psychiatry, 44*, 100.

Lees, A.J. (1985). *Tics and related disorders*. New York: Churchill Livingstone.

Lichter, D.G., Jackson, L.A., & Schachter, M. (1995). Clinical evidence of genomic imprinting in Tourette's syndrome. *Neurology, 45*, 924–928.

Lohr, J.B., & Wisniewski, A.A. (1987). *Movement disorders: A neuropsychiatric approach*. New York: Guilford Press.

Lombroso, P.J., Mack, G., Scahill, L., King, R.A., & Leckman, J.F. (1992). Exacerbation of Tourette's syndrome associated with thermal stress: A family study. *Neurology, 41*, 1984–1987.

Lombroso, P.J., Scahill, L.D., Chappell, P.B., Pauls, D.L., Cohen, D.J., & Leckman, J.F. (1995). Tourette's syndrome: A multigenerational, neuropsychiatric disorder. In W.J. Weiner & A.E. Lang (Eds.), *Behavioral neurology of movement disorders: Advances in neurology* (pp. 305–318). New York: Raven Press.

Ludlow, C.L., Polinsky, R.J., Caine, E.D., Bassich, C.J., & Ebert, M.H. (1982). Language and speech abnormalities in Tourette syndrome. *Advances of Neurology, 35*, 351–361.

Micheli, F., Gatto, M., Gershanik, O., Steinschnaider, A., Fernandez Pardal, M., & Massaro, M. (1995). Gilles de la Tourette syndrome: Clinical features of 75 cases from Argentina. *Behavioural Neurology, 8*, 75–80.

Nee, L.E., Caine, E.D., Polinsky, R.J., Eldridge, R., & Ebert, M.H. (1980). Gilles de la Tourette syndrome: Clinical and family studies of 50 cases. *Annals of Neurology, 7*, 41–49.

Obeso, J.A, Rothwell, J.C., & Marsden, C.D. (1981). Simple tics in Gilles de la Tourette's syndrome are not prefaced by a normal premovement EEG potential. *Journal of Neurology, Neurosurgery and Psychiatry, 44*, 735–738.

Pakstis, A.J., Heutinik, P., Pauls, D.L., Kurlan, R., van de Wetering, B.J., Leckman, J.F., Sandkuyl, L.A., Kidd, J.R., Breedveld, G.J., & Castiglione, C.M. (1991). Progress in the search of genetic linkage with Tourette syndrome: An exclusion map covering more than 50% of the autosomal genome. *American Journal of Human Genetics, 48*, 281–294.

Palumbo, D., Maughan, A., & Kurlan, R. (1997). Tourette syndrome is only one of several causes of basal ganglia syndrome. *Archives of Neurology, 54*, 475–483.

Parent, A. (1986). *Comparative neurobiology of the basal ganglia*. New York: Wiley.

Pauls, D.L., Alsobrook, J.P. 2nd, Goodman, W., Rasmussen, S., & Leckman, J.F. (1995). A family study of obsessive-compulsive disorder. *American Journal of Psychiatry, 152(1)*, 76–84.

Pauls, D.L., & Leckman, J.F. (1986). The inheritance of Gilles de la Tourette's syndrome and associated behaviours: Evidence for autosomal dominant transmission. *New England Journal of Medicine, 315*, 993–997.

Pauls, D.L., Pakstis, A.J., Kurlan, R., Kidd, K.K., Leckman, J.F., Cohen, D.J., Kidd, J.R., Como, P., & Sparkes, R. (1990). Segregation and linkage analysis of Gilles de la Tourette's syndrome and related disorders. *Journal of the American Academy of Child and Adolescent Psychiatry, 48*, 195–203.

Pauls, D.L., Raymond, C.L., & Robertson, M. (1991). The genetics of obsessive-compulsive disorder: A review. In J. Zohar, T. Insel, & S. Rasmussen (Eds.), *The psychobiology of obsessive-compulsive disorder* (pp. 89–100). New York: Springer.

Pauls, D.L., Raymond, C.L., Stevenson, J.F., & Leckman, J.F. (1991). A family study of Gilles de la Tourette. *American Journal of Human Genetics, 48*, 154–163.

Petersen, B., Riddle, M.A., Cohen, D.J., Katz, L.D., Smith, J.C, Hardin, M.T., & Leckman, J.F. (1993). Reduced basal ganglia volumes in Tourette's syndrome using three-dimensional reconstruction techniques from magnetic resonance images. *Neurology, 43*, 941–949.

Price, R.A., Pauls, D.L., & Caine, E.D. (1984). Pedigree and segregation analysis of clinically defined subgroups of Tourette's syndrome. *American Journal of Human Genetics, 36*, 178s.

Robertson, I.H. (1989). Anomalies in the laterality of omissions in unilateral left visual neglect: Implications for an attentional theory of neglect. *Neuropsychologia, 27*, 157–165.

Robertson, M., Channon, S., Baker, J., & Flynn, D. (1993). The psychopathology of Gilles de la Tourette syndrome: A controlled study. *British Journal of Psychiatry, 162*, 114–117.

Robertson, M.M., Trimble, M.R., & Lees, A.J. (1988). The psychopathology of Gilles de la Tourette's syndrome: A phenomenological analysis. *British Journal of Psychiatry, 152*, 383–390.

Robertson, M.M., & Yakeley, J. (1996). Gilles de la Tourette syndrome and obsessive compulsive disorder. In B.S. Fugel, R.B. Schiffer, & S.M. Rao (Eds.), *Neuropsychiatry* (pp. 827–870). Baltimore: Willcome & Wilkins.

Sacks, O. (1986). *The man who mistook his wife for a hat.* London: Duckworth.

Sacks, O. (1992). Tourette's syndrome and creativity: Exploiting the ticcy witticisms and witty ticcicisms. *British Medical Journal, 305*, 1515–1516.

Schultz, R.T., Carter, A.S., Scahill, L., & Leckman, J. (1999). Neuropsychological findings. In J.F. Leckman & D.J. Cohen (Eds.)., *Tourtee's syndrome: Tics, obsessions, compulsions* (pp. 80–103). New York: Wiley.

Seignot, M.J.N. (1961). Un cas de maladie des tics de Gilles de la Tourette gueri par le R-1625. *Annals Medico-Psychologiques, 119*, 578–579.

Shapiro, A.K., Shapiro, E.S, Bruun, R.D., & Sweet, R.D. (1978). *Gilles de la Tourette syndrome.* New York: Raven Press.

Shapiro, A.K., & Shapiro, E.S. (1988). Treatment of tic disorders with haloperidol. In D.J. Cohen, R.D. Bruun, & J.F. Leckman (Eds.), *Tourette's syndrome and tics disorders.* New York: Wiley.

Shapiro, E.S., Shapiro, A.K., Fulop, G., Hubbard, M., Mandeli, J., Nordlie, J., & Phillips, R.A. (1989). Controlled study of haloperidol, pimozide, and placebo for the treatment of Gilles de la Tourette's syndrome. *Archives of General Psychiatry, 46*, 722.

Shapiro, A.K., Shapiro, E.S., Young, J.G., & Feinberg, T.E (1988). *Gilles de la Tourette Syndrome.* New York: Raven Press.

Sheppard, D. (1999). *Attentional and motor correlates of frontostriatal disorders.* Unpublished doctoral dissertation, Monash University, Clayton, Victoria, Australia.

Sheppard, D.M., Bradshaw, J.L., Georgiou, N., Bradshaw, J.A., & Lee, P. (2000). Movement sequencing in children with Tourette's syndrome and attention deficit hyperactivity disorder. *Movement Disorders, 15*, 1184–1193.

Shytle, R.D., Silver, A.A., & Sanberg, P.R. (1996). Clinical assessment of Tourette's syndrome. In P.R. Sanberg, K.P. Ossenkopp, & M. Kavaliers (Eds.), *Motor activity and movement disorders* (pp. 343–357). Totowa, NJ: Human Press.

Singer, H.S., Allen, R., Brown, J., Salam, M., & Hahn, I-H. (1990). Sleep disorders in Tourette syndrome: A primary or unrelated problem? *Annals of Neurology, 28*, 424 (abstract).

Singer, H.S., Reiss, A.L., Brown, J.E., Aylward, E.H., Shih, B., Chee, E., Harris, E.L., Reader, M.J., Chase, G.A., Bryan, R.N., & Denckla, M.B. (1993). Volumetric MRI changes in basal ganglia of children with Tourette's syndrome. *Neurology, 43*, 950–956.

Singer, H.S., & Rosenberg, L.A. (1989). Development of behavioural and emotional problems in Tourette syndrome. *Pediatric Neurology, 5*, 41–44.

Singer, H.S., & Walkup, J.T. (1991). Tourette syndrome and other tic disorders: Diagnosis, pathophysiology, and treatment. *Medicine, 70*, 15–32.

Stevens, H. (1971). Gilles de la Tourette and his syndrome by serendipity. *American Journal of Psychiatry, 128*, 489–492.

Walkup, J.T., Scahill, L.D., & Riddle, M.A. (1995). Disruptive behavior, hyperactivity, and learning disabilities in children with Tourette's syndrome. In W.J. Weiner & A.E. Lang (Eds.), *Behavioral neurology of movement disorders: Advances in neurology* (pp. 259–272). New York: Raven Press.

Wallesch, C.-W. (1990). Repetitive verbal behaviour: Functional and neurological considerations. *Aphasiology*, *4*, 133–154.

APPENDIX: QUOTATIONS FROM TOURETTE (1885): TRANSLATIONS BY JOHN L. BRADSHAW

- There is no premonitory aura
  La maladie ... sans cause appréciable, sans qu'il puisse rendre compte d'aucune sensation prémonitoire qui puisse ressembler à une aura (p. 159)
- There is no loss of consciousness
  Il ne perd jamais connaissance (p. 159)
- Mostly males are affected
  Elle semble de plus affecter particulièrement le sexe masculin (p. 165)
- Hereditary often noted
  Ces tics sont bien souvent héréditaires (p. 165)
  Cette affection est héréditaire (p. 188)
- Motor tics—begin often in the face or upper limbs
  Ces mouvements incoordonnés ou plutòt ces secousses musculaires débutent le plus souvent par la face ou par les membres supérieurs (p. 166)
- The patient taps with the foot, squats, gets up again, but the commonest movement is the jump
  Le malade frappe du pied, se baisse, se relève; mais, le mouvement qu'il accomplit le plus souvent est le saut ... (p. 167)
- Classic characteristics include suddenness and rapidity of movement
  Un de ces caractères réside dans la soudaineté ... et la rapidité (p. 168)
- Vocal tics—emission of articulate or inarticulate sounds
  Cette incoordination peut s'accompagner de l'émission de sons inarticulés ou articulés (p. 188)
- There is no anosognosia
  Ces malades sont particuliérement sensibles à toutes les actions (p. 169)
  Ils ont parfaitement conscience de leur état (p. 172)
- Tics can be suppressed—by sleep
  Ces secousses peuvent être ... totalement supprimées par ... le sommeil (p. 169)
  —and by fever
  Febris solvit spasmos (Latin: p. 170)
- Intelligence ... and moral development is normal for the age
  Quant à l'état mental, il est parfaitement régulier et normal: les sujets raisonnent trés bien ... la plupart sont fort intelligents. Quant à l'état moral, il est variable suivant l'âge de l'individu (p. 172)
- Voluntary suppression/control is possible, briefly, at the cost of a subsequent violent rebound
  Pendant l'entrevue ... si celle-ci était trés brève, il pouvait mettre un frein à tous ses mouvements insolites et les arrêter complètement. Mais, aussitôt après cette cessation qui ne s'obtenait qu'au prix de la plus violente contention d'esprit, les mouvements revenaient avec une violence inaccoutumée (p. 173)
- A permanent condition
  Une fois sauteur, on est toujours sauteur (p. 187)
- Though there may be remissions
  Périodes de rémission ou d'accalmie (p. 185)
- Echolalia
  Le sujet deviendra écholalique. ... il répète ... les derniers mots de la phrase qu'il vient d'entendre (p. 175)

- There may even be echolalia of a foreign, unknown tongue
  Le malade répètera parfaitement des mots prononcés dans une langue qui lui est tout à fait inconnue (p. 177)
- Coprolalia
  Il prononce. . . . des mots qu'il ne voudrait pas dire, en particulier 'zut' ou 'merde' (p. 160)
  Ce caractère d'obscénité est pathognomique (p. 183)
- Echopraxia
  La faculté d'imitation irrésistible (p. 178)
- The cook on a steamer had long-standing *latah*. One day, on the bridge, he was cradling his child in his arms. Then a sailor began to copy the cook's action with a belaying pin. He threw it on a sail, amusing himself rolling it on the canvas. The cook immediately did the same with his child. The sailor, dropping the canvas, let the belaying pin fall to the bridge. The cook did the same with his infant who died from the blow.
  Le cook d'un steamer était un latah des plus corsés. Il berçait un jour, sur le pont du navire, son enfant dans ses bras, lorsque survint un matelot qui se mit, à l'instar du cook, à bercer dans ses bras un billot de bois. Puis ce matelot jeta son billot sur un tendelet et s'amusa à le faire rouler sur la toile, ce que fit immédiatement le cook avec son enfant. Le matelot, lâchant alors la toile, laissa retomber son billot sur le pont; le cook en fit de même pour son petit garçon qui se tua sur le coup. (pp. 179–180).

CHAPTER TWENTY

Can a cognitive deficit elicit an exceptional ability? A case of savant syndrome in drawing abilities: Nadia

Laurent Mottron, Elyse Limoges, and Patricia Jelenic
Hôpital Rivière-des-Prairies and Department of Psychiatry, University of Montreal, Canada

INTRODUCTION

The case study of a prodigious autistic draftsperson, Nadia, by Selfe (1977) has been discussed at length in the literature, and has attracted a good deal of attention in the media. Although her handicap has been attributed to a neurological dysfunction, nothing is known about its nature and localisation. Interestingly, her neuropsychological profile presents the reverse pattern of a typical dissociation between a well-circumscribed cognitive deficit coupled with normal overall functioning. Instead, her exceptional performance in a very restricted area is coupled with an abnormal level of overall functioning. Since autism is a relatively new topic in neuropsychology, no major attempts have been made in this discipline to account for Nadia's remarkable developmental discrepancy in skill attainment. The goal of this chapter is to review explanatory theories and relevant findings published since Selfe's report, and to discuss and put forward a neuropsychological model for Nadia's performance resulting from our own work on drawing and perception in autism.

CASE REPORT

Nadia was a 6-year-old child when she was first examined at the Child Development Research unit in Nottingham in 1974. She was second born of a family of three children, after a normal pregnancy and delivery. Both of her parents were scientists who immigrated to England in the mid-1970s. Parents and siblings did not present any pathological features and did not demonstrate any particular artistic talent. The first symptoms reported by the mother were a cephalic hypotonia and a lack of emotional response. At the age of 2.5 years, Nadia seemed unaware of danger and was unresponsive to verbal demands. In addition, she exhibited an important motor delay: she did not sit at a normal age and learned to walk only at the age of 2 years. She remained clumsy and slow, and would often stumble over objects. Nevertheless, her physical development was normal, with normal feeding and weaning.

Information regarding her medical examination at the age of 5 years and 4 months is limited. Results indicated that her auditory system was normal. A cranial X-ray showed no intracranial calcifications, with a small sella and a thick dorsum sellae. Her bone structure was similar to that of a 7–8-year-old child (she was large and considerably overweight) and her skull had a brachycephalic vault. EEG records indicated a slight excess of irregular intermediate slow activity, mainly in the right hemisphere, a few sharp elements in the resting record, and an abnormal response to photic stimulation, without clinical epilepsy.

She developed expressive language in two steps. First, she learned a few Ukrainian words—her parent's first language—when she was nine months old, which she used less and less over the course of the second year. She did not use any two-word utterances. At 6 years of age she possessed almost no language skills (i.e. she only used 10 or less single- or two-word utterances in a stereotyped way, and could not creatively combine two words). She could recognise a small number of objects to which references were made, and she could label a few objects when asked. Her spontaneous speech consisted mainly of delayed, out-of-context echolalia and some song lyrics. She also babbled to herself when disturbed. At approximately 12 years of age she began to use two-word utterances to express basic needs, but her language capability remained extremely poor. Language comprehension, as assessed through the execution of simple orders, was very low. However, her level of understanding was slightly better in Ukrainian, the language spoken at home. She was unable to read, even simple letters. At a behavioural level, she was a rather lethargic child. However, her passive attitude towards school and family life was disrupted by occasional tantrums and screaming. She also exhibited violence towards objects or persons when frustrated.

A diagnosis of autism with mental retardation was established after her first examination. Although the diagnostic criteria have changed somewhat since 1974, this diagnosis is still valid today, based on a detailed description of her behaviour in the relevant areas of communication, social behaviour, play, and repetitive behaviours. Disruption in the area of communication was characterised by gaze avoidance, and by the observation that she communicated only to satisfy personal needs. For example, she was able to point to objects that she needed or to the direction in which she wanted to move. In addition, she was generally unresponsive to any form of language. Impairment in social development was first characterised by a lack of emotional response as a baby. Later, she would follow another child or adult obsessively without socially interacting with that person. She could manifest excitement when going out, but presented no evidence of socially generated emotions. She was particularly affected in the domain of repetitive behaviour and restricted interests. She played repetitively with perceptual motor toys such as shoe-lace threading toys, form boards, and jig-saw puzzles. In addition, she would finger play with water and tear paper into strips. She also exhibited some peculiar mannerisms, especially when looking at her own drawings. Her ritualistic behaviours consisted of arranging toys (teddy bears and dolls) in special places; such arrangements could not be displaced without causing an aversive reaction. In addition, she exhibited sameness reactions for changing of clothes or time schedules. She also presented remarkable visual repetitive behaviour. She moved objects in front of her eyes without moving her head, and would look at objects and people from the corners of her eyes. Although her visual acuity appeared normal in a standard examination, she used to bring objects close to her eyes and lean close to the paper when drawing. She also stared at her drawing while modifying the visual angle under which the drawing was seen. Some visual stimuli yielded aversive responses, as she covered her eyes with her hands when exposed to bright lights.

Psychological assessment

Psychological testing was incomplete due to a low level of compliance. Furthermore, motor slowness usually prevented her from reaching a performance score that was adequate for her chronological age. The results of the tests revealed that she was mainly interested in non-verbal tasks, in which she reached a 4-year-old level at 5.6 years of age. She performed best on puzzle tasks (she could complete a form board without having the original figure as a model). She also had excellent copying abilities with wood pieces and pens. Her poor performance on the Block-design and Object Assembly WISC sub-tests, which is unusual in autism, could be attributed to non-compliance or to motor slowness. Repeated assessment of perceptual matching revealed that she was able to match identical pictures of objects and silhouettes. However, she was unable to match objects from different views or of different sizes. Furthermore, she failed to point to a picture that mismatched other pictures at a categorical level. In contrast to her moderately good performance in visuo-spatial non-verbal tasks, she performed below a mental age of 18 months on the verbal sub-tests of the Merrill Palmer. Her global IQ, as retrospectively estimated from the available testing, did not exceed 50.

Drawing behaviour

Her special drawing skill first appeared at the age of 3.5 years. Detection of the talent was sudden, and no support or encouragement had preceded the original drawing performance. This is supported by the observation that she was completely unresponsive to reward (food or social) or admiration concerning her drawings, nor could she be compelled to draw. She began to draw, from memory, stationary views of objects, animals (mostly horses), and some faces and solid objects (trains), with an apparent utilisation of linear perspective. Drawings were not preceded by a scribbling phase and were photographically realistic, in total contrast to the intellectual realism used in the drawings of normal children. Her exploitation of perspective, foreshortening, accurate proportions, and diminishing size with distance and quality of drawing were undoubtedly above her mental and chronological age. She studied the original picture, sometimes scribbling the outline, but did not copy from it. Her dexterity while drawing contrasted with her clumsiness on other tasks. She could draw firm lines (regardless of their orientation relative to her body) and perfect circles. She showed no interest in colours, but sometimes used a coloured ball-point pen to make her usual drawings.

Her drawing strategies presented some remarkable peculiarities. For example, she began by drawing less important parts, such as the neck of a person. She also drew objects or facial parts at their perfectly correct position (for example, the ears) prior to the outline that connects them (face outline). If an object was hidden behind another, she did not draw the hidden part. Also, she never modified the size or orientation of a figure in order to represent it fully on a sheet of paper, often resulting in figures that were cut off at the edge of the sheet. In some cases, she stopped drawing a picture prior to completion. According to Selfe, her drawing strategy appeared not to be governed by the previous line drawn but by 'a very strong image of the finished product'. Nevertheless, although she did not adapt her drawing to the paper size, an examination of her drawings and of the original models revealed that she could completely reverse the model or modify its size or orientation. When she made successive representations of the same object, she could add details, creating composite figures from previous drawings. She could also finish a picture and add details a *posteriori* by returning to the exact point on an interrupted line. Her drawings of cockerels are a remarkable example. A few days after having encountered a drawing of a cockerel in a book, she began to draw several orientations of the same animal, as if she were able to conceive the transformation of a 3D object through rotation. This was surprising, considering her lack of experience with real cockerels.

Although she used photographic realism from when she first began to draw, her skill developed only between the ages of 3.5 to 6 years and did not progress thereafter. Educated in a special school for severely subnormal

Figure 20.1 Example of Nadia's drawing at approximately age 4.

children, she participated in intensive art courses that did not improve her talent. At the age of 12, her drawings were still highly skilled, but only to the same extent of a gifted, normal child of identical age. During adolescence she lost interest in drawing and the quality of her work degraded markedly, resembling ordinary childish productions.

HISTORICAL SIGNIFICANCE OF NADIA'S CASE

The publication of Nadias's drawings by Selfe in 1977 produced an astounding effect in the world of child psychology and psychiatry. The precocity and quality of Nadia's abilities changed common notions about the natural developmental drawing process, and the cultural versus natural aspect of visual perspective in drawings. However, these aspects are only marginally relevant for cognitive neuropsychology and will not be discussed here.

Instead, we will focus on the consequences of this case to cognitive models of autism.

Nadia was not the first 'savant syndrome' case to be published. The interest in exceptional abilities in subjects with mental retardation goes back to the 19th century. Cases of prodigious calculators, as well as intellectually retarded persons with outstanding calendar and list memory, had been anecdotally reported. These individuals were typically described using the term 'idiot savant' and the relation between giftedness among the mentally retarded and the yet unknown autism was not established. Generally, the performance of these individuals was attributed to the existence of a spared cognitive area as opposed to the abnormal consequence of early brain damage. Nadia was the first case to be presented as an example of an association between a general cognitive deficit, a special ability, and a clinical picture of autism (however, Scheerer, Rothman, & Goldstein, 1945, had described 'savant' skills in terms of compensation between abstract and concrete thought).

To our knowledge, Nadia's case was also the first scientific account of a special ability in the visuo-spatial domain. We shall examine the historical significance of Nadia's case by considering (a) the theoretical accounts of her condition, (b) the influence of the publication of her case on the understanding of graphic abilities and cognitive deficits in autism, and (c) the importance of the case today.

THEORETICAL ACCOUNTS OF NADIA'S CASE

Selfe thoughtfully discarded the photographic or eidetic memory explanation of Nadia's drawing ability that was proposed for savant calendar calculators by Jaensch (1930), and maintained in Treffert's (1989) book. One argument against eidetic memory was that Nadia could operate on her visual representations, add details, rotate images, and keep representations in memory for a much longer amount of time than persons with eidetic memory. Furthermore, having a photographic memory does not automatically explain the ability to reproduce its content on paper with a photographic quality. Selfe also quickly discarded the idea of a simple compensatory overdevelopment of the right hemisphere due to language delay, as suggested by the theory of brain laterality in use at that time. This hypothesis was rejected because (1) evidence of Nadia's cerebral functioning was incongruent with this hypothesis, (2) other individuals with savant syndrome developed good language abilities, and (3) deaf-mute children display the same course of graphic development as normal children. However, it is worth noting that as Nadia developed a basic level of language, a coincidental decline in her drawing ability was observed.

As an alternative explanation, Selfe attributed Nadia's exceptional drawing ability to a visual or photographic realism, resulting from the impossibility of reliance on intellectual realism. She would draw what she sees because she cannot draw what she understands. According to Harris (1963), children's drawings of objects reveal the development of the discriminations and generalisations they make about these objects. Hence, intellectual realism results from semantic knowledge about objects. Selfe also based her interpretation on Paivio's (1971) dual-coding hypothesis. According to this view, there are two types of thought processes—a pictorial one involving visual imagery, and a verbal and discursive one. This author claims that verbal coding interferes with the development of viewer-centred representations. In contrast, Selfe's model of the drawings of normal subjects involved a more subtle representation of visual cognitive processes—visual perception, on the one hand, and semantic categorisation of the visual display through its matching with a visual prototype on the other hand.

The first clear finding of the investigation was that Nadia did not make use of intellectual realism, but instead relied on visual realism. Also, she did not use conventional representations that reflected a universal, conventional, and semantically oriented representation of the world (e.g. placing the sun in the top corner of the sheet, or using a straight line to represent a landscape). In contrast, Nadia appeared to draw what she saw from her point of view, without exhibiting what is now known as top-down influence. This resulted in a natural utilisation of linear perspective without having any knowledge of this concept. Nadia also used complex representation devices that can be culturally taught to teenagers, but which her age as well as her mental deficiency precluded her from learning. For example, she used partial concealment, foreshortening, and diminution of size with distance. The predominance, in her drawing, of what she saw, can be illustrated by her performance in a task requiring children to draw incomplete or non-symmetrical figures (Graham, Berman; & Ernhart, 1960). Nadia, contrary to subjects in the control group, preserved the integrity of figures while drawing them, without transforming them into symmetrical or closed figures. This empirical finding might help to understand why she, in contrast to normal children who preferred complete forms, drew incomplete drawings or finished a drawing past the edge of a sheet of paper. Nadia could also draw unfamiliar and complex objects such as the harness of a horse, as well as objects that were unfamiliar to any child of her age and that were far too complicated for her limited lexical knowledge. In today's terms, we could say that Selfe interpreted Nadia's condition as a developmental associative agnosia. For example, she drew realistic objects that she could not interpret semantically, just as patients with associative agnosia draw and match objects that they are unable to name. Nevertheless, in her 1983 book, Selfe later gave up this hypothesis based on the fact that all persons with autism display a deficit in abstract thoughts, but that they do not present special abilities as a group—a point that we shall discuss later.

WHAT HAS BEEN LEARNED ABOUT DRAWING ABILITIES IN AUTISM SINCE NADIA'S CASE: STEPHEN AND EC

In her work (1977, 1983, 1995), Selfe documented the facts of the case with enough clarity and perspicacity to convince the scientific community of its theoretical importance. The interest in her description is not diminished by the obsolete nature of some of the models she used. The next step was to establish the way in which such a case could possibly modify cognitive models of autism on the one hand, and visual processing models on the other hand. This objective appears to be only partially fulfilled today. Due to Nadia's young age and low level of intellectual performance, psychological assessment using models of cognitive functioning built for subjects with normal intelligence was impossible to realise with Nadia.

Recently, Oliver Sacks (1996) reported the case of Stephen, a brilliant autistic draftsman. The main outcome of Stephen's case was to suggest that Nadia's graphic peculiarities might belong to autistic draftsmen in general. Nevertheless, Sacks did not try to establish this connection on scientific grounds. After the publication of Nadia's case, one savant draftsman, EC, received an in-depth empirical assessment of graphic performance (Mottron & Belleville, 1993, 1995). EC is a French-speaking adult, with an IQ in the low average level. He is able to read and speak fluently, with a clear clinical picture of high-functioning autism. Since late childhood, EC exhibited an exceptional graphic ability that probably surpasses that of Nadia and Stephen from a technical point of view, although the artistic value of his drawings is less convincing. Unlike Nadia and Stephen, he did not draw before the age of 7–8 years. EC's strengths lie in perspective drawing with an ability to accurately draw the same object under varying sizes and visual angles without being exposed to it more than once. For example, he can draw complex 3D objects under two reverse and symmetrical orientations. He has an astonishing, almost incredible ability to draw the deformation by rotation of a 3D object with curvilinear shape (for example, a chair, a sink, a modern tap), without any graphic corrections, and beginning with any part of the object.

EC's graphic behaviour was similar in some ways to Nadia's behaviour. He did not go through the normal scribbling phase. He only used black outline without textures and did not spontaneously add colours to his drawings (except for surfaces coloured after the end of the drawing). He had rigid drawing habits, using only a ball-point pen or sharpened pencil on A4 paper. Like Nadia, he began his drawings with unimportant parts, and placed parts at the correct position before drawing the lines that joined them. He never used an eraser to correct his productions, even when using a pencil to draw. He only drew restricted numbers of objects (boilers, mechanical objects,

trains). In addition, drawings of human faces were rare and did not particularly resemble the human form. As he got older, he became inspired by comic
books, modifying his drawing style using '*ligne claire*' (i.e. colour surfaces
without nuances with a black, slightly over-marked outline). Contrary to
Nadia, EC used visual realism despite the presence of fluent language. This
undermines the often quoted statement that Nadia's regression in drawing
skill could be related to her improvement in language.

EC usually did his drawings from memory, but when asked to copy real
objects, he would stare at the object for a short period of time and would not
look back at it again during the drawing phase. The orientation of the drawing was independent from the orientation of his body. Like Stephen and
Nadia, he creatively added details to real objects. Like Nadia, EC presented
idiosyncratic visual behaviours while drawing. When a drawing was complete,
he would often place the sheet in an horizontal plane slightly under his eyes
and contemplate it in that position. He would also place the drawing in front
of a mirror and look alternately at the drawing and at its reverse image.

In contemporary models of visual perception, perceptual processes are
divided into three main levels: (1) low-level (texture, luminance, contrast,
movement); (2) intermediate-level (construction of visual patterns, local-
global hierarchy); and (3) high-level (object and face labelling, semantic

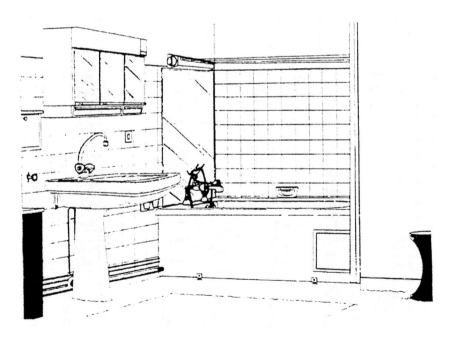

Figure 20.2 One of EC's drawings.

interpretation) (Humpreys & Riddoch, 1987). We first thought that EC's special ability might result from an abnormality in the low or intermediate level of visual perception, an hypothesis Selfe also proposed to explain Nadia's special ability. To verify this hypothesis, we assessed EC's visual perception through concepts and paradigms derived from neuropsychological studies in normal and brain-injured subjects. Results of the basic perceptual tasks revealed that he had a perfect ability to copy, to match canonical and non-canonical views, and to identify various objects. He could identify colours and use the appropriate colour for a particular object, but he reduced the number of hues when copying a coloured picture. In summary, he could extract and use, at a normal level, the three-dimensional properties of an object and derive from it an object-centred representation (i.e. independent of the viewer's point of view). His performance on object recognition under degraded (Gollin, 1960) and fragmented (Hooper, 1958) conditions was normal but not exceptional. EC performed at ceiling level in an object decision task, and in a word-to-picture matching task in the intra- and extra-categorical condition.

Based on his normal performance in basic perceptual tasks, we then proceeded to more complex perceptual tasks. We first assessed the hierarchical organisation of visual information through local/global tasks. Indeed, to account for his special abilities we hypothesised that EC perceives and retains global and local aspects of a visual display without the global bias displayed by normal subjects. In these tasks, visual hierarchical stimuli, composed of large letters made of small letters, were used (for example, a large A made of small Hs). Results indicated that, like control subjects, EC committed more detection errors for local than global targets in a condition where local and global levels were congruent, but that he behaved differently in the presence of incongruent local and global targets. In this incongruent condition, he presented more global than local errors, an effect not observed in controls. This peculiarity was interpreted as an absence of hierarchical status for global level. Another perceptual experiment assessed the order of figure construction and the stability of this order under successive copies of the same object. The results revealed that EC could begin by drawing local features and vary his order of graphic construction along successive copies. A video analysis of his drawing construction revealed that he followed a proximity rule and not a hierarchical order in his copies. Finally, we investigated EC's ability to detect the impossible aspect of impossible figures for a short exposure time. Impossible figures are geometrical designs in which local aspects are globally incompatible in the real world. Results indicated that EC was unable to detect the impossible aspect of geometrical figures for short exposures, but that he understood the concept of impossibility for long exposures.

In a second series of experiments, EC's ability to produce and appreciate perspective was investigated (Mottron & Belleville, 1995). Results revealed that he approximated linear perspective, but that he did not make use of the vanishing point. This excluded the possibility that he used linear perspective as a top-down, conscious strategy. In both EC's and Nadia's drawings, the appearance of perspective was perfect despite technical perspective errors (e.g. lack of co-termination of vanishing points). EC was also able to complete 3D volumes (parts of elliptical cylinders in various rotations) with a level of precision exceeding that of trained architects and professional draftsmen. These findings were interpreted as a demonstration of abnormal construction of visual representation for complex objects, and therefore inside the realm of visual perception. We concluded that in EC, abnormal hierarchical perception resulted in a local bias that in turn might explain the random order of drawing.

In the absence of valid ideas about the relationship between EC's presumed perceptual abnormalities and his drawing *ability*, we decided to explore the generality of these findings with a group of high-functioning autistic subjects without graphic gifts. Surprisingly, the findings revealed that persons with autism behaved like normal controls and presented a global bias in hierarchical stimuli (Mottron, Burack, Stauder, & Robaey, 1999). Interference between local and global parts, emerging or 'holistic' properties and relative primacy according to various experimental conditions appeared normal, as long as very high-functioning subjects were tested, and geometric figures or letters were used. This finding was in opposition to our own model of an absence of hierarchy in visual perception, and also with the predictions of the Central Coherence theory. Based on her broad experience in empirical research in autism, Frith had proposed in 1989 a 'central coherence' principle stating that persons with autism lacked the general tendency to integrate information of a given level into a higher one. This principle predicts a local bias in visual perception, as well as failure to process incoming stimuli in their context.

By using graphic copy tasks, and not purely perceptual tasks, our search for a cognitive explanation of the graphic peculiarities in autism became easier. In another series of experiments (Mottron, Belleville, & Ménard, 1999) we explored copying strategies for objects and geometrical designs in very high-functioning adolescents with autism. It was indeed possible that, at a behavioural level, graphic tasks would reveal peculiarities where perceptual tasks would only lead to ambiguous results. Persons with autism as a group presented, like EC, with a local bias in graphic construction. Also, like EC, they did not perceive geometrical impossibility normally: they displayed an absence of effect of impossibility on copy time. When asked to copy possible figures, they did so with the same speed and accuracy as controls. However, their drawing time on impossible figures was faster than that of the control group.

Due to previous findings obtained in local–global perception of hierarchical stimuli, and the excellent results obtained in the graphic copy task with the clinical group, we discarded a purely perceptual interpretation in favour of a more complex model involving visual working memory. Perceptual interpretations are concerned with the construction of perceptual representations in the temporo-occipital areas of the brain or extra-striate, visual associative areas. In contrast, executive interpretations are concerned with the planning processes that act upon perceptual representations stored in working memory. An executive interpretation of the lack of primacy of global features in graphic construction can be related to deficits in graphic planning or to idiosyncratic planning strategies. It can be argued that initiation of a copy of a drawing with global traits requires a strategy decision, especially if one considers the fact that local features are more numerous than global ones. For the same reason, a planning impairment would result in the initiation of a copy of a drawing with any part of the object, creating a tendency to favour the more numerous local features and resulting in a 'piecemeal' copy with a local bias. This interpretation, however, cannot account for the facilitation observed in reproducing impossible figures.

A slightly different version of the executive interpretation would attribute the idiosyncratic graphic strategies of individuals with autism to a limitation in the level of complexity of the operations performed upon spatial representations. Complexity could be defined in terms of number of independent elements involved in the manipulation of information (Mottron, 1989; see Zelazo, Burack, Benedetto, & Frye, 1996, and Halford, Wilson, & Phillips, 1998 for related theoretical constructs). Copying tasks require the concurrent activation of several elements in working memory in order to successfully plan the motor components of the task. For example, a local line must be copied in relation to other local parts in order to ensure that it co-terminates with adjacent parts and that its size is properly scaled relative to the global size of the model. Limitations in the capacity to maintain local and global traits of the model in working memory, in order to plan graphic construction, might not allow for the elaboration of the 'global traits first' strategy. This would result in a copying sequence favouring local features. On the other hand, the attenuation of the effect of impossibility might be caused by a deficit in the ability to maintain several local parts in working memory during graphic planning. This would cancel the geometric conflict between the local parts of impossible figures. This theoretical trend attributes anomalies in a specific domain of data processing to a general, non-modular problem in information processing (Frith, 1989; but see also Minshew, Goldstein, & Siegel, 1997).

Nevertheless, the interpretation of expertise in terms of a deficit is not completely convincing. It does not account for the capacity to reproduce, at a high level of accuracy, several phenomenal properties of the object such as its modification under rotation, its diminishing size with distance, or the relative proportions among parts. In studies of infant drawings, it is generally agreed that spontaneous use of intellectual realism as opposed to visual realism results from the combined influence of semantic memory and motor immaturity. Our interpretation stating that a better ability to draw phenomenal properties of objects results from a modified relation between perception and planning in short-term memory is also weak in this regard, because it does not account for exceptional ability in visual realism. We shall address this aspect in the following section.

RELATION BETWEEN DEFICIT AND GIFT

The interpretation of Nadia's outstanding ability diverges markedly according to the relation postulated between deficit and gift. As in any association described in single-case studies, there is a choice to make between random co-occurrence and causality. Some of the first commentators on Nadia's case chose the co-occurrence alternative. In what could be called the 'genius' interpretation, Nadia was considered to be a genius draftsperson *who also happened* to be mentally retarded and autistic. This interpretation implies that her precocity and gift requires no further explanation than that for geniuses in general. The theoretical consequence of this interpretation questions the existence of a general 'g' factor equivalently distributed in all cognitive performances. This line of interpretation is presented in Gardner's (1983) account of Nadia. According to this author, Nadia's case demonstrates that intelligence involves multiple faculties, some being independent of others. A similar interpretation, though in a somewhat different context, has been proposed by Cossu and Marshall (1990) involving another 'special ability' in autism, hyperlexia. They used the case of a savant Italian autistic reader to defend a modular model of reading ability, but this interpretation was strongly criticised from a developmental point of view (Marcel, 1990). Gardner's use of Nadia also raises the problem of building one hypothesis— multiple intelligence—on the basis of another hypothesis—independence between gift and deficiency: if there is a causal relation between deficit and mental deficiency, the hypothesis fails. On the other hand, the 'genius' interpretation prevents any generalisation of Nadia's graphic or atypical perceptual processing to autism in general, because Nadia's gift would result from an outstanding ability and not from a deficit.

Another explanation of Nadia's ability is the executive/training interpretation. Executive deficit would be responsible for the limitation of interests and the behavioural focus on a limited number of operations. This limitation would produce a training, which in turn would result in exceptional abilities identical to those found in trained, normal subjects. This interpretation has proven to be the most plausible in the case of QC, an autistic woman with exceptional ability in music perception (Mottron, Peretz, Belleville, & Rouleau, 1999). An in-depth assessment of QC's perception, hierarchical processing for visual and musical material, and executive function revealed that she performed at her mental age on all of the tasks, except those tapping perseveration and cognitive flexibility. On the other hand, her absolute pitch did not differ from the same ability in a gifted non-autistic subject. This was highly suggestive of executive deficit yielding a training in music, without modifying common laws for music perception. Nevertheless, such an explanation cannot account for special abilities where atypical processing can be demonstrated in the domain of gift.

An alternative explanation involves a deeper, functional relation of compensation between cognitive operations concerned with the impaired domain and those concerned with the exceptional ability. We have already reported that the separation between the impaired domain and the spared cognitive functions may be searched for in the realm of perceptual processing. On this account, if abnormal hierarchical visual processing causes Nadia or EC to initiate their drawings by local parts, it is thus a deficit that is responsible for some of the characteristics of the special ability. In the recent literature on brain-injured adult subjects, there are numerous examples of dissociation in visual perception. For example, Goodale (1995) described the case of a woman who was perfectly able to use visual orientation in the course of an action but who performed at chance level when asked to judge parallelism of two lines. In this line of interpretation, Nadia would present the same dissociation as patients with associative agnosia. She would present a normal functioning of certain aspects of visual perception (2D and 3D outline detection) with a deficit in others (colours, object identification), combined with a larger deficit in object identification. Compensation processes through development would then turn normal functioning into a special ability. A neighbouring account proposes that the separation between impaired and spared cognitive functions (and, consequently, of the compensation relation during development) does not lie between low and intermediate levels of perception, but between intermediate and high levels (i.e., between construction of representation and semantic interpretation of visual displays), as proposed by Lorna Selfe.

When Selfe published her book, Nadia was the first autistic savant draftsperson reported. The association between the two factors, autism and perspective drawing, might have been a random one, although Selfe had the perspicacity to suspect that the phenomenon was a pathological one connected to the deficits seen in autism (Selfe, 1995, p. 214). More than 20 years later, numerous cases have been described. Selfe reported seven other cases, all with clear autistic features. Today, there are more than 20 published cases of autistic draftsmen who exhibit precocious use of visual realism, including Stephen (Sacks, 1996), EC, (Mottron & Belleville, 1993) and Hermelin and O'Connor's cases (Hermelin & O'Connor, 1990). Conversely, no cases of subjects with this type of ability and without autism have been published in the last 10 years.

Another important argument in favour of a relation between peaks of performance and autism comes from what Happé and Frith (1996) call the WAIS 'spiky' profile among autistic subjects. This clinical group exhibits, with an impressive constancy, a higher performance in block-design (reproducing of geometrical figures with blocks) and object assembly (a sort of puzzle) than their average performance on other verbal and non-verbal tasks would predict. Remarkably, these two tasks involve manipulation and memorisation of the phenomenal appearance of objects without requiring labelling or semantic interpretation. However, this result could be considered as an 'obscurus per obscurior' type of explanation. It does not explain the enigma of Nadia's drawing, but extends the mystery to the whole autistic population.

The serious consideration of this 'spiky profile' led Frith and Happé (1994) to remark that numerous symptoms in autism cannot be accounted for by a 'social explanation'. These include the symptoms found in the area of repetitive behaviours, restricted interest, and special abilities. At least two cognitive impairments—one in the social-communication area, the other in the structuring of information in general—would be required to account for the complete set of autistic symptoms. The nature of the impairment responsible for the non-social symptoms of autism is still unknown. Indeed, models of abnormal structuring of information (global coherence deficit and hierarchical deficit models) have led to interesting findings (Happé, 1996; Jolliffe & Baron-Cohen, 1997; Mottron, Belleville, & Ménard, 1999) as well as incorrect predictions (Mottron, Burack, Stauder, & Robaey, 1999; Ozonoff, Strayer, MacMahon, & Filloux, 1995).

We now propose a model to account for Nadia's uneven profile of performance developed from our findings in the impossible figure task. This model is based on the format under which data are maintained in short-term memory. It is generally accepted that in normal subjects (for a review see Van Sommers, 1989), the perceptual information comprised in a copy is stored in a transient mode in working memory during graphic planning. Nevertheless, it is never copied as such. Perceptual content is modified by an input from long-term memory or by manipulation itself. This interaction results in a modification of the phenomenal properties of the objects by perceptual prototypes, but also by the network of rules that forms one of the major components of long-term memory. For visual information, this coding operation replaces phenomenal, analogue information with abstract, digitised information. During this process, some phenomenal properties (e.g. texture, luminance, viewer-centred representation) are lost when an object-centred representation is attained, and/or when operations are performed on visual representations.

In this 'Enhanced Perceptual Functioning' model (Mottron & Burack, 2001), we propose that, for savant syndrome individuals and the autistic draftsmen in particular, the perceptual content would be transmitted to short-term memory and from there, to graphic planning with a lower level of modification. In other words, savant subjects would manipulate in working memory, during mental rotation or graphic planning, dimensions of information lost during the coding process of visual information in normal subjects. Why does perceptual information remain accessible to Nadia? Several possibilities are currently under scrutiny. Operations in working memory involve fewer elements in persons with autism than in typically developing persons, as suggested by their local bias in graphic construction and the absence of impossibility effect in copy tasks. One of our hypotheses is *that there might be a relation between diminishing the complexity of operations performed in working memory and raising the phenomenal quality of data manipulated in working memory*. For example, it might be because working memory is not used by complex operations that more resources are vacant for phenomenal information. Nevertheless, the direction of causality may be the opposite. Using a spatial metaphor, it is also possible that when one phenomenal aspect of the object fills the working memory space, there is no room for anything else, in the sense that data stored in an analogue format occupy more space on a computer than data stored in a digitised format. The reduction in the number of independent elements that can be simultaneously manipulated in working memory would then result from excessive analogic storage. In sum, a relation of compensation may take place, whatever its level (neuronal or cognitive) or its direction of causality.

At a developmental level, there might also be a relation between an increase in the phenomenal precision of visual data and a delay in the construction of visual prototypes and rules about the phenomenal world.

CONCLUSION

What is remarkable about Selfe's description of Nadia is that, although Selfe was a clinician and not a researcher, she probably understood the theoretical importance of her discovery better than scientists who refer to her book in order to serve their own theoretical purposes on intelligence or modularity. Her case study may be considered important per se, but also with respect to the innovative method she used in testing her subject extensively in her area of expertise as well as in other areas, with paradigms and concepts originating from the study of normal subjects. Several years later, it appears that single-case and group studies of drawing abilities in autism have allowed researchers, directly or indirectly, to establish important cognitive deficits or particularities in individuals with autism as a group. Although the hope of finding a single, clear-cut cognitive locus for savant syndrome performances appears highly hypothetical, we can now dispose of some empirical findings with non-savant persons with autism that can be accounted for by cognitive models with an explanatory power on savant syndrome in drawing. The reverse is also true, as some findings obtained with savant autistic draftsmen subjects may be extended to autism without special abilities. The cases of Nadia and EC initiated a field of research in which special abilities are used to investigate the cognitive systems related to these abilities, in search of subtle anomalies responsible for the outstanding performance. In turn, these cases oriented research towards a generalisation of these abnormalities in the autistic population as a group, either gifted or ungifted.

ACKNOWLEDGEMENTS

This work was made possible by a grant from the Fonds de la Recherche en Santé du Québec/Fonds Québequois de la Recherche Sociale no. RS2530N94, and a grant from the Conseil de la Recherche Médicale du Canada, no. MT14332.

REFERENCES

Cossu, G., & Marshall, J.C. (1990). Are cognitive skills a prerequisite for learning to read and write? *Cognitive Neuropsychology, 7(1)*, 21–40.

Frith, U. (1989). *Autism: Explaining the enigma.* Oxford: Basil Blackwell.

Frith, U., & Happé, F. (1994). Autism: Beyond 'theory of mind' (Review). *Cognition, 50*, 115–132.

Gardner, H. (1983). *Frames of mind: The theory of multiple intelligences.* New York: Basic Books.

Goodale, M.A. (1995). The cortical organisation of visual perception. In M. Kosslyn & D.N. Osherson (Eds.), *Visual cognition* (Vol. 2, pp. 167–213). London: Bradford Books.

Graham, F.K., Berman, P.W., & Ernhart, C.B. (1960). Development in pre-school children of the ability to copy forms. *Child Development, 31*, 339–359.

Gollin, E.S. (1960). Developmental studies of visual recognition of incomplete objects. *Perceptual and Motor Skills, 11*, 189–298

Halford, G.S., Wilson, W.H., & Phillips, S. (1998). Processing capacity defined by relational complexity: Implications for comparative, developmental, and cognitive psychology. *Behavioral & Brain Sciences. 21(6)*, 803–831; discussion 831–864.

Happé, F. (1996). Studying weak central coherence at low levels: Children with autism do not succumb to visual illusions. A research note. *Journal of Child Psychology and Psychiatry, 37*, 873–877.

Happé, F., & Frith, U. (1996). The neuropsychology of autism. *Brain, 119*, 1377–1400.

Harris, D.B. (1963). *Children's drawings as measures of intellectual maturity.* New York: Harcourt, Brace and World.

Hermelin, B., & O'Connor, N. (1990). Art and accuracy: The drawing ability of idiots-savants. *Journal of Child Psychology and Psychiatry, 31*, 217–228.

Hooper, H.E., (1958). Hooper Visual Organisation Test (HVOT). In H.E. Hooper, *The Hooper Visual Organization Test, Manual.* Los Angeles: Western Psychological Services.

Humphreys, G.W., & Riddoch, M.J. (1987). The fractionation of visual agnosia. In G.W. Humphreys & M.J. Riddoch (Eds.), *Visual object processing: A cognitive neuropsychological approach* (pp. 281–306). Hillsdale, NJ: Lawrence Erlbaum Associates Inc.

Jaensch, E. (1930). *Eidetic imagery and typological methods of investigation.* London: Routledge & Kegan Paul.

Jolliffe, T., & Baron-Cohen, S. (1997). Are people with autism and Asperger Syndrome faster than normal on the embedded figures test? *Journal of Child Psychology and Psychiatry*, *38*(5), 527–534.

Marcel, A.J. (1990). What does it mean to ask whether cognitive skills are prerequisite for learning to read and write?- A response to Cossu and Marshall. *Cognitive Neuropsychology*, *7*(1), 41–48.

Minshew, N.J., Goldstein. G., & Siegel, D.J. (1997). Neuropsychologic functioning in autism: Profile of a complex information processing disorder. *Journal of the International Neuropsychological Society*, *3(4)*, 303–16.

Mottron, L., (1989). René Thom's semiotics: An application to the pathological limitations of semiosis. In T. Sebeok & J. Umiker-Sebeok (Eds.), *The semiotic web 1988* (pp. 91–127). Berlin: Mouton de Gruyter.

Mottron, L., & Belleville, S. (1993). A study of perceptual analysis in a high-level autistic subject with exceptional graphic abilities. *Brain and Cognition*, *23*, 279–309.

Mottron, L., & Belleville, S. (1995). Perspective production in a savant autistic draughtsman. *Psychological Medicine*, *25*, 639–648.

Mottron, L., Belleville, S., & Ménard, E. (1999). Local bias in autistic subjects as evidenced by graphic tasks: Perceptual hierarchization or working memory deficit? *Journal of Child Psychology and Psychiatry*, *40(5)*, 743–755.

Mottron, L., & Burack, J. (2001). Enhanced perceptual functioning in the development of autism. In J.A. Burack, T. Charman, N. Yirmiya, & P.R. Zelazo (Eds.), *The development of autism: Perspectives from theory and research* (pp. 131–148). Mahwah, NJ: Lawrence Erlbaum Associates Inc.

Mottron, L., Burack, J., Stauder, J.E., & Robaey, P. (1999). Perceptual processing among high-functioning persons with autism. *Journal of Child Psychology and Psychiatry*, *40(2)*, 201–211.

Mottron, L., Peretz, I., Belleville, S., & Rouleau, N. (1999). Absolute pitch in autism: A case study. *Neurocase*, *5(6)*, 485–501.

Ozonoff, S., Strayer, D.L., MacMahon, W.M., & Filloux, F. (1995). Executive function abilities in autism and Tourette syndrome: An information processing approach. *Journal of Child Psychology and Psychiatry*, *35*, 1015–1037.

Paivio, A. (1971). *Imagery and verbal processes*. New York: Holt, Rheinhart and Winston.

Sacks, O. (1996). *An anthropologist on Mars*. Toronto: Vintage Canada.

Selfe, L. (1977). *Nadia: A case of extraordinary drawing ability in an autistic child*. London: Academic Press.

Selfe, L. (1983). *Normal and anomalous representational drawing ability in children*. London: Academic Press.

Selfe, L. (1995). Nadia reconsidered. In C. Golomb (Ed.), *The development of gifted child artists: Selected case studies* (pp. 197–236). Hillsdale, NJ: Lawrence Erlbaum Associates Inc.

Scheerer, M., Rothmann, E., & Goldstein, K.A. (1945). A case of idiot savant: An experimental study of personality organisation. *Psychological Monographs*, *58*, 1–16.

Treffert, D.A. (1989). *Extraordinary people: Understanding 'idiot savants'*. New York: Harper and Row.

Van Sommers, P. (1989). A system for drawing and drawing-related neuropsychology. *Cognitive Neuropsychology*, *6*, 117–164.

Zelazo, P.D., Burack, J.A., Benedetto, E., & Frye, D. (1996). Theory of mind and rule use in individuals with Down's syndrome: A test of the uniqueness and specificity claims. *Journal of Child Psychology and Psychiatry*, *37*, 479–484.

Case index

Author index

Adair, J.C. 183, 185
Adams, R.J. 170
Agid, Y. 211–212
Aglioti, S. 160
Aimard, G. 164, 184, 186
Albert, M.L. 28, 159–160, 181–182, 229, 258
Allen, M.E. 170
Allen, R. 309
Allport, A. 3, 20, 28–29, 31–32, 81
Alpert, N. 95
Alsobrook, J.P. 2nd, 308
Amaral, D.G. 106
American Psychiatric Association, 309
Anderson, B. 271
Anderson, D.N. 246, 251
Anderson, G.M. 307–308, 313
Andreewsky, E. 15
Angelini, R. 271, 274
Ankerhus, J. 182
Annoni, J.-M. 273–275
Anton, G. 173–175, 181–182, 199–207, 210–215, 217, 221
Antonucci, G. 160, 165
Arguin, M. 58, 61–62, 65–66, 69
Armstrong, E. 125

Arnsten, A.F.T. 307–308
Asari, Y. 68
Ashbridge, E. 196
Assal, G. 68
Atkins, P. 62
Axenfeld, D. 191
Aylward, E.H. 306, 313

Babinski, J. 176–177, 180, 217
Baddeley, A.D. 4, 19–27, 32–33, 88–89, 91, 268
Baker, C. 88, 91
Baker, J. 309
Bálint, R. 193
Ball, C.J. 215
Balogh, J. 91, 93
Baloh, R.W. 164
Bamford, K.A. 308
Banich, M.T. 264–265
Barbieri, C. 185
Barbut, D. 270
Baron-Cohen, S. 337
Barr, W.B. 214–215, 218
Barré, J.A. 180
Barrett, A.M. 64
Barry, C. 80

Subject index